Introduction to AI Law and Policy

Primary Legal and Policy Sources on AI Governance

ASPEN COURSEBOOK SERIES

Introduction to AI Law and Policy

PRIMARY LEGAL AND POLICY SOURCES ON AI GOVERNANCE

Margaret Hu
Davison M. Douglas Professor of Law
William & Mary Law School

ASPEN PUBLISHING

Cover image credit: angel_nt/stock.adobe.com

To contact Customer Service, e-mail customer.service@aspenpublishing.com, call 1-800-950-5259, or mail correspondence to:

Aspen Publishing
Attn: Order Department
1 Wall Street
Burlington, MA 01803

Printed in the United States of America.

1 2 3 4 5 6 7 8 9 0

ISBN 979-8-8996-3938-8

Library of Congress Cataloging-in-Publication Data

Names: Hu, Margaret (Professor of Law) author
Title: Introduction to AI law and policy: primary legal and policy sources on AI governance/Margaret Hu, Davison M. Douglas Professor of Law, William & Mary Law School.
Other titles: Introduction to artificial intelligence law and policy
Description: First edition. | Burlington, MA : Aspen Publishing, 2026. | Series: Aspen coursebook series | Includes bibliographical references and index. | Summary: "Law school coursebook offering an introductory overview of law and policy challenges introduced by AI and other emerging technologies"– Provided by publisher.
Identifiers: LCCN 2026021372 (print) | LCCN 2026021373 (ebook) | ISBN 9798899639388 paperback | ISBN 9798899639401 ebook
Subjects: LCSH: Artificial intelligence–Law and legislation–United States | Artificial intelligence–Government policy–United States | Technological innovations–Law and legislation–United States | LCGFT: Course materials
Classification: LCC KF390.5.C6 H823 2026 (print) | LCC KF390.5.C6 (ebook)
LC record available at https://lccn.loc.gov/2026021372
LC ebook record available at https://lccn.loc.gov/2026021373

ABOUT ASPEN PUBLISHING

Aspen Publishing is a leading provider of legal education content and digital learning solutions in the United States and globally. Our innovative products and platforms—designed based on best practices in learning science—engage students and enhance outcomes. From textbooks and audiobooks authored by renowned experts to digital platforms and products like LEAF, Connected eBooks, Connected Quizzing, PracticePerfect, and JD-Next, we empower the next generation of legal professionals with innovative, trusted, and accessible resources.

The Aspen Casebook Series, affectionately known as the "red and black" casebooks among law faculty and students, includes hundreds of highly regarded textbooks across more than 80 disciplines. These range from foundational courses like Torts and Contracts to emerging electives such as Sustainability and the Law of Policing. Our study aids, including the popular *Examples & Explanations* series, help law students master complex topics with clarity and confidence.

Aspen's expertise extends to undergraduate education with our Paralegal, Criminal Justice, and Business Law series, offering the same hallmark quality to a broader audience. JD-Next, our groundbreaking online law school prep course and admissions test, provides a realistic preview of law school, equips students with essential skills for academic success, and evaluates their readiness for legal studies.

Aspen Publishing Is Proud to Be a UWorld Company

Since 2003, UWorld has been a global leader in developing high-quality learning tools for students preparing for high-stakes exams. With a commitment to excellence, UWorld has helped millions of students in undergraduate, graduate, and professional programs in fields such as medicine, nursing, finance, and law achieve their academic and career goals.

Founded by Chandra S. Pemmasani, M.D., during his medical residency, UWorld began focusing on medical education and has since expanded into various academic fields, including law. In 2020, UWorld launched its Legal vertical, starting with its comprehensive Multistate Bar Exam (MBE®) Question Bank, followed by the acquisition of Themis Bar Review, which integrated resources to provide a complete bar exam preparation experience. In 2024, UWorld expanded its offerings by acquiring Aspen Publishing, enhancing its suite of legal education products.

Today, UWorld offers an unparalleled range of study materials that blend active learning methods with expert content, ensuring students and educators can access the most effective resources. From bar preparation to law school success, UWorld is committed to supporting the next generation of legal professionals. Learn more at uworld.com.

To my family, including my professional and academic one; to my friends, known and unknown; and to anyone aspiring to stay human.

Summary of Contents

Contents

Preface

The universal implications of artificial intelligence (AI) demand a radical reconsideration of how we approach all fields of study and research. AI law and policy is no different. Grappling with AI law and policy means considering how AI—and topics surrounding its regulation and litigation arising from its use—affects all aspects of society and government. This can involve theories of justice and governance structures, social and political movements, the digital economy and political economy, knowledge production and ethics, labor and employment, rights and privileges, freedom of expression and association, power and defense, security and sovereignty, and other frameworks relevant to the rule of law.

AI law and policy is an evolving field of legal inquiry that intersects with a wide range of other legal fields. Depending on one's legal perspective, AI law and policy can be seen as either encompassing or being encompassed by other areas of technology law and policy: data privacy and data protection, information security and cybersecurity, cybercrime and cyber law, algorithms and the law, intellectual property, Internet law and the Internet of Things, social media and platform regulation, First Amendment law, criminal procedure, and other areas of law. AI is embedded in a wide range of systems, such as surveillance, financial technology or fintech, and biometrics, to name just a few. Because AI systems are embedded within other systems unfolding in an information society and digital economy, AI law and policy is part of the DNA of other legal organisms and other legal ecosystems. Many of these topics are beyond the scope of this introductory text.

Additionally, AI architecture and the uses of AI are evolving. As the technology adapts, so, too, the laws, definitions, and standards surrounding AI are also adapting. The data market ecosystems and enabling applications, the digital infrastructures and other foundational data and technological structures, and other AI systems and structures are also accommodating the speed and nature of innovation. Scientists, corporations, nongovernmental organizations, and governmental bodies are setting different standards and establishing different definitions for AI and machine learning to address their unique needs and goals.

Reconciling law and technology—assessing AI's legal impact while also simultaneously assessing AI's technological impact—is an enormously complex undertaking for those in the field of AI law and policy. Many are struggling to grasp the technological capacities and impact of AI. Because of the emerging nature of the law and policy surrounding AI, which is developing as the technology is developing, the law surrounding AI is far from clear. Where AI regulations are lacking, and when AI technology has already been deployed, the significant legal implications of AI necessitate an evaluation of what laws currently exist that might be available in the future to redress AI's harms and risks, leaving AI law and policy often in a reactive state.

Consequently, there is no consensus on what constitutes the field of AI law and policy. This project does not purport to state definitively the parameters of the field of AI law and policy. Rather, it serves a more modest goal: it offers the scaffolding of a pedagogical tool. It presents one method for how to approach a discussion on the state of an evolving field that is referred to as AI law and policy, and in particular, how to conceptualize AI governance. The first few chapters aim to support the conceptualization of various methods available to institute AI guardrails. Many of the first few chapters specifically focus on the White House's historic release of the *Blueprint for an AI Bill of Rights* in October 2022. The *Blueprint for an AI Bill of Rights* provides a conceptual pathway for understanding a principles-based or rights-based approach to AI governance under several pillars: (1) Safe and Effective AI and Automated Decisionmaking Systems; (2) Antidiscrimination and Algorithmic Discrimination Protections; (3) Data Privacy Protections; (4) Notice and Explanation; and (5) Human-Centered Alternatives and Human Oversight.

Additionally, this text incorporates a survey of complaints and soft law, such as policy guidance documents, due to the inchoate nature of the field. Representative complaints have been included in this book to reflect newly emerging legal theories in AI cases. Complaints do not reflect conclusions of law. Similarly, guidance documents have been included to reflect theories of how to enforce voluntary forms of AI oversight. Guidance documents also do not reflect instruments that possess the force of law. The field of AI law is awaiting legislative and judicial developments to set more conclusively the parameters of the field. Future editions will be adjusted accordingly.

This book, as a snapshot in a moment of time, provides a range of primary sources—complaints, cases, statutes, regulations, guidance documents, congressional reports, government press releases, and other materials— to contextualize how laws and policies are developing as we encounter new consequences of the integration of AI into our lives and digital economy. Because AI law and policy is still a work in progress, only a limited number of illustrative primary sources have been included. The excerpts of these primary sources reflect a case study approach to introduce the subject matter. This does not represent a comprehensive survey, but, rather, an introduction to AI governance concepts through the vehicle of select primary sources and source summaries. The page constraints of this book required that in some instances, only summaries of the sources are included—for example, a press release or a public announcement. In other instances, I intentionally selected summaries and excerpts to increase accessibility, such as news articles over academic articles. The full text of many of the sources can be found in the statutory supplement and elsewhere.

Finally, the focus of this book project, intended for a survey course that can be offered in a wide range of disciplines, is on primary sources. Citations to secondary sources are few. References to the rich academic debates surrounding AI law and policy, and an engagement with ongoing and important scholarly research in this exciting field, have been limited. Similarly, the sometimes conflicting goals of both simplicity and breadth, and the reality of page limitations, led to the development of a structure that is more akin to a sourcebook and that offers only limited introductions to the sources. Each chapter is intended to offer introductory concepts only and, to exemplify select introductory concepts, provide an overview of limited case studies to serve illustrative purposes. I recognize that it is not exhaustive and may incentivize a search for greater context. This is available in supplementary materials provided by this publisher and others.

Editorial decisions to exclude certain sources in any book project like this are arduous. The aims of the project undertaken here made these decisions particularly difficult, given the scale and tempo of the subject matter. The editorial team and I acknowledge how contested these decisions might be in a field of law as nascent as AI law and policy. I invite a conversation on revisions and expansions in future editions.

Author's Note on Editorial and Research Process

Introduction to AI Law and Policy includes excerpts of eleven chapters from a larger book project: *AI Law and Policy, First Edition.* Because I have been asked often about the research method and editing decisions behind *AI Law and Policy,* below is a summary of this book's genesis and progeny.

After I was approached by Aspen Publishing to undertake the project of developing a casebook and textbook, hundreds of potential primary sources were reviewed and catalogued, and drafts of multiple outlines emerged. The outlines and annotated summaries of proposed content tables served not only as a classification system to sort through and make sense of the source materials but also as a type of scaffolding for a potential pedagogical approach and theory. A small army of students, colleagues, research librarians, experts, and editors and advisors joined me in hunting down and reviewing the sources. Hundreds of secondary and primary sources were downloaded and read, classified, stored, analyzed, re-analyzed, and discussed with my research team and team of advisors. Sources are saved in both physical and digital files. All sources cited in this book are on file with the author. As a research team, we continuously gather and study source materials on a weekly, sometimes daily, basis. Both the classification system and scaffolding will evolve as the law evolves.

To document the birth of the field of AI law and policy, this book spotlights a wide variety of primary sources to serve as an archival resource: the panorama of sources is allowed to speak for itself as part of the scaffolding for this sweeping subject matter. For *AI Law and Policy,* excerpts from the wide range of potential primary sources were selected one by one. Due to page limitations, many sources were not included. Like all serious and intensive curation protocols, this has been and will continue to be a painfully deliberative process. Sources that remained for publication were then edited for clarity and consistency. Weblinks, often broken or at risk of being broken in the future, were removed.

Given the historical approach of the book, this collection of source material strives to represent and recognize the complex decisionmaking processes—spanning both domestic and international realms of legal and advisory authorities—exercised by executive administrations and governing agencies, the judiciary and administrative hearing bodies, congressional and legislative bodies, corporate and industry leaders, experts and civil society, and nongovernmental organizations.

I express my gratitude in advance to generous readers and reviewers who might be gracious enough to point out any errors or concerns; share ideas for improvement; and support the iterative process that makes each successive edition and companion project stronger, clearer, more relevant, and more accurate.

Acknowledgments

This book represents a multiyear effort of an extraordinary team. It is the result of a dedicated collection of editors, research librarians, research and administrative assistants, reviewers, and expert advisors. For helping to guide the First Edition to its completion, I thank Jocelyn Aqua, John Bagby, Kim Houser, Davi Liang, Steve Miskinis, Daniel Shin, and Tara Wang. It is a pleasure to offer additional thanks to Leslie Street, Director of William & Mary Law Library, and the dedicated leadership of members of her team, including Christopher Byrne, Head of Research & Instructional Services, and Fred Dingledy, Senior Reference Librarian.

For thoughtful discussions on AI law and policy, including feedback on the First Edition, I thank Kira Allmann, Roy Austin, Merritt Baer, Chiraag Bains, Jeff Bellin, Laura Berger, danah boyd, Stuart Brotman, Paul Burgess, Jenna Burrell, Julie Cohen, Kat Duffy, Liz Losh, Trenton Ford, Brandon Garrett, Keesha Gaskins-Nathan, Laura Heymann, Merve Hickok, Kristin Johnson, Sylvester Johnson, Nathan Letts, Brenda Leong, Mike Madison, Peter Margulies, Christ Marsden, Andrea Matwyshyn, Sarah Nicole, Davi Ottenheimer, Spencer Overton, Sunita Patel, Lala Qadir, Elisa Poteat, Catherine Powell, Christabel Randolph, Rashida Richardson, Marc Rotenberg, David Restrepo, Eric Sears, Jaime Settle, Chris Shenefiel, Andreen Soley, Daniel Susser, Steve Tapia, Taylor Treece, Anne Washington, Paul Waters, and Roger Yee. The student research team for this First Edition was exceptional: Shreya Bariki, Emma Battin, Stephanie Bruno, Anna Buri, Taylor Cannatelli, Malcolm Edwards, Naomi Hampton, Angelina Han, Sally Harnish, Matt Heller, Jesse Hsu, John Kearney, Sang Hwan Lee, Vivian Li, Xueyan Liu, Logan Losito, Alison Munden, Alex Perkowski, Janelle Radcliffe, Jack Reuter, Caleb Saunders, Katie Smart, Genevieve Stegner-Freitag, Cecelia Tate, and Alec Whipple. I greatly appreciate the administrative support and the leadership of Cody Watson, Director of William & Mary Law Faculty Support Services, and the excellent members of his team, Katie Blackman and Tonya Green. Deepest gratitude to A. Benjamin Spencer, Dean of William & Mary Law School; Alyson Wilson and Dennis Manos, current and former Vice Provost for Research at William & Mary, respectively, who both provided generous support; Iria Giuffrida, Associate Provost for Faculty Affairs & Development; William & Mary Law Deans and Center and Institute Directors: Kami Chavis, Evan Criddle, Mike Dick, Rebecca Green, Allison Larsen, Fred Lederer, and James Stern; and William & Mary Dean of the School of Computing, Data Sciences & Physics Doug Schmidt;

William & Mary Democracy Initiative Co-Chairs Ginger Ambler and Carrie Cooper, current and former, respectively; William & Mary Whole of Government Center for Excellence Director Kay Floyd; and William & Mary Global Research Institute (GRI) Director Mike Tierney.

For the generosity of their expertise, I thank the leadership and participants of multiple research workshops and convenings, including: 2025 events hosted by Information Society Project, Yale Law School, led by Founder and Director Jack Balkin, and Executive Director Chinmayi Arun—and much gratitude to Jack and Chinmayi for test piloting chapters of the book in their Spring 2025 AI seminar; 2025 Data Law and AI Ethics Research Colloquium, cohosted by Kevin Werbach at Wharton, University of Pennsylvania, co-led by Janine Hiller and Angie Raymond, and including Josh Fairfield, Mark Graber, Andrea Matwyshyn, and others; Duke Law School's Center on Law, Race & Policy's 2024 conference and 2025 research workshop on AI, hosted and led by Director Trina Jones and Executive Director Geovanny Martinez, including Ifeoma Ajunwa, Chaz Arnett, April Dawson, Jessica Eaglin, Sonia Gipson Rankin, and others; 2025 Ohio State University Data Points Lecture, hosted by Dennis Hirsch, Director, Program on Data and Governance; 2024 New York University's Center for Critical Race and Digital Studies (CR+DS) Research Workshop and CR+DS Founder and Director Charlton McIlwain; 2024 and 2025 Annual Meetings of the Future of Privacy Forum (FPF), including my co-faculty FPF CEO Jules Polonetsky; 2023 Blueprint for an AI Bill of Rights: One Year Later, cohosted by William & Mary Data Science and Offices of the President and Provost, Data & Society (D&S), and the Center for Democracy & Technology (CDT), including inspiration from the leadership of President Katherine Rowe, Provost Peggy Agouris, Data Science Director Tony Stefanidis, D&S President Charlton McIlwain and D&S Executive Director Janet Haven, CDT CEO Alex Givens and CDT Vice President of Policy Samir Jain, former Acting Director of the White House OSTP Alondra Nelson, former White House OSTP Assistant Director of Data and Democracy Sorelle Friedler, and former White House OSTP Assistant Director for Science and Justice Suresh Venkatasubramanian, and others; 2021-23 conferences and research workshops on AI cohosted by Pennsylvania State University's Institute for Computational and Data Sciences (ICDS) and Duke University's Kenan Institute for Ethics (KIE), and the leadership of former ICDS Director Jenni Evans, Interim ICDS Director Guido Cervone, and former KIE Director Suzanne Shanahan.

For the past decade, I have been fortunate to be in collaboration and partnership with experts and leaders from multiple academic and civil society organizations. Particularly at the earliest stages of the book's development, the project benefited from a community of expert advisors from my affiliation with the FPF Advisory Board; CDT Non-Resident Fellowship; D&S Scholars Council; CR+DS Advisory Board; Oxford University Press AI in

Society series co-editor of the AI Governance Unit, together with Charlton McIlwain; Center for AI and Digital Policy (CAIDP) Global Academic Network; and American Bar Association Standing Committee on Law and National Security Advisory Committee.

I am indebted to the support of many mentors and colleagues, including Jack Balkin, Katherine Bartlett, Guy-Uriel Charles, Walter Dellinger, Trina Jones, Jeff Powell, and Elizabeth Schultz. I am also indebted to Aspen Publishing and their editors, including Aiden Blasi, Elizabeth Dobkowski, Kathy Langone, and Anton Yakovlev, who worked tirelessly and offered invaluable editorial leadership throughout. Special thanks to Joe Terry, President, and Justin Billing, former Managing Editor, at Aspen for recruiting me and lending their invaluable support.

Finally, sincerest appreciation is extended to those granting permission to include excerpts from the following published works:

ChatGPT - the Impact of Large Language Models on Law Enforcement. Europol, 19 Dec. 2023. Copyright © European Union Agency for Law Enforcement Cooperation 1999-2025.

European Court of Auditors. *Artificial Intelligence Initial Strategy and Deployment Roadmap 2024–2025.* ECA, 2024, https://www.eca.europa.eu/ECAPublications/ECA-AI-Strategy-2024-2025/ECA-AI-Strategy-2024-2025_EN.pdf. Licensed under Creative Commons Attribution 4.0 International License (CC BY 4.0), https://creativecommons.org/licenses/by/4.0/.

Genna, Innocenzo. "The Regulation of Foundation Models in the EU AI Act." Ibanet.org, International Bar Association, 12 Apr. 2024, www.ibanet.org/the-regulation-of-foundation-models-in-the-eu-ai-act.

Mastercard. "Data Responsibility & Governance Practices." Mastercard, https://www.mastercard.us/en-us/vision/corp-responsibility/data-responsibility.html.

Microsoft. *Microsoft Responsible AI Standard v2: General Requirements.* June 2022, https://blogs.microsoft.com/wp-content/uploads/prod/sites/5/2022/06/Microsoft-Responsible-AI-Standard-v2-General-Requirements-3.pdf.

Recommendation of the Council on AI. Organization for Economic Cooperation and Development, 2019. Copyright © 2019 OECD.

Russell, Stuart, et al. "Updates to the OECD's Definition of an AI System Explained." OECD.org, Organization for Economic Cooperation and Development, 29 Nov. 2023, oecd.ai/en/wonk/ai-system-definition-update. Copyright © 2023 OECD.

Turner, Jacob, and Simmons & Simmons. *AI Short-Form Explainability Statement.* HireVue, April 2022, https://www.hirevue.com/wp-content/uploads/2022/04/HV_AI_Short-Form_Explainability_1pager.pdf.

UNESCO. *Readiness Assessment Methodology: A Tool of the Recommendation on the Ethics of Artificial Intelligence, 2023.* Licensed under CC BY-SA 3.0 IGO, https://creativecommons.org/licenses/by-sa/3.0/igo/deed.en.

UNESCO. *Recommendation on the Ethics of Artificial Intelligence. United Nations Educational, Scientific and Cultural Organization, 2023.* Licensed under CC BY-SA 3.0 IGO, https://creativecommons.org/licenses/by-sa/3.0/igo/deed.en.

United Nations General Assembly. *Enhancing International Cooperation on Capacity-Building of Artificial Intelligence.* Resolution A/RES/78/311, 1 July 2024, United Nations Digital Library, https://digitallibrary.un.org/record/4054005/files/A_RES_78_311-EN.pdf.

Writers Guild of America West et al. *Letter to Senate Majority Leader Chuck Schumer (D-NY).* 27 Mar. 2023, https://www.wgaeast.org/wp-content/uploads/sites/4/2024/06/Letter_to_Leader_Schumer_on_AI-legislation.pdf.

Chapter 1

Introduction

What is artificial intelligence (AI)? "Simply put, AI is a collection of technologies that combine data, algorithms and computing power."[1]

Introduction to AI Law and Policy should be understood as a project that is deliberately historical. Each chapter is an exercise in photojournalism, not unlike snapshots from the frontlines. This book and its counterpart, *AI Law and Policy*, aspire to provide a panoramic view of a fast-moving phenomenon in a transformative moment of history. The primary sources curated for this project offer a wide-angle view of both disruptive technology and an area of law undergoing the earliest stages of experimentation, captured at the time of publication. They tell a story through the historical value and voice of each excerpt. The story is this: the history of AI law and policy at its nascent stages will inform how AI law and policy develops over its longer trajectory.

This book offers a series of introductory and interlocking concepts that are foundational to the project of effective AI governance. Chapters 1 and 2 offer an introduction to and definitions of AI, respectively. Chapter 3 discusses contrasting frameworks of AI governance. The need to strive for safe and effective AI and automated decisionmaking systems is discussed in Chapter 2 within the context of how AI is defined in multiple legal instruments. Chapter 3 offers a comparative approach to AI governance that examines risk-based AI governance frameworks side-by-side with rights-based AI governance frameworks and other hybrid frameworks that blend characteristics of both.

Chapters 4 through 6 address algorithmic discrimination, transparency and explanation, and data privacy. Chapter 7 addresses the topics of personhood and citizenship. Chapter 8 explores some of the challenges associated with human oversight, especially in the context of generative AI developments. In short, these first few chapters facilitate an understanding of why and how AI systems are complex to govern in a constitutional democracy and how anchoring AI governance upon a rights-based approach can be useful in meeting those challenges. AI law and policy is not only about grasping the legal consequences and liabilities that may be

1. Eur. Comm'n, *White Paper on Artificial Intelligence: A European Approach to Excellence and Trust*, at 2, COM (2020) 65 final (Feb. 19, 2020).

attached to designing, deploying, and using AI systems. AI law and policy is also about AI governance, an approach to structuring oversight of AI and related emerging technologies that is a conceptual project as much as a legal one.

The final three chapters introduce topics that are especially relevant to understanding the future arc of AI law and policy, and the shifting paradigms that experts, professionals, and policymakers are now confronting in light of the expanding capacities of AI systems.

To begin this look to the future, Chapter 9 first discusses ethical AI frameworks that are being created to guide AI development and use. Ethical AI frameworks and proposed rules required for AI auditing and monitoring are being instituted for developers and operators. To better understand the future of potential prescriptions to redress AI risks and harms, Chapter 10 includes case studies of proposed preventive testing measures and remedies. These options recommend methods for identifying potential harms and biases, preventing the use of AI in certain instances and structuring remedies when harms occur. Chapter 11 concludes with key issues that encompass societal concerns, including labor, research and education, and environmental sustainability.

Understanding AI law and policy at an operational level inherently demands some attention to gaining proficiency in the technical aspects of AI and other emerging technologies. Careful evaluation of the legal consequences and policy dimensions of AI, machine learning, algorithmic decisionmaking, and automated or semi-automated systems, depends upon this proficiency. The chapters ahead pose particularized questions that are tethered to whatever technology is the focus of the complaint or judicial opinion, statute or regulation, or other primary source. The law or policy question presented and the technological question presented are often intertwined. The illustrative case studies reveal how AI law and policy may be impacting technology and innovation, and vice versa.

Future technological and legal developments will be reserved for exploration in future editions. Examining the historical record of the interrelationships between AI and AI governance opens the door to deepening the discourse on both. Pragmatically speaking, it is impossible to offer a comprehensive representation, or even a satisfactory sampling, of these rapid developments. By attempting to outline the trajectories of AI governance as they are unfolding at the time of publication, this book aims to historicize an inflection point, and, simultaneously, it invites a conversation on what primary source materials comprise the historical record of AI law and policy as we witness how the field is formed.

Chapter 2
Definitions

How is AI defined in legal instruments? For the purposes of grasping AI governance, it is important to recognize who is defining AI and what aspects of an AI system are being defined. To inquire why AI or an AI system has been defined one way or another, ask who and what purposes are served by the definition. Scientists, researchers, and industry leaders may approach a definition of AI that deviates from the definition adopted by judges and litigants, lawmakers, regulators, and policymakers. Because law and policy often attempt to regulate to protect against risks and preempt anticipated harms to citizens and society, law and policy are likely to adopt a broadly encompassing definition and approach AI from an outcomes-centered perspective in policy development discussions.

AI law and policy leads with the importance of the rule of law. In this book, it leads with the question of how the law animates a constitutional democracy. The AI definitions offered below are not focused so much on technological components or capacity. Rather the definitions illuminate how the law, governing bodies, or administrative agencies encompass the technological impact within a necessity or consequence of regulation or public oversight.

In defining AI within the field of AI law and policy, it is also significant to recognize how and why the risks posed by AI systems and many emerging technologies are distinct from the risks posed by traditional computational systems. Consequently, the definitions and classifications presented below are included to help illustrate why the capacities of AI create evolving liabilities that are seen as unprecedented.

A. *CASE STUDIES IN DEFINING AI IN LAW AND STANDARDS*

As case studies, we include two examples of how AI has been defined in federal and state law. In the examples below, the lawmakers focus on automation by machine. Neither is limited to the technical understanding of AI as one developed by a machine learning technique; rather, the legal definitions encompass any sort of autonomous algorithm. These both represent intentionally broad definitions that are likely to influence the use of many currently developed tools.

1. *AI Definitions in Federal and State Law*

The *Advancing American AI Act* requires U.S. federal agencies to inventory AI systems used by the federal government and to assess the risks of AI prior to procurement and deployment.[1] The *Advancing American AI Act* itself relies upon a definition of AI that was referenced in the *National Defense Authorization Act (NDAA) of 2019*, referring to the *NDAA* definition of AI by incorporation. It is worth noting the expansive and inclusive nature of how AI can be interpreted and defined within a federal statute.

a. Advancing American AI Act

The *Advancing American AI Act* is included in the *James M. Inhofe National Defense Authorization Act for Fiscal Year 2023*. Enacted in 2022, the *Advancing American AI Act*'s AI definition places key focus on the machine learning aspects of AI, with accommodation for other forms of AI systems not yet made available.

The *Advancing American AI Act* defines "Artificial Intelligence," as provided in Section 7223(3) below, and also defines an "AI System" in Section 7223(4), as a separate legal definition distinct from "Artificial Intelligence."

Advancing American AI Act

P.L. 117-263—James M. Inhofe National Defense Authorization Act for Fiscal Year 2023
Title LXXII—Government Affairs, Subtitle B—Advancing American AI Act

Sec. 7223. Definitions

In this subtitle:

(3) Artificial Intelligence.—The term "artificial intelligence" has the meaning given the term in section 238(g) of the John S. McCain National Defense Authorization Act for Fiscal Year 2019 (10 U.S.C. 2358 note).

(4) Artificial Intelligence System.—The term "artificial intelligence system"—

(A) means any data system, software, application, tool, or utility that operates in whole or in part using dynamic or static machine learning algorithms or other forms of artificial intelligence, whether—

(i) the data system, software, application, tool, or utility is established primarily for the purpose of researching, developing, or implementing artificial intelligence technology; or

---

1. P.L. 117-263 (2022), Division G—Homeland Security Matters, Title LXXII—Governmental Affairs, Subtitle B—Advancing American AI Act, James M. Inhofe National Defense Authorization Act for Fiscal Year 2023.

(ii) artificial intelligence capability is integrated into another system or agency business process, operational activity, or technology system; and

(B) does not include any common commercial product within which artificial intelligence is embedded, such as a word processor or map navigation system. . . .

b. John S. McCain National Defense Authorization Act for Fiscal Year 2019

The *Advancing American AI Act* refers to the definition of artificial intelligence as it was included in the *John S. McCain National Defense Authorization Act for Fiscal Year 2019* (10 U.S.C. 2358 note), P.L. 115-232, Sec. 238(g). The *John S. McCain National Defense Authorization Act* "included the first definition of AI in federal statute" in the U.S.[2] It defines artificial intelligence as follows.

John S. McCain National Defense Authorization Act for Fiscal Year 2019

P.L. 115-232

Sec. 238. Joint Artificial Intelligence Research, Development, and Transition Activities

(g) Artificial Intelligence Defined.—In this section, the term "artificial intelligence" includes the following:

(1) Any artificial system that performs tasks under varying and unpredictable circumstances without significant human oversight, or that can learn from experience and improve performance when exposed to data sets.

(2) An artificial system developed in computer software, physical hardware, or other context that solves tasks requiring human-like perception, cognition, planning, learning, communication, or physical action.

(3) An artificial system designed to think or act like a human, including cognitive architectures and neural networks.

(4) A set of techniques, including machine learning, that is designed to approximate a cognitive task.

(5) An artificial system designed to act rationally, including an intelligent software agent or embodied robot that achieves goals using perception, planning, reasoning, learning, communicating, decision making, and acting.

c. Colorado AI Consumer Protection Act

Colorado S.B. 24-205, often referred to as the *Colorado AI Consumer Protection Act*, is one of the first examples of state AI legislation that has been successfully passed. Colorado became one of the few states that required developers of "high-risk artificial intelligence systems" to use reasonable

---

2. Laurie A. Harris, Cong. Rsch. Serv., R 47644, Artificial Intelligence: Overview, Recent Advances, and Considerations for the 118th Congress 8 (2023).

care to protect consumers from algorithmic discrimination risks arising from such systems.

The Colorado law defines "Artificial intelligence system" as:[3]

> any machine-based system that, for any explicit or implicit objective, infers from the inputs the system receives how to generate outputs, including content, decisions, predictions, or recommendations, that can influence physical or virtual environments.

d. California Government Code

In 2024, California amended its code to update its definitions of AI and automated decision system. In Assembly Bill No. 2885, the legislature adopted the definitions below in amending Section 11546.45.5 of the Government Code.

California Government Code

2024 Statutes of California, Ch. 843 (A.B. 2885)
An Act to Amend [] the Government Code, Relating to Artificial Intelligence

> 11546.45.5. (a) For purposes of this section:
>
> **(1)** "Artificial intelligence" means an engineered or machine-based system that varies in its level of autonomy and that can, for explicit or implicit objectives, infer from the input it receives how to generate outputs that can influence physical or virtual environments.
>
> **(2)** "Automated decision system" means a computational process derived from machine learning, statistical modeling, data analytics, or artificial intelligence that issues simplified output, including a score, classification, or recommendation, that is used to assist or replace human discretionary decisionmaking and materially impacts natural persons. "Automated decision system" does not include a spam email filter, firewall, antivirus software, identity and access management tools, calculator, database, dataset, or other compilation of data. . . .

e. California AI Training Data Transparency Act

California further adopted definitions of generative AI and synthetic data generation in the passage of the *California AI Training Data Transparency Act* in 2024.

California AI Training Data Transparency Act

2024 Statutes of California, Ch. 817 (A.B. 2013)
Title 15.2 added to Part 4 of Division 3 of the California Civil Code

Title 15.2 of the California Civil Code

---

3. Colo. Rev. Stat. § 6-1-1701 *et seq.* (2024).

3110. For purposes of this title, the following definitions shall apply:

(c) "Generative artificial intelligence" means artificial intelligence that can generate derived synthetic content, such as text, images, video, and audio, that emulates the structure and characteristics of the artificial intelligence's training data. . . .

(e) "Synthetic data generation" means a process in which seed data are used to create artificial data that have some of the statistical characteristics of the seed data.

(f) "Train a generative artificial intelligence system or service" includes testing, validating, or fine tuning by the developer of the artificial intelligence system or service.

2. *AI Definitions in Organisation for Economic Cooperation and Development (OECD) AI Principles*

The Organisation for Economic Cooperation and Development (OECD) is an international intergovernmental organization. OECD's definition of AI establishes an initial common global understanding of the emerging technology.[4]

a. Original OECD Definition of AI

OECD promulgated a definition of AI in 2019 that was widely adopted by 42 nations globally, including the U.S. The OECD Directorate for Science, Technology and Innovation oversees several committees, including the Committee on Digital Economy Policy (CDEP). "In order to support implementation of the Recommendation [of the Council on Artificial Intelligence], the [OECD] Council instructed the CDEP to develop practical guidance for implementation."[5] The *Recommendation of the Council on Artificial Intelligence*, art. 1, adopted the 2019 OECD definition of AI below[6] and then revised the definition in 2023 to reflect the broadening consequences and evolving nature of AI, as presented by generative AI. Both are presented below for a side-by-side comparison.

Original AI Definition Recommended by the OECD Council on AI (2019)

Organisation for Economic Cooperation and Development (OECD)
May 21, 2019 (adopted); March 5, 2024 (amended)

AI system: An AI system is a machine-based system that can, for a given set of human-defined objectives, make predictions, recommendations,

---

4. OECD, Recommendation of the Council on Artificial Intelligence (Adopted May 21, 2019, Amend. May 2, 2024).

5. *Id.*

6. Stuart Russell et al., *Updates to the OECD's Definition of an AI System Explained,* OECD (Nov. 29, 2023).

or decisions influencing real or virtual environments. AI systems are designed to operate with varying levels of autonomy.

b. Revised OECD Definition to Encompass General Purpose AI (GPAI) and Generative AI

As will be discussed in Chapter 8, rapidly evolving technological developments have led to new proposed regulations and revisions of governmental definitions of AI to encompass the consequences of generative AI. OECD is widely recognized as the first international intergovernmental body to create a standard on AI.[7] After the release of Chat-GPT by OpenAI, OECD expanded its definition of AI to encompass generative AI capacities. OECD released a revised version of its definition of AI in 2023, included below without annotation.[8]

Revised AI Definition by OECD to Accommodate Generative AI (2023)

Organisation for Economic Cooperation and Development (OECD)
November 29, 2023

An AI system is a machine-based system that, for explicit or implicit objectives, infers, from the input it receives, how to generate outputs such as predictions, content, recommendations, or decisions that can influence physical or virtual environments. Different AI systems vary in their levels of autonomy and adaptiveness after deployment.

HOW OECD COUNTRIES UPDATED THE DEFINITION

Here are the revisions to the current text of the definition of "AI System" in detail, with additions set out in **bold** and subtractions in ~~strikethrough~~:

An AI system is a machine-based system that ~~can~~, for ~~a given set of human-defined~~ **explicit or implicit** objectives, **infers, from the input it receives, how to generate outputs such as** ~~makes~~ predictions, **content**, recommendations, or decisions **that can** influenc~~eing~~ **physical** ~~real~~ or virtual environments. **Different** AI systems ~~are designed to operate with~~ vary~~ing~~ **in their** levels of autonomy **and adaptiveness after deployment**.

---

7. Fiona Alexander, *U.S. Joins with OECD in Adopting Global AI Principles*, U.S. Dep't Com., Nat'l Telecomm. Info. Admin. (May 22, 2019).

8. Stuart Russell et al., *supra* note 6.

These changes reflect the following observations:

Description of the objectives: These edits seek to reflect the scientific consensus that an AI system's objectives may be explicit (e.g., where they are directly programmed in the system by a human developer) or implicit (e.g., via a set of rules specified by a human, or when the system is capable of learning new objectives).

Examples of systems with implicit objectives include self-driving systems that are programmed to comply with traffic rules (but do not "know" their implicit objective of protecting lives) or a large language model like ChatGPT where the objectives of the system are not explicitly programmed but acquired in part through the process of imitation learning from human-generated text and partly from the process of reinforcement learning from human feedback (RLHF).

Inputs: The addition of "infer, from the input it receives" underscores the important role of input, including rules and data, which may be provided by humans or machines, in operating AI systems. An AI system is said to "infer how to generate outputs" when it receives input from the environment and computes an output by processing the input through one or more models and underlying algorithms. For example, a visual object recognition system implemented by a deep neural network performs "inference", i.e., infers how to generate its output (in this case, a classification of the object in the image) by passing its input (the pixels of the image) through the deep network (a parameterized algebraic expression composed of addition, multiplication, and certain nonlinear operations).

Outputs: The addition of the word "content" clarifies that the Recommendation applies to generative AI systems, which produce "content" (technically, a sub-set of "predictions, recommendations, or decisions") such as text, video, or images.

Environment: Substituting "real" with "physical" clarifies and aligns with other international processes. Furthermore, contrasting real with virtual suggests that virtual environments are not real, which is not the case: they are real in that they accept real actions from the AI system and generate real sensory inputs to the AI system.

Adaptiveness: This reflects that some AI systems can continue to evolve after their design and deployment (for example, recommender systems that adapt to individual preferences or voice recognition systems that adapt to user's voice) and is an additional characterization of an important group of AI systems. Also, the previous wording, "operate with varying levels", might be read as describing a single system whose level of autonomy and adaptiveness might change over time, which was not the intended reading.

c. Revised EU AI Act Definition to Encompass General Purpose AI (GPAI) and Generative AI

In 2023, the European Union (EU) provisionally passed the *EU AI Act.* The finalization of the *Act* in 2024 required trilogues between three governing bodies of the EU who engaged in a series of negotiations: the European Parliament, Council of the European Union, and European Commission. In the final stages of negotiation, the trilogue meetings involved debates on how best to define AI and whether to limit the definition to machine learning systems, and logic and knowledge-based approaches to AI systems, rather than expand the Act to encompass general purpose AI such as generative AI.[9]

The *EU AI Act* relies heavily on the approach recommended by OECD. The revised OECD definition of AI currently focuses on machine-based systems that have the capacity to act within autonomous levels that generate outputs such as decisions and predictions as a result of data inputs. The *EU AI Act* attempted to adopt a definition that distinguished the AI technologies covered by the regulation from systems that represented simple software systems. Article 3 of the *EU AI Act* proposes a series of definitions relevant to the Act.[10] Article 3(1) defines AI broadly, and a definition of general-purpose AI Model is provided in Article 3(63).

EU AI Act

Article 3. Definitions

For the purposes of this Regulation, the following definitions apply:

> **(1)** 'AI system' means a machine-based system that is designed to operate with varying levels of autonomy and that may exhibit adaptiveness after deployment, and that, for explicit or implicit objectives, infers, from the input it receives, how to generate outputs such as predictions, content, recommendations, or decisions that can influence physical or virtual environments; . . .
>
> **(63)** 'general-purpose AI model' means an AI model, including where such an AI model is trained with a large amount of data using self-supervision at scale, that displays significant generality and is capable of competently performing a wide range of distinct tasks regardless of the way the model is placed on the market and that can be integrated into a variety of downstream systems or applications, except AI models that are used for research, development or prototyping activities before they are placed on the market[.]

---

9. Tambiana Madiega, *General-Purpose Artificial Intelligence: Digital Issues in Focus* 2 (2023).

10. Regulation 2024/1689, of the European Parliament and of the Council of 13 June, 2024 on laying down harmonised rules on artificial intelligence and amending Regulations, (EU) 2020/1828 (Artificial Intelligence Act), O.J. (L 1689), Art. 3 [hereinafter *EU AI Act*].

B. AI COMPONENTS AND TERMS

If viewed in technical terms alone, standing outside of law and policy, AI is often described as a branch of computer science that represents a family of technologies. "AI is not a single piece of hardware or software, but rather a constellation of technologies that give a computer system the ability to solve problems and to perform tasks that would otherwise require human intelligence."[11] As a result, many AI definitions proposed in law are representative of a "field of fields," or an interdisciplinary field that is comprised of multiple other fields.

There is no universal consensus on how to define the components of AI. *The Advancing American AI Act* establishes that the Director of the Office of Management and Budget within the White House must "ensure that contracts for the acquisition of an artificial intelligence system or service . . . include considerations for securing the training data, algorithms, and other components of any artificial intelligence system against misuse, unauthorized alteration, degradation, or rendering inoperable" and "ensure appropriate use and protection of privacy[.]"[12] Therefore, the components of AI that are contemplated by this act include, at a minimum, both training data and algorithms. In the discussion below, examples are provided of how law and policy define and regulate a range of AI components, including 1. Datasets and Training Models; 2. Algorithms; 3. Reasoning and Problem Solving; 4. Planning and Scheduling; 5. Learning; and 6. Processing and Sensors.

1. Datasets and Training Models

AI requires training data to build models, also referred to as training models, to feed algorithms and requires machine learning in order to generate responses to prompts and other queries. Particularly with generative AI, the training models necessitate extraordinarily high volumes of curated training data to increase the accuracy of the response. "At its core, an AI model is both a set of selected algorithms and the data used to train those

---

11. A.B.A. [American Bar Ass'n] Report to the House of Delegates [in support of A.B.A. Resolution 604] 1 n.1 (adopted Feb. 6, 2023) (citing Nat'l Sec. Comm'n on A.I. (NSCAI), Final Report, Artificial Intelligence in Context 31-40, (2021); Nat'l Coordination Off. (NCO) Networking and Info. Tech. Rsch. and Dev. (NITRD) Program, Nat'l Artificial Intelligence Research and Development Strategic Plan: 2019 Update (Nov. 12, 2020)).

12. P.L. 117-263, Division G—Homeland Security Matters, Title LXXII—Governmental Affairs, Subtitle B—Advancing American AI Act, James M. Inhofe National Defense Authorization Act for Fiscal Year 2023, Sec. 7224(d)(1)(A)(iv)-7224(d)(1)(B).

algorithms so that they can make the most accurate predictions."[13] Training and testing AI models is often iterative. "AI model training is an iterative process whose success depends on the quality and depth of the input as well as the ability of trainers to identify and compensate for deficiencies . . . balancing the many different possible variables, outliers, and complications in data."[14]

Regulators have struggled to set forth the definitions and standards required to measure when greater oversight might be required over an AI system or the AI model itself. One metric that has been used by policymakers is Floating-Point Operations Per Second (FLOP). FLOPs measure how many calculations a computer can perform per second. Under the *EU AI Act*, "general purpose AI models that were trained using a total computing power of more than 10^{25} FLOPs are considered to pose systemic risks."[15]

The risks to national security posed by AI are particularly acute. "These risks may be exacerbated when countries of concern use bulk sensitive personal data to develop AI capabilities and algorithms that, in turn, enable the use of large datasets in increasingly sophisticated and effective ways to the detriment of United States national security."[16] With AI, for example, adversaries can "recogniz[e] patterns across multiple unrelated datasets to identify potential individuals whose links to the Federal Government would be otherwise obscured in a single dataset."[17]

a. Protecting Americans' Data from Foreign Adversaries Act of 2024

The *Protecting Americans' Data from Foreign Adversaries Act* was passed by Congress and signed into law in 2024. The bill defines categories of data designated as particularly sensitive that require additional protection for national security purposes.

Protecting Americans' Data from Foreign Adversaries Act of 2024

P.L. 118-50, Division I—Protecting Americans' Data from Foreign Adversaries Act of 2024

(5) Personally Identifiable Sensitive Data.—The term "personally identifiable sensitive data" means any sensitive data that identifies or is linked or

---

13. Michael Chen, *What Is AI Training and Why Is It Important?*, Oracle Cloud Infrastructure (Dec. 6, 2023).

14. *Id.*

15. *Artificial Intelligence: Questions and Answers*, Eur. Comm'n (Jul. 31, 2024) (referencing *EU AI Act*, Reg. 2024/1689, Art. 51.2).

16. Exec. Order No. 14117, § 1, 89 Fed. Reg. 15421, *Preventing Access to Americans' Bulk Sensitive Personal Data and United States Government-Related Data by Countries of Concern* (Feb. 28, 2024).

17. *Id.*

reasonably linkable, alone or in combination with other data, to an individual or a device that identifies or is linked or reasonably linkable to an individual.

(6) Precise Geolocation Information.—The term "precise geolocation information" means information that—

(A) is derived from a device or technology of an individual; and

(B) reveals the past or present physical location of an individual or device that identifies or is linked or reasonably linkable to 1 or more individuals, with sufficient precision to identify street level location information of an individual or device or the location of an individual or device within a range of 1,850 feet or less.

(7) Sensitive Data.—The term "sensitive data" includes the following:

(A) A government-issued identifier, such as a Social Security number, passport number, or driver's license number.

(B) Any information that describes or reveals the past, present, or future physical health, mental health, disability, diagnosis, or healthcare condition or treatment of an individual.

(C) A financial account number, debit card number, credit card number, or information that describes or reveals the income level or bank account balances of an individual.

(D) Biometric information.

(E) Genetic information.

(F) Precise geolocation information.

(G) An individual's private communications such as voicemails, emails, texts, direct messages, mail, voice communications, and video communications, or information identifying the parties to such communications or pertaining to the transmission of such communications, including telephone numbers called, telephone numbers from which calls were placed, the time calls were made, call duration, and location information of the parties to the call.

(H) Account or device log-in credentials, or security or access codes for an account or device.

(I) Information identifying the sexual behavior of an individual.

(J) Calendar information, address book information, phone or text logs, photos, audio recordings, or videos, maintained for private use by an individual, regardless of whether such information is stored on the individual's device or is accessible from that device and is backed up in a separate location.

(K) A photograph, film, video recording, or other similar medium that shows the naked or undergarment-clad private area of an individual.

(L) Information revealing the video content requested or selected by an individual.

(M) Information about an individual under the age of 17.

(N) An individual's race, color, ethnicity, or religion.

(O) Information identifying an individual's online activities over time and across websites or online services.

(P) Information that reveals the status of an individual as a member of the Armed Forces.

(Q) Any other data that a data broker sells, licenses, rents, trades, transfers, releases, discloses, provides access to, or otherwise makes available to a foreign adversary country, or entity that is controlled by a foreign adversary, for the purpose of identifying the types of data listed in subparagraphs (A) through (P).

2. *Algorithms*

Many references to AI in law and policy contexts refer to algorithms and algorithmic decisionmaking, including algorithmic profiling and predictive risk assessments. In AI law and policy, algorithms are highly consequential because of the legal risks and potential infringement of rights that can result from algorithmic decisionmaking. For example, constitutional and other legal rights may be implicated by risk assessment algorithms that may unfairly and inaccurately predict that an individual will be more likely to commit a crime based on data that is correlative to an individual's geography, race, or gender.[18]

Legal consequences involving algorithmic decisionmaking can be considered a part of AI law and policy. In mathematics, statistics, and computer and data sciences, algorithms are relied upon to perform essential functions in machine learning and AI. There are many types of algorithms, which in the machine learning context are often understood as a "set of instructions a computer executes to learn from data[,]" where "the resulting structured information is typically called a model."[19]

The operations performed upon the input variables are decided by the programmer of the algorithm. In machine learning, "information the computer learns from the data via the algorithm may look like 'weights' by which to multiply each input factor" to create the output.[20] Complexity can vary significantly, but the result and goal of development can be to produce a new model or algorithm that can take in novel inputs (e.g., one week's worth of weather data) and produce a new output from the algorithm (e.g., whether it will rain tomorrow). The following graphic from the National Institute of Standards and Technology (NIST) provides a visualization of the relationship between data sets, training models, algorithms, and machine learning.

---

18. Julia Angwin, et al., *Machine Bias*, PROPUBLICA (May 23, 2016).

19. Kristian Lum, et al., What is an "Algorithm"? It Depends on Whom You Ask, MIT TECH. REV. (Feb. 26, 2021). (In some instances, "a model is itself called an algorithm" because "models are rules (learned by the computer's training algorithm instead of stated directly by humans) that define a sequence of operations.")

20. *Id.*

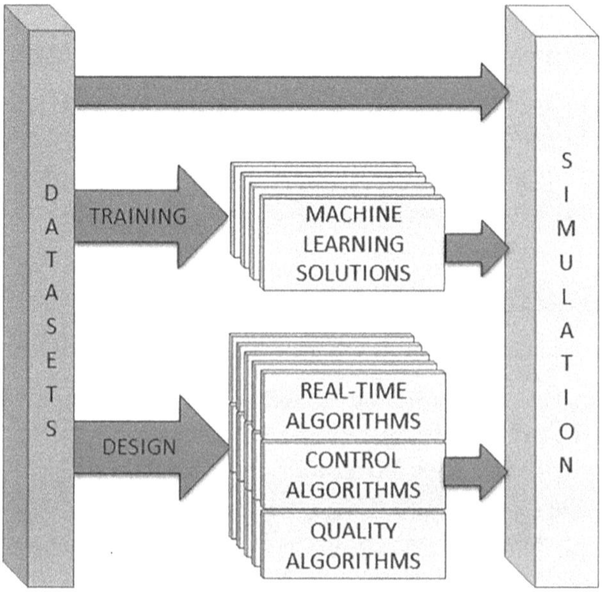

Source: Edited graphic from NIST, Data-Driven Network Optimization for Future Wireless Systems

Models and algorithms can be built by hand for purposes besides machine learning, with data scientists and statisticians painstakingly combing through mountains of recorded data. These manually constructed datasets in cancer research, for instance, mean that scientists have considered enough data to distinguish between cancerous and healthy cells through direct examination.[21] However, advances in AI have led to machine learning based on computed tomography (CT) scans with "researchers assembl[ing] as many CT images as possible to use as training data . . . [to] show tissue with cancerous cells [and] . . . healthy tissues."[22] Additionally, "they create rules on the relationship between data in the images and what doctors know about identifying cancer . . . [and] give these rules and the training data to the machine learning system."[23] Finally, the AI system "uses the rules and the training data to teach itself how to recognize cancerous tissue."[24]

21. *See, e.g.*, Peter W. Hamilton, et al., *Automated Tumor Analysis for Molecular Profiling in Lung Cancer*, 6 ONCOTARGET 27938, 27948 (2015) ("[D]igital slides and every tumor and non-tumor cells [were] manually counted by hand . . . to derive an accurate percentage tumor figure. . . . Over 500,000 cells were counted manually for this exercise.").

22. *DOE Explains . . . Machine Learning*, U.S. DEP'T ENERGY, OFF. SCIENCE.

23. *Id.*

24. *Id.*

a. Use and Disclosure of Predictive Modeling in Medicare Programs

Title 42 of the United States Code, governing public health and welfare, states that the Secretary of Health and Human Services "shall use predictive modeling and other analytics technologies" to detect fraud in the Medicare program. The definition of "covered algorithm" is included in this statutory provision.

United States Code

Title 42. The Public Health and Welfare[;] Chapter 7. Social Security

§ 1320a-7m. Use of Predictive Modeling and Other Analytics Technologies to Identify and Prevent Waste, Fraud, and Abuse in the Medicare Fee-for-Service Program[25]

(a) Use in the Medicare fee-for-service program

The Secretary shall use predictive modeling and other analytics technologies (in this section referred to as "predictive analytics technologies") to identify improper claims for reimbursement and to prevent the payment of such claims under the Medicare fee-for-service program. . . .

§ 1320a-7n. Disclosure of Predictive Modeling and Other Analytics Technologies to Identify and Prevent Waste, Fraud, and Abuse[26]

(b) Limiting disclosure of predictive modeling technologies

In implementing such provisions under such section 1320a-7m with respect to covered algorithms (as defined in subsection (c)), the following shall apply:

(1) Nonapplication of FOIA

The covered algorithms used or developed for purposes of such section 1320a-7m (including by the Secretary or a State (or an entity operating under a contract with a State)) shall be exempt from disclosure[27] . . .

(c) Covered algorithm defined

In this section, the term "covered algorithm"—

(1) means a predictive modeling or other analytics technology, as used for purposes of section 1320a-7m(a) of this title to identify and prevent waste, fraud, and abuse with respect to the Medicare program . . . and

(2) includes the mathematical expressions utilized in the application of such technology and the means by which such technology is developed.

---

25. P.L. 111-240—Small Business Jobs Act of 2010, Title IV—Additional Small Business Provisions, Subtitle B—Other Provisions, Part II Medicare Fraud (Sept. 27, 2010) (42 U.S.C. 1320a-7m).

26. P.L.114-198—Comprehensive Addiction and Recovery Act of 2016, Title VII—Miscellaneous (July 22, 2016) (42 U.S.C. 1320a-7n).

27. Exempt from disclosure under the Freedom of Information Act (FOIA), 5 U.S.C. 552(b)(3).

3. *Reasoning and Problem Solving*

An algorithm by itself is not necessarily AI, as it is simply "a process or set of rules to be followed in calculations or other problem-solving operations,"[28] and can be conducted without computing assistance. Algorithms, even complex algorithms, therefore, do not necessarily involve AI or machine learning.[29] A decision tree that can be followed with pen and paper can be an algorithm.[30] Reasoning and problem solving in AI often reflects an attempt to mimic human processes.

a. Mississippi Computer Science and Cyber Education Equality Act

The Mississippi Code for K-12 education provides curricular guidance on developing educational materials that support primary and secondary education for career readiness in computer science.

Mississippi Computer Science and Cyber Education Equality Act

2021 Mississippi Laws, Amending Title 37. Education[;] Ch. 13. Curriculum (H.B. 633)

§ 37-13-207. K-12 Computer Science Curriculum; Subjects of Instruction; Implementation

(1) The State Department of Education is authorized and directed to implement K-12 computer science curriculum based on the 2018 Mississippi College and Career-Readiness Standards for computer science, which includes instruction in, but not limited to:

(a) Computational thinking;
(b) Problem solving;
(c) Programming;
(d) Cyber security;
(e) Data science;
(f) Robotics;
(g) Artificial intelligence and machine learning; and
(h) Other computer science and cyber-related content. . . .

4. *Planning and Scheduling*

The Artificial Intelligence Group at Jet Propulsion Laboratory developed a system referred to as the ASPEN (Automated Scheduling and Planning Environment) system, leveraging AI to conduct analysis for optimization of task management.

---

28. *Algorithm*, Oxford English Dictionary.

29. Lum et al., *supra* note 19.

30. Eileen Guo, et al., This is the Stanford Vaccine Algorithm that Left Out Frontline Doctors, MIT Tech. Rev. (Dec. 21, 2020).

a. NASA Jet Propulsion Laboratory, ASPEN (Automated Scheduling and Planning Environment)

Utilizing AI technologies, the ASPEN system provides a modular and reconfigurable application framework that supports planning and scheduling applications, which include: "an expressive modeling language, a resource management system, a temporal reasoning system, and a graphical interface."[31]

5. Learning

As discussed below, machine learning is considered a branch of AI or a subset of AI that facilitates learning from data inputs and extracting patterns from training data. This can occur, for example, through machine learning algorithms that learn from the data inputs.

To draw a contrast between traditional computational methods and AI, experts have analogized algorithmic functions with baking processes. A recipe for baking a cake can be considered an algorithm. "[Y]ou can ask the computer to bake a cake, but it will only be able to complete the task if you have given the computer the recipe to follow[,]" because "[r]egular computing is reliant upon pre-determined instruction[.]"[32] In AI, however, "rather than pre-programming a specific cake recipe," developers input raw data, such as "multiple different cake recipes[.]"[33] Next, the AI program, through machine learning algorithms, engages in inductive reasoning to generate what it predicts or infers to be "the most appropriate steps to follow based on the recipes in the input data set."[34]

In other words, there is a distinction between classic computational systems and AI systems. AI is often probabilistic and dependent upon data-driven inputs and algorithms. In machine learning, the algorithms inform the computer system on how to learn from patterns of voluminous data. In traditional computing, the results are programmed to be deterministic and predefined. Every condition that leads to the computational result is defined in the system.[35]

Machine learning systems are often divided into either supervised or unsupervised systems. If the training data uses labeled data that identifies the nature of the data, it is considered supervised. If the machine learning system is unsupervised, the training data is not labeled. "Some machine learning

---

31. NASA Jet Propulsion Laboratory, Artificial Intelligence Group, *ASPEN*, Nat'l Aeronautic Space Administrat. Jet Propulsion Lab'y.

32. *What's the Difference between AI and Regular Computing?*, Royal Inst. (Dec. 12, 2023).

33. *Id.*

34. *Id.*

35. *Id.*

systems can improve their abilities based on feedback received on the predictions. These are called reinforcement machine learning systems. . . . [that] tweak [their] algorithms to produce more accurate predictions in the future."[36] Machine learning can identify results through a "learning" process that involves a trial-and-error protocol whereby the system is trained to reach specific results that have been structured by the programmer.[37]

a. National Artificial Intelligence Initiative Act of 2020 [Definitions]

The *National Artificial Intelligence Initiative Act* provides a definition for machine learning, excerpted below.

National Artificial Intelligence Initiative Act of 2020 Definitions: 15 U.S.C. 19401

Title 15. Commerce and Trade[;] Chapter 119. National Artificial Intelligence Initiative Act

§ 9401. Definitions

(11) Machine learning

The term "machine learning" means an application of artificial intelligence that is characterized by providing systems the ability to automatically learn and improve on the basis of data or experience, without being explicitly programmed.[38]

6. *Processing and Sensors*

One of the core components of AI is the capacity of the AI system through the deployment of processing technologies and sensors. Processing and sensors can analyze, assess and exploit, and disseminate and integrate data. Robotics that rely upon complex sensors are increasingly dependent upon AI systems.

a. Virginia Hospital and Nursing Home Licensure and Inspection

The State Board of Health of Virginia guides the regulatory requirements for licensing and inspection of hospitals and nursing homes. The excerpt of the Virginia state health code below requires the promulgation of regulations that protect health data when using AI and virtual assistants in hospitals, nursing homes, and certified nursing facilities.

---

36. *DOE Explains . . . Machine Learning, supra* note 22.

37. Janelle Shane, You Look Like a Thing and I Love You: How Artificial Intelligence Works and Why It's Making the World a Weirder Place 9 (2019).

38. P.L. 116-283, Div. E, § 5002, Jan. 1, 2021, 134 Stat. 4523.

Code of Virginia

2025 Virginia Acts, Ch. 254 (H. 2255)
An Act to Amend and Reenact [] § 32.1-127 [Title 32.1. Health[;] Chapter 5. Regulation of Medical Care Facilities and Services[;] Article 1. Hospital and Nursing Home Licensure and Inspection]

§ 32.1-127. Regulations

A. The regulations promulgated by the [State Board of Health] to carry out the provisions of this article . . .

B. Such regulations: . . .

29. Shall require each hospital, nursing home, and certified nursing facility to establish and implement policies to ensure the permissible access to and use of an intelligent personal assistant provided by a patient, in accordance with such regulations, while receiving inpatient services. Such policies shall ensure protection of health information in accordance with the requirements of the federal Health Insurance Portability and Accountability Act of 1996, 42 U.S.C. § 1320d *et seq.*, as amended. For the purposes of this subdivision, "intelligent personal assistant" means a combination of an electronic device and a specialized software application designed to assist users with basic tasks using a combination of natural language processing and artificial intelligence, including such combinations known as "digital assistants" or "virtual assistants." . . .

C. AI FIELDS, DOMAINS, AND SUBDOMAINS

Legal definitions of AI often focus on AI systems that reach machine-enabled predictions, assessments and inferences, recommendations, and other results. In some instances, AI systems are trained to reach specific results that are predictive or correlative in nature. The problem-solving and predictive capacities of AI and machine learning often deploy supercomputing architecture that is dependent upon unthinkably large amounts of data and models of data. The data-driven nature of AI architecture and its data-centric infrastructure—for instance, the foundational AI models used for generative AI, the supercomputing storage capacities of cloud computing, or the web-based accessibility of AI—means that AI is a field of fields legally as well as technologically.

1. AI Systems and Taxonomy

Although AI and AI systems are distinguishable technically and legally, both have been defined under the law as capable of influencing outcomes that may have legal consequences. This distinction is important, as some definitions not only cover AI tools that are tasked with a machine-based decision but also cover algorithmic decisionmaking systems, and other automated or semiautomated decisionmaking systems, that have the potential to influence both public and private decisionmakers, potentially impacting constitutional rights and other legal rights. Some algorithmic decisionmaking systems and AI systems are also referred to as expert systems, "a subfield of computer science" and AI.[39] "Expert systems are computer programs that can perform some task which typically requires the capabilities of a skilled human."[40]

There is no universal consensus on how best to categorize all possible AI branches and fields of AI. Many include the following: machine learning; natural language processing; data science, big data, and data analytics; perception and robotics, including computer vision; and fuzzy logic.

Some experts provide a taxonomy that divides AI domains into two classifications: core and transversal. Core domain characteristics of AI define specific AI capacities and functionalities. Transversal domain characteristics span all capacities and functionalities and are "not specifically related to a particular academic discipline or area of knowledge, but [represent] issues common to all the core domains."[41] The following graphic illustrates a proposed AI taxonomy.

Table 1 AI Domains and Subdomains Constituting One Part of the Operational Definition of AI

	AI taxonomy	
	AI domain	**AI subdomain**
Core	**Reasoning**	Knowledge representation
		Automated reasoning
		Common sense reasoning
	Planning	Planning and Scheduling
		Searching
		Optimisation
	Learning	Machine learning
	Communication	Natural language processing
	Perception	Computer vision
		Audio processing
Transversal	**Integration and Interaction**	Multi-agent systems
		Robotics and Automation
		Connected and Automated vehicles
	Services	AI Services
	Ethics and Philosophy	AI Ethics
		Philosophy of AI

Source: European Commission Joint Research Centre, AI Watch, Defining Artificial Intelligence

39. Daniel L. Schmoldt, *Expert Systems and the Environment*, *in* ENCYCLOPEDIA OF ENVIRONMENTAL SCIENCE 243 (David E. Alexander and Rhodes W. Fairbridge eds., (1999)).

40. *Id.*

41. EUR. COMM'N JOINT RSCH. CTR., AI WATCH, DEFINING ARTIFICIAL INTELLIGENCE (2020).

2. *Machine Learning*

The broad nature of AI means that it is divided into subsets of developmental methods and forms. Machine learning (ML) is one subset of AI, a "branch of AI that deals with enabling machines to learn from data."[42] ML learns from data inputs, often "using algorithms that are able to 'learn' by extracting patterns from a large body of data."[43] This is distinct from "traditional rule-based algorithms[,]" as ML often learns through an iterative approach that relies upon a training dataset of structured or unstructured data.[44] There are generally three categories of ML: supervised learning, unsupervised learning, and reinforcement learning.[45] In some complex systems, these categories are combined.[46] Other subsets of learning are used to create AI of different complexity and purpose, such as deep learning, a form of ML that extracts information from inputs autonomously, and neural networks, a form of ML that mimics human brain neurons.[47]

3. *Natural Language Processing*

Natural Language Processing (NLP) enables AI systems to assess and process human language. It analyzes text and speech to extract meaning from it. NLP is a necessary element of many chatbots and virtual assistants, and is critical to generative AI.[48] NLP has been defined as a body of knowledge:[49]

> For a computer program to interpret a relatively unrestricted natural language communication, a great deal of knowledge is required. Knowledge is needed of:
>
> - the structure of sentences
> - the meaning of words
> - the morphology of words

---

42. Fabio Cuzzolin, et al., *Knowing Me, Knowing You: Theory of Mind in AI,* 50 PSYCH. MED. 1057, 1057 (2020).

43. General Services Administration [GSA] IT [Information Technology]. Modernization Centers for Excellence [COE], *AI Guide for Government: A Living and Evolving Guide to the Application of Artificial Intelligence for the U.S. Federal Government, Key AI Terminology,* GEN. SERV. ADMIN.

44. *Id.*

45. *Id.*

46. *Id.*

47. IBM Data and AI Team, *AI Versus Machine Learning Versus Deep Learning Versus neural Networks: What's the Difference?,* IBM (July 6, 2023).

48. Sanjith David, *Natural Language Processing: An Overview,* CTRS. FOR DISEASE CONTROL TECH. R&D LAB'Y (Feb. 10, 2023).

49. WILLIAM B. GEVARTER, AN OVERVIEW OF COMPUTER-BASED NATURAL LANGUAGE PROCESSING 2 (Nat'l Bureau of Standards Info. Rep. NBSIR 83-2687 Apr. 1983).

- a model of the beliefs of the sender
- the rules of conversation, and
- an extensive shared body of general information about the world.

This body of knowledge can enable a computer (like a human) to use expectation-driven processing in which knowledge about the usual properties of known objects, concepts, and what typically happens in situations, can be used to understand incomplete or ungrammatical sentences in appropriate contexts.

4. Data Science, Big Data, and Data Analytics

AI and its modeling require vast amounts of data to build upon and train their models. A related subfield of AI is big data. Advancements in computing power, data storage, and internet communication have permitted far greater amounts of data to be produced, shared, and collected, be it by thousands of meteorology stations around the globe, sensors placed around a car, surveillance devices around a city, Internet browser cookies collecting data on billions of users from their social media profiles and web activity, or any other source of data that can be collected or centralized.

The term "big data" enjoys multiple definitions depending on the context. It typically refers to four V's that often characterize big data: volume (i.e., the size of a dataset), velocity (i.e., the rate of flow of collected data and speed by which it's processed), variety (i.e., how data can come from multiple sources, or types), and variability (i.e., how structure or other characteristics can change). Existing data models, infrastructure, and analytics have adapted and scaled up to efficiently manage big data.[50] The following graphic created by NASA demonstrates the interconnectivity between AI infrastructure, AI components, and AI applications.

The vast amount of web activity has motivated a change from a focus on studying structured data (data predefined in its collection or organization) to studying and analyzing unstructured data (data that is not predefined in its collection or organization). Big data, thus, consists of "'large, diverse, complex, longitudinal, and/or distributed datasets generated from instruments, sensors, Internet transactions, email, video, click streams, and/or all other digital sources available today and in the future.'"[51]

---

50. Nat'l Inst. of Standards & Tech. [NIST], U.S. Dep't of Commerce, *NIST Big Data Interoperability Framework: Volume 1, Definitions Version 3*, (NIST Special Publ'n 1500-1r2, Oct. 2019).

51. Exec. Off. of President, Big Data: Seizing Opportunities, Preserving Values (May 2014) 3 n.8 (2014) (quoting Nat'l Sci. Found., Solicitation 12-499: Core Techniques and Technologies for Advancing Big Data Science & Engineering (BIGDATA) (2012)).

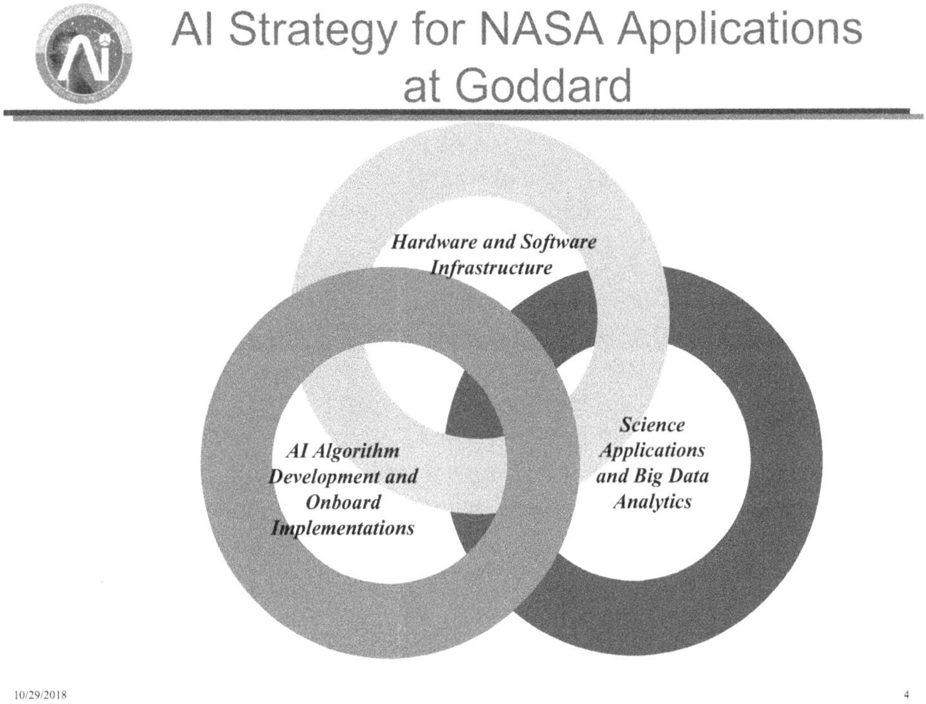

Source: Edited slide from NASA Earth Science Technology Office's (ESTO) Advanced Information Systems Technology (AIST) Program.

Big data tools, for example, are viewed as critical in the fields of data analytics, bioinformatics, and cancer research. "Cancer data can be fragmented and compartmentalized[.]"[52] "[T]o overcome the challenges this poses," cancer researchers use big data to "[establish] an infrastructure to help researchers store, analyze, integrate, access, and visualize large amounts of biological data and related information[.]"[53]

5. Perception and Robotics

Perception as part of AI incorporates sensor technologies, including computer or machine vision and audio processing. The integration of multiple AI technologies can facilitate the development of robotics and other multi-agent systems and automation.

Robotics are "technologies that enable automatically controlled, reprogrammable, multi-purpose machines to perform actions in the physical

---

52. Nat'l Cancer Inst., *Bioinformatics, Big Data, and Cancer,* NAT'L INSTS. HEALTH [NIH] (May 10, 2024).

53. *Id. See also* Kewei Cheng et al., *Inductive or Deductive? Rethinking the Fundamental Reasoning Abilities of LLMs,* CORNELL UNIV., ARXIV (Aug. 7, 2024).

world traditionally performed or initiated by human beings, including by way of artificial intelligence or related technologies."[54] For example, NASA's Jet Propulsion Laboratory (JPL), a division of the California Institute of Technology, has researched the incorporation of both neural networks and fuzzy logic into its robotics research, deploying AI and other emerging technologies to increase robotic functions.[55] Neural networks facilitate robotic learning. This can come from associating perceptions to adapt to environmental situations.[56] Fuzzy logic, on the other hand, incorporates linguistic rather than mathematical tools into the engineering technology to create more humanistic robotic responses.[57]

D. REPRESENTATIVE FUNCTIONALITIES OF AI

Many experts provide a range of categorizations and classifications of AI based on technological capacities. The categories in the following sections identify several proposed categories of AI that are representative of real and imagined capacities of AI and other emerging technologies.[58] This discussion is included for illustrative purposes only. It does not purport to represent a definitive classification of the range of academic and scientific discourse on all categories of AI, or the criteria proposed for each representative category. Additionally, the categories below are fluid and are not mutually exclusive. AI tools and systems can represent capacities and technologies that experts contend can span and cross over from one category to another.

1. Narrow AI, Reactive AI, and Predictive AI

Definitions of AI are still evolving. Some experts contend that there are two predominant categories of AI: (1) Narrow AI, also referred to as Weak AI, such as machine learning and generative AI that is programmed to generate reactive or predictive results; and (2) General AI or Theoretical AI, Sentient AI, or Artificial General Intelligence (AGI) that, theoretically, can rival human consciousness and intelligence.

---

54. European Parliament resolution of 20 October 2020 with recommendations to the Commission on a framework of ethical aspects of artificial intelligence, robotics and related technologies, 2020/2012(INL), Art. 4(c).

55. *People are Robots, too. Almost*, NAT'L AERONAUTIC SPACE ADMINISTRAT. JET PROPULSION LAB'Y (Oct. 28, 2003).

56. *Id.*

57. *Id.*

58. Arend Hintz, *Understanding the Four Types of AI, from Reactive Robots to Self-Aware Beings*, THE CONVERSATION, (Nov. 13, 2016).

The National Institute of Standards and Technology (NIST), a division of the U.S. Department of Commerce, has offered the following chart to distinguish the characteristics between Narrow AI and General AI.[59]

Narrow AI	General AI
• Application specific/task limited	• Perform general (human) intelligent actions
• Fixed domain models provided by programmers	• Self-learns and reasons with its operating environment
• Learns from thousands of labeled examples	• Learns from few examples and/or from unstructured data
• Reflexive tasks with no understanding	• Full range of human cognitive abilities
• Knowledge does not transfer to other domains or tasks	• Leverages knowledge transfer to new domains and tasks
• Today's AI	• Future AI?

Source: NIST; National Science and Technology Council, Subcommittee on Machine Learning and AI Technology.

Narrow AI, for example, is an AI system designed for a specific task, like an AI program that is trained on millions of chess games. In these systems, the AI is trained to be reactive or predictive, such as the Deep Blue program trained by IBM that famously defeated world chess champion Garry Kasparov.[60] "[A]chievements in the field today have been in task-specific AI or 'narrow AI', as opposed to what is commonly called artificial general intelligence [AGI] that can learn a wide range of tasks—like humans."[61] AGI or Sentient AI does not yet exist. Many ubiquitous technologies incorporate Narrow AI or Weak AI. These include, for example, algorithmic recommendations in social media feeds, automated suggestions for entertainment selections, navigation systems, autocorrect and calendaring tools, adaptive cruise control and other autonomous features in vehicles, robotic vacuums, smart biowearables and implanted medical devices, facial recognition and other biometric identity systems, and many other technologies.

2. *Limited Memory AI and Generative AI*

Limited memory AI is a form of Narrow AI or Weak AI. Through a combination of algorithmic and machine learning, it builds upon experiential

59. Michael Garris, Nat'l Inst. of Standards & Tech. [NIST], U.S. Dep't of Commerce & Nat'l Sci. & Tech. Council, Subcomm. on Machine Learning and AI Tech., Presentation: *Demystifying Today's Artificial Intelligence,* Nat'l Inst. Standards Tech. (May 22, 2018).

60. Garry Kasparov, Deep Thinking: Where Machine Intelligence Ends and Human Creativity Begins (2017).

61. GSA, *supra* note 43.

knowledge and historical reference models by learning from data inputs or observations. Generative AI may in some instances fall within the categories of reactive and predictive AI, and limited memory AI. Generative AI "refers to AI systems, in particular those using machine learning (ML) and trained on large volumes of data, that are able to generate new content[,]"[62] and "is a complex mix of data and computational algorithms[.]"[63] Generative AI "can create various outputs, including text responses (e.g., OpenAI's ChatGPT and Google's Bard [now Google Gemini]), images (e.g., Stability AI's Stable Diffusion and Midjourney's self-titled program), videos, computer code, or music."[64]

Generative AI is also comprised of foundation models or foundational model AI. Foundation models are considered a form of generative AI, or a "class of AI models that emulate the structure and characteristics of input data in order to generate derived synthetic content[,]" including: "images, videos, audio, text, and other digital content."[65] AI models are "a component of an information system that implements AI technology and uses computational, statistical, or machine-learning techniques to produce outputs from a given set of inputs."[66] The introduction of chatbots and virtual assistants, such as Siri, Alexa, and ChatGPT, led to the reference of AI foundation models as frontier AI or frontier foundational model AI, as these AI and generative AI tools rely on newly developing models.[67]

Multiple generative AI systems are reliant on Large Language Models (LLMs) and Natural Language Processing (NLP). Through a "prompt"—a statement, command, question, or other engagement of communication—a user inputs text or voice command into a generative AI system in a natural or conversational way. The generative AI system then responds to the prompt by generating content. LLMs and NLP allow the AI system to process a conversational prompt and to be trained to respond in a conversationally appropriate manner. "Large language models (LLMs) are AI systems that aim to model language, sometimes using millions or billions of parameters (i.e., numbers in the model that determine how inputs are converted to outputs). Repeatedly tweaking these parameters, using mathematical optimization techniques, and large amounts of data and computational power, increases model performance."[68]

---

62. *Id.*

63. Elham Tabassi, *Minimizing Harms and Maximizing the Potential of Generative* AI, Nat'l Inst. of Standards & Tech., U.S. Dep't of Commerce Blog (Nov. 20, 2023).

64. Laurie A. Harris, Cong. Rsch. Serv., IF 12426, Generative Artificial Intelligence: Overview, Issues, and Questions for Congress 1 (2023).

65. Exec. Order No. 14110, § 3(p), 3 C.F.R. 657, *Safe, Secure, and Trustworthy Development and Use of AI* (Oct. 30, 2023).

66. *Id.*

67. *See, e.g.*, Nathan Sanders & Bruce Schneier, *How the "Frontier" Became the Slogan of Uncontrolled AI*, Jacobin (Feb. 27, 2024).

68. *Id.*

3. *Theory of Mind AI*

Theory of Mind AI encompasses robotic research focusing on AI that aims to develop emotionally intelligent machines.[69] The humanoid robot Sophia, created by Hanson Robotics, can recognize faces and was developed to emotionally respond to interactions with unique and emotionally appropriate conversations and facial expressions.[70] As another example, the Kismet robot head, developed by Cynthia Breazeal at MIT, was programmed to recognize emotional signals and reproduce human emotions and expressions.[71] The topics of AI, robotics, and personhood will be discussed below.

4. *Sentient AI and Artificial General Intelligence as Theoretical AI*

The most advanced form of AI is Sentient AI or Self-Aware AI that expresses consciousness and human conscience capacities[72] and can rival human intelligence.[73] Theoretically, Artificial General Intelligence (AGI) is distinct from Sentient AI. It does not necessarily aim to achieve a Sentient AI level of cognitive and emotional capability, expressing self-generated emotions and engaging with humans with a level of consciousness that, theoretically, will be similar to human beings.[74] AGI, rather, aims at rivaling human intelligence. Sentient AI and AGI do not yet exist, and they are sometimes referred to as Theoretical AI, as it is debated among experts whether these types of AI are technically possible or whether they are only theoretically possible. Other experts debate the ethics and other consequences of Theoretical AI.

E. *AI LIFECYCLES*

The term "AI lifecycle" is an increasingly used phrase in AI development, AI business, and AI regulation.[75] An AI lifecycle, also known as AI project lifecycle, is the process by which an AI system is designed, developed, verified, deployed, and used. These steps are not a strictly sequential

---

69. *See, e.g.*, Cuzzolin, et al., *supra* note 42.

70. *Sophia*, Hanson Robotics.

71. *See, e.g.*, Duncan Graham-Rowe, *Meet Kismet*, New Scientist (Aug. 22, 1998).

72. Cuzzolin, et al., *supra* note 42.

73. *Id.*

74. Ralph Lewis, *What Would It Take to Build Sentient AI?*, Psych. Today (Oct. 8, 2023).

75. *See* Ted Chiang, The Lifecycle of Software Objects (2010) (one of the earliest uses of the word "lifecycle" in reference to AI is from science fiction).

process from problem to algorithmic solution, but one that can take place iteratively or reverse if issues occur and continues in development past deployment. New data can be collected, new plans can be made about new data, new models can be built upon new plans or new data, all before reemerging into the verification, deployment, and operation phases.[76]

The specific term AI lifecycle is not used in all current pieces of AI regulation. The *EU AI Act*, for instance, refers to the AI lifecycle to help contextualize an understanding of AI systems and development. By viewing an AI system as a developmental lifecycle, the regulation is not limited to targeting the issues that may result from one stage or the impacts of that stage's implementation. It permits parties to see the need to respect the rule of law and human rights through the entire AI system lifecycle.[77]

Another reason to refer to the AI lifecycle as an entirety is to mandate requirements across the entire lifecycle to prevent risks of harms that are difficult to reverse. The incorporation of sensitive information in AI foundational models and generative AI, for instance, is hard to reverse or retract once deployed. Other requirements, such as traceability of datasets and ensuring analysis of outputs, must be incorporated into the design from the beginning to enable AI system analysis.

Upon adoption of the *Recommendation of the Council on AI*, OECD instructed the OECD Directorate for Science, Technology and Innovation Committee on Digital Economy Policy to develop draft outlines for "developing practical guidance on the implementation" of the recommendation.[78]

The *Recommendation of the Council on AI* also included the following additional definitions:[79]

> AI system lifecycle: AI system lifecycle phases involve: i) 'design, data and models', which is a context-dependent sequence encompassing planning and design, data collection and processing, as well as model building; ii) 'verification and validation'; iii) 'deployment'; and iv) 'operation and monitoring'. These phases often take place in an iterative manner and are not necessarily sequential. The decision to retire an AI system from operation may occur at any point during the operation and monitoring phase.
> AI knowledge: AI knowledge refers to the skills and resources, such as data, code, algorithms, models, research, know-how, training programmes, governance, processes and best practices, required to understand and participate in the AI system lifecycle.

76. OECD, Artificial Intelligence in Society (2019).
77. *AI Principles*, OECD (see Principle 1.2).
78. Stuart Russell et al., *supra* note 6.
79. OECD, Recommendation of the Council on Artificial Intelligence ¶ I, OECD/LEGAL/0449 (May 21, 2019).

> AI actors: AI actors are those who play an active role in the AI system lifecycle, including organisations and individuals that deploy or operate AI.

The *OECD AI Principles* were adopted shortly after the adoption of the OECD AI definition. The principles recommended how governments and others could "shape a human-centric approach to trustworthy AI."[80]

The *EU AI Act* recognizes that AI definitions may need to evolve as the technological capacity of AI and other emerging technologies evolve. The *EU AI Act* excludes AI uses for national security or military and defense purposes and provides exceptions for law enforcement and border security. Similarly, the *EU AI Act* does not apply to AI systems used solely for the purpose of advancing research and innovation or for deployment of AI for non-professional objectives in purely private contexts.

In summary, the definitions of AI above are distinct from technical definitions of AI that might focus on AI's technological aspects. These AI definitions are broad and focus on operational aspects of AI, such as the ability to conduct assessment and prediction with levels of autonomy, and also focus on the way in which AI systems can influence both physical and virtual spheres of operation. They reflect law and policy developments that surround AI governance. Consequently, the materials in this book have been curated to provide examples of how governmental and nongovernmental entities are addressing the human impact of AI: how law and policy developments that adopt specific AI definitions are currently addressing the consequences, risks, and harms posed by AI and other emerging technologies.

AI systems, automated or semi-automated decisonmaking or assessment protocols, profoundly impact individuals and the public and private sectors. This impact is felt across all areas of law and fields of study, including commerce and international trade, innovation research and development, labor and employment, human rights and civil rights, and national security. Because the impact of AI is vast and the technologies surrounding AI are fast moving, the definitions of AI adopted by various governing bodies have tended to be broad and capable of enduring multiple phases of innovations.

80. OECD Working Party on Artificial Intel. Governance, AI Data Governance and Privacy: Synergies and Areas of International Co-Operation 16 (2024).

CHAPTER 3

CONCEPTUALIZING AI GOVERNANCE

Chapter 3 examines structures of governance in the regulation of AI. AI governance is one form of governance. AI governance, data governance, and corporate governance are distinct concepts; however, they can be interrelated. The discussion below uses the term AI governance to reflect frameworks of AI oversight and AI accountability. AI governance endeavors to design the laws and standards and oversight policies and principles necessary to ensure that AI systems are developed and deployed responsibly. Independently, outside of AI, governance topics are theoretically and conceptually complex. In the field of AI law and policy, the complexities are often compounded. The processes of conceptualizing AI governance may involve questions of a specific political environment and political economy, alignment or misalignment of economic and behavioral incentives, geopolitical conflicts and national security strategies, practicality and technological feasibility of proposed oversight, known and unknown risks posed by AI systems, assessments of AI benefits weighed against potential harms, long-term social impact and potential disparate impact, and other critical considerations. It also considers how the oversight mechanism or regulation maps into preexisting policy and legal frameworks, as well as into other governance and governmental practices and processes.

A. *INTRODUCTION TO OVERSIGHT MECHANISMS*

Integrated within the field of AI law and policy are philosophies of AI governance and power, which are sometimes visible and debated, and sometimes obscured, shielded from active discourse. Chapter 3 invites an interrogation of these philosophies, and their interaction with legal and policy developments in AI governance. It focuses on historical developments in AI governance and potential efficacies of proposed governance methods. A key question is how AI governance structures, unfolding rapidly and globally, may or may not conform to the legal and philosophical commitments that underscore a constitutional democracy. To launch this conversation on oversight mechanisms, some legal instruments and broad approaches to AI governance are outlined below. Laws, policies, and strategies will often leverage multiple philosophies and oversight mechanisms. Therefore, the categories below should not be read as rigid and siloed classifications, but rather, potentially integrated concepts.

1. Hard Law v. Soft Law

Globally, statutory and regulatory frameworks providing AI oversight are quickly proliferating. Yet, preceding an examination of AI statutory and regulatory frameworks is a question of how AI governance unfolds under both hard law and soft law approaches. A foundational conversation in AI law and policy is ascertaining the line between hard law and soft law. Hard law is generally understood to include statutory frameworks with enforceable consequences, regulations that are promulgated from originating statutes, and common law, such as judicial opinions. In contrast, soft law is generally understood to include ethical principles, policies and procedures, and other executive and agency policy guidance that can be structured within the administrative state. Admittedly, ascertaining what is appropriately categorized as hard law and soft law in the field of AI law and policy is a fast-moving target.

In the U.S., many national AI governance developments have occurred within the category of soft law. For over a decade, the White House, spanning multiple administrations, has issued reports and executive orders addressing AI policy, inclusive of AI subfields and interstitial fields.[1] For the past few Congresses, several statutes have been enacted and fall within the category of hard law. These include: the *National Artificial Intelligence Initiative Act of 2020*;[2] the *AI in Government Act of 2020*;[3] the *Advancing American AI Act* [2022];[4] the *AI Training Act* [2022];[5] and the *John S. McCain National Defense Authorization Act for Fiscal Year 2019*.[6]

1. *See, e.g.*, White House, Exec. Off. Pres., Big Data: Seizing Opportunities, Preserving Values 3 n.8 (2014) (quoting National Science Foundation, Solicitation 12-499: Core Techniques and Technologies for Advancing Big Data Science & Engineering (BIG-DATA), 2 (2012); White House, Exec. Off. Pres., Big Data: A Report on Algorithmic Systems, Opportunity, and Civil Rights (2016); Exec. Order No. 13859, 3 C.F.R. 254, *Maintaining American Leadership in Artificial Intelligence* (Feb. 11, 2019).

2. P.L. 116-283, Division E—National Artificial Intelligence Initiative Act of 2020, William M. (Mac) Thornberry National Defense Authorization Act for Fiscal Year 2021.

3. P.L. 116-260, Division U—Homeland Security and Governmental Affairs Provisions, Title I—AI in Government Act of 2020, Consolidated Appropriations Act, 2021.

4. P.L. 117-263, Division G—Homeland Security Matters, Title LXXII—Governmental Affairs, Subtitle B—Advancing American AI Act, James M. Inhofe National Defense Authorization Act for Fiscal Year 2023.

5. P.L. 117-207, Sec. 1 ("This Act may be cited as the 'Artificial Intelligence Training for the Acquisition Workforce Act' or the 'AI Training Act'.").

6. P.L. 115-232, John S. McCain National Defense Authorization Act for Fiscal Year 2019.

As will be discussed later in this chapter, in recent years the Executive Branch of the U.S. government released important documents providing national policy guidance on AI governance. In October 2022, the White House Office of Science and Technology Policy (OSTP) released the *Blueprint for an AI Bill of Rights.* Shortly thereafter, the U.S. Department of Commerce, National Institute of Standards and Technology (NIST), released Version 1.0 of the *NIST Artificial Intelligence (AI) Risk Management Framework* in January 2023. Federal agencies in the U.S. were also invited to comply with the *Executive Order on the Safe, Secure, and Trustworthy Development and Use of Artificial Intelligence* (E.O. 14110), released by the White House in October 2023. Following the directives of E.O. 14110, the White House Office of Management and Budget (OMB) published the *OMB Memorandum on Advancing Governance, Innovation, and Risk Management in Federal Agencies' Use of Artificial Intelligence* in March 2024. Paralleling the *Executive Order on the Safe, Secure, and Trustworthy Development and Use of Artificial Intelligence,* other national and state legislative proposals, and other global AI governance developments, the OMB Memorandum on AI directed federal agencies to focus on balancing AI risk mitigation with AI innovation and economic growth goals. On January 20, 2025, the Trump administration rescinded E.O. 14110, and on April 3, 2025, rescinded the OMB policies that were promulgated pursuant to E.O. 11410.[7] On January 23, 2025, the administration published the *Executive Order on Removing Barriers to American Leadership in Artificial Intelligence,* E.O. 14179.[8]

The *Blueprint,* the *NIST AI Risk Management Framework,* E.O. 14179, and other federal programs and policies reflect soft law approaches to AI governance. The non-binding nature of the *Blueprint* is explained in this disclaimer:[9]

> The Blueprint for an AI Bill of Rights is non-binding and does not constitute U.S. government policy. It does not supersede, modify, or direct an interpretation of any existing statute, regulation, policy, or international instrument. It does not constitute binding guidance for the public or Federal agencies and therefore does not require compliance with the principles described herein. It also is not determinative of what the U.S. government's position will be in any international negotiation. Adoption

---

7. Exec. Order No. 14148, 90 Fed. Reg. 8237, *Initial Rescissions of Harmful Executive Orders and Actions* (Jan. 28, 2025); OMB Memorandum M-25-21, *Accelerating Federal Use of AI through Innovation, Governance, and Public Trust* (Apr. 3, 2025); OMB Memorandum M-25-22, *Driving Efficient Acquisition of Artificial Intelligence in Government* (Apr. 3, 2025). These two OMB memos implement Exec. Order No. 14179, 90 Fed. Reg. 8741, *Removing Barriers to American Leadership in Artificial Intelligence* (Jan. 31, 2025), rescinding and replacing the two OMB memos promulgated during the Biden administration on AI use and AI procurement, OMB Memorandum M-24-10, *Advancing Governance, Innovation, and Risk Management for Agency Use of Artificial Intelligence* (Mar. 28, 2024) and OMB Memorandum M-24-18, *Advancing the Responsible Acquisition of Artificial Intelligence in Government* (Sept. 24, 2024).

8. Exec. Order No. 14179, 90 Fed. Reg. 8741, *Removing Barriers to American Leadership in Artificial Intelligence* (Jan. 31, 2025).

9. White House, Off. Sci. and Tech. Pol'y, Blueprint for an AI Bill of Rights (2022).

> of these principles may not meet the requirements of existing statutes, regulations, policies, or international instruments, or the requirements of the Federal agencies that enforce them. These principles are not intended to, and do not, prohibit or limit any lawful activity of a government agency, including law enforcement, national security, or intelligence activities.

Soft law approaches to AI governance by the executive branch have embraced voluntary measures such as the *NIST AI Risk Management Framework,* which "is intended for voluntary use and to improve the ability to incorporate trustworthiness considerations into the design, development, use, and evaluation of AI products, services, and systems."[10]

The presence of soft law helps to govern AI through a wide range of actions, including proposing methodologies for how to assess and mitigate AI risks; providing technology and AI companies with information on pre-existing federal laws and mandates and what types of harms federal agencies might investigate; and offering published guidance on what federal agencies might not advise for procurement and use in state and federal governmental contexts.

2. *Horizontal Oversight v. Vertical Oversight*

Another way to approach oversight is in the breadth of the scope of the regulation. There are generally two approaches to regulating AI: horizontal AI regulation and vertical AI regulation. Horizontal regulation generally applies to all applications of AI throughout all different sectors of industry, government, and application. Vertical regulation is a regulation that applies to specific use cases or sectors of AI, being narrowly focused on a more limited field or purpose.

The *EU AI Act* is a high-profile example of what the EU represents as a form of horizontal AI regulation. It applies to all uses of AI across all sectors, applying the same risk assessments and safety requirements to follow. There are also many examples of vertical AI regulation, primarily among state and local jurisdictions in the U.S. The *Illinois Artificial Intelligence Video Interview Act,*[11] for instance, only applies to the use of AI when it is used to analyze video taken during recruitment interviews, also a very narrow application.

Some jurisdictions adopt both approaches. The People's Republic of China, for example, has adopted both horizontal regulation that applies

10. U.S. Dep't Commerce, Nat'l Inst. Standards and Tech., Info. Tech. Lab., *AI Risk Management Framework* (Jan. 2023).

11. Illinois Artificial Intelligence Video Interview Act, 820 Ill. Comp. Stat. 42/5 (2022).

broadly to all uses of AI and vertical regulations that regulate specific industry sectors.

3. Internal Governance and Self-Governance v. External Governance

Similar to the method of understanding AI oversight as hard law or soft law, or as horizontal or vertical, AI governance can also be categorized as internal or external. In the absence of omnibus federal legislation that comprehensively regulates AI and emerging technologies, both the public and private sectors in the U.S., including, importantly, leading AI companies and technology companies, have adopted AI risk management frameworks, AI ethics principles, and other internal governance strategies. External governance can take shape through hard law, such as developments in proposed legislation and rulemaking by agencies in federal and state governments. Statutory and regulatory frameworks are emerging to provide hard law approaches to AI governance. External governance of AI systems can include soft law and policy developments, such as public-private partnerships, voluntary commitments, and procurement guidelines. In addition, governance can include shareholder action, reporting and revelations that shape internal reform, governance through litigation strategies, and other tools.

Under self-governance models, leading AI and technology companies, along with many others, have adopted guidance to provide internal corporate oversight to the development and deployment of AI. Specifically, as will be discussed in Chapters 9 and 10, companies have adopted AI ethics principles and other AI oversight methods, such as AI auditing and impact assessments. Some lawmakers and policymakers have looked to the potential of codifying internal governance practices into law, advocating for the transition from an internal to an external governance approach. In other contexts, governments globally have sought a cooperative approach to AI governance.

4. Multistakeholder Governance and Cooperative Governance

The need for effective stakeholder engagement is seen as particularly critical in AI policy. In public policy, stakeholders are often defined in terms of consultative roles, those groups or individuals that should serve in a consultatory or advisory role in policy development due to their expertise, for example, or their potential to influence or be impacted by the policy matter. Under one definition, in the context of European Industrial Relations, "[a] stakeholder is an individual, group of persons or organization that can affect or is affected by the decisions of another organization . . . includ[ing] interest groups."[12]

The examples below suggest methods undertaken by governmental bodies to incentivize multistakeholder engagement and cooperative AI governance efforts. On July 21, 2023, the White House convened a meeting with seven leading AI companies: Amazon, Anthropic, Google, Inflection, Meta, Microsoft, and OpenAI. The excerpts below include the announcement that followed this meeting. As the Fact Sheet and the *Voluntary AI Commitments* were published by the prior administration, policies are subject to revision. Additionally, the excerpts also include provisions of the *EU General Data Protection Regulation* and *EU AI Act* that refer to the need for stakeholder engagement and multistakeholder efforts.

a. White House Voluntary Commitments with Leading AI Companies

Fact Sheet: Biden-Harris Administration Secures Voluntary Commitments from Leading Artificial Intelligence Companies to Manage the Risks Posed by AI

July 21, 2023

Companies that are developing these emerging technologies have a responsibility to ensure their products are safe. . . . These commitments, which the companies have chosen to undertake immediately, underscore three principles that must be fundamental to the future of AI – safety, security, and trust – and mark a critical step toward developing responsible AI. . . .

Voluntary AI Commitments

[White House Voluntary Commitments with Leading AI Companies]
September 12, 2023

These voluntary commitments are consistent with existing laws and regulations, and designed to advance a generative AI legal and policy regime. These voluntary commitments also recognize that different AI actors have different responsibilities depending on their roles in the AI development lifecycle and in AI systems, and that risk prioritization and management of each commitment is specific to the capabilities of each AI system. Companies intend these voluntary commitments to remain in effect until regulations covering substantially the same issues come into force. Individual companies may make additional commitments beyond those included here. . . .

---

12. *Stakeholder*, EUROPEAN INDUSTRIAL RELATIONS DICTIONARY (published Aug. 6, 2019, updated Dec. 3, 2019).

b. EU General Data Protection Regulation (GDPR), Article 50 [International Cooperation for the Protection of Personal Data]

GDPR

Article 50. International Cooperation for the Protection of Personal Data

In relation to third countries and international organisations, the Commission and supervisory authorities shall take appropriate steps to: . . .

> **(c)** engage relevant stakeholders in discussion and activities aimed at furthering international cooperation in the enforcement of legislation for the protection of personal data[.] . . .

c. EU AI Act, Article 40 [Harmonised Standards and Standardisation Deliverables]

EU AI Act

Article 40. Harmonised Standards and Standardisation Deliverables

> **3.** The participants in the standardisation process shall seek to promote investment and innovation in AI, including through increasing legal certainty, as well as the competitiveness and growth of the Union market, to contribute to strengthening global cooperation on standardisation and taking into account existing international standards in the field of AI that are consistent with Union values, fundamental rights and interests, and to enhance multi-stakeholder governance ensuring a balanced representation of interests and the effective participation of all relevant stakeholders[.] . . .

B. CASE STUDIES IN RISK ELIMINATION AND RISK MITIGATION APPROACHES

A constitutional democracy is reliant upon multiple structures of governance and government, such as parliamentary systems and bicameralism, federalism, and other forms of executive decisionmaking and elected representation; regulatory regimes; and the enforcement and investigatory arms of an administrative state. The centering axis of a constitutional democracy is the rule of law. The U.S. Constitution manifests this through a decentralized philosophy of power and incorporates power-balancing methods, such as the separation of powers and a system of checks and balances. These methods and other constitutional tools that limit and restrict exercises of power have been referred to as "risk-management devices" in constitutional management and design.[13] The Bill of Rights, the first ten amendments of

---

13. Adrian Vermeule, The Constitution of Risk 1 (2013).

the U.S. Constitution, followed to explicitly articulate a series of foundational rights for the new republic.

This is a useful metaphor in understanding AI governance. Constitutional law developments mirror AI law developments in significant ways. Both are concerned with restraint and accountability, on the one hand, and preserving fundamental rights, on the other. Many conversations in AI governance frame regulation in terms of AI rights and AI risks. These are sometimes presented as two separate approaches to AI oversight: a rights-based approach and a risk-based approach. As will be explored in more detail below, there are legislative and regulatory developments that represent a mixture of the two approaches. The hybrid approach includes elements of both in an attempt to manage and mitigate risks posed by AI and emerging technologies.

1. *Rights-Based Framework*

In a rights-based approach to AI governance, the goal is to eliminate, to the extent possible, risks posed by AI. To achieve this, the regulatory model and oversight tools seek to identify rights and preserve those rights from infringement by AI and automated systems. These rights can be derived from constitutional rights, such as those enshrined within the Bill of Rights, human rights, or other sources of cognizable rights. What human rights and privileges must be preserved and protected when using AI in government decision making, policing and military action, courts and administrative procedures, and industry? How, and when, does AI infringe upon those rights?

The *Blueprint for an AI Bill of Rights* is neither a legal regulation nor a technical framework. Instead, the White House Office of Science and Technology Policy (OSTP), in promulgating the *Blueprint*, sought to provide a shared vision of harnessing the positive benefits of AI while maintaining an eye on fair information principles and fundamental rights.

a. White House Office of Science and Technology Policy (OSTP) Blueprint for an AI Bill of Rights

The *Blueprint for an AI Bill of Rights* takes a rights-based approach to AI governance. It has been selected to illustrate of this approach because it forces a conversation on how we conceptualize what fundamental rights are, how we need to envision those rights in the deployment of AI and automated systems, and how those fundamental rights might be infringed upon by those systems.

Although policies are subject to revision in the transition between administrations, the *Blueprint for an AI Bill of Rights* is historically enduring. It offers conceptual scaffolding and a legal theory for a rights-based method of AI governance.

The *Blueprint for an AI Bill of Rights* provides a series of examples to "illustrate the breadth of automated systems" to demonstrate how "they have the potential to meaningfully impact rights, opportunities, or access to critical resources or services[.]"[14] The examples of how AI and automated systems can impact constitutional rights and privileges in the *Blueprint for an AI Bill of Rights* underscore the need for a discussion on a new set of principles to guide a conceptualization of AI rights.

The purpose of setting forth the following examples provided by the *Blueprint for an AI Bill of Rights* is to illustrate the first part of conceptualizing AI governance: What is at stake? What are the goals and aspirations for AI oversight? The White House attempted to answer these questions in the following:[15]

> **Examples of Automated Systems for Which the Blueprint for an AI Bill of Rights Should be Considered Include Those That Have the Potential to Meaningfully Impact:**
>
> - **Civil rights, civil liberties, or privacy, including but not limited to:**
>   - Speech-related systems such as automated content moderation tools;
>   - Surveillance and criminal justice system algorithms such as risk assessments, predictive policing, automated license plate readers, real-time facial recognition systems (especially those used in public places or during protected activities like peaceful protests), social media monitoring, and ankle monitoring devices;
>   - Voting-related systems such as signature matching tools;
>   - Systems with a potential privacy impact such as smart home systems and associated data, systems that use or collect health-related data, systems that use or collect education-related data, criminal justice system data, ad-targeting systems, and systems that perform big data analytics in order to build profiles or infer personal information about individuals; and
>   - Any system that has the meaningful potential to lead to algorithmic discrimination.
> - **Equal opportunities, including but not limited to:**
>   - Education-related systems such as algorithms that purport to detect student cheating or plagiarism, admissions algorithms, online or virtual reality student monitoring systems, projections of student progress or outcomes, algorithms that determine access to resources or programs, and surveillance of classes (whether online or in-person);
>   - Housing-related systems such as tenant screening algorithms, automated valuation systems that estimate the value of homes used in mortgage underwriting or home insurance, and automated valuations from online aggregator websites; and

---

14. White House, Off. Sci. and Tech. Pol'y, Blueprint for an AI Bill of Rights: *Examples of Automated Systems* (2022).

15. *Id.*

- Employment-related systems such as workplace algorithms that inform all aspects of the terms and conditions of employment including, but not limited to, pay or promotion, hiring or termination algorithms, virtual or augmented reality workplace training programs, and electronic workplace surveillance and management systems.
- **Access to critical resources and services, including but not limited to:**
  - Health and health insurance technologies such as medical AI systems and devices, AI-assisted diagnostic tools, algorithms or predictive models used to support clinical decision making, medical or insurance health risk assessments, drug addiction risk assessments and associated access algorithms, wearable technologies, wellness apps, insurance care allocation algorithms, and health insurance cost and underwriting algorithms;
  - Financial system algorithms such as loan allocation algorithms, financial system access determination algorithms, credit scoring systems, insurance algorithms including risk assessments, automated interest rate determinations, and financial algorithms that apply penalties (e.g., that can garnish wages or withhold tax returns);
  - Systems that impact the safety of communities such as automated traffic control systems, electrical grid controls, smart city technologies, and industrial emissions and environmental impact control algorithms; and
  - Systems related to access to benefits, services, or assignment of penalties such as systems that support decision makers who adjudicate benefits such as collating or analyzing information or matching records, systems which similarly assist in the adjudication of administrative or criminal penalties, fraud detection algorithms, services or benefits access control algorithms, biometric systems used as access control, and systems which make benefits or services related decisions on a fully or partially autonomous basis (such as a determination to revoke benefits).

The *Blueprint for an AI Bill of Rights* explained that AI governance required a commitment to a new conceptualization of AI rights. It explained that all citizens were impacted by AI systems in ways that required envisioning a scope of protections that could safeguard citizens from growing harms and risks posed by AI and AI systems. The five proposed pillars of fundamental AI rights included: (1) Safe and Effective Systems; (2) Algorithmic Discrimination Protections; (3) Data Privacy; (4) Notice and Explanation; and (5) Human-Centered Alternatives and Remedies.

The *Blueprint for an AI Bill of Rights* next articulated each one of these principles. This non-binding document suggested a new conceptualization of fundamental AI rights under a theory of what was termed an "AI Bill of Rights." The excerpt below provides a summary of each of these principles, which the drafters invited the reader to visualize as a new type of fundamental constitutional right.

Blueprint for an AI Bill of Rights

White House Office of Science and Technology Policy
October 4, 2022

PRINCIPLE 1: SAFE AND EFFECTIVE SYSTEMS

Safe and Effective Systems: You Should Be Protected from Unsafe or Ineffective Systems

You Should Be Protected from Unsafe or Ineffective Systems

Automated systems should be developed with consultation from diverse communities, stakeholders, and domain experts to identify concerns, risks, and potential impacts of the system.

Systems should undergo pre-deployment testing, risk identification and mitigation, and ongoing monitoring that demonstrate they are safe and effective based on their intended use, mitigation of unsafe outcomes including those beyond the intended use, and adherence to domain-specific standards.

Outcomes of these protective measures should include the possibility of not deploying the system or removing a system from use.

Automated systems should not be designed with an intent or reasonably foreseeable possibility of endangering your safety or the safety of your community.

They should be designed to proactively protect you from harms stemming from unintended, yet foreseeable, uses or impacts of automated systems.

You should be protected from inappropriate or irrelevant data use in the design, development, and deployment of automated systems, and from the compounded harm of its reuse.

Independent evaluation and reporting that confirms that the system is safe and effective, including reporting of steps taken to mitigate potential harms, should be performed and the results made public whenever possible.

PRINCIPLE 2: ALGORITHMIC DISCRIMINATION PROTECTIONS

Algorithmic Discrimination Protections: You Should Not Face Discrimination by Algorithms and Systems Should Be Used and Designed in an Equitable Way

You Should Not Face Discrimination by Algorithms and Systems Should Be Used and Designed in an Equitable Way

Algorithmic discrimination occurs when automated systems contribute to unjustified different treatment or impacts disfavoring people based on their race, color, ethnicity, sex (including pregnancy, childbirth, and related medical conditions, gender identity, intersex status, and sexual orientation), religion, age, national origin, disability, veteran status, genetic information, or any other classification protected by law.

Depending on the specific circumstances, such algorithmic discrimination may violate legal protections.

Designers, developers, and deployers of automated systems should take proactive and continuous measures to protect individuals and communities from algorithmic discrimination and to use and design systems in an equitable way.

This protection should include proactive equity assessments as part of the system design, use of representative data and protection against proxies for demographic features, ensuring accessibility for people with disabilities in design and development, pre-deployment and ongoing disparity testing and mitigation, and clear organizational oversight.

Independent evaluation and plain language reporting in the form of an algorithmic impact assessment, including disparity testing results and mitigation information, should be performed and made public whenever possible to confirm these protections.

PRINCIPLE 3: DATA PRIVACY

Data Privacy: You Should Be Protected from Abusive Data Practices Via Built-in Protections and You Should Have Agency Over How Data About You Is Used

You Should Be Protected from Abusive Data Practices Via Built-In Protections and You Should Have Agency Over How Data About You Is Used

You should be protected from violations of privacy through design choices that ensure such protections are included by default, including ensuring that data collection conforms to reasonable expectations and that only data strictly necessary for the specific context is collected.

Designers, developers, and deployers of automated systems should seek your permission and respect your decisions regarding collection, use, access, transfer, and deletion of your data in appropriate ways and to the greatest extent possible; where not possible, alternative privacy by design safeguards should be used.

Systems should not employ user experience and design decisions that obfuscate user choice or burden users with defaults that are privacy invasive.

Consent should only be used to justify collection of data in cases where it can be appropriately and meaningfully given. Any consent requests should be brief, be understandable in plain language, and give you agency over data collection and the specific context of use; current hard-to-understand notice-and-choice practices for broad uses of data should be changed.

Enhanced protections and restrictions for data and inferences related to sensitive domains, including health, work, education, criminal justice, and finance, and for data pertaining to youth should put you first. In sensitive domains, your data and related inferences should only be used for necessary functions, and you should be protected by ethical review and use prohibitions.

You and your communities should be free from unchecked surveillance; surveillance technologies should be subject to heightened oversight that includes at least pre-deployment assessment of their potential harms and scope limits to protect privacy and civil liberties.

Continuous surveillance and monitoring should not be used in education, work, housing, or in other contexts where the use of such surveillance technologies is likely to limit rights, opportunities, or access.

Whenever possible, you should have access to reporting that confirms your data decisions have been respected and provides an assessment of the potential impact of surveillance technologies on your rights, opportunities, or access.

PRINCIPLE 4: NOTICE AND EXPLANATION

Notice and Explanation: You Should Know That an Automated System Is Being Used and Understand How and Why It Contributes to Outcomes That Impact You

You Should Know That An Automated System Is Being Used and Understand How and Why It Contributes to Outcomes That Impact You

Designers, developers, and deployers of automated systems should provide generally accessible plain language documentation including clear descriptions of the overall system functioning and the role automation plays, notice that such systems are in use, the individual or organization responsible for the system, and explanations of outcomes that are clear, timely, and accessible.

Such notice should be kept up-to-date and people impacted by the system should be notified of significant use case or key functionality changes.

You should know how and why an outcome impacting you was determined by an automated system, including when the automated system is not the sole input determining the outcome.

Automated systems should provide explanations that are technically valid, meaningful and useful to you and to any operators or others who need to understand the system, and calibrated to the level of risk based on the context.

Reporting that includes summary information about these automated systems in plain language and assessments of the clarity and quality of the notice and explanations should be made public whenever possible.

PRINCIPLE 5: HUMAN-CENTERED ALTERNATIVES AND REMEDIES

Human Alternatives, Consideration, and Fallback: You Should Be Able to Opt Out, Where Appropriate, and Have Access to a Person Who Can Quickly Consider and Remedy Problems You Encounter

You Should Be Able to Opt Out, Where Appropriate, and Have Access to a Person Who Can Quickly Consider and Remedy Problems You Encounter

You should be able to opt out from automated systems in favor of a human alternative, where appropriate.

Appropriateness should be determined based on reasonable expectations in a given context and with a focus on ensuring broad accessibility and protecting the public from especially harmful impacts. In some cases, a human or other alternative may be required by law.

You should have access to timely human consideration and remedy by a fallback and escalation process if an automated system fails, it produces an error, or you would like to appeal or contest its impacts on you.

Human consideration and fallback should be accessible, equitable, effective, maintained, accompanied by appropriate operator training, and should not impose an unreasonable burden on the public.

Automated systems with an intended use within sensitive domains, including, but not limited to, criminal justice, employment, education, and health, should additionally be tailored to the purpose, provide meaningful access for oversight, include training for any people interacting with the system, and incorporate human consideration for adverse or high-risk decisions.

Reporting that includes a description of these human governance processes and assessment of their timeliness, accessibility, outcomes, and effectiveness should be made public whenever possible.

2. *Risk-Based Framework*

The risk-based approach to AI regulation focuses on risk management, often requiring greater levels of compliance for areas of greater risk. Risk-based approaches can incorporate elements of rights-based approaches. One of the typical goals of a risk-based approach is the minimization of risks to civil rights. But the overall focus of a risk-based approach centers upon addressing AI risks.

Voluntary compliance in the U.S. is a hallmark of early attempts to adopt risk-based approaches to AI governance. The U.S. Department of Commerce, through the leadership of the National Institute of Standards and Technology (NIST), for example, introduced the 2023 *NIST AI Risk Management Framework*. The *AI Risk Management Framework* adopts a risk-based approach to AI governance and invites the public and private sectors to voluntarily follow guidance on how best to evaluate the potential harms of AI. Executive policies and federal agency frameworks are subject to change from one administration to the next. Like the *Blueprint for an AI Bill of Rights*, the *NIST AI Risk Management Framework* also holds enduring historical value for understanding risk-based models of AI governance.

a. National Institute of Standards and Technology (NIST) AI Risk Management Framework

The *NIST AI Risk Management Framework 1.0* provides a definition of "Trustworthy AI" that encompasses characteristics of AI systems ready for safe and responsible deployment. "In collaboration with the private and public sectors," NIST "developed a framework to better manage risks to individuals, organizations, and society associated with artificial intelligence (AI)."[16] The *AI Risk Management Framework* also stresses a robust governance system to ensure the organization's successful implementation of the framework. It "is intended for voluntary use and to improve the ability to incorporate trustworthiness considerations into the design, development, use, and evaluation of AI products, services, and systems."[17] The *AI Risk Management Framework* defines AI trustworthiness as necessary because:[18]

> Highly secure but unfair systems, accurate but opaque and uninterpretable systems, and inaccurate but secure, privacy-enhanced, and transparent systems are all undesirable. A comprehensive approach to risk management calls for balancing tradeoffs among the trustworthiness characteristics. It is the joint responsibility of all AI actors to determine whether AI technology is an appropriate or necessary tool for a given context or purpose, and how to use it responsibly. The decision to commission or deploy an AI system should be based on a contextual assessment of trustworthiness characteristics and the relative risks, impacts, costs, and benefits, and informed by a broad set of interested parties.

The following excerpts from the *AI Risk Management Framework* illustrate how the U.S. attempts to guide a voluntary effort through public-private cooperation to incentivize trustworthy AI in the development and deployment of AI technologies. Policies are subject to revision in the transition between administrations.

NIST AI Risk Management Framework (AI RMF 1.0)

U.S. Department of Commerce, National Institute of Standards and Technology (NIST)
January 26, 2023

EXECUTIVE SUMMARY

. . . While there are myriad standards and best practices to help organizations mitigate the risks of traditional software or information-based

---

16. U.S. Dep't Commerce, Nat'l Inst. Standards and Tech., Info. Tech. Lab., *AI Risk Management Framework* (Jan. 2023).

17. *Id.*

18. *Id.*

systems, the risks posed by AI systems are in many ways unique. AI systems, for example, may be trained on data that can change over time, sometimes significantly and unexpectedly, affecting system functionality and trustworthiness in ways that are hard to understand. AI systems and the contexts in which they are deployed are frequently complex, making it difficult to detect and respond to failures when they occur. AI systems are inherently socio-technical in nature, meaning they are influenced by societal dynamics and human behavior. AI risks – and benefits – can emerge from the interplay of technical aspects combined with societal factors related to how a system is used, its interactions with other AI systems, who operates it, and the social context in which it is deployed.

These risks make AI a uniquely challenging technology to deploy and utilize both for organizations and within society. Without proper controls, AI systems can amplify, perpetuate, or exacerbate inequitable or undesirable outcomes for individuals and communities. With proper controls, AI systems can mitigate and manage inequitable outcomes.

AI risk management is a key component of responsible development and use of AI systems. Responsible AI practices can help align the decisions about AI system design, development, and uses with intended aim and values. Core concepts in responsible AI emphasize human centricity, social responsibility, and sustainability. AI risk management can drive responsible uses and practices by prompting organizations and their internal teams who design, develop, and deploy AI to think more critically about context and potential or unexpected negative and positive impacts. Understanding and managing the risks of AI systems will help to enhance trustworthiness, and in turn, cultivate public trust. . . .

As directed by the National Artificial Intelligence Initiative Act of 2020 (P.L. 116-283), the goal of the AI RMF is to offer a resource to the organizations designing, developing, deploying, or using AI systems to help manage the many risks of AI and promote trustworthy and responsible development and use of AI systems. The Framework is intended to be voluntary, rights-preserving, non-sector-specific, and use-case agnostic, providing flexibility to organizations of all sizes and in all sectors and throughout society to implement the approaches in the Framework . . . .

PART 1: FOUNDATIONAL INFORMATION

1. Framing Risk

AI risk management offers a path to minimize potential negative impacts of AI systems, such as threats to civil liberties and rights, while also providing opportunities to maximize positive impacts. Addressing, documenting, and managing AI risks and potential negative impacts effectively can lead to more trustworthy AI systems.

1.1 Understanding and Addressing Risks, Impacts, and Harms

In the context of the AI RMF, *risk* refers to the composite measure of an event's probability of occurring and the magnitude or degree of the consequences of the corresponding event. The impacts, or consequences, of AI systems can be positive, negative, or both and can result in opportunities or threats (Adapted from: ISO 31000:2018). When considering the negative impact of a potential event, risk is a function of 1) the negative impact, or magnitude of harm, that would arise if the circumstance or event occurs and 2) the likelihood of occurrence (Adapted from: OMB Circular A-130:2016). Negative impact or harm can be experienced by individuals, groups, communities, organizations, society, the environment, and the planet. . . .

While risk management processes generally address negative impacts, this Framework offers approaches to minimize anticipated negative impacts of AI systems *and* identify opportunities to maximize positive impacts. Effectively managing the risk of potential harms could lead to more trustworthy AI systems and unleash potential benefits to people (individuals, communities, and society), organizations, and systems/ecosystems. Risk management can enable AI developers and users to understand impacts and account for the inherent limitations and uncertainties in their models and systems, which in turn can improve overall system performance and trustworthiness and the likelihood that AI technologies will be used in ways that are beneficial.

The AI RMF is designed to address new risks as they emerge. This flexibility is particularly important where impacts are not easily foreseeable and applications are evolving. While some AI risks and benefits are well-known, it can be challenging to assess negative impacts and the degree of harms. Figure 1 provides examples of potential harms that can be related to AI systems.

AI risk management efforts should consider that humans may assume that AI systems work – and work well – in *all* settings. For example, whether correct or not, AI systems are often perceived as being more objective than humans or as offering greater capabilities than general software.

1.2 Challenges for AI Risk Management

Several challenges are described below. They should be taken into account when managing risks in pursuit of AI trustworthiness.

1.2.1 Risk Measurement

AI risks or failures that are not well-defined or adequately understood are difficult to measure quantitatively or qualitatively. The inability to appropriately measure AI risks does not imply that an AI system necessarily poses either a high or low risk. Some risk measurement challenges include:

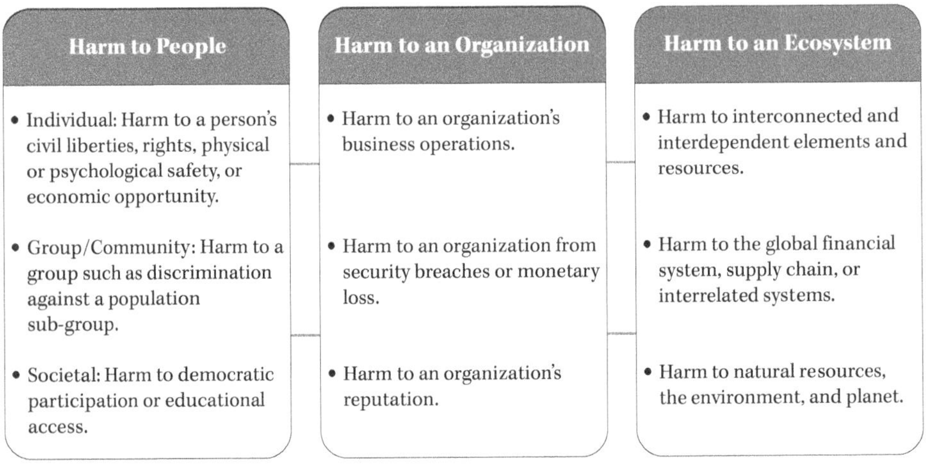

Fig. 1. Examples of potential harms related to AI systems. Trustworthy AI systems and their responsible use can mitigate negative risks and contribute to benefits for people, organizations, and ecosystems.

Risks related to third-party software, hardware, and data: Third-party data or systems can accelerate research and development and facilitate technology transition. They also may complicate risk measurement. Risk can emerge both from third-party data, software or hardware itself and how it is used. Risk metrics or methodologies used by the organization developing the AI system may not align with the risk metrics or methodologies uses by the organization *deploying or operating* the system. Also, the organization developing the AI system may not be transparent about the risk metrics or methodologies it used. Risk measurement and management can be complicated by how customers use or integrate third-party data or systems into AI products or services, particularly without sufficient internal governance structures and technical safeguards. Regardless, all parties and AI actors should manage risk in the AI systems they develop, deploy, or use as standalone or integrated components.

Tracking emergent risks: Organizations' risk management efforts will be enhanced by identifying and tracking emergent risks and considering techniques for measuring them. AI system impact assessment approaches can help AI actors understand potential impacts or harms within specific contexts.

Availability of reliable metrics: The current lack of consensus on robust and verifiable measurement methods for risk and trustworthiness, and applicability to different AI use cases, is an AI risk measurement challenge. Potential pitfalls when seeking to measure negative risk or harms include the reality that development of metrics is often an institutional endeavor and may inadvertently reflect factors unrelated to the underlying impact. In addition, measurement approaches can be oversimplified, gamed, lack critical nuance, become relied upon in unexpected ways, or fail to account for differences in affected groups and contexts.

Approaches for measuring impacts on a population work best if they recognize that contexts matter, that harms may affect varied groups or sub-groups differently, and that communities or other sub-groups who may be harmed are not always direct users of a system.

Risk at different stages of the AI lifecycle: Measuring risk at an earlier stage in the AI lifecycle may yield different results than measuring risk at a later stage; some risks may be latent at a given point in time and may increase as AI systems adapt and evolve. Furthermore, different AI actors across the AI lifecycle can have different risk perspectives. For example, an AI developer who makes AI software available, such as pre-trained models, can have a different risk perspective than an AI actor who is responsible for deploying that pre-trained model in a specific use case. Such deployers may not recognize that their particular uses could entail risks which differ from those perceived by the initial developer. All involved AI actors share responsibilities for designing, developing, and deploying a trustworthy AI system that is fit for purpose.

Risk in real-world settings: While measuring AI risks in a laboratory or a controlled environment may yield important insights pre-deployment, these measurements may differ from risks that emerge in operational, real-world settings.

Inscrutability: Inscrutable AI systems can complicate risk measurement. Inscrutability can be a result of the opaque nature of AI systems (limited explainability or interpretability), lack of transparency or documentation in AI system development or deployment, or inherent uncertainties in AI systems.

Human baseline: Risk management of AI systems that are intended to augment or replace human activity, for example decision making, requires some form of baseline metrics for comparison. This is difficult to systematize since AI systems carry out different tasks – and perform tasks differently – than humans.

1.2.2 Risk Tolerance

While the AI RMF can be used to prioritize risk, it does not prescribe risk tolerance. *Risk tolerance* refers to the organization's or AI actor's readiness to bear the risk in order to achieve its objectives. Risk tolerance can be influenced by legal or regulatory requirements (Adapted from: ISO GUIDE 73). Risk tolerance and the level of risk that is acceptable to organizations or society are highly contextual and application and use-case specific. Risk tolerances can be influenced by policies and norms established by AI system owners, organizations, industries, communities, or policy makers. Risk tolerances are likely to change over time as AI systems, policies, and norms evolve. Different organizations may have varied risk tolerances due to their particular organizational priorities and resource considerations.

Emerging knowledge and methods to better inform harm/cost-benefit tradeoffs will continue to be developed and debated by businesses, governments, academia, and civil society. To the extent that challenges for specifying AI risk tolerances remain unresolved, there may be contexts where a risk management framework is not yet readily applicable for mitigating negative AI risks.

The Framework is intended to be flexible and to augment existing risk practices which should align with applicable laws, regulations, and norms. Organizations should follow existing regulations and guidelines for risk criteria, tolerance, and response established by organizational, domain, discipline, sector, or professional requirements. Some sectors or industries may have established definitions of harm or established documentation, reporting, and disclosure requirements. Within sectors, risk management may depend on existing guidelines for specific applications and use case settings. Where established guidelines do not exist, organizations should define reasonable risk tolerance. Once tolerance is defined, this AI RMF can be used to manage risks and to document risk management processes.

1.2.3 Risk Prioritization

Attempting to eliminate negative risk entirely can be counterproductive in practice because not all incidents and failures can be eliminated. Unrealistic expectations about risk may lead organizations to allocate resources in a manner that makes risk triage inefficient or impractical or wastes scarce resources. A risk management culture can help organizations recognize that not all AI risks are the same, and resources can be allocated purposefully. Actionable risk management efforts lay out clear guidelines for assessing trustworthiness of each AI system an organization develops or deploys. Policies and resources should be prioritized based on the assessed risk level and potential impact of an AI system. The extent to which an AI system may be customized or tailored to the specific context of use by the AI deployer can be a contributing factor.

When applying the AI RMF, risks which the organization determines to be highest for the AI systems within a given context of use call for the most urgent prioritization and most thorough risk management process. In cases where an AI system presents unacceptable negative risk levels – such as where significant negative impacts are imminent, severe harms are actually occurring, or catastrophic risks are present – development and deployment should cease in a safe manner until risks can be sufficiently managed. If an AI system's development, deployment, and use cases are found to be low-risk in a specific context, that may suggest potentially lower prioritization.

Risk prioritization may differ between AI systems that are designed or deployed to directly interact with humans as compared to AI systems that are not. Higher initial prioritization may be called for in settings where the

AI system is trained on large datasets comprised of sensitive or protected data such as personally identifiable information, or where the outputs of the AI systems have direct or indirect impact on humans. AI systems designed to interact only with computational systems and trained on non-sensitive datasets (for example, data collected from the physical environment) may call for lower initial prioritization. Nonetheless, regularly assessing and prioritizing risk based on context remains important because non-human-facing AI systems can have downstream safety or social implications.

Residual risk – defined as risk remaining after risk treatment [] – directly impacts end users or affected individuals and communities. Documenting residual risks will call for the system provider to fully consider the risks of deploying the AI product and will inform end users about potential negative impacts of interacting with the system.

1.2.4 Organizational Integration and Management of Risk

AI risks should not be considered in isolation. Different AI actors have different responsibilities and awareness depending on their roles in the lifecycle. For example, organizations developing an AI system often will not have information about how the system may be used. AI risk management should be integrated and incorporated into broader enterprise risk management strategies and processes. Treating AI risks along with other critical risks, such as cybersecurity and privacy, will yield a more integrated outcome and organizational efficiencies.

The AI RMF may be utilized along with related guidance and frameworks for managing AI system risks or broader enterprise risks. Some risks related to AI systems are common across other types of software development and deployment. Examples of overlapping risks include: privacy concerns related to the use of underlying data to train AI systems; the energy and environmental implications associated with resource-heavy computing demands; security concerns related to the confidentiality, integrity, and availability of the system and its training and output data; and general security of the underlying software and hardware for AI systems.

Organizations need to establish and maintain the appropriate accountability mechanisms, roles and responsibilities, culture, and incentive structures for risk management to be effective. Use of the AI RMF alone will not lead to these changes or provide the appropriate incentives. Effective risk management is realized through organizational commitment at senior levels and may require cultural change within an organization or industry. In addition, small to medium-sized organizations managing AI risks or implementing the AI RMF may face different challenges than large organizations, depending on their capabilities and resources.

2. Audience

Identifying and managing AI risks and potential impacts – both positive and negative – requires a broad set of perspectives and actors across the AI lifecycle. Ideally, AI actors will represent a diversity of experience, expertise, and backgrounds and comprise demographically and disciplinarily diverse teams. The AI RMF is intended to be used by AI actors across the AI lifecycle and dimensions.

The OECD has developed a framework for classifying AI lifecycle activities according to five key socio-technical dimensions, each with properties relevant for AI policy and governance, including risk management [OECD (2022) OECD Framework for the Classification of AI systems—OECD Digital Economy Papers]. Figure 2 shows these dimensions, slightly modified by NIST for purposes of this framework. The NIST modification highlights the importance of test, evaluation, verification, and validation (TEVV) processes throughout an AI lifecycle and generalizes the operational context of an AI system.

AI dimensions displayed in Figure 2 are the Application Context, Data and Input, AI Model, and Task and Output. AI actors involved in these dimensions who perform or manage the design, development, deployment, evaluation, and use of AI systems and drive AI risk management efforts are the *primary* AI RMF audience.

Representative AI actors across the lifecycle dimensions are listed in Figure 3[.] Within the AI RMF, all AI actors work together to manage risks and achieve the goals of trustworthy and responsible AI. AI actors with TEVV-specific expertise are integrated throughout the AI lifecycle and are especially likely to benefit from the Framework. Performed regularly, TEVV tasks can provide insights relative to technical, societal, legal, and ethical standards or norms, and can assist with anticipating impacts and assessing and tracking emergent risks. As a regular process within an AI lifecycle, TEVV allows for both mid-course remediation and post-hoc risk management.

The People & Planet dimension at the center of Figure 2 represents human rights and the broader well-being of society and the planet. The AI actors in this dimension comprise a separate AI RMF audience who *informs* the primary audience. These AI actors may include trade associations, standards developing organizations, researchers, advocacy groups, environmental groups, civil society organizations, end users, and potentially impacted individuals and communities. These actors can:

- assist in providing context and understanding potential and actual impacts;
- be a source of formal or quasi-formal norms and guidance for AI risk management;
- designate boundaries for AI operation (technical, societal, legal, and ethical); and
- promote discussion of the tradeoffs needed to balance societal values and priorities related to civil liberties and rights, equity, the environment and the planet, and the economy.

Successful risk management depends upon a sense of collective responsibility among AI actors shown in Figure 3. The AI RMF functions . . . require diverse perspectives, disciplines, professions, and experiences. Diverse teams contribute to more open sharing of ideas and assumptions about

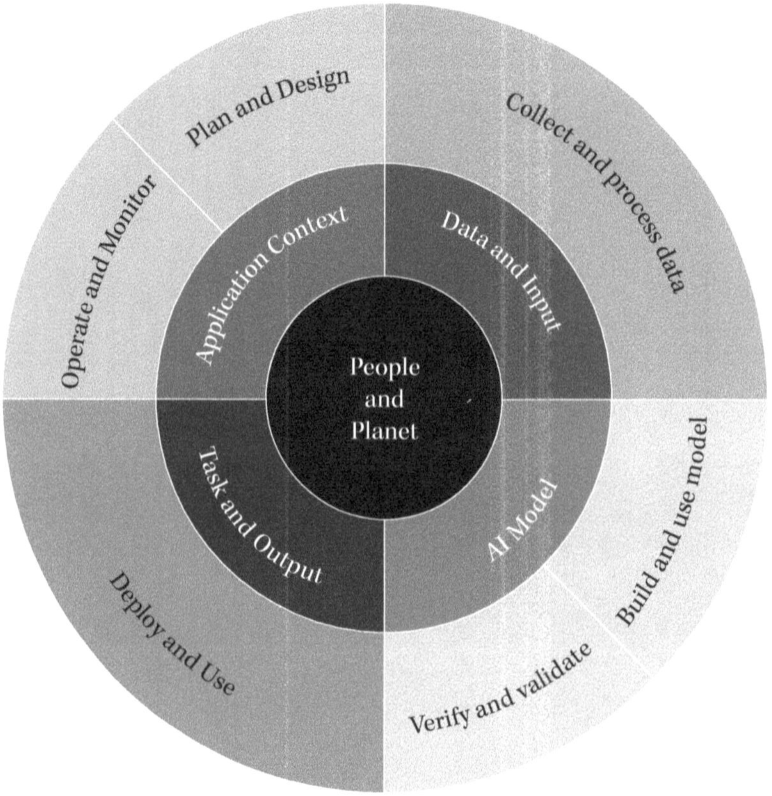

Fig. 2. Lifecycle and Key Dimensions of an AI System. Modified from OECD (2022) OECD Framework for the Classification of AI systems—OECD Digital Economy Papers. The two inner circles show AI systems' key dimensions, and the outer circle shows AI lifecycle stages. Ideally, risk management efforts start with the Plan and Design function in the application context and are performed throughout the AI system lifecycle. See Figure 3 for representative AI actors.

the purposes and functions of technology – making these implicit aspects more explicit. This broader collective perspective creates opportunities for surfacing problems and identifying existing and emergent risks.

3. AI Risks and Trustworthiness

For AI systems to be trustworthy, they often need to be responsive to a multiplicity of criteria that are of value to interested parties. Approaches which enhance AI trustworthiness can reduce negative AI risks. This Framework articulates the following characteristics of trustworthy AI and offers guidance for addressing them. Characteristics of trustworthy AI systems include: **valid and reliable, safe, secure and resilient, accountable and trans- parent, explainable and interpretable, privacy-enhanced, and fair with harmful bias managed**. Creating trustworthy AI requires balancing each of these characteristics based on the AI system's context of use. While

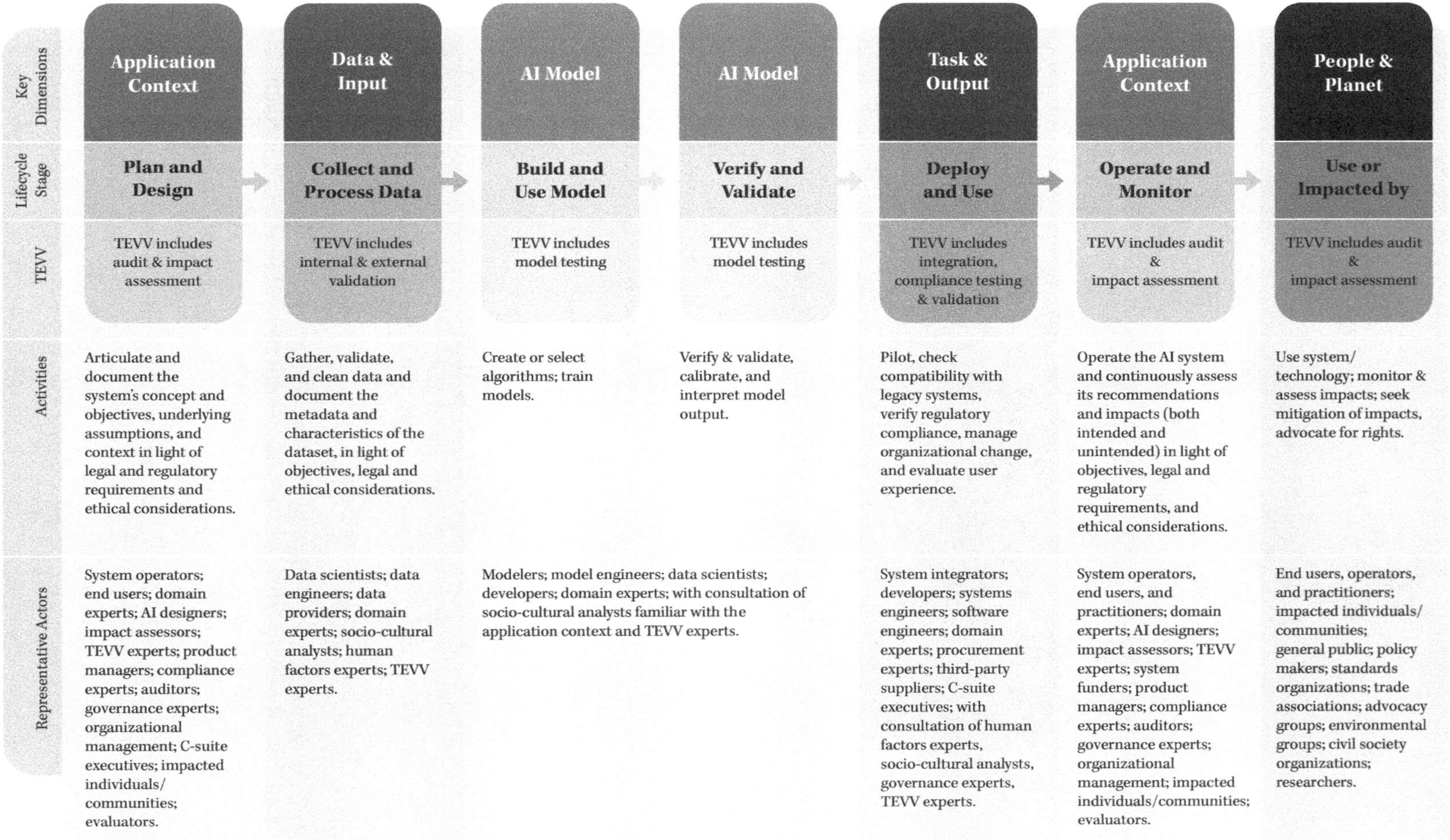

Fig. 3. AI actors across AI lifecycle stages. Note that AI actors in the AI Model dimension (Figure 2) are separated as a best practice, with those building and using the models separated from those verifying and validating the models.

all characteristics are socio-technical system attributes, accountability and transparency also relate to the processes and activities internal to an AI system and its external setting. Neglecting these characteristics can increase the probability and magnitude of negative consequences.

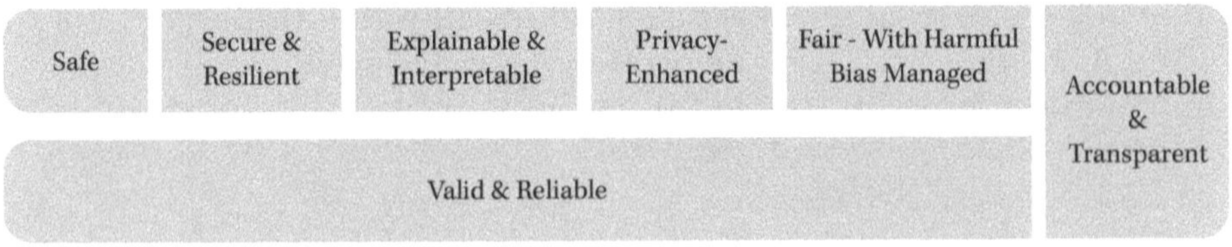

Fig. 4. Characteristics of trustworthy AI systems. Valid & Reliable is a necessary condition of trustworthiness and is shown as the base for other trustworthiness characteristics. Accountable & Transparent is shown as a vertical box because it relates to all other characteristics.

Trustworthiness characteristics (shown in Figure 4) are inextricably tied to social and organizational behavior, the datasets used by AI systems, selection of AI models and algorithms and the decisions made by those who build them, and the interactions with the humans who provide insight from and oversight of such systems. Human judgment should be employed when deciding on the specific metrics related to AI trustworthiness characteristics and the precise threshold values for those metrics.

Addressing AI trustworthiness characteristics individually will not ensure AI system trustworthiness; tradeoffs are usually involved, rarely do all characteristics apply in every set- ting, and some will be more or less important in any given situation. Ultimately, trustworthiness is a social concept that ranges across a spectrum and is only as strong as its weakest characteristics.

When managing AI risks, organizations can face difficult decisions in balancing these characteristics. For example, in certain scenarios tradeoffs may emerge between optimizing for interpretability and achieving privacy. In other cases, organizations might face a tradeoff between predictive accuracy and interpretability. Or, under certain conditions such as data sparsity, privacy-enhancing techniques can result in a loss in accuracy, affecting decisions about fairness and other values in certain domains. Dealing with tradeoffs requires taking into account the decision-making context. These analyses can highlight the existence and extent of tradeoffs between different measures, but they do not answer questions about how to navigate the tradeoff. Those depend on the values at play in the relevant *context* and should be resolved in a manner that is both transparent and appropriately justifiable.

There are multiple approaches for enhancing contextual awareness in the AI lifecycle. For example, subject matter experts can assist in the evaluation of TEVV findings and work with product and deployment teams to align TEVV parameters to requirements and deployment conditions. When properly resourced, increasing the breadth and diversity of input from interested parties and relevant AI actors throughout the AI lifecycle can enhance opportunities for informing contextually sensitive evaluations, and for identifying AI system benefits and positive impacts. These practices can increase the likelihood that risks arising in social contexts are managed appropriately.

Understanding and treatment of trustworthiness characteristics depends on an AI actor's particular role within the AI lifecycle. For any given AI system, an AI designer or developer may have a different perception of the characteristics than the deployer. . . .

3.1 Valid and Reliable

Validation is the "confirmation, through the provision of objective evidence, that the requirements for a specific intended use or application have been fulfilled" []. Deployment of AI systems which are inaccurate, unreliable, or poorly generalized to data and settings beyond their training creates and increases negative AI risks and reduces trustworthiness.

Reliability is defined in the same standard as the "ability of an item to perform as required, without failure, for a given time interval, under given conditions" []. Reliability is a goal for overall correctness of AI system operation under the conditions of expected use and over a given period of time, including the entire lifetime of the system.

Accuracy and robustness contribute to the validity and trustworthiness of AI systems and can be in tension with one another in AI systems.

Accuracy is defined . . . as "closeness of results of observations, computations, or estimates to the true values or the values accepted as being true." Measures of accuracy should consider computational-centric measures (e.g., false positive and false negative rates), human-AI teaming, and demonstrate external validity (generalizable beyond the training conditions). Accuracy measurements should always be paired with clearly defined and realistic test sets – that are representative of conditions of expected use – and details about test methodology; these should be included in associated documentation. Accuracy measurements may include disaggregation of results for different data segments.

Robustness or *generalizability* is defined as the "ability of a system to maintain its level of performance under a variety of circumstances" []. Robustness is a goal for appropriate system functionality in a broad set of conditions and circumstances, including uses of AI systems not initially anticipated. Robustness requires not only that the system perform exactly as it does under expected uses, but also that it should perform in ways that minimize potential harms to people if it is operating in an unexpected setting.

Validity and reliability for deployed AI systems are often assessed by ongoing testing or monitoring that confirms a system is performing as intended. Measurement of validity, accuracy, robustness, and reliability contribute to trustworthiness and should take into consideration that certain types of failures can cause greater harm. AI risk management efforts should prioritize the minimization of potential negative impacts, and may need to include human intervention in cases where the AI system cannot detect or correct errors.

3.2 Safe

AI systems should "not under defined conditions, lead to a state in which human life, health, property, or the environment is endangered" []. Safe operation of AI systems is improved through:

- responsible design, development, and deployment practices;
- clear information to deployers on responsible use of the system;
- responsible decision-making by deployers and end users; and
- explanations and documentation of risks based on empirical evidence of incidents.

Different types of safety risks may require tailored AI risk management approaches based on context and the severity of potential risks presented. Safety risks that pose a potential risk of serious injury or death call for the most urgent prioritization and most thorough risk management process.

Employing safety considerations during the lifecycle and starting as early as possible with planning and design can prevent failures or conditions that can render a system dangerous. Other practical approaches for AI safety often relate to rigorous simulation and in-domain testing, real-time monitoring, and the ability to shut down, modify, or have human intervention into systems that deviate from intended or expected functionality.

AI safety risk management approaches should take cues from efforts and guidelines for safety in fields such as transportation and healthcare and align with existing sector- or application-specific guidelines or standards.

3.3 Secure and Resilient

AI systems, as well as the ecosystems in which they are deployed, may be said to be *resilient* if they can withstand unexpected adverse events or unexpected changes in their environment or use – or if they can maintain their functions and structure in the face of internal and external change and degrade safely and gracefully when this is necessary []. Common security concerns relate to adversarial examples, data poisoning, and the exfiltration of models, training data, or other intellectual property through AI system endpoints. AI systems that can maintain confidentiality, integrity, and availability through protection mechanisms that prevent unauthorized access and use may be said to be *secure*. . . .

Security and resilience are related but distinct characteristics. While resilience is the ability to return to normal function after an unexpected adverse event, security includes resilience but also encompasses protocols to avoid, protect against, respond to, or recover from attacks. Resilience relates to robustness and goes beyond the provenance of the data to encompass unexpected or adversarial use (or abuse or misuse) of the model or data.

3.4 Accountable and Transparent

Trustworthy AI depends upon accountability. Accountability presupposes transparency. *Transparency* reflects the extent to which information about an AI system and its outputs is available to individuals interacting with such a system – regardless of whether they are even aware that they are doing so. Meaningful transparency provides access to appropriate levels of information based on the stage of the AI lifecycle and tailored to the role or knowledge of AI actors or individuals interacting with or using the AI system. By promoting higher levels of understanding, transparency increases confidence in the AI system.

This characteristic's scope spans from design decisions and training data to model training, the structure of the model, its intended use cases, and how and when deployment, post-deployment, or end user decisions were made and by whom. Transparency is often necessary for actionable redress related to AI system outputs that are incorrect or otherwise lead to negative impacts. Transparency should consider human-AI interaction: for example, how a human operator or user is notified when a potential or actual adverse outcome caused by an AI system is detected. A transparent system is not necessarily an accurate, privacy-enhanced, secure, or fair system. However, it is difficult to determine whether an opaque system possesses such characteristics, and to do so over time as complex systems evolve.

The role of AI actors should be considered when seeking accountability for the outcomes of AI systems. The relationship between risk and accountability associated with AI and technological systems more broadly differs across cultural, legal, sectoral, and societal contexts. When consequences are severe, such as when life and liberty are at stake, AI developers and deployers should consider proportionally and proactively adjusting their transparency and accountability practices. Maintaining organizational practices and governing structures for harm reduction, like risk management, can help lead to more accountable systems.

Measures to enhance transparency and accountability should also consider the impact of these efforts on the implementing entity, including the level of necessary resources and the need to safeguard proprietary information.

Maintaining the provenance of training data and supporting attribution of the AI system's decisions to subsets of training data can assist with both transparency and accountability. Training data may also be subject to copyright and should follow applicable intellectual property rights laws.

As transparency tools for AI systems and related documentation continue to evolve, developers of AI systems are encouraged to test different types of transparency tools in cooperation with AI deployers to ensure that AI systems are used as intended.

3.5 Explainable and Interpretable

Explainability refers to a representation of the mechanisms underlying AI systems' operation, whereas *interpretability* refers to the meaning of AI systems' output in the context of their designed functional purposes. Together, explainability and interpretability assist those operating or overseeing an AI system, as well as users of an AI system, to gain deeper insights into the functionality and trustworthiness of the system, including its out- puts. The underlying assumption is that perceptions of negative risk stem from a lack of ability to make sense of, or contextualize, system output appropriately. Explainable and interpretable AI systems offer information that will help end users understand the purposes and potential impact of an AI system.

Risk from lack of explainability may be managed by describing how AI systems function, with descriptions tailored to individual differences such as the user's role, knowledge, and skill level. Explainable systems can be debugged and monitored more easily, and they lend themselves to more thorough documentation, audit, and governance.

Risks to interpretability often can be addressed by communicating a description of why an AI system made a particular prediction or recommendation. . . .

Transparency, explainability, and interpretability are distinct characteristics that support each other. Transparency can answer the question of "what happened" in the system. Explainability can answer the question of "how" a decision was made in the system. Interpretability can answer the question of "why" a decision was made by the system and its meaning or context to the user.

3.6 Privacy-Enhanced

Privacy refers generally to the norms and practices that help to safeguard human autonomy, identity, and dignity. These norms and practices typically address freedom from intrusion, limiting observation, or individuals' agency to consent to disclosure or control of facets of their identities (e.g., body, data, reputation). . . .

Privacy values such as anonymity, confidentiality, and control generally should guide choices for AI system design, development, and deployment. Privacy-related risks may influence security, bias, and transparency and come with tradeoffs with these other characteristics. Like safety and security, specific technical features of an AI system may promote or reduce privacy. AI systems can also present new risks to privacy by allowing inference to identify individuals or previously private information about individuals.

Privacy-enhancing technologies ("PETs") for AI, as well as data minimizing methods such as de-identification and aggregation for certain model outputs, can support design for privacy-enhanced AI systems. Under certain conditions such as data sparsity, privacy- enhancing techniques can result in a loss in accuracy, affecting decisions about fairness and other values in certain domains.

3.7 Fair – with Harmful Bias Managed

Fairness in AI includes concerns for equality and equity by addressing issues such as harmful bias and discrimination. Standards of fairness can be complex and difficult to define because perceptions of fairness differ among cultures and may shift depending on application. Organizations' risk management efforts will be enhanced by recognizing and considering these differences. Systems in which harmful biases are mitigated are not necessarily fair. For example, systems in which predictions are somewhat balanced across demographic groups may still be inaccessible to individuals with disabilities or affected by the digital divide or may exacerbate existing disparities or systemic biases.

Bias is broader than demographic balance and data representativeness. NIST has identified three major categories of AI bias to be considered and managed: systemic, computational and statistical, and human-cognitive. Each of these can occur in the absence of prejudice, partiality, or discriminatory intent. Systemic bias can be present in AI datasets, the organizational norms, practices, and processes across the AI lifecycle, and the broader society that uses AI systems. Computational and statistical biases can be present in AI datasets and algorithmic processes, and often stem from systematic errors due to non-representative samples. Human-cognitive biases relate to how an individual or group perceives AI system information to make a decision or fill in missing information, or how humans think about purposes and functions of an AI system. Human-cognitive biases are omnipresent in decision-making processes across the AI lifecycle and system use, including the design, implementation, operation, and maintenance of AI.

Bias exists in many forms and can become ingrained in the automated systems that help make decisions about our lives. While bias is not always a negative phenomenon, AI systems can potentially increase the speed and scale of biases and perpetuate and amplify harms to individuals, groups, communities, organizations, and society. Bias is tightly associated with the concepts of transparency as well as fairness in society. . . .

4. Effectiveness of the AI RMF

Evaluations of AI RMF effectiveness – including ways to measure bottom-line improvements in the trustworthiness of AI systems – will be part of future NIST activities, in conjunction with the AI community.

Organizations and other users of the Framework are encouraged to periodically evaluate whether the AI RMF has improved their ability to manage AI risks, including but not limited to their policies, processes, practices, implementation plans, indicators, measurements, and expected outcomes. NIST intends to work collaboratively with others to develop metrics, methodologies, and goals for evaluating the AI RMF's effectiveness, and to broadly share results and supporting information. . . .

C. CASE STUDY IN HYBRID FRAMEWORK: RIGHTS- AND RISK-BASED MODEL

While the rights-based and the risk-based frameworks are often used to describe the structure of AI regulation, multiple regulatory approaches can actually be viewed as a hybrid framework. Like the risk-based approach, a hybrid approach views threats to civil and human rights in terms of risks, and regulates those risks in accordance to the potential threat to rights.

The *EU AI Act* is one example of a hybrid approach. As seen in Article 27 and reinforced by Recital 1 below, the *EU AI* Act focuses on both innovation policy and on protecting fundamental European human rights through risk management. Article 27 and Recital 1 of the *EU AI Act* describe a framework for requiring a higher tier of impact assessment for AI systems that are classified as a "high-risk AI system." High-risk AI systems require greater scrutiny and obligations, including impact assessments based on their impact on fundamental rights. Article 6(2) and Annex III help to clarify how classifications of high-risk AI systems are determined.

1. EU AI Act: Rights-Based Approach

a. EU AI Act, Article 27 [Rights Impact Assessment]

EU AI Act

Article 27. Fundamental Rights Impact Assessment for High-Risk AI Systems

1. Prior to deploying a high-risk AI system . . . deployers that are bodies governed by public law, or are private entities providing public services, and deployers of high-risk AI systems . . . shall perform an assessment of the impact on fundamental rights that the use of such system may produce. For that purpose, deployers shall perform an assessment consisting of:

(**a**) a description of the deployer's processes in which the high-risk AI system will be used in line with its intended purpose;

(**b**) a description of the period of time within which, and the frequency with which, each high-risk AI system is intended to be used;

(**c**) the categories of natural persons and groups likely to be affected by its use in the specific context;

(**d**) the specific risks of harm likely to have an impact on the categories of natural persons or groups of persons identified pursuant to point (c) of this paragraph, taking into account the information given by the provider . . . ;

(**e**) a description of the implementation of human oversight measures, according to the instructions for use;

(**f**) the measures to be taken in the case of the materialisation of those risks, including the arrangements for internal governance and complaint mechanisms. . . .

b. EU AI Act, Recital 1 [Regulation Purpose]

EU AI Act

Recital 1

The purpose of this Regulation is to improve the functioning of the internal market by laying down a uniform legal framework in particular for the development, the placing on the market, the putting into service and the use of artificial intelligence systems (AI systems) in the Union, in accordance with Union values, to promote the uptake of human centric and trustworthy artificial intelligence (AI) while ensuring a high level of protection of health, safety, fundamental rights as enshrined in the Charter of Fundamental Rights of the European Union (the 'Charter'), including democracy, the rule of law and environmental protection, to protect against the harmful effects of AI systems in the Union, and to support innovation. This Regulation ensures the free movement, cross-border, of AI-based goods and services, thus preventing Member States from imposing restrictions on the development, marketing and use of AI systems, unless explicitly authorised by this Regulation.

2. *EU AI Act: Risk-Based Approach*

a. EU AI Act, Article 6 [High-Risk AI System Classifications]

EU AI Act

Article 6. Classification Rules for High-Risk AI Systems

1. Irrespective of whether an AI system is placed on the market or put into service independently of the products referred to in points (a) and (b), that AI system shall be considered to be high-risk where both of the following conditions are fulfilled:

(a) the AI system is intended to be used as a safety component of a product, or the AI system is itself a product, covered by the Union harmonisation legislation[;]

(b) the product whose safety component pursuant to point (a) is the AI system, or the AI system itself as a product, is required to undergo a third-party conformity assessment, with a view to the placing on the market or the putting into service of that product pursuant to the Union harmonisation legislation[.]

2. In addition to the high-risk AI systems referred to in paragraph 1, AI systems referred to in Annex III shall be considered high-risk. . . .

b. EU AI Act, Annex III [High-Risk AI Systems]

EU AI Act

Annex III. High-Risk AI Systems Referred to in Article 6(2)[19]

High-risk AI systems pursuant to Article 6(2) are the AI systems listed in any of the following areas:

1. Biometrics, in so far as their use is permitted under relevant Union or national law:

(a) remote biometric identification systems. This shall not include AI systems intended to be used for biometric verification the sole purpose of which is to confirm that a specific natural person is the person he or she claims to be;

---

19. *Id.*

(b) AI systems intended to be used for biometric categorisation, according to sensitive or protected attributes or characteristics based on the inference of those attributes or characteristics;

(c) AI systems intended to be used for emotion recognition.

2. Critical infrastructure: AI systems intended to be used as safety components in the management and operation of critical digital infrastructure, road traffic, or in the supply of water, gas, heating or electricity.

3. Education and vocational training:

[AI systems intended to be used . . .]

(a) . . . to determine access or admission or to assign natural persons to educational and vocational training institutions at all levels;

(b) . . . to evaluate learning outcomes, including when those outcomes are used to steer the learning process of natural persons in educational and vocational training institutions at all levels;

(c) . . . for the purpose of assessing the appropriate level of education[;]

(d) . . . for monitoring and detecting prohibited behavior of students during tests[.]

4. Employment, workers management and access to self-employment:

[AI systems intended to be used . . .]

(a) . . . for recruitment or selection of natural persons, in particular to place targeted job advertisements, to analyse and filter job applications, and to evaluate candidates;

(b) . . . to make decisions affecting terms of work-related relationships, the promotion or termination of work-related contractual relationships, to allocate tasks based on individual behaviour or personal traits or characteristics or to monitor and evaluate the performance and behaviour of persons in such relationships.

5. Access to and enjoyment of essential private services and essential public services and benefits:

[AI systems intended to be used . . .]

(a) . . . by public authorities or on behalf of public authorities to evaluate the eligibility of natural persons for essential public assistance benefits and services, including healthcare services, as well as to grant, reduce, revoke, or reclaim such benefits and services;

(b) . . . to evaluate the creditworthiness of natural persons or establish their credit score, with the exception of AI systems used for the purpose of detecting financial fraud;

(c) . . . for risk assessment and pricing in relation to natural persons in the case of life and health insurance;

(d) AI systems intended to evaluate and classify emergency calls by natural persons or to be used to dispatch, or to establish priority in the dispatching of, emergency first response services, including by police, firefighters and medical aid, as well as emergency healthcare patient triage systems.

6. Law enforcement[:]

[AI systems intended to be used by or on behalf of law enforcement authorities . . .]

(a) . . . to assess the risk of a natural person becoming the victim of criminal offences;

(b) . . . as polygraphs or similar tools;

(c) . . . to evaluate the reliability of evidence in the course of the investigation or prosecution of criminal offences;

(d) . . . for assessing the risk of a natural person offending or re-offending not solely on the basis of the profiling of natural persons . . . or to assess personality traits and characteristics or past criminal behaviour[;]

(e) . . . for the profiling of natural persons . . . in the course of the detection, investigation or prosecution of criminal offences.

7. Migration, asylum and border control management[:]

[AI systems intended to be used by or on behalf of competent public authorities . . .]

(a) . . . as polygraphs or similar tools;

(b) . . . to assess a risk, including a security risk, a risk of irregular immigration, or a health risk, posed by a natural person who intends to enter or has entered into the territory of a Member State;

(c) . . . for the examination of applications for asylum, visa and residence permits and associated complaints with regard to the eligibility of the natural persons applying for a status, including related assessments of the reliability of evidence;

(d) . . . for the purpose of detecting, recognising or identifying natural persons, with the exception of the verification of travel documents.

8. Administration of justice and democratic processes:

(a) AI systems intended to assist a judicial authority or on their behalf to assist a judicial authority in researching and interpreting facts and the law and in applying the law to a concrete set of facts, or to be used in a similar way in alternative dispute resolution;

(b) AI systems intended to be used by a judicial authority on their behalf for influencing the outcome of an election or referendum or the voting behaviour of natural persons in the exercise of their vote in elections or referenda. This does not include AI systems to the output of which natural persons are not directly exposed, such as tools used to organise, optimise or structure political campaigns from an administrative or logistical point of view.

D. CASE STUDIES IN EVOLUTIONARY GOVERNANCE THROUGH STATUTORY REFORM AND LITIGATION

The rise of AI regulation in its different forms can be contrasted to AI governance reliant on generally applicable trade and products liability laws. The case of *Rodgers v. Christie* was brought against the developer of an algorithm and its deployer, suing under a strict liability tort law. Examine the difficulty of applying this law to algorithms and AI and consider the novelty of an approach like this.

1. Testing Developer and Deployer Liability in Litigation

The following case, *Rodgers v. Christie*, is a part of a growing number of examples where plaintiffs seek to bring tort claims based on alleged defects in algorithmic decisionmaking, or other alleged harms that result from AI and automated systems. Although the case was ultimately dismissed, the liability landscape for AI developers and deployers may stretch into areas where risk management may be emphasized in multiple stages of the AI lifecycle.

a. Rodgers v. Christie

Rodgers v. Christie

United States Court of Appeals for the Third Circuit
795 F. App'x 878-880 (3d Cir. 2020)
Unpublished

KRAUSE, United States Circuit Judge.

June Rodgers's son was tragically murdered, allegedly by a man who days before had been granted pretrial release by a New Jersey state court. She brought products liability claims against the foundation responsible for the Public Safety Assessment (PSA), a multifactor risk estimation model that forms part of the state's pretrial release system.[20] The District Court dismissed the complaint, concluding that the PSA is not a "product" under the New Jersey Products Liability Act (NJPLA). We agree and therefore will affirm.

DISCUSSION

The NJPLA imposes strict liability on manufacturers or sellers of certain defective "product[s]."[21] But the Act does not define that term. To fill the gap, the District Court looked to the Third Restatement of Torts, which defines "product" as "tangible personal property distributed commercially for use or consumption" or any "[o]ther item[ ]" whose "context of . . . distribution and use is sufficiently analogous to [that] of tangible personal property."[22] It had good reason to do so, as New Jersey courts often look to the Third Restatement in deciding issues related to the state's products liability regime.[23] And on appeal, both parties agree the Third Restatement's definition is the appropriate one. We therefore assume that to give rise to an NJPLA action, the "product" at issue must fall within section 19 of the Third Restatement.

The PSA does not fit within that definition for two reasons. First, as the District Court concluded, it is not distributed commercially. Rather,

---

20. [Fn. 1 in original] Rodgers also sued two New Jersey officials, who were later dismissed without prejudice, as well as the PSA's "chief architect," App. 29, who is not at issue in this appeal.

21. [In text in original] N.J. Stat. Ann. § 2A:58C-2.

22. [In text in original] App. 6 (quoting Restatement (Third) of Torts: Products Liability § 19(a) (Am. Law Inst. 1998)).

23. [In text in original] *See, e.g.*, Myrlak v. Port Auth. of N.Y. & N.J., 157 N.J. 84, 723 A.2d 45, 48 (1999); Lewis v. Am. Cyanamid Co., 155 N.J. 544, 715 A.2d 967, 975, 979 (1998); Boyle v. Ford Motor Co., 399 N.J.Super. 18, 942 A.2d 850, 853-54, 860-61 (N.J. Super. Ct. App. Div.), *cert. denied*, 196 N.J. 597, 960 A.2d 393 (2008); Mathews v. Univ. Loft Co., 387 N.J.Super. 349, 903 A.2d 1120, 1126-27 (N.J. Super. Ct. App. Div.), *cert. denied*, 188 N.J. 577, 911 A.2d 69 (2006).

it was designed as an "objective, standardized, and . . . empirical" "risk assessment instrument" to be used by pretrial services programs like New Jersey's.[24] Rodgers makes no effort to challenge this conclusion in her briefing and has thus forfeited the issue.[25] Second, the PSA is neither "tangible personal property" nor remotely "analogous to" it.[26] As Rodgers' complaint recognizes, it is an "algorithm" or "formula" using various factors to estimate a defendant's risk of absconding or endangering the community.[27] As the District Court recognized, "information, guidance, ideas, and recommendations" are not "product[s]" under the Third Restatement, both as a definitional matter and because extending strict liability to the distribution of ideas would raise serious First Amendment concerns.[28] Rodgers's only response is that the PSA's defects "undermine[ ]" New Jersey's pretrial release system, making it "not reasonably fit, suitable or safe" for its intended use.[29] But the NJPLA applies only to defective *products*, not to anything that causes harm or fails to achieve its purpose. . . .

2. *Treatment of Developers and Deployers in AI Statutes*

Colorado's approach to mitigating AI and algorithmic risks stems from two prongs: first, developers must focus their efforts on transparency and provide certain information regarding their products; and second, deployers of AI systems must implement proper risk management and governance programs to ensure the safe use of AI.

a. Colorado AI Consumer Protection Act, Definitions

A key part of AI regulation is setting the duties and responsibilities for those who develop and deploy AI, as well as those who use the AI. As discussed in Chapter 2, AI regulation has taken a greater focus on regulating AI lifecycles, acknowledging that AI will change in technology, purpose, and use in both the developmental stage and the deployment stage.

Current laws are evolving to regulate AI at multiple stages of the AI lifecycle. The following Colorado law, often referred to as the *Colorado AI Consumer Protection Act,* or sometimes as the *Colorado AI Act,* considers both developers and deployers in its language. The Colorado lawmakers, in passing the first-of-its-kind consumer protection law regulating AI, considered which steps are the responsibility of the developer, deployer, or both. The *Colorado AI Consumer Protection Act* opens with a series of definitions, including definitions for consumer, deploy, deployer, developer, and high-risk AI

---

24. [In text in original] N.J. Stat. Ann. § 2A:162-25(c)(1).
25. [In text in original] In re Wettach, 811 F.3d 99, 105 (3d Cir. 2016).
26. [In text in original] Restatement (Third) of Torts: Products Liability § 19(a).
27. [In text in original] App. 30.
28. [In text in original] App. 7-8 (citing Restatement (Third) of Torts § 19 cmt. d).
29. [In text in original] Appellant's Br. 18-19 (quoting N.J. Stat. Ann. § 2A:58C-2).

system. It also includes a list of technologies and systems that are excluded from the definition of high-risk AI systems.

Colorado AI Consumer Protection Act

2024 Colorado Session Laws, Ch. 198 (S.B. 24-205)

SECTION 1. In Colorado Revised Statutes, **add** part 17 to article 1 of title 6 as follows:

6-1-1701. Definitions

(4) "Consumer" means an individual who is a Colorado resident.

(5) "Deploy" means to use a high-risk artificial intelligence system.

(6) "Deployer" means a person doing business in this state that deploys a high-risk artificial intelligence system.

(7) "Developer" means a person doing business in this state that develops or intentionally and substantially modifies an artificial intelligence system. . . .

(9) **(a)** "High-risk artificial intelligence system" means any artificial intelligence system that, when deployed, makes, or is a substantial factor in making, a consequential decision.

(b) "High-risk artificial intelligence system" does not include:

(I) An artificial intelligence system if the artificial intelligence system is intended to:

(A) Perform a narrow procedural task; or

(B) Detect decision-making patterns or deviations from prior decision-making patterns and is not intended to replace or influence a previously completed human assessment without sufficient human review; or

(II) The following technologies, unless the technologies, when deployed, make, or are a substantial factor in making, a consequential decision:

(A) Anti-fraud technology that does not use facial recognition technology;

(B) Anti-malware;

(C) Anti-virus;

(D) Artificial intelligence-enabled video games;

(E) Calculators;

(F) Cybersecurity;

(G) Databases;

(H) Data storage;

(I) Firewall;

(J) Internet domain registration;

(K) Internet website loading;

(L) Networking;

(M) Spam- and robocall-filtering;

(N) Spell-checking;

(O) Spreadsheets;

(P) Web caching;

(Q) Web hosting or any similar technology; or

(R) Technology that communicates with consumers in natural language for the purpose of providing users with information, making referrals or recommendations, and answering questions and is subject to an accepted use policy that prohibits generating content that is discriminatory or harmful.

b. California AI Training Data Transparency Act

The *California AI Training Data Transparency Act* was passed in 2024. The legislation was specifically aimed at generative AI developers and required the release of high-level summaries of datasets to provide greater transparency in AI system development. The state law also required the disclosure of how synthetic data generation may have been used in generative AI systems.

AI Training Data Transparency Act

2024 Statutes of California, Ch. 817 (A.B. 2013)
Title 15.2 added to Part 4 of Division 3 of the California Civil Code

Title 15.2 of the California Civil Code

3111. . . . [A] generative artificial intelligence system or service, or a substantial modification to a generative artificial intelligence system or service, released on or after January 1, 2022, is made publicly available to Californians for use, regardless of whether the terms of that use include compensation, the developer of the system or service shall post on the developer's internet website documentation regarding the data used by the developer to train the generative artificial intelligence system or service, including, but not be limited to, all of the following:

(a) A high-level summary of the datasets used in the development of the generative artificial intelligence system or service, including, but not limited to:

(1) The sources or owners of the datasets.

(2) A description of how the datasets further the intended purpose of the artificial intelligence system or service.

(3) The number of data points included in the datasets, which may be in general ranges, and with estimated figures for dynamic datasets.

(4) A description of the types of data points within the datasets. For purposes of this paragraph, the following definitions apply:

(A) As applied to datasets that include labels, "types of data points" means the types of labels used.

(B) As applied to datasets without labeling, "types of data points" refers to the general characteristics.

(5) Whether the datasets include any data protected by copyright, trademark, or patent, or whether the datasets are entirely in the public domain.

(6) Whether the datasets were purchased or licensed by the developer.

(7) Whether the datasets include personal information, as defined in subdivision (v) of Section 1798.140.

(8) Whether the datasets include aggregate consumer information, as defined in subdivision (b) of Section 1798.140.

(9) Whether there was any cleaning, processing, or other modification to the datasets by the developer, including the intended purpose of those efforts in relation to the artificial intelligence system or service.

(10) The time period during which the data in the datasets were collected, including a notice if the data collection is ongoing.

(11) The dates the datasets were first used during the development of the artificial intelligence system or service.

(12) Whether the generative artificial intelligence system or service used or continuously uses synthetic data generation in its development. A developer may include a description of the functional need or desired purpose of the synthetic data in relation to the intended purpose of the system or service. . . .

This book takes a historical approach to understanding the foundations for AI law and policy. Understanding the history of AI oversight commences with an investigation of the goals and ambitions of rights-based and risk-based AI governance at the time these terms were introduced as law and policy concepts. Some experts use the terms Trustworthy AI or Trusted AI, Accountable AI, and Responsible AI interchangeably to emphasize the need to mitigate the greatest potential risks and harms of AI. Trustworthy AI is often discussed in terms of a risk-based approach to AI governance solutions. AI governance can also encapsulate other goals such as preserving rights, accelerating AI innovation and growth, and safeguarding national security, among other policy and legal objectives.

At the earliest stages of a push to adopt a national standard for AI governance in the U.S., the White House Office of Science and Technology Policy (OSTP); the U.S. Department of Commerce, National Institute of Standards and Technology (NIST); and other federal agencies have released multiple guidance documents to provide governmental oversight for AI and other emerging technologies. OSTP's *Blueprint for an AI Bill of Rights* and the *NIST AI Risk Management Framework* both adopt fair principles to guide the development and deployment of safe and effective AI and automated systems.[30]

---

30. Colo. Rev. Stat. § 6-1-1706(3)(b)(I)-(III) (2025):

(3) In any action commenced by the attorney general to enforce this part 17, it is an affirmative defense that the developer, deployer, or other person: . . .

(b) Is otherwise in compliance with:

(I) The latest version of the "Artificial Intelligence Risk Management Framework" published by the [N]ational [I]nstitute of [S]tandards and [T]echnology in the United States [D]epartment of [C]ommerce and standard ISO/IEC 42001 of the International Organization for Standardization;

(II) Another nationally or internationally recognized risk management framework for artificial intelligence systems, if the standards are substantially equivalent to or more stringent than the requirements of this part 17; or

(III) Any risk management framework for artificial intelligence systems that the attorney general, in the attorney general's discretion, may designate and, if designated, shall publicly disseminate.

The *EU AI Act* and other AI regulatory developments represent a hybrid approach, integrating a combination of rights-based and risk-based approaches to AI governance. Questions surrounding whether and how the rights-based or risk-based approaches to AI governance are meaningfully distinguishable are worthy of future discourse. This careful study is critical because how we integrate AI governance into new and existing legal and technical frameworks impacts the ecosystem of AI oversight mechanisms and democratic governance prioritization of rights and responsibilities.

Although some core principles may be shared between a rights-based and risk-based conceptualization of AI governance, the emphases on each conceptualization will be different and warrants careful attention. Also warranting careful attention are the ways in which hybrid approaches integrate rights-based and risk-based methods, the evolution of developer and deployer duties through statutory reform and amendments to existing legislation, and other developments in ongoing litigation. Core to this inquiry is debating to what extent these goals may come into conflict with each other, and whether they are consistent or inconsistent with constitutional law or other legal commitments.

Chapter 4

Algorithmic Discrimination and Disparate Impact

Chapter 4 addresses one of the most pressing concerns surrounding AI governance: algorithmic discrimination and disparate impact in AI and automated systems. The black box nature of AI and automated systems adds a layer of complexity to AI law and policy. This is particularly true in AI civil rights matters. Uncovering the sources of bias in AI systems and how discrimination might result is challenging. Further, there is a distinction between civil rights law and civil rights and human rights as reflected in fundamental fairness principles. Similarly, there is a distinction between what is understood to be the government's jurisdiction under antidiscrimination laws and the government's commitment to antidiscrimination objectives under an AI rights-based framework of governance.

A. *ALGORITHMIC DISCRIMINATION AND BIAS HARMS*

In October 2022, the White House Office of Science and Technology Policy (OSTP) released the *Blueprint for an AI Bill of Rights*. The *Blueprint for an AI Bill of Rights* articulated a set of principles. The non-binding document recommended that each one of the principles could be conceptualized as new forms of fundamental constitutional rights. The drafters of the *Blueprint*, for example, invited the reader to visualize freedom from algorithmic discrimination as a new type of fundamental constitutional right.

As discussed previously, the document was non-enforceable and did not impact other legal instruments. It was published by OSTP to provide a framework for policy conversation.

1. *Algorithmic Discrimination Protections*

a. Blueprint for an AI Bill of Rights

The *Blueprint for an AI Bill of Rights* emphasizes that reducing algorithmic discrimination harms requires commitments from AI designers, developers, and deployers to pursue proactive and continuous measures to mitigate risks in AI and automated systems. This guidance document was published during the Biden administration, and it should be noted that policies are subject to revision in the change of administrations. The excerpt below from the *Blueprint for an AI Bill of Rights* provides principles for mitigating algorithmic discrimination.

Blueprint for an AI Bill of Rights

White House Office of Science and Technology Policy
October 4, 2022

PRINCIPLE 2: ALGORITHMIC DISCRIMINATION PROTECTIONS

Algorithmic Discrimination Protections: You Should Not Face Discrimination by Algorithms and Systems Should Be Used and Designed in an Equitable Way

You should not face discrimination by algorithms, and systems should be used and designed in an equitable way. Algorithmic discrimination occurs when automated systems contribute to unjustified different treatment or impacts disfavoring people based on their race, color, ethnicity, sex (including pregnancy, childbirth, and related medical conditions, gender identity, intersex status, and sexual orientation), religion, age, national origin, disability, veteran status, genetic information, or any other classification protected by law.

Depending on the specific circumstances, such algorithmic discrimination may violate legal protections.

Designers, developers, and deployers of automated systems should take proactive and continuous measures to protect individuals and communities from algorithmic discrimination and to use and design systems in an equitable way.

This protection should include proactive equity assessments as part of the system design, use of representative data and protection against proxies for demographic features, ensuring accessibility for people with disabilities in design and development, pre-deployment and ongoing disparity testing and mitigation, and clear organizational oversight.

Independent evaluation and plain language reporting in the form of an algorithmic impact assessment, including disparity testing results and mitigation information, should be performed and made public whenever possible to confirm these protections.

2. *Managing AI Bias*

a. NIST AI Risk Management Framework

Shortly after the White House Office of Science and Technology Policy (OSTP) released the *Blueprint for an AI Bill of Rights* in October 2022, the U.S. Department of Commerce, National Institute of Standards & Technology (NIST), released Version 1.0 of the *NIST Artificial Intelligence (AI) Risk Management Framework.* Published in January 2023, the *NIST AI Risk Management Framework* approach to mitigating algorithmic bias focuses on a context-driven understanding of fairness and recognizes that cognitive biases and implicit bias may be omnipresent across all stages of the AI lifecycle, including all development and deployment phases of AI systems. Policies and guidance documents such as the *NIST AI Risk Management Framework* may be revised under the leadership of successive administrations.

The *NIST AI Risk Management Framework* recommends testing and evaluating AI technologies and automated systems to reduce the risk of bias and aim for fairness.

NIST AI Risk Management Framework

U.S. Department of Commerce, National Institute of Standards and Technology (NIST)
January 26, 2023

3.7 FAIR – WITH HARMFUL BIAS MANAGED

"*Fairness* in AI includes concerns for equality and equity by addressing issues such as harmful bias and discrimination. Standards of fairness can be complex and difficult to define because perceptions of fairness differ among cultures and may shift depending on application." "Bias is tightly associated with the concepts of transparency as well as fairness in society."

1. "Systemic bias can be present in AI datasets, the organizational norms, practices, and processes across the AI lifecycle, and the broader society that uses AI systems."
2. "Computational and statistical biases can be present in AI datasets and algorithmic processes, and often stem from systematic errors due to non-representative samples."
3. "Human-cognitive biases relate to how an individual or group perceives AI system information to make a decision or fill in missing information, or how humans think about purposes and functions of an AI system. Human-cognitive biases are omnipresent in decision-making processes across the AI lifecycle and system use, including the design, implementation, operation, and maintenance of AI."

"Bias exists in many forms and can become ingrained in the automated systems that help make decisions about our lives." "AI systems can potentially increase the speed and scale of biases and perpetuate and amplify harms to individuals, groups, communities, organizations, and society."

3. *EU AI Act and General Data Protection Regulation (GDPR)*

The *EU AI Act* approach examines the foreseeable consequences of the use of AI systems. To address algorithmic discrimination and other harms, the *EU AI Act* structures the categorization of AI systems within classifications of risk. As discussed in Chapter 3, high-risk AI systems are subject to greater oversight. High-risk AI systems are defined by Article 6 and identified in Annex III of the *EU AI Act.* Some potential dangers associated with high-risk AI systems, as set forth in Annex III, include biometric identification and verification, surveillance, assessments, scoring, and profiling.

To provide greater understanding of Annex III of the *EU AI Act*, the European Commission released a graphic that is referred to as the high-risk AI system pyramid.[1] The pyramid connotes various classifications of risk in AI systems: unacceptable risk, high risk, limited risk, and minimal risk. Potential duties and responsibilities are attached to the highest levels of risk, including increasing liabilities for high risk and unacceptable risk categories.

EU AI Act

Risk-Based AI System Pyramid

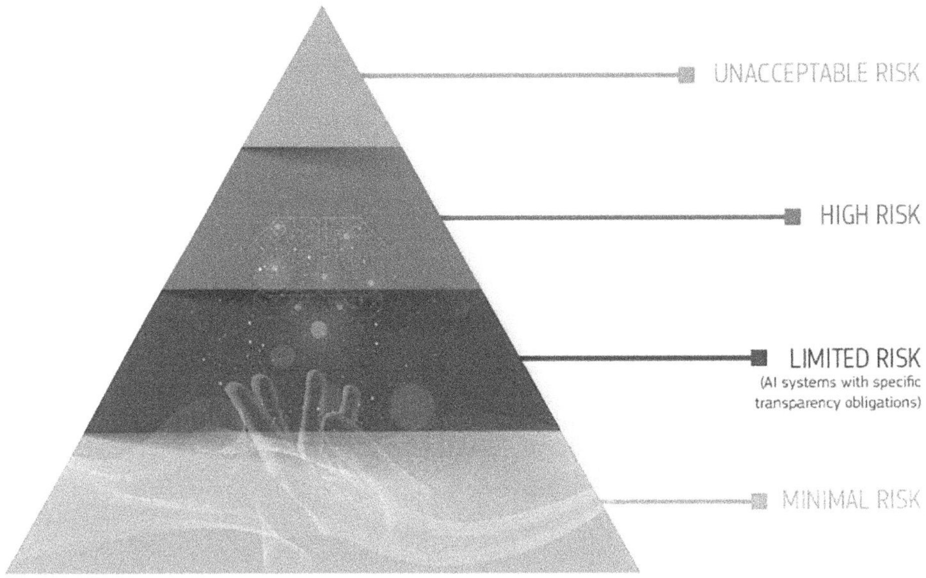

Fig. 1. *EU AI Act* Pyramid of Criticality, denoting categories of AI risk.

1. European Comm'n, *Shaping Europe's Digital Future: AI Act* (updated Oct. 14, 2024).

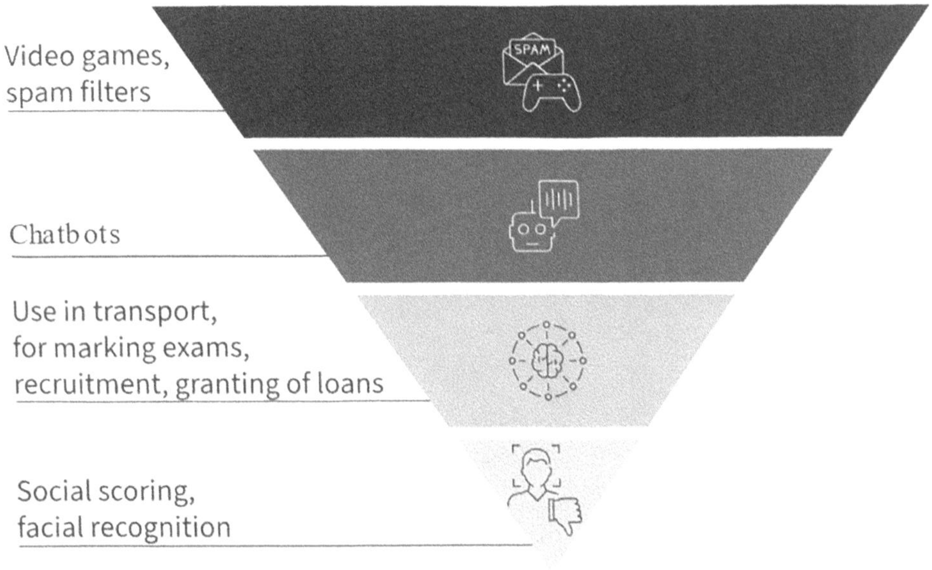

Fig. 2. *EU AI Act.* Inverted Pyramid of Criticality.

The following excerpt from the European Council and the Council of the European Union provides accompanying text to contextualize the inverted pyramid graphic above.

The [*EU AI Act's*] four risk levels and their corresponding rules are:[2]

Minimal or No Risks

Most AI systems do not pose risks. AI-powered games or spam filters can be used freely. They are not regulated or affected by the EU's AI act.

Limited Risks

AI systems that present only limited risks, such as chatbots or AI systems that generate content, are subject to transparency obligations, such as informing users that their content was generated by AI so that they can make informed decisions concerning further use.

High Risks

High-risk AI systems, such as those used in disease diagnoses, autonomous driving and the biometric identification of individuals involved in criminal activities or investigations, must meet strict requirements and obligations to gain access to the EU market. These include rigorous testing, transparency and human supervision.

Unacceptable Risks

AI systems that pose a threat to people's safety, rights or livelihoods are banned from use in the EU. These include cognitive behavioural manipulation, predictive policing, emotion recognition in the workplace and educational institutions,

2. Council of the EU and European Council, *Artificial Intelligence Act.*

and social scoring. The use of real-time remote biometric identification systems such as facial recognition by law enforcement authorities in public spaces is also prohibited, with some limited exceptions.

a. EU AI Act, Article 3 [Definition of Profiling]

The types of harms associated with high-risk AI systems include scoring and profiling. Algorithmic discrimination and disparate impact are often seen as inextricably linked to these concerns. The *EU AI Act* and the *EU General Data Protection Regulation (GDPR)* utilize the same definition of profiling.

EU AI Act

Article 3. Definitions

> **(52)** 'profiling' means profiling as defined in Article 4, point (4), of Regulation (EU) 2016/679[.]

The *EU AI Act*'s definition of profiling refers to the *EU GDPR*, Article 4(4) definition of profiling, as shown below.

GDPR

Article 4(4). Definitions

> **(4)** 'profiling' means any form of automated processing of personal data consisting of the use of personal data to evaluate certain personal aspects relating to a natural person, in particular to analyse or predict aspects concerning that natural person's performance at work, economic situation, health, personal preferences, interests, reliability, behaviour, location or movements[.]

b. EU AI Act, Article 7 [Amendments to Annex III (High-Risk AI Systems)]

The *EU AI Act*, and many other statutory and regulatory developments in AI oversight in the U.S. and globally, focuses on how to mitigate the risk of health and safety harms that may be posed by AI systems. In addition to the classification of high-risk AI systems identified in Annex III, the *EU AI Act* anticipates the need to amend the criteria and potential use cases that may lead to the nomination of additional AI systems to the classification of a high-risk AI system.

EU AI Act

Article 7. Amendments to Annex III [High-Risk AI Systems]

> **1.** The Commission is empowered to adopt delegated acts in accordance with Article 97 to amend Annex III by adding or modifying use-cases of high-risk AI systems where both of the following conditions are fulfilled:

(a) the AI systems are intended to be used in any of the areas listed in Annex III;

(b) the AI systems pose a risk of harm to health and safety, or an adverse impact on fundamental rights, and that risk is equivalent to, or greater than, the risk of harm or of adverse impact posed by the high-risk AI systems already referred to in Annex III.

2. When assessing the condition under paragraph 1, point (b), the Commission shall take into account the following criteria:

(a) the intended purpose of the AI system;

(b) the extent to which an AI system has been used or is likely to be used;

(c) the nature and amount of the data processed and used by the AI system, in particular whether special categories of personal data are processed;

(d) the extent to which the AI system acts autonomously and the possibility for a human to override a decision or recommendations that may lead to potential harm;

(e) the extent to which the use of an AI system has already caused harm to health and safety, has had an adverse impact on fundamental rights or has given rise to significant concerns in relation to the likelihood of such harm or adverse impact, as demonstrated, for example, by reports or documented allegations submitted to national competent authorities or by other reports, as appropriate;

(f) the potential extent of such harm or such adverse impact, in particular in terms of its intensity and its ability to affect multiple persons or to disproportionately affect a particular group of persons;

(g) the extent to which persons who are potentially harmed or suffer an adverse impact are dependent on the outcome produced with an AI system, in particular because for practical or legal reasons it is not reasonably possible to opt-out from that outcome;

(h) the extent to which there is an imbalance of power, or the persons who are potentially harmed or suffer an adverse impact are in a vulnerable position in relation to the deployer of an AI system, in particular due to status, authority, knowledge, economic or social circumstances, or age;

(i) the extent to which the outcome produced involving an AI system is easily corrigible or reversible, taking into account the technical solutions available to correct or reverse it, whereby outcomes having an adverse impact on health, safety or fundamental rights, shall not be considered to be easily corrigible or reversible;

(j) the magnitude and likelihood of benefit of the deployment of the AI system for individuals, groups, or society at large, including possible improvements in product safety;

(k) the extent to which existing Union law provides for:

(i) effective measures of redress in relation to the risks posed by an AI system, with the exclusion of claims for damages;

(ii) effective measures to prevent or substantially minimise those risks.

c. EU AI Act, Article 14 [Human Oversight]

Automation bias is a related concept to algorithmic bias. Although algorithmic discrimination and algorithmic bias are not coterminous, the definitions of high-risk AI systems may encompass both. In Article 14 of the *EU AI Act*, under a discussion of the need for human oversight and accountability, the law recognizes that regulating high-risk AI systems involves the potential of overreliance and harmful impact from automation bias. Article 14 discusses automation bias below.

EU AI Act

Article 14. Human Oversight

4. . . . [T]he high-risk AI system shall be provided to the deployer in such a way that natural persons to whom human oversight is assigned are enabled, as appropriate and proportionate: . . .

(b) to remain aware of the possible tendency of automatically relying or over-relying on the output produced by a high-risk AI system (automation bias), in particular for high-risk AI systems used to provide information or recommendations for decisions to be taken by natural persons; . . .

4. Colorado AI Consumer Protection Act

Colorado's approach to managing AI risks is based on specific identified areas of concern that were deemed necessary for enhanced protections. The *Colorado AI Consumer Protection Act* requires the developer of a high-risk AI system to use reasonable care to protect consumers from any known or reasonably foreseeable risks of algorithmic discrimination in the high-risk system.[3] The *Colorado AI Consumer Protection Act* defines both algorithmic discrimination and high-risk AI systems and sets forth algorithmic discrimination protections.[4]

a. Colo. Rev. Stat. Sec. 6-1-1701(1), (9). Definitions—Algorithmic Discrimination; High-Risk Artificial Intelligence System

Colorado AI Consumer Protection Act

2024 Colorado Session Laws, Ch. 198 (S.B. 24-205)

6-1-1701(1). Definitions

(1) (a) "Algorithmic discrimination" means any condition in which the use of an artificial intelligence system results in an unlawful differential treatment or impact that disfavors an individual or group of individuals on the basis

3. Colo. Rev. Stat. § 6-1-1702 *et seq.* (2024).
4. *Id.* at § 6-1-1701(1)(a)-(b) *et seq.*

of their actual or perceived age, color, disability, ethnicity, genetic information, limited proficiency in the English language, national origin, race, religion, reproductive health, sex, veteran status, or other classification protected under the laws of this state or federal law.

(b) "Algorithmic discrimination" does not include:

(I) The offer, license, or use of a high-risk artificial intelligence system by a developer or deployer for the sole purpose of:

(A) The developer's or deployer's self-testing to identify, mitigate, or prevent discrimination or otherwise ensure compliance with state and federal law; or

(B) Expanding an applicant, customer, or participant pool to increase diversity or redress historical discrimination; or

(II) An act or omission by or on behalf of a private club or other establishment that is not in fact open to the public, as set forth in Title II of the federal "Civil Rights Act of 1964", 42 U.S.C. sec. 2000a(e), as amended. . . .

6-1-1701(9). Definitions

(9) (a) "High-risk artificial intelligence system" means any artificial intelligence system that, when deployed, makes, or is a substantial factor in making, a consequential decision.

(b) "High-risk artificial intelligence system" does not include:

(I) An artificial intelligence system if the artificial intelligence system is intended to:

(A) Perform a narrow procedural task; or

(B) Detect decision-making patterns or deviations from prior decision-making patterns and is not intended to replace or influence a previously completed human assessment without sufficient human review; . . .

b. Colo. Rev. Stat. Sec. 6-1-1702. Developer Duty to Avoid Algorithmic Discrimination — Required Documentation

6-1-1702. Developer Duty to Avoid Algorithmic Discrimination — Required Documentation

(1) . . . [A] developer of a high-risk artificial intelligence system shall use reasonable care to protect consumers from any known or reasonably foreseeable risks of algorithmic discrimination arising from the intended and contracted uses of the high-risk artificial intelligence system. In any enforcement action brought [by the attorney general] . . . there is a rebuttable presumption that a developer used reasonable care as required under this section if the developer complied with this section and any additional requirements or obligations as set forth in rules promulgated by the attorney general[.] . . .

c. Colo. Rev. Stat. Sec. 6-1-1703. Deployer Duty to Avoid Algorithmic Discrimination—Risk Management Policy and Program

6-1-1703. Deployer Duty to Avoid Algorithmic Discrimination—Risk Management Policy and Program

(1) . . . [A] deployer of a high-risk artificial intelligence system shall use reasonable care to protect consumers from any known or reasonably foreseeable risks of algorithmic discrimination. In any enforcement action brought [by the attorney general] . . . there is a rebuttable presumption that a deployer of a high-risk artificial intelligence system used reasonable care as required under this section if the deployer complied with this section and any additional requirements or obligations as set forth in rules promulgated by the attorney general[.] . . .

B. CASE STUDIES IN ALGORITHMIC BIAS AND DISPARATE IMPACT

1. Risk Assessment Automation as Case Study

Multiple cases filed in state and federal courts represent the effort to address algorithmic bias and disparate impact through legal redress. The following case, filed in Wisconsin, *State v. Loomis*, is the first comprehensive judicial examination of the usage of algorithmic systems to consider a defendant's sentencing by a judge.

a. State v. Loomis

State [of Wisconsin] v. Loomis is foundational to understanding algorithmic discrimination. *State v. Loomis* involved the use of COMPAS, an algorithmically-based risk-assessment tool.[5] COMPAS purports to assess a defendant's risk of recidivism, the likelihood that a given defendant may reoffend.[6] In 2012, the Wisconsin Department of Corrections incorporated COMPAS into "each step in the prison system, from sentencing to parole."[7]

COMPAS determinations were thereafter incorporated into defendants' presentence investigation (PSI) reports, even as increasing evidence determined that the tool resulted in a disparate impact on the basis of race.[8] The *Loomis* case involves a challenge by a criminal defendant to the use of COMPAS against him in his sentencing. The state court upheld the use of COMPAS.

---

5. Julia Angwin et al., *Machine Bias*, ProPublica (May 23, 2016).
6. *Id.*
7. *Id.*
8. *Id.*

State v. Loomis

Wisconsin Supreme Court
881 N.W.2d 749 (Wis. 2016)

Delivered by Justice BRADLEY.

I

. . . The facts of this case are not in dispute. The State [Wisconsin] contends that Loomis was the driver in a drive-by shooting. It charged him with five counts, all as a repeater: (1) First-degree recklessly endangering safety (PTAC); (2) Attempting to flee or elude a traffic officer (PTAC); (3) Operating a motor vehicle without the owner's consent; (4) Possession of a firearm by a felon (PTAC); (5) Possession of a short-barreled shotgun or rifle (PTAC).[9]

Loomis denies involvement in the drive-by shooting. He waived his right to trial and entered a guilty plea to only two of the less severe charges, attempting to flee a traffic officer and operating a motor vehicle without the owner's consent. The plea agreement stated that the other counts would be dismissed but read in:

> The other counts will be dismissed and read in for sentencing, although the defendant denies he had any role in the shooting, and only drove the car after the shooting occurred. The State believes he was the driver of the car when the shooting happened.
>
> The State will leave any appropriate sentence to the Court's discretion but will argue aggravating and mitigating factors.

After accepting Loomis's plea, the circuit court ordered a presentence investigation. The Presentence Investigation Report ("PSI") included an attached COMPAS risk assessment.

COMPAS is a risk-need assessment tool designed by Northpointe, Inc. to provide decisional support for the Department of Corrections when making placement decisions, managing offenders, and planning treatment.[10] The COMPAS risk assessment is based upon information gathered from the defendant's criminal file and an interview with the defendant.

A COMPAS report consists of a risk assessment designed to predict recidivism and a separate needs assessment for identifying program needs in areas such as employment, housing and substance abuse.[11] The risk assessment portion of COMPAS generates risk scores displayed in the form of a bar chart, with three bars that represent pretrial recidivism risk, general recidivism risk, and violent recidivism risk.[12] Each bar indicates a defendant's level of risk on a scale of one to ten.[13]

---

9. [Fn. 13 in original] "PTAC" refers to party to a crime.

10. [Fn. 14 in original] Northpointe, Inc., *Practitioner's Guide to COMPAS Core*, at 1 (Mar. 19, 2015).

11. [Fn. 15 in original] *Id.* at 12, 16.

12. [Fn. 16 in original] *Id.* at 3, 26.

13. [Fn. 17 in original] *Id.* at 8.

As the PSI explains, risk scores are intended to predict the general likelihood that those with a similar history of offending are either less likely or more likely to commit another crime following release from custody. However, the COMPAS risk assessment does not predict the specific likelihood that an individual offender will reoffend. Instead, it provides a prediction based on a comparison of information about the individual to a similar data group.

Loomis's COMPAS risk scores indicated that he presented a high risk of recidivism on all three bar charts. His PSI included a description of how the COMPAS risk assessment should be used and cautioned against its misuse, instructing that it is to be used to identify offenders who could benefit from interventions and to target risk factors that should be addressed during supervision.

The PSI also cautions that a COMPAS risk assessment should not be used to determine the severity of a sentence or whether an offender is incarcerated:

> *For purposes of Evidence Based Sentencing, actuarial assessment tools are especially relevant to: 1. Identify offenders who should be targeted for interventions. 2. Identify dynamic risk factors to target with conditions of supervision. 3.* ***It is very important to remember that risk scores are not intended to determine the severity of the sentence or whether an offender is incarcerated****. (Emphasis added.)* [Italics added].

At sentencing, the State argued that the circuit court should use the COMPAS report when determining an appropriate sentence:

> In addition, the COMPAS report that was completed in this case does show the high risk and the high needs of the defendant. There's a high risk of violence, high risk of recidivism, high pre-trial risk; and so all of these are factors in determining the appropriate sentence.

Ultimately, the circuit court referenced the COMPAS risk score along with other sentencing factors in ruling out probation:

> *You're identified, through the COMPAS assessment, as an individual who is at high risk to the community.* [Italics added].
>
> In terms of weighing the various factors, I'm ruling out probation because of the seriousness of the crime and because your history, your history on supervision, and the risk assessment tools that have been utilized, suggest that you're extremely high risk to re-offend. . . .

Loomis filed a motion for post-conviction relief requesting a new sentencing hearing. He argued that the circuit court's consideration of the COMPAS risk assessment at sentencing violated his due process rights. Loomis further asserted that the circuit court erroneously exercised its discretion by improperly assuming that the factual bases for the read-in charges were true.

The circuit court held two hearings on the post-conviction motion. At the first hearing, the circuit court addressed Loomis's claim that it had erroneously exercised its discretion in how it considered the read-in charges. Considering the relevant case law and legal standards, the circuit court concluded that it had applied the proper standard and denied Loomis's motion on that issue.

During the first post-conviction motion hearing, the circuit court reviewed the plea hearing transcript and the sentencing transcript and explained that it did not believe Loomis's explanation:

> *I felt Mr. Loomis's explanation was inconsistent with the facts. The State's version was more consistent with the facts and gave greater weight to the State's version at sentencing.* [Italics added].

At the second hearing, the circuit court addressed the due process issues. The defendant offered the testimony of an expert witness, Dr. David Thompson, regarding the use at sentencing of a COMPAS risk assessment. Dr. Thompson opined that a COMPAS risk assessment should not be used for decisions regarding incarceration because a COMPAS risk assessment was not designed for such use. According to Dr. Thompson, a circuit court's consideration at sentencing of the risk assessment portions of COMPAS runs a "tremendous risk of over estimating an individual's risk and . . . mistakenly sentencing them or basing their sentence on factors that may not apply. . . ."

Dr. Thompson further testified that sentencing courts have very little information about how a COMPAS assessment analyzes the risk:

> *The Court does not know how the COMPAS compares that individual's history with the population that it's comparing them with. The Court doesn't even know whether that population is a Wisconsin population, a New York population, a California population. . . . There's all kinds of information that the court doesn't have, and what we're doing is we're mis-informing the court when we put these graphs in front of them and let them use it for sentence.* [Italics added].

In denying the post-conviction motion, the circuit court explained that it used the COMPAS risk assessment to corroborate its findings and that it would have imposed the same sentence regardless of whether it considered the COMPAS risk scores. Loomis appealed and the court of appeals certified the appeal to this court. . . .

III

At the outset we observe that the defendant is not challenging the use of a COMPAS risk assessment for decisions other than sentencing, and he is not challenging the use of the needs portion of the COMPAS report at sentencing. Instead, Loomis challenges only the use of the risk assessment portion of the COMPAS report at sentencing.

Specifically, Loomis asserts that the circuit court's use of a COMPAS risk assessment at sentencing violates a defendant's right to due process for three reasons: (1) it violates a defendant's right to be sentenced based upon accurate information, in part because the proprietary nature of COMPAS prevents him from assessing its accuracy; (2) it violates a defendant's right to an individualized sentence; and (3) it improperly uses gendered assessments in sentencing. . . .

The question of whether COMPAS can be used at sentencing has previously been addressed.

. . . We encouraged circuit courts to seek "more complete information upfront, at the time of sentencing. Judges would be assisted in knowing about a defendant's propensity for causing harm [and] the circumstances likely to precipitate the harm[.]'" . . .

VII

Next, we address the permissible uses for a COMPAS risk assessment at sentencing. Then we set forth the limitations and cautions that a sentencing court must observe when using COMPAS.

Although it cannot be determinative, a sentencing court may use a COMPAS risk assessment as a relevant factor for such matters as: (1) diverting low-risk prison-bound offenders to a non-prison alternative; (2) assessing whether an offender can be supervised safely and effectively in the community; and (3) imposing terms and conditions of probation, supervision, and responses to violations.[14]

First, COMPAS may be useful in identifying prison-bound offenders who are at low risk to reoffend for purposes of diverting them to non-prison alternatives and aids in the decision of whether to suspend all or part of an offender's sentence.[15]

Second, risk assessment tools such as COMPAS can be helpful to assess an offender's risk to public safety and can inform the decision of whether the risk of re-offense presented by the offender can be safely managed and effectively reduced through community supervision and services.[16]

Third, COMPAS may be used to inform decisions about the terms and conditions of probation and supervision.[17] Risk assessments can be useful in identifying low-risk offenders who do not require intensive supervision and treatment programs.[18] Together with a need assessment, a risk assessment may inform public safety considerations related to offender risk management, and therefore may be used to provide guidance about the level of supervision and control needed for an offender placed on probation

14. [Fn. 49 in original] *Tallarico, supra* note 20, at 20-21.

15. [Fn. 50 in original] Casey, *Using Offender Risk and Needs Assessment Information at Sentencing, supra* note 7, at 8, 9, 13.

16. [Fn. 51 in original] *Id.* at 9, 13-14.

17. [Fn. 52 in original] *Id.* at 16.

18. [Fn. 53 in original] *Id.*

or released to extended supervision.[19] Specifically, it may inform decisions such as reporting requirements, drug testing, electronic monitoring, community service, and the most appropriate treatment strategies.[20]

Thus, a COMPAS risk assessment may be used to "enhance a judge's evaluation, weighing, and application of the other sentencing evidence in the formulation of an individualized sentencing program appropriate for each defendant."[21] As the court of appeals explained in *Samsa*, "COMPAS is merely one tool available to a court at the time of sentencing and a court is free to rely on portions of the assessment while rejecting other portions."[22]

However, the use of a COMPAS risk assessment at sentencing must be subject to certain limitations. As noted above, the DOC already recognizes these limitations on the PSI, instructing that "[i]t is very important to remember that risk scores are not intended to determine the severity of the sentence or whether an offender is incarcerated." This is also the first "Guiding Principle" of the National Center for State Courts ("NCSC") report on using offender risk and needs assessment at sentencing, which instructs that:

> *Risk and need assessment information should be used in the sentencing decision to inform public safety considerations related to offender risk reduction and management. It should not be used as an aggravating or mitigating factor in determining the severity of an offender's sanction.*[23] [Italics added].

Additionally, we set forth the corollary limitation that risk scores may not be used as the determinative factor in deciding whether the offender can be supervised safely and effectively in the com- munity. This is consistent with the second "Guiding Principle" of the National Center for State Courts.[24]

The decision of the Indiana Supreme Court in *Malenchik*, provides additional guidance here. It limited the use of risk assessments, explaining that they "are not intended to serve as aggravating or mitigating circumstances nor to determine the gross length of sentence, but a trial court may employ such results in formulating the manner in which a sentence is to be served."[25]

Additionally, a COMPAS risk assessment was not designed to address all of the goals of a sentence. Its aim is addressing the treatment needs of an

---

19. [Fn. 54 in original] *Id.* at 11; Casey, *Offender Risk & Needs Assessment Instruments: A Primer for Courts, supra* note 32, at 2.

20. [Fn. 55 in original] Casey, *Using Offender Risk and Needs Assessment Information at Sentencing, supra* note 7, at 14, 16.

21. [In text in original] *See Malenchik*, 928 N.E.2d at 573.

22. [In text in original] [State v. Samsa] 359 Wis.2d 580, ¶ 13, 859 N.W.2d 149.

23. [Fn. 56 in original] *Id.* at 11.

24. [Fn. 57 in original] *Id.* at 14.

25. [In text in original] 928 N.E.2d at 575.

individual and identifying the risk of recidivism. Sentencing, on the other hand, is meant to address additional purposes.[26]

Because of these disparate goals, using a risk assessment tool to determine the length and severity of a sentence is a poor fit. As scholars have observed, "[a]ssessing the risk of future crime plays no role in sentencing decisions based solely on backward-looking perceptions of blame-worthiness, TTT is not relevant to deterrence, TTT and should not be used to sentence offenders to more time than they morally deserve."[27]

Thus, a sentencing court may consider a COMPAS risk assessment at sentencing subject to the following limitations. As recognized by the Department of Corrections, the PSI instructs that risk scores may not be used: (1) to determine whether an offender is incarcerated; or (2) to determine the severity of the sentence. Additionally, risk scores may not be used as the determinative factor in deciding whether an offender can be supervised safely and effectively in the community.[28]

Importantly, a circuit court must explain the factors in addition to a COMPAS risk assessment that independently support the sentence imposed. A COMPAS risk assessment is only one of many factors that may be considered and weighed at sentencing.

Any Presentence Investigation Report ("PSI") containing a COMPAS risk assessment filed with the court must contain a written advisement listing the limitations.[29] Additionally, this written advisement should inform sentencing courts of the following cautions as discussed throughout this opinion:

- *The proprietary nature of COMPAS has been invoked to prevent disclosure of information relating to how factors are weighed or how risk scores are determined.*
- *Because COMPAS risk assessment scores are based on group data, they are able to identify groups of high-risk offenders — not a particular high-risk individual.*
- *Some studies of COMPAS risk assessment scores have raised questions about whether they disproportionately classify minority offenders as having a higher risk of recidivism.*

---

26. [In text in original] *See* State v. Dowdy, 2012 WI 12, ¶ 97, 338 Wis.2d 565, 808 N.W.2d 691 (Abrahamson, C.J., dissenting) ("It is commonly understood that there are four main purposes of sentencing: (1) deterrence; (2) rehabilitation; (3) retribution; and (4) segregation.").

27. [Fn. 58 in original] John Monahan and Jennifer L. Skeem, *Risk Assessment in Criminal Sentencing*, 12 Annual Rev. Clinical Psychol. 489, 492-93. *See also* Melissa Hamilton, *Risk–Needs Assessment: Constitutional and Ethical Challenges*, 52 Am. Crim. L. Rev. 231, 277 (2015) ("Retributive and deterrence orientations are less amenable to evidence-based practices").

28. [Fn. 59 in original] Casey, *Using Offender Risk and Needs Assessment Information at Sentencing, supra* note 7, at 14.

29. [Fn. 60 in original] A circuit court may order a presentence investigation pursuant to Wis. Stat. § 972.15(1). When filed with the court, any presentence investigative report that attaches or incorporates a COMPAS risk assessment must contain, consistent with due process, a written advisement regarding the cautions and limitations.

- *A COMPAS risk assessment compares defendants to a national sample, but no cross-validation study for a Wisconsin population has yet been completed. Risk assessment tools must be constantly monitored and re-normed for accuracy due to changing populations and subpopulations.*
- *COMPAS was not developed for use at sentencing, but was intended for use by the Department of Corrections in making determinations regarding treatment, supervision, and parole.*

It is important to note that these are the cautions that have been identified in the present moment. For example, if a cross-validation study for a Wisconsin population is conducted, then flexibility is needed to remove this caution or explain the results of the cross-validation study. Similarly, this advisement should be regularly updated as other cautions become more or less relevant as additional data becomes available. . . .

2. *Biometrics and Facial Recognition Technology as Case Study*

The next two cases examine privacy concerns arising from facial recognition technology. In *ACLU v. ClearviewAI,* the Plaintiffs are the ACLU and ACLU of Illinois, Chicago Alliance Against Sexual Exploitation, Sex Workers Outreach Project Chicago, Illinois Public Interest Research Group, and Mujeres Latinas en Acción. The Plaintiffs alleged that ClearviewAI captured over three billion faceprints from images found online to create a facial recognition identification system that the ACLU alleged violated the *Illinois Biometric Information Privacy Information Act* (*BIPA*). *BIPA* requires that prior written consent must be obtained from an Illinois resident from companies that collect, capture, or obtain biometric identifiers, such as digital fingerprint, faceprint, and iris scans.

The second case, *FTC v. Rite Aid,* demonstrates the enforcement jurisdiction of the Federal Trade Commission (FTC) to regulate unfair and deceptive trade practices in U.S. commerce. In *FTC v. Rite Aid,* the FTC requested the suspension of the use of facial recognition technology by Rite Aid due to its alleged failure to implement reasonable procedures and prevent harm to consumers.

a. ACLU v. ClearviewAI (Consent Order)

In *ACLU v. ClearviewAI,* the Plaintiffs argued that the lawsuit was the first in the nation to focus explicitly on the harm caused by facial recognition technology to vulnerable communities, including: "survivors of domestic violence and sexual assault, undocumented immigrants, communities of color, and members of other vulnerable communities."[30] The Plaintiffs

30. ACLU v. Clearview AI, No. 2020-CH-04353, (Ill. Cir. Ct. May 11, 2022).

alleged that the ClearviewAI technology violated the Illinois BIPA protections. The plaintiffs sought multiple remedies, including deletion of all faceprints gathered without consent from Illinois residents.

On May 11, 2022, the circuit court released a consent order that permanently enjoined ClearviewAI from releasing its faceprint database to most businesses and private entities nationwide and also barred selling access to entities within Illinois for five years.[31]

ACLU v. Clearview AI (Consent Order)

Circuit Court of Cook County, Illinois, County Department, Chancery Division
Consent Order of Permanent and Time-Limited Injunctions Against Defendant
Case No. 2020 CH 04353
May 11, 2022

MEYERSON, Cook County Circuit Judge.

CONSENT ORDER

2. Clearview is permanently enjoined from granting paid or free access to the Clearview database of alleged facial vectors at issue in Plaintiffs' complaint and Clearview's counterclaim anywhere in the United States (the "Clearview App") to: (1) any private entity or private individuals, except (a) as consistent with 740 ILCS 14/25 (and applicable law referred to therein) or (b) in compliance with the requirements of 740 ILCS 14/15 and (2) any individual government employee who is not acting in their official capacity on behalf of a State or federal government agency, or local unit of government. For the avoidance of doubt, the private entity and private individual injunction in no way limits Clearview's ability to work with federal or other State government agencies arid contractors engaged in authorized support for and under contracts with such federal or other State government agencies at all levels and locations. . . .

4. For a period of five (5) years from the date of the entry of this Order, Clearview is enjoined from granting either paid or free access to Illinois state, county, local, or other government agencies (but is not restricted from permitting such access for federal or other State government agencies and contractors engaged in authorized support for and under contracts with such federal and other State government agencies at all levels and locations) and contractors working for those agencies in Illinois, including state and local police departments and other state and local law enforcement agencies (the "Illinois State and Local Agencies"), to the Clearview App.

5. Clearview is further enjoined for a period of five (5) years from the date of the entry of this Order from granting either paid or free access to the Clearview App to any private entity located in Illinois, even if said transaction

31. *Id.*

is otherwise permissible under 740 ILCS 14/25 (and applicable law referred to therein), or 740 ILCS' 14/15. Clearview also may not grant either paid or free access to any individual employees of Illinois State and Local Agencies during this period. including when they are working in their official capacities. . . .

IT IS SO ORDERED.

b. FTC v. Rite Aid (Complaint)

In *FTC v. Rite Aid*, the FTC alleged that from 2012 until 2020, the company utilized facial recognition technology in many of its pharmacy locations to detect criminal activity and shoplifting. Through its facial recognition and databasing technology, alerts were made to Rite Aid employees via "match alerts" sent to their email and phone. The notifications indicated that certain individuals who had entered the store were potential criminal matches. Rite Aid employees would then take action against "match alert" individuals. This included subjecting them to increased surveillance, keeping patrons from making purchases, and, in some instances, banning them from the store. There were alleged instances where patrons were publicly shamed for past criminal activity. Some patrons were detained or subjected to searches, while employees called the police to notify them of alleged criminal activity.

In numerous instances, the complaint alleged, match alerts were false positives where an individual had been misidentified. The complaint further alleged that these false positives caused and were likely to cause injuries to patrons, especially to Black, Asian, and Latino female patrons. The FTC contended that Rite Aid failed to deploy the technology and train service providers in a manner that safeguarded personal information and failed to maintain records relating to its information security program.[32]

FTC v. Rite Aid (Complaint)

United States District Court for the Eastern District of Pennsylvania
Complaint for Permanent Injunction and Other Relief
Case No. 2:23-cv-05023
December 19, 2023

SUMMARY

3. From at least approximately October 2012 until July 2020, Rite Aid has used facial recognition technology in hundreds of its retail pharmacy locations to identify patrons that it had previously deemed likely to engage in shoplifting or other criminal behavior in order to "drive and keep persons of interest out of [Rite Aid's] stores." The technology generated alerts sent

---

32. Fed. Trade Comm'n, Rite Aid Banned from Using AI Facial Recognition After FTC Says Retailer Deployed Technology without Reasonable Safeguards (Dec. 19, 2023).

to Rite Aid's employees, including by email or mobile phone application notifications ("match alerts"), indicating that individuals who had entered Rite Aid stores were matches for entries in Rite Aid's watchlist database.

4. In whole or in part due to facial recognition match alerts, Rite Aid employees took action against the individuals who had triggered the supposed matches, including subjecting them to increased surveillance; banning them from entering or making purchases at the Rite Aid stores; publicly and audibly accusing them of past criminal activity in front of friends, family, acquaintances, and strangers; detaining them or subjecting them to searches; and calling the police to report that they had engaged in criminal activity. In numerous instances, the match alerts that led to these actions were false positives (i.e., instances in which the technology incorrectly identified a person who had entered a store as someone in Rite Aid's database). . . .

6. Rite Aid's failures caused and were likely to cause substantial injury to consumers, and especially to Black, Asian, Latino, and women consumers.

7. . . . Rite Aid routinely failed to use reasonable steps in selecting and retaining service providers capable of appropriately safeguarding personal information they received from Rite Aid; require service providers by contract to implement and maintain appropriate safeguards for personal information they received from Rite Aid; and maintain written records relating to its information security program. Furthermore, Rite Aid failed to produce documents relating to its compliance with the 2010 Order, including documents that contradict, qualify, or call into question its compliance.

C. CASE STUDIES IN FEDERAL RESPONSES

The *White House Executive Order on the Safe, Secure, and Trustworthy Development and Use of AI*, Executive Order 14110 (E.O. 14110), published in October 2023, proposed a comprehensive federal government-wide approach to the safe use of AI while managing risks. Other actions within U.S. federal agencies prior to and immediately after the publication of E.O. 14110 demonstrated various soft law approaches to AI governance. On January 20, 2025, the Trump administration rescinded E.O. 14110. It also later rescinded the OMB Policy that had been promulgated pursuant E.O. 14110.[33] On January

33. Exec. Order No. 14148, 90 Fed. Reg. 8237, *Initial Rescissions of Harmful Executive Orders and Actions* (Jan. 28, 2025); OMB Memorandum M-25-21, *Accelerating Federal Use of AI through Innovation, Governance, and Public Trust* (Apr. 3, 2025); OMB Memorandum M-25-22, *Driving Efficient Acquisition of Artificial Intelligence in Government* (Apr. 3, 2025). These two OMB memos implement Executive Order 14179. (Jan. 23, 2025), rescinding and replacing the two OMB memos promulgated during the Biden administration on AI use and AI procurement, OMB Memorandum M-24-10, *Advancing Governance, Innovation, and Risk Management for Agency Use of Artificial Intelligence* (Mar. 28, 2024) and OMB Memorandum M-24-18, *Advancing the Responsible Acquisition of Artificial Intelligence in Government* (Sept. 24, 2024).

23, 2025, the administration published the *Executive Order on Removing Barriers to American Leadership in Artificial Intelligence*, E.O. 14179.[34]

1. *White House Executive Orders and Federal Interagency Coordination as Case Studies*

The *Executive Order on the Safe, Secure, and Trustworthy Development and Use of AI* was published by the Biden administration on October 30, 2023, to address a wide range of governance objectives, including mitigating unlawful discrimination and other harms that might be aggravated by AI. In conjunction, the Assistant Attorney General of the Civil Rights Division, U.S. Department of Justice, and other federal agencies pledged to use pre-existing legal authorities to prevent and address discrimination in the use of automated systems including algorithmic discrimination. The executive order was rescinded by the Trump administration on January 20, 2025.

a. White House Executive Order on Removing Barriers to American Leadership in Artificial Intelligence

The excerpt below is from the *Executive Order on Removing Barriers to American Leadership in Artificial Intelligence*, released on January 23, 2025.

White House Executive Order 14179:
Removing Barriers to American Leadership in Artificial Intelligence

January 23, 2025

Section 1. *Purpose.* The United States has long been at the forefront of artificial intelligence (AI) innovation, driven by the strength of our free markets, world-class research institutions, and entrepreneurial spirit. To maintain this leadership, we must develop AI systems that are free from ideological bias or engineered social agendas. With the right Government policies, we can solidify our position as the global leader in AI and secure a brighter future for all Americans. This order revokes certain existing AI policies and directives that act as barriers to American AI innovation, clearing a path for the United States to act decisively to retain global leadership in artificial intelligence.

Section 2. *Policy.* It is the policy of the United States to sustain and enhance America's global AI dominance in order to promote human flourishing, economic competitiveness, and national security. . . .

Section 5. *Implementation of Order Revocation.*

34. Exec. Order No. 14179, 90 Fed. Reg. 8741, *Removing Barriers to American Leadership in Artificial Intelligence* (Jan. 31, 2025)

(a) The [Assistant to the President for Science and Technology] APST, the Special Advisor for AI and Crypto, and the [Assistant to the President for National Security Affairs] APNSA shall immediately review, in coordination with the heads of all agencies as they deem relevant, all policies, directives, regulations, orders, and other actions taken pursuant to the revoked Executive Order 14110 of October 30, 2023 (Safe, Secure, and Trustworthy Development and Use of Artificial Intelligence). The APST, the Special Advisor for AI and Crypto, and the APNSA shall, in coordination with the heads of relevant agencies, identify any actions taken pursuant to Executive Order 14110 that are or may be inconsistent with, or present obstacles to, the policy set forth in section 2 of this order. For any such agency actions identified, the heads of agencies shall, as appropriate and consistent with applicable law, suspend, revise, or rescind such actions, or propose suspending, revising, or rescinding such actions. If in any case such suspension, revision, or rescission cannot be finalized immediately, the APST and the heads of agencies shall promptly take steps to provide all available exemptions authorized by any such orders, rules, regulations, guidelines, or policies, as appropriate and consistent with applicable law, until such action can be finalized.

(b) . . . [T]he OMB Director, in coordination with the APST, shall revise OMB Memoranda M-24-10 [*Advancing Governance, Innovation, and Risk Management for Agency Use of Artificial Intelligence* (March 2024)] and M-24-18 [*Advancing the Responsible Acquisition of Artificial Intelligence in Government* (September 2024)] as necessary to make them consistent with the policy set forth in section 2 of this order. . . .

b. White House Executive Order on the Safe, Secure, and Trustworthy Development and Use of AI (Rescinded)

On January 20, 2025, the Trump administration rescinded E.O. 14110, the Biden administration's *Executive Order on the Safe, Secure, and Trustworthy Development and Use of AI.* An excerpt from the *Executive Order on the Safe, Secure, and Trustworthy Development and Use of AI* is included for historical reference.

White House Executive Order 14110 (Rescinded): Safe, Secure, and Trustworthy Development and Use of Artificial Intelligence

October 30, 2023

Sec. 7. Advancing Equity and Civil Rights

7.1. Strengthening AI and Civil Rights in the Criminal Justice System

(a) To address unlawful discrimination and other harms that may be exacerbated by AI, the Attorney General shall:

(i) . . . coordinate with and support agencies in their implementation and enforcement of existing Federal laws to address civil rights and civil liberties violations and discrimination related to AI;

(ii) direct the Assistant Attorney General in charge of the Civil Rights Division to convene, within 90 days of the date of this order, a meeting of the heads of Federal civil rights offices—for which meeting the heads of civil rights offices within independent regulatory agencies will be encouraged to join—to discuss comprehensive use of their respective authorities and offices to: prevent and address discrimination in the use of automated systems, including algorithmic discrimination; increase coordination between the Department of Justice's Civil Rights Division and Federal civil rights offices concerning issues related to AI and algorithmic discrimination; improve external stakeholder engagement to promote public awareness of potential discriminatory uses and effects of AI; and develop, as appropriate, additional training, technical assistance, guidance, or other resources; and

(iii) consider providing, as appropriate and consistent with applicable law, guidance, technical assistance, and training to State, local, Tribal, and territorial investigators and prosecutors on best practices for investigating and prosecuting civil rights violations and discrimination related to automated systems, including AI.

(b) To promote the equitable treatment of individuals and adhere to the Federal Government's fundamental obligation to ensure fair and impartial justice for all, with respect to the use of AI in the criminal justice system, the Attorney General shall, in consultation with the Secretary of Homeland Security and the Director of OSTP:

(i) within 365 days of the date of this order, submit to the President a report that addresses the use of AI in the criminal justice system, including any use in:

(A) sentencing;

(B) parole, supervised release, and probation;

(C) bail, pretrial release, and pretrial detention;

(D) risk assessments, including pretrial, earned time, and early release or transfer to home-confinement determinations;

(E) police surveillance;

(F) crime forecasting and predictive policing, including the ingestion of historical crime data into AI systems to predict high-density "hot spots";

(G) prison-management tools; and

(H) forensic analysis;

(ii) within the report set forth in subsection 7.1(b)(i) of this section:

(A) identify areas where AI can enhance law enforcement efficiency and accuracy, consistent with protections for privacy, civil rights, and civil liberties; and

(B) recommend best practices for law enforcement agencies, including safeguards and appropriate use limits for AI, to address the concerns set forth in section 13(e)(i) of Executive Order 14074 as well as the best practices and the guidelines set forth in section 13(e)(iii) of Executive Order 14074; and

(iii) supplement the report set forth in subsection 7.1(b)(i) of this section as appropriate with recommendations to the President, including with respect to requests for necessary legislation.

(c) To advance the presence of relevant technical experts and expertise (such as machine-learning engineers, software and infrastructure engineering, data privacy experts, data scientists, and user experience researchers) among law enforcement professionals[.] . . .

7.2. Protecting Civil Rights Related to Government Benefits and Programs

(a) To advance equity and civil rights . . . and in addition to complying with the guidance on Federal Government use of AI . . . agencies shall use their respective civil rights and civil liberties offices and authorities—as appropriate and consistent with applicable law—to prevent and address unlawful discrimination and other harms that result from uses of AI in Federal Government programs and benefits administration. This directive does not apply to agencies' civil or criminal enforcement authorities. Agencies shall consider opportunities to ensure that their respective civil rights and civil liberties offices are appropriately consulted on agency decisions regarding the design, development, acquisition, and use of AI in Federal Government programs and benefits administration. To further these objectives, agencies shall also consider opportunities to increase coordination, communication, and engagement about AI as appropriate with community-based organizations; civil-rights and civil-liberties organizations; academic institutions; industry; State, local, Tribal, and territorial governments; and other stakeholders.

(b) To promote equitable administration of public benefits[.] . . .

7.3. Strengthening AI and Civil Rights in the Broader Economy

(a) . . . prevent unlawful discrimination from AI used for hiring, the Secretary of Labor shall publish guidance for Federal contractors regarding nondiscrimination in hiring involving AI and other technology-based hiring systems.

(b) To address discrimination and biases against protected groups in housing markets and consumer financial markets, the Director of the Federal Housing Finance Agency and the Director of the Consumer Financial Protection Bureau are encouraged to consider using their authorities, as they deem appropriate, to require their respective regulated entities, where possible, to use appropriate methodologies including AI tools to ensure compliance with Federal law and:

(i) evaluate their underwriting models for bias or disparities affecting protected groups; and

(ii) evaluate automated collateral-valuation and appraisal processes in ways that minimize bias.

(c) . . . to combat unlawful discrimination enabled by automated or algorithmic tools used to make decisions about access to housing and in other real estate-related transactions, the Secretary of Housing and Urban Development shall, and the Director of the Consumer Financial Protection Bureau is encouraged to, issue additional guidance:

(i) addressing the use of tenant screening systems in ways that may violate the Fair Housing Act (Public Law 90-284), the Fair Credit Reporting Act (Public Law 91-508), or other relevant Federal laws, including how the use of data, such as criminal records, eviction records, and credit information, can lead to discriminatory outcomes in violation of Federal law; and

(ii) addressing how the Fair Housing Act, the Consumer Financial Protection Act of 2010 (title X of Public Law 111-203), or the Equal Credit Opportunity Act (Public Law 93-495) apply to the advertising of housing, credit, and other real estate-related transactions through digital platforms, including those that use algorithms to facilitate advertising delivery, as well as on best practices to avoid violations of Federal law.

(d) To help ensure that people with disabilities benefit from AI's promise while being protected from its risks, including unequal treatment from the use of biometric data like gaze direction, eye tracking, gait analysis, and hand motions, the Architectural and Transportation Barriers Compliance Board is encouraged, as it deems appropriate, to solicit public participation and conduct community engagement; to issue technical assistance and recommendations on the risks and benefits of AI in using biometric data as an input; and to provide people with disabilities access to information and communication technology and transportation services. . . .

c. Federal Interagency Public Statement: Joint Statement on Enforcement Efforts Against Discrimination and Bias in Automated Systems

Federal interagency efforts have coordinated enforcement commitments to address algorithmic discrimination and other forms of AI discrimination. The leaders of multiple agencies "issued the following joint statement about enforcement efforts to protect the public from bias in automated systems and artificial intelligence[.]"[35]

In April 2023, months after the White House publication of the *Blueprint for an AI Bill of Rights* and the release of the *NIST AI Risk Management Framework*, four agencies released a joint interagency statement on the enforcement of civil rights and consumer protection laws. The federal agencies "jointly pledged" to "uphold America's commitment to the core principles of fairness, equality, and justice as emerging automated systems, including those sometimes marketed as 'artificial intelligence' or 'AI,' become increasingly common in our daily lives—impacting civil rights, fair competition, consumer protection, and equal opportunity."[36]

The following four governmental entities signed the pledge to uphold the enforcement of current antidiscrimination laws and consumer protection laws—the U.S. Civil Rights Division of the U.S. Department of Justice, Equal Employment Opportunity Commission, Federal Trade Commission, and Consumer Financial Protection Bureau. The interagency statement was signed by Rohit Chopra, Director of the Consumer Financial Protection

---

35. Rohit Chopra et al., *Joint Statement on Enforcement Efforts Against Discrimination and Bias in Automated Systems*, FTC (Apr. 25, 2023).

36. Fed Trade Comm'n, FTC Chair Khan and Officials from DOJ, CFPB and EEOC Release Joint Statement on AI (Apr. 25, 2023).

Bureau; Kristen Clarke, Assistant Attorney General for the U.S. Justice Department's Civil Rights Division; Charlotte A. Burrows, Chair of the Equal Employment Opportunity Commission; and Lina M. Khan, Chair of the Federal Trade Commission. This Federal Interagency Joint Statement was issued during the Biden administration. An excerpt from the April 2023 *Joint Statement on the Enforcement Efforts Against Discrimination and Bias in Automated Systems* is included for historical reference.

Joint Statement on Enforcement Efforts Against Discrimination and Bias in Automated Systems

U.S. Civil Rights Division of the U.S. Department of Justice, Equal Employment Opportunity Commission, Federal Trade Commission, and Consumer Financial Protection Bureau
April 25, 2023

America's commitment to the core principles of fairness, equality, and justice is deeply embedded in the federal laws that our agencies enforce to protect civil rights, fair competition, consumer protection, and equal opportunity. These established laws have long served to protect individuals even as our society has navigated emerging technologies. Responsible innovation is not incompatible with these laws. Indeed, innovation and adherence to the law can complement each other and bring tangible benefits to people in a fair and competitive manner, such as increased access to opportunities as well as better products and services at lower costs.

Today, the use of automated systems, including those sometimes marketed as "artificial intelligence" or "AI," is becoming increasingly common in our daily lives. We use the term "automated systems" broadly to mean software and algorithmic processes, including AI, that are used to automate workflows and help people complete tasks or make decisions. Private and public entities use these systems to make critical decisions that impact individuals' rights and opportunities, including fair and equal access to a job, housing, credit opportunities, and other goods and services. These automated systems are often advertised as providing insights and breakthroughs, increasing efficiencies and cost-savings, and modernizing existing practices. Although many of these tools offer the promise of advancement, their use also has the potential to perpetuate unlawful bias, automate unlawful discrimination, and produce other harmful outcomes.

OUR AGENCIES' ENFORCEMENT AUTHORITIES APPLY TO AUTOMATED SYSTEMS

Existing legal authorities apply to the use of automated systems and innovative new technologies just as they apply to other practices. The Consumer Financial

Protection Bureau, the Department of Justice's Civil Rights Division, the Equal Employment Opportunity Commission, and the Federal Trade Commission are among the federal agencies responsible for enforcing civil rights, non-discrimination, fair competition, consumer protection, and other vitally important legal protections. We take seriously our responsibility to ensure that these rapidly evolving automated systems are developed and used in a manner consistent with federal laws, and each of our agencies has previously expressed concern about potentially harmful uses of automated systems. For example:

- The **Consumer Financial Protection Bureau** (CFPB) supervises, sets rules for, and enforces numerous federal consumer financial laws and guards consumers in the financial marketplace from unfair, deceptive, or abusive acts or practices and from discrimination. The CFPB published a circular confirming that federal consumer financial laws and adverse action requirements apply regardless of the technology being used. The circular also made clear that the fact that the technology used to make a credit decision is too complex, opaque, or new is not a defense for violating these laws.
- The **Department of Justice's Civil Rights Division** (Division) enforces constitutional provisions and federal statutes prohibiting discrimination across many facets of life, including in education, the criminal justice system, employment, housing, lending, and voting. Among the Division's other work on issues related to AI and automated systems, the Division recently filed a statement of interest in federal court explaining that the Fair Housing Act applies to algorithm-based tenant screening services.
- The **Equal Employment Opportunity Commission** (EEOC) enforces federal laws that make it illegal for an employer, union, or employment agency to discriminate against an applicant or employee due to a person's race, color, religion, sex (including pregnancy, gender identity, and sexual orientation), national origin, age (40 or older), disability, or genetic information (including family medical history). In addition to the EEOC's enforcement activities on discrimination related to AI and automated systems, the EEOC issued a technical assistance document explaining how the Americans with Disabilities Act applies to the use of software, algorithms, and AI to make employment-related decisions about job applicants and employees.
- The **Federal Trade Commission** (FTC) protects consumers from deceptive or unfair business practices and unfair methods of competition across most sectors of the U.S. economy by enforcing the FTC Act and numerous other laws and regulations. The FTC issued a report evaluating the use and impact of AI in combatting online harms identified by Congress. The report outlines significant

concerns that AI tools can be inaccurate, biased, and discriminatory by design and incentivize relying on increasingly invasive forms of commercial surveillance. The FTC has also warned market participants that it may violate the FTC Act to use automated tools that have discriminatory impacts, to make claims about AI that are not substantiated, or to deploy AI before taking steps to assess and mitigate risks. Finally, the FTC has required firms to destroy algorithms or other work product that were trained on data that should not have been collected.

AUTOMATED SYSTEMS MAY CONTRIBUTE TO UNLAWFUL DISCRIMINATION AND OTHERWISE VIOLATE FEDERAL LAW

Many automated systems rely on vast amounts of data to find patterns or correlations, and then apply those patterns to new data to perform tasks or make recommendations and predictions. While these tools can be useful, they also have the potential to produce outcomes that result in unlawful discrimination. Potential discrimination in automated systems may come from different sources, including problems with:

- **Data and Datasets:** Automated system outcomes can be skewed by unrepresentative or imbalanced datasets, datasets that incorporate historical bias, or datasets that contain other types of errors. Automated systems also can correlate data with protected classes, which can lead to discriminatory outcomes.
- **Model Opacity and Access:** Many automated systems are "black boxes" whose internal workings are not clear to most people and, in some cases, even the developer of the tool. This lack of transparency often makes it all the more difficult for developers, businesses, and individuals to know whether an automated system is fair.
- **Design and Use:** Developers do not always understand or account for the contexts in which private or public entities will use their automated systems. Developers may design a system on the basis of flawed assumptions about its users, relevant context, or the underlying practices or procedures it may replace.

Today, our agencies reiterate our resolve to monitor the development and use of automated systems and promote responsible innovation. We also pledge to vigorously use our collective authorities to protect individuals' rights regardless of whether legal violations occur through traditional means or advanced technologies.[37]

37. *Joint Statement*, *supra* note 35 ("Note: This document is for informational purposes only and does not provide technical assistance about how to comply with federal law. It does not constitute final agency action and does not have an immediate and direct legal effect. It does not create any new rights or obligations and it is not enforceable.")

2. *AI and Federal Procurement and Contract Compliance Policy as Case Studies*

Prior to revocation in January 2025, the following examples showed different approaches to regulating AI through procurement and contract compliance regulations.

a. White House Office of Management and Budget (OMB) Memorandum: Advancing Governance, Innovation, and Risk Management in Federal Agencies' Use of Artificial Intelligence (Rescinded)

On March 28, 2024, approximately five months after the White House publication of Executive Order 14110 on *Safe, Secure, and Trustworthy Development and Use of AI*, the White House Office of Management and Budget (OMB) released a memorandum for all leaders of departments and federal agencies within the U.S. Federal Executive branch on AI guidance for AI innovation and risk management: *Advancing Governance, Innovation, and Risk Management in Federal Agencies' Use of Artificial Intelligence.*

The *Executive Order on Removing Barriers to American Leadership in Artificial Intelligence*, released January 23, 2025, stated that the OMB Director and the Assistant to the President for Science and Technology "shall revise OMB Memoranda M-24-10 [*Advancing Governance, Innovation, and Risk Management for Agency Use of Artificial Intelligence* (March 2024)] and M-24-18 [*Advancing the Responsible Acquisition of Artificial Intelligence in Government* (September 2024)] as necessary[.]"[38] The excerpt below, although rescinded, is included for historical reference.

Advancing Governance, Innovation, and Risk Management for Agency Use of Artificial Intelligence (Rescinded)

White House Office of Management and Budget (OMB)
M-24-10 Memorandum for the Heads of Executive Departments and Agencies
March 28, 2024

Managing Risks from the Use of AI. While agencies will realize significant benefits from AI, they must also manage a range of risks from the use of AI. Agencies are subject to existing risk management requirements relevant to AI, and this memorandum does not replace or supersede these requirements. Instead, it establishes new requirements and recommendations that, both independently and collectively, address the specific risks from relying on AI to inform or carry out agency decisions and actions,

38. Exec. Order No. 14179, 90 Fed. Reg. 8741, *Removing Barriers to American Leadership in Artificial Intelligence* (Jan. 31, 2025).

particularly when such reliance impacts the rights and safety of the public. To address these risks, this memorandum requires agencies to follow minimum practices when using safety-impacting AI and rights-impacting AI, and enumerates specific categories of AI that are presumed to impact rights and safety. Finally, this memorandum also establishes a series of recommendations for managing AI risks in the context of Federal procurement . . .

4. ADVANCING RESPONSIBLE ARTIFICIAL INTELLIGENCE INNOVATION

If implemented responsibly, AI can improve operations and deliver efficiencies across the Federal Government. Agencies must improve their ability to use AI in ways that benefit the public and increase mission effectiveness, while recognizing the limitations and risks of AI and when it is not suited for a given task. In particular, agencies are encouraged to prioritize AI development and adoption for the public good and where the technology can be helpful in understanding and tackling large societal challenges, such as using AI to improve the accessibility of government services, reduce food insecurity, address the climate crisis, improve public health, advance equitable outcomes, protect democracy and human rights, and grow economic competitiveness in a way that benefits people across the United States.

To achieve this, agencies should build upon existing internal enterprise capacity to support responsible AI innovation, take actions to strengthen their AI and AI-enabling talent,[39] and improve their ability to develop and procure AI. Agencies should both explore joint efforts to scale these opportunities as well as take steps to responsibly share their AI resources across the Federal Government and with the public.

a. AI Strategies

viii. the agency's plan to encourage diverse perspectives throughout the AI development or **procurement** lifecycle, including how to determine whether a particular use of AI is meeting the agency's equity goals and civil rights commitments; [emphasis added] . . .

e. Harmonization of Artificial Intelligence Requirements

ii. sharing best practices and lessons learned, including for achieving meaningful participation from affected communities and the public in AI development and **procurement**, updating organizational processes to better accommodate AI, removing barriers to responsible AI innovation, responding to AI incidents that may

---

39. [Fn. 18 in original] Agencies should also ensure that they consider and satisfy applicable collective bargaining obligations regarding their implementation of AI.

have resulted in harm to an individual, and building a diverse AI workforce to meet the agency's needs; [emphasis added] . . .

5. MANAGING RISKS FROM THE USE OF ARTIFICIAL INTELLIGENCE

c. Minimum Practices for Safety-Impacting and Rights-Impacting Artificial Intelligence

v. Additional Minimum Practices for Rights-Impacting AI

A. **Identify and assess AI's impact on equity and fairness, and mitigate algorithmic discrimination when it is present**. Agencies must:
   1. Identify and document in their AI impact assessment when using data that contains information about a class protected by Federal nondiscrimination laws (e.g., race, age, etc.). Given the risks arising when AI may correlate demographic information with other types of information, agencies should also assess and document whether the AI model could foreseeably use other attributes as proxies for a protected characteristic and whether such use would significantly influence model performance;
   2. Assess the AI in a real-world context to determine whether the AI model results in significant disparities in the model's performance (e.g., accuracy, precision, reliability in predicting outcomes) across demographic groups;
   3. Mitigate disparities that lead to, or perpetuate, unlawful discrimination or harmful bias, or that decrease equity as a result of the government's use of the AI; and
   4. Consistent with applicable law, cease use of the AI for agency decision making if the agency is unable to adequately mitigate any associated risk of unlawful discrimination against protected classes. Agencies should maintain appropriate documentation to accompany this decision-making, and should disclose it publicly to the extent consistent with applicable law and governmentwide policy.

B. **Consult and incorporate feedback from affected communities and the public**. Consistent with applicable law and governmentwide guidance, agencies must consult affected communities, including underserved communities, and they must solicit public feedback, where appropriate, in the design, development, and use of the AI and use such feedback to inform agency decision-making regarding the AI. The consultation and feedback process must include seeking input on the agency's approach to implementing the minimum risk management practices established in Section 5(c) of this memorandum, such as applicable opt-out procedures. Agencies should consider and manage the risks of public consultation in contexts like fraud prevention and law enforcement investigations, where consulting with the targeted individual is impractical but consulting with a representative group may be appropriate.[40]

Agencies are strongly encouraged to solicit feedback on an ongoing basis from affected communities in particular as well as from the public broadly, especially after significant modifications to the AI or the conditions or context in which it is used.[41] In the course of assessing such feedback, if an agency determines that the use of AI in a given context would cause more harm than good, the agency should not use the AI.

To carry out such consultations and feedback processes, agencies must take appropriate steps to solicit input from the communities and individuals affected by the AI, which could include:[42]

1. direct usability testing, such as observing users interacting with the system;
2. general solicitations of comments from the public, such as a request for information in the Federal Register or a "Tell Us About Your Experience" sheet with an open-ended space for responses;
3. post-transaction customer feedback collections;[43]
4. public hearings or meetings, such as a listening session;
5. outreach to relevant Federal employee groups and Federal labor organizations, including on the appropriate fulfillment of collective bargaining obligations, where applicable; or
6. any other transparent process that seeks public input, comments, or feedback from the affected groups in a meaningful, equitable, accessible, and effective manner. . . .

C. **Conduct ongoing monitoring and mitigation for AI-enabled discrimination**. As part of the ongoing monitoring requirement established in Section 5(c)(iv)(D), agencies must also monitor rights-impacting AI to specifically assess and mitigate AI-enabled

40. [Fn. 45 in original] For example, an agency using an AI tool to detect Federal benefits fraud is not required to consult with the target of their investigation. However, an agency should discern when it is appropriate to consult with civil society groups, academia, or other experts in the field to understand the technology's impact.

41. [Fn. 46 in original] The affected communities will vary depending on an agency's deployment context, but may include customers (for example, individuals, businesses, or organizations that interact with an agency) or Federal employee groups and employees' union representatives, when applicable.

42. [Fn. 47 in original] Agencies are encouraged to engage with OMB on whether they are required to submit information collection requests for OMB clearance under the Paperwork Reduction Act (44 U.S.C. § 3507) for the purposes of these consultations and feedback processes.

43. [Fn. 48 in original] Information on post-transaction customer feedback surveys can be found in OMB Circular A-11, Section 280 – Managing Customer Experience and Improving Service Delivery.

discrimination against protected classes, including discrimination that might arise from unforeseen circumstances, changes to the system after deployment, or changes to the context of use or associated data. Where sufficient mitigation is not possible, agencies must safely discontinue use of the AI functionality.

D. **Notify negatively affected individuals**. Consistent with applicable law and governmentwide guidance, agencies must notify individuals when use of the AI results in an adverse decision or action that specifically concerns them, such as the denial of benefits or deeming a transaction fraudulent.[44] Agencies should consider the timing of their notice and when it is appropriate to provide notice in multiple languages and through alternative formats and channels, depending on the context of the AI's use. The notice must also include a clear and accessible means of contacting the agency and, where applicable, provide information to the individual on their right to appeal. Agencies must also abide by any existing obligations to provide explanations for such decisions and actions.[45]. . .

d. Managing Risks in Federal Procurement of Artificial Intelligence

This section provides agencies with recommendations for responsible procurement of AI, supplementing an agency's required risk management practices above for rights-impacting AI and safety-impacting AI. In addition to these recommendations and consistent with section 7224(d) of the Advancing American AI Act and Section 10.1(d)(ii) of Executive Order 14110, OMB will also develop an initial means to ensure that Federal contracts for the acquisition of an AI system or service align with the guidance in this memorandum.

i. **Aligning with the Law**. Agencies should ensure that procured AI is consistent with the Constitution and complies with all other applicable laws, regulations, and policies, including those addressing privacy, confidentiality, intellectual property, cybersecurity, human and civil rights, and civil liberties.

---

44. [Fn. 49 in original] In some instances, such as an active law enforcement investigation, providing immediate notice may be inappropriate or impractical, or disclosure may be more appropriate at a later stage (for example, prior to a defendant's trial).

45. [Fn. 50 in original] Explanations might include, for example, how and why the AI-driven decision or action was taken. This does not mean that agencies must provide a perfect breakdown of how a machine learning system came to a conclusion, as exact explanations of AI decisions may not be technically feasible. However, agencies should still characterize the general nature of such AI decisions through context such as the data that the decision relied upon, the design of the AI, and the broader decision-making context in which the system operates. Such explanations should be technologically valid, meaningful, useful, and as simply stated as possible, and higher-risk decisions should be accompanied by more comprehensive explanations.

ii. **Transparency and Performance Improvement**. Agencies should take steps to ensure transparency and adequate performance for their procured AI, including by: A. obtaining adequate documentation to assess the AI's capabilities, such as through the use of model, data, and system cards; . . .

vi. **Responsible Procurement of AI for Biometric Identification**. When procuring systems that use AI to identify individuals using biometric identifiers—e.g., faces, irises, fingerprints, or gait—agencies are encouraged to:

A. Assess and address the risks that the data used to train or operate the AI may not be lawfully collected or used, or else may not be sufficiently accurate to support reliable biometric identification. This includes the risks that the biometric information was collected without appropriate consent, was originally collected for another purpose, embeds unwanted bias, or was collected without validation of the included identities; and

B. Request supporting documentation or test results to validate the accuracy, reliability, and validity of the AI's ability to match identities.

vii. **Responsibly Procuring Generative AI**. Agencies are encouraged to include risk management requirements in contracts for generative AI, and particularly for dual-use foundation models, including:

A. requiring adequate testing and safeguards,

B. requiring results of internal or external testing and evaluation, to include AI red teaming against risks from generative AI, such as discriminatory, misleading, inflammatory, unsafe, or deceptive outputs;

C. requiring that generative AI models have capabilities, as appropriate and technologically feasible, to reliably label or establish provenance for their content as generated or modified by AI; and

D. incorporating relevant NIST standards, defined pursuant to Sections 4.1(a) and 10.1(d) of Executive Order 14110, as appropriate. . . .

b. U.S. Department of Labor, Office of Federal Contract Compliance Programs: AI Guidance for Federal Contractors (Guidance Removed)

For the past few decades, government procurement protocols have been used to serve antidiscrimination goals. The Office of Federal Contract Compliance Programs (OFCCP) within the U.S. Department of Labor has shaped civil rights policies through federal procurement and contracting protocols. It enforces both soft and hard law to execute civil rights goals through procurement. OFCCP enforces several authorities to ensure equal employment opportunities, a cornerstone of the *Civil Rights Act of 1964*. OFCCP's enforcement jurisdiction includes Executive Order 11246; the *Rehabilitation Act of 1973*, Section 503; and the *Vietnam Era Veterans' Readjustment Assistance Act of 1974*.

The agency offers procurement guidance to mitigate discriminatory risks associated with AI and automated systems in employment contexts. OFCCP issued the following policy guidance in accordance with the October 2023 E.O. 14110, *Executive Order on the Safe, Secure, and Trustworthy Development and Use of Artificial Intelligence*, and the March 2024 OMB Memorandum, *OMB Policy to Advance Governance, Innovation, and Risk Management in Federal Agencies' Use of Artificial Intelligence*, discussed previously. The October 2023 E.O. 14110 and the March 2024 OMB Memorandum were rescinded,[46] and policies are subject to revision in the transition between administrations.

Artificial Intelligence and Equal Employment Opportunity for Federal Contractors (Guidance Removed)

U.S. Department of Labor, Office of Federal Contract Compliance Programs (OFCCP)
April 29, 2024

INTRODUCTION

On October 30, 2023, President Joseph R. Biden, Jr. issued Executive Order 14110 ("Executive Order on the Safe, Secure, and Trustworthy Development and Use of Artificial Intelligence"), calling for a coordinated U.S. government approach to ensuring the responsible and safe development and use of Artificial Intelligence (AI). The Executive Order requires that "Within 365 days of the date of this order, to prevent unlawful discrimination from AI used for hiring, the Secretary of Labor shall publish guidance for Federal contractors regarding nondiscrimination in hiring involving AI and other technology-based hiring systems." In keeping with Executive Order 14110, the Office of Federal Contract Compliance Programs (OFCCP) developed this guide addressing AI in the Equal Employment Opportunity (EEO) context. The guide addresses obligations enforced by OFCCP and applies to both federal contractors and subcontractors, collectively referred to as federal contractors.

While some federal contractors may use AI systems to increase productivity and efficiency in their employment decision-making, the use of AI systems also has the potential to perpetuate unlawful bias and automate unlawful discrimination, among other harmful outcomes. OFCCP answers

---

46. Exec. Order No. 14148, 90 Fed. Reg. 8237, *Initial Rescissions of Harmful Executive Orders and Actions* (Jan. 28, 2025); OMB Memorandum M-25-21, *Accelerating Federal Use of AI through Innovation, Governance, and Public Trust* (Apr. 3, 2025); OMB Memorandum M-25-22, *Driving Efficient Acquisition of Artificial Intelligence in Government* (Apr. 3, 2025).

questions and shares promising practices . . . to clarify federal contractors' legal obligations, promote EEO, and mitigate the potentially harmful impacts of AI in employment decisions. . . .

4. What Are Some Examples of Federal Contractors' EEO Compliance Obligations Related to the Use of AI in Employment Decisions?

Covered federal contractors are obligated by law to ensure that they do not discriminate in employment and that they take affirmative action to ensure employees and applicants are treated without regard to their race, color, religion, sex, sexual orientation, gender identity, national origin, disability, or status as a protected veteran. These EEO obligations extend to the federal contractor's use of automated systems, including AI, when making employment decisions. . . .

c. Advancing American AI Act

The *Advancing American AI Act* was proposed to achieve multiple objectives. The law, for example, proposes privacy, civil rights and civil liberties, and other protections in the government procurement of AI systems. Federal agencies are required to satisfy minimum transparency requirements and publish inventories of the AI systems that are currently used and deployed.

Advancing American AI Act

P.L. 117-263—James M. Inhofe National Defense Authorization Act for Fiscal Year 2023
Title LXXII—Government Affairs, Subtitle B—Advancing American AI Act

Sec. 7224. Principles and policies for use of artificial intelligence in government.

(b) Department policies and processes for procurement and use of artificial intelligence-enabled systems. . . .

(1) the Secretary of Homeland Security, with the participation of the Chief Procurement Officer, the Chief Information Officer, the Chief Privacy Officer, and the Officer for Civil Rights and Civil Liberties of the Department and any other person determined to be relevant by the Secretary of Homeland Security, shall issue policies and procedures for the Department related to—

(A) the acquisition and use of artificial intelligence; and

(B) considerations for the risks and impacts related to artificial intelligence-enabled systems, including associated data of machine learning systems, to ensure that full consideration is given to—

(i) the privacy, civil rights, and civil liberties impacts of artificial intelligence-enabled systems; and

(ii) security against misuse, degradation, or rending inoperable of artificial intelligence-enabled systems; and

(2) the Chief Privacy Officer and the Officer for Civil Rights and Civil Liberties of the Department shall report to Congress on any additional staffing or funding resources that may be required to carry out the requirements of this subsection. . . .

The *GDPR* and the *EU AI Act* include provisions that address algorithmic discrimination. Similarly, in the U.S., civil rights and consumer protection laws are currently relied upon by the federal government to address algorithmic discrimination. The antidiscrimination provisions of the *Civil Rights Act of 1964* are enforced by the U.S. Civil Rights Division of the U.S. Department of Justice and the Equal Employment Opportunity Commission. The Federal Trade Commission enforces Section 5 of the *Federal Trade Commission Act*, which prohibits unfair and deceptive trade practices. The Consumer Financial Protection Bureau also enforces federal statutes against algorithmic discrimination, including the *Consumer Financial Protection Act* and Title X of the *Dodd-Frank Reform and Consumer Protection Act.*

Additionally, as discussed above, the *Colorado AI Consumer Protection Act* and other state and local laws explicitly address algorithmic discrimination harms. For instance, the *Colorado AI Consumer Protection Act* requires public statements summarizing the types of high-risk systems created by the developer, or intentionally and substantially modified, and how the developer manages any known risks of algorithmic discrimination that may arise from the development or intentional modification of the high-risk systems. The law requires developers of high-risk systems to disclose to the Colorado Attorney General any known or reasonably foreseeable risks of algorithmic discrimination. The act also requires implementing a risk management policy and program for the high-risk system, along with an impact assessment. Annual review of the deployment of each system is required to ensure that there is no algorithmic discrimination. It also provides a consumer with opportunities to correct any incorrect personal data that a high-risk system processed in making a consequential decision.

In future chapters, related topics will be addressed in the context of constitutional law and public law. Those chapters will focus on AI and automated systems and their intersection with due process and equal protection, criminal procedure, antidiscrimination law, and consumer and financial protections.

CHAPTER 5

TRANSPARENCY AND EXPLANATION

Although AI technologies bring unprecedented capacity to automate complicated tasks, the complex nature of these systems makes it difficult to provide the same level of transparency and explainability of how these systems operate compared to classical algorithm-based systems. As AI plays an increasingly direct role in shaping people's ideas and behaviors, transparency and explainability of these systems' operations are paramount in determining how much of a consequential role they may have in influencing individuals' and communities' thoughts and actions. The increasing embedding of AI systems in everyday uses introduces a multitude of risks. Chapter 5 explores how transparency and explainability play a crucial role in mitigating such AI harms in AI law and policy developments.

A. *TRANSPARENCY, EXPLANATION, AND NOTICE AND DISCLOSURE*

Two principles are frequently used in discussing AI governance and regulation: transparency and explanation. These two principles cover the understanding of how AI is developed, deployed, and used and how it produces the output that people rely on.

1. *Case Studies of Transparency Requirements*

A core part of the *EU AI Act* focuses on requirements of transparency, explainability, and human oversight. Consider how the following articles encourage better transparency and explainability in AI and algorithm design.

a. EU AI Act, Articles 13 and 50 [Principle of Transparency]

The following provides the legal duty of transparency for both the deployers and users of AI systems.

EU AI Act

Article 13. Transparency and Provision of Information to Deployers

1. High-risk AI systems shall be designed and developed in such a way as to ensure that their operation is sufficiently transparent to enable deployers to interpret a system's output and use it appropriately. An appropriate type and degree of transparency shall be ensured with a view to achieving compliance with the relevant obligations of the provider and deployer set out in Section 3.

2. High-risk AI systems shall be accompanied by instructions for use in an appropriate digital format or otherwise that include concise, complete, correct and clear information that is relevant, accessible and comprehensible to deployers.

3. The instructions for use shall contain at least the following information:

(a) the identity and the contact details of the provider and, where applicable, of its authorised representative;

(b) the characteristics, capabilities and limitations of performance of the high-risk AI system, including:

(i) its intended purpose;

(ii) the level of accuracy, including its metrics, robustness and cybersecurity referred to in Article 15 against which the high-risk AI system has been tested and validated and which can be expected, and any known and foreseeable circumstances that may have an impact on that expected level of accuracy, robustness and cybersecurity;

(iii) any known or foreseeable circumstance, related to the use of the high-risk AI system in accordance with its intended purpose or under conditions of reasonably foreseeable misuse, which may lead to risks to the health and safety or fundamental rights referred to in Article 9(2);

(iv) where applicable, the technical capabilities and characteristics of the high-risk AI system to provide information that is relevant to explain its output;

(v) when appropriate, its performance regarding specific persons or groups of persons on which the system is intended to be used;

(vi) when appropriate, specifications for the input data, or any other relevant information in terms of the training, validation and testing data sets used, taking into account the intended purpose of the high-risk AI system;

(vii) where applicable, information to enable deployers to interpret the output of the high-risk AI system and use it appropriately;

(c) the changes to the high-risk AI system and its performance which have been pre-determined by the provider at the moment of the initial conformity assessment, if any;

(d) the human oversight measures referred to in Article 14, including the technical measures put in place to facilitate the interpretation of the outputs of the high-risk AI systems by the deployers;

(e) the computational and hardware resources needed, the expected lifetime of the high-risk AI system and any necessary maintenance and care measures, including their frequency, to ensure the proper functioning of that AI system, including as regards software updates;

(f) where relevant, a description of the mechanisms included within the high-risk AI system that allows deployers to properly collect, store and interpret the logs in accordance with Article 12.

EU AI Act

Article 50. Transparency Obligations for Providers and Deployers of Certain AI Systems

1. Providers shall ensure that AI systems intended to interact directly with natural persons are designed and developed in such a way that the natural persons concerned are informed that they are interacting with an AI system, unless this is obvious from the point of view of a natural person who is reasonably well-informed, observant and circumspect, taking into account the circumstances and the context of use. This obligation shall not apply to AI systems authorised by law to detect, prevent, investigate or prosecute criminal offences, subject to appropriate safeguards for the rights and freedoms of third parties, unless those systems are available for the public to report a criminal offence.

2. Providers of AI systems, including general-purpose AI systems, generating synthetic audio, image, video or text content, shall ensure that the outputs of the AI system are marked in a machine-readable format and detectable as artificially generated or manipulated. Providers shall ensure their technical solutions are effective, interoperable, robust and reliable as far as this is technically feasible, taking into account the specificities and limitations of various types of content, the costs of implementation and the generally acknowledged state-of-the-art, as may be reflected in relevant technical standards. This obligation shall not apply to the extent the AI systems perform an assistive function for standard editing or do not substantially alter the input data provided by the deployer or the semantics thereof, or where authorised by law to detect, prevent, investigate or prosecute criminal offences.

3. Deployers of an emotion recognition system or a biometric categorisation system shall inform the natural persons exposed thereto of the operation of the system, and shall process the personal data in accordance with Regulations (EU) 2016/679 and (EU) 2018/1725 and Directive (EU) 2016/680, as applicable. This obligation shall not apply to AI systems used for biometric categorisation and emotion recognition, which are permitted by law to detect, prevent or investigate criminal offences, subject to appropriate safeguards for the rights and freedoms of third parties, and in compliance with Union law.

4. Deployers of an AI system that generates or manipulates image, audio or video content constituting a deep fake, shall disclose that the content has been artificially generated or manipulated. This obligation shall not apply where the use is authorised by law to detect, prevent, investigate or prosecute criminal offence. Where the content forms part of an evidently artistic, creative, satirical, fictional analogous work or programme, the transparency obligations set out in this paragraph are limited to disclosure of the existence of

such generated or manipulated content in an appropriate manner that does not hamper the display or enjoyment of the work.

Deployers of an AI system that generates or manipulates text which is published with the purpose of informing the public on matters of public interest shall disclose that the text has been artificially generated or manipulated. This obligation shall not apply where the use is authorised by law to detect, prevent, investigate or prosecute criminal offences or where the AI-generated content has undergone a process of human review or editorial control and where a natural or legal person holds editorial responsibility for the publication of the content. . . .

b. GDPR, Articles 12 and 15 [Principle of Transparency]

As the following section notes, transparency in AI systems entails record keeping and accuracy during the system's lifecycle.

GDPR

Article 12. Transparent Information, Communication and Modalities for the Exercise of the Rights of the Data Subject

1. The controller shall take appropriate measures to provide any information referred to in Articles 13 and 14 and any communication under Articles 15 to 22 and 34 relating to processing to the data subject in a concise, transparent, intelligible and easily accessible form, using clear and plain language, in particular for any information addressed specifically to a child. The information shall be provided in writing, or by other means, including, where appropriate, by electronic means. When requested by the data subject, the information may be provided orally, provided that the identity of the data subject is proven by other means.

2. The controller shall facilitate the exercise of data subject rights under Articles 15 to 22. In the cases referred to in Article 11(2), the controller shall not refuse to act on the request of the data subject for exercising his or her rights under Articles 15 to 22, unless the controller demonstrates that it is not in a position to identify the data subject.

3. The controller shall provide information on action taken on a request under Articles 15 to 22 to the data subject without undue delay and in any event within one month of receipt of the request. That period may be extended by two further months where necessary, taking into account the complexity and number of the requests. The controller shall inform the data subject of any such extension within one month of receipt of the request, together with the reasons for the delay. Where the data subject makes the request by electronic form means, the information shall be provided by electronic means where possible, unless otherwise requested by the data subject.

4. If the controller does not take action on the request of the data subject, the controller shall inform the data subject without delay and at the latest within one month of receipt of the request of the reasons for not taking action and on the possibility of lodging a complaint with a supervisory authority and seeking a judicial remedy.

5. Information provided under Articles 13 and 14 and any communication and any actions taken under Articles 15 to 22 and 34 shall be provided free of charge. Where requests from a data subject are manifestly unfounded or excessive, in particular because of their repetitive character, the controller may either:

(**a**) charge a reasonable fee taking into account the administrative costs of providing the information or communication or taking the action requested; or

(**b**) refuse to act on the request.

The controller shall bear the burden of demonstrating the manifestly unfounded or excessive character of the request.

6. Without prejudice to Article 11, where the controller has reasonable doubts concerning the identity of the natural person making the request referred to in Articles 15 to 21, the controller may request the provision of additional information necessary to confirm the identity of the data subject.

7. The information to be provided to data subjects pursuant to Articles 13 and 14 may be provided in combination with standardised icons in order to give in an easily visible, intelligible and clearly legible manner a meaningful overview of the intended processing. Where the icons are presented electronically they shall be machine-readable.

8. The Commission shall be empowered to adopt delegated acts in accordance with Article 92 for the purpose of determining the information to be presented by the icons and the procedures for providing standardised icons.

GDPR

Article 15. Right of Access by the Data Subject

1. The data subject shall have the right to obtain from the controller confirmation as to whether or not personal data concerning him or her are being processed, and, where that is the case, access to the personal data and the following information:

(**a**) the purposes of the processing;

(**b**) the categories of personal data concerned;

(**c**) the recipients or categories of recipient to whom the personal data have been or will be disclosed, in particular recipients in third countries or international organisations;

(**d**) where possible, the envisaged period for which the personal data will be stored, or, if not possible, the criteria used to determine that period;

(**e**) the existence of the right to request from the controller rectification or erasure of personal data or restriction of processing of personal data concerning the data subject or to object to such processing;

(**f**) the right to lodge a complaint with a supervisory authority;

(**g**) where the personal data are not collected from the data subject, any available information as to their source;

(**h**) the existence of automated decision-making, including profiling, referred to in Article 22(1) and (4) and, at least in those cases, meaningful information about the logic involved, as well as the significance and the envisaged consequences of such processing for the data subject.

2. Where personal data are transferred to a third country or to an international organisation, the data subject shall have the right to be informed of the appropriate safeguards pursuant to Article 46 relating to the transfer.

3. The controller shall provide a copy of the personal data undergoing processing. For any further copies requested by the data subject, the controller may charge a reasonable fee based on administrative costs. Where the data subject makes the request by electronic means, and unless otherwise requested by the data subject, the information shall be provided in a commonly used electronic form.

4. The right to obtain a copy referred to in paragraph 3 shall not adversely affect the rights and freedoms of others.

2. *Case Studies of Explanation and Interpretability*

Although an AI system's complexity makes it far more difficult to explain that system's behavior, the *EU AI Act* nevertheless places key emphasis on the right by European subjects to a clear, meaningful explanation of the role of AI systems whenever a decisionmaking procedure negatively impacts them.

a. EU AI Act, Article 86 [Principle of Right to Explanation]

EU AI Act

Article 86. Right to Explanation of Individual Decision-Making

1. Any affected person subject to a decision which is taken by the deployer on the basis of the output from a high-risk AI system listed in Annex III, with the exception of systems listed under point 2 thereof, and which produces legal effects or similarly significantly affects that person in a way that they consider to have an adverse impact on their health, safety or fundamental rights shall have the right to obtain from the deployer clear and meaningful explanations of the role of the AI system in the decision-making procedure and the main elements of the decision taken.

2. Paragraph 1 shall not apply to the use of AI systems for which exceptions from, or restrictions to, the obligation under paragraph 1 follow from Union or national law in compliance with Union law.

3. This Article shall apply only to the extent that the right referred to in paragraph 1 is not otherwise provided for under Union law.

b. EU AI Act, Article 14(4) [Principle of Human Oversight]

This next section provides details of the human oversight role for AI systems.

EU AI Act

Article 14(4). Human Oversight

4. For the purpose of implementing paragraphs 1, 2 and 3, the high-risk AI system shall be provided to the user in such a way that natural persons to whom human oversight is assigned are enabled, as appropriate and proportionate to the following circumstances:

(a) to properly understand the relevant capacities and limitations of the high-risk AI system and be able to duly monitor its operation, including in view of detecting and addressing anomalies, dysfunctions and unexpected performance;

(b) to remain aware of the possible tendency of automatically relying or over-relying on the output produced by a high-risk AI system (automation bias), in particular for high-risk AI systems used to provide information or recommendations for decisions to be taken by natural persons;

(c) to correctly interpret the high-risk AI system's output, taking into account, for example, the interpretation tools and methods available;

(d) to decide, in any particular situation, not to use the high-risk AI system or to otherwise disregard, override or reverse the output of the high-risk AI system;

(e) to intervene in the operation of the high-risk AI system or interrupt the system through a 'stop' button or a similar procedure that allows the system to come to a halt in a safe state.

3. Case Studies of Notice and Disclosure

a. GDPR, Articles 13 and 14 [Right to Notice and to be Informed]

Within the European privacy regulatory space, European subjects have the *right* to be informed about the collection and use of their personal data by third parties.

GDPR

Article 13. Information to be Provided Where Personal Data are Collected from the Data Subject

1. Where personal data relating to a data subject are collected from the data subject, the controller shall, at the time when personal data are obtained, provide the data subject with all of the following information:

(a) the identity and the contact details of the controller and, where applicable, of the controller's representative;

(b) the contact details of the data protection officer, where applicable;

(c) the purposes of the processing for which the personal data are intended as well as the legal basis for the processing;

(d) where the processing is based on point (f) of Article 6(1), the legitimate interests pursued by the controller or by a third party;

(e) the recipients or categories of recipients of the personal data, if any;

(f) where applicable, the fact that the controller intends to transfer personal data to a third country or international organisation and the existence or absence of an adequacy decision by the Commission, or in the case of transfers referred to in Article 46 or 47, or the second subparagraph of Article 49(1), reference to the appropriate or suitable safeguards and the means by which to obtain a copy of them or where they have been made available.

2. In addition to the information referred to in paragraph 1, the controller shall, at the time when personal data are obtained, provide the data subject with the following further information necessary to ensure fair and transparent processing:

(a) the period for which the personal data will be stored, or if that is not possible, the criteria used to determine that period;

(b) the existence of the right to request from the controller access to and rectification or erasure of personal data or restriction of processing concerning the data subject or to object to processing as well as the right to data portability;

(c) where the processing is based on point (a) of Article 6(1) or point (a) of Article 9(2), the existence of the right to withdraw consent at any time, without affecting the lawfulness of processing based on consent before its withdrawal;

(d) the right to lodge a complaint with a supervisory authority;

(e) whether the provision of personal data is a statutory or contractual requirement, or a requirement necessary to enter into a contract, as well as whether the data subject is obliged to provide the personal data and of the possible consequences of failure to provide such data;

(f) the existence of automated decision-making, including profiling, referred to in Article 22(1) and (4) and, at least in those cases, meaningful information about the logic involved, as well as the significance and the envisaged consequences of such processing for the data subject.

3. Where the controller intends to further process the personal data for a purpose other than that for which the personal data were collected, the controller shall provide the data subject prior to that further processing with information on that other purpose and with any relevant further information as referred to in paragraph 2.

4. Paragraphs 1, 2 and 3 shall not apply where and insofar as the data subject already has the information.

GDPR

Article 14. Information to be Provided Where Personal Data Have Not Been Obtained from the Data Subject

1. Where personal data have not been obtained from the data subject, the controller shall provide the data subject with the following information:

(a) the identity and the contact details of the controller and, where applicable, of the controller's representative;

(b) the contact details of the data protection officer, where applicable;

(c) the purposes of the processing for which the personal data are intended as well as the legal basis for the processing;

(d) the categories of personal data concerned;

(e) the recipients or categories of recipients of the personal data, if any;

(f) where applicable, that the controller intends to transfer personal data to a recipient in a third country or international organisation and the existence or absence of an adequacy decision by the Commission, or in the case of transfers referred to in Article 46 or 47, or the second subparagraph of Article 49(1), reference to the appropriate or suitable safeguards and the means to obtain a copy of them or where they have been made available.

2. In addition to the information referred to in paragraph 1, the controller shall provide the data subject with the following information necessary to ensure fair and transparent processing in respect of the data subject:

(a) the period for which the personal data will be stored, or if that is not possible, the criteria used to determine that period;

(b) where the processing is based on point (f) of Article 6(1), the legitimate interests pursued by the controller or by a third party;

(c) the existence of the right to request from the controller access to and rectification or erasure of personal data or restriction of processing concerning the data subject and to object to processing as well as the right to data portability;

(d) where processing is based on point (a) of Article 6(1) or point (a) of Article 9(2), the existence of the right to withdraw consent at any time, without affecting the lawfulness of processing based on consent before its withdrawal;

(e) the right to lodge a complaint with a supervisory authority;

(f) from which source the personal data originate, and if applicable, whether it came from publicly accessible sources;

(g) the existence of automated decision-making, including profiling, referred to in Article 22(1) and (4) and, at least in those cases, meaningful information about the logic involved, as well as the significance and the envisaged consequences of such processing for the data subject.

3. The controller shall provide the information referred to in paragraphs 1 and 2:

(a) within a reasonable period after obtaining the personal data, but at the latest within one month, having regard to the specific circumstances in which the personal data are processed;

(b) if the personal data are to be used for communication with the data subject, at the latest at the time of the first communication to that data subject; or

(c) if a disclosure to another recipient is envisaged, at the latest when the personal data are first disclosed.

4. Where the controller intends to further process the personal data for a purpose other than that for which the personal data were obtained, the controller shall provide the data subject prior to that further processing with information on that other purpose and with any relevant further information as referred to in paragraph 2.

5. Paragraphs 1 to 4 shall not apply where and insofar as:

(a) the data subject already has the information;

(b) the provision of such information proves impossible or would involve a disproportionate effort, in particular for processing for archiving purposes in the public interest, scientific or historical research purposes or statistical purposes, subject to the conditions and safeguards referred to in Article 89(1) or in so far as the obligation referred to in paragraph 1 of this Article is likely to render impossible or seriously impair the achievement of the objectives of that processing. In such cases the controller shall take appropriate measures to protect the data subject's rights and freedoms and legitimate interests, including making the information publicly available;

(c) obtaining or disclosure is expressly laid down by Union or Member State law to which the controller is subject and which provides appropriate measures to protect the data subject's legitimate interests; or

(d) where the personal data must remain confidential subject to an obligation of professional secrecy regulated by Union or Member State law, including a statutory obligation of secrecy.

b. Colo. Rev. Stat. Sec. 6-1-1704—Disclosure of an Artificial Intelligence System to Consumer

Colorado AI Consumer Protection Act

2024 Colorado Session Laws, Ch. 198 (S.B. 24-205)

6–1–1704. Disclosure of an Artificial Intelligence System to Consumer

(1) . . . except as provided in subsection (2) of this section, a deployer or other developer that deploys, offers, sells, leases, licenses, gives, or otherwise makes available an artificial intelligence system that is intended to interact with consumers shall ensure the disclosure to each consumer who interacts with the artificial intelligence system that the consumer is interacting with an artificial intelligence system.

(2) Disclosure is not required under subsection (1) of this section under circumstances in which it would be obvious to a reasonable person that the person is interacting with an artificial intelligence system.

B. ATTEMPTS TO ASSERT BLACK BOX ACCOUNTABILITY

With the use of algorithms throughout different sectors, from how data searching functions to very impactful purposes like determining job hiring, uses of data for certain activities that have been deemed "high risk" have resulted in the passage of limiting legislation that requires stricter controls, such as needing heightened levels of privacy and security to prevent sensitive data from leaking, or requiring greater explanation or transparency in use.

The *Illinois Biometric Information Privacy Act* (*BIPA*) is older compared to many of the other data protection and AI regulations discussed in this book, having been passed in 2008. The law focuses on the control of biometric data, requiring that companies clearly inform users when biometric data are being collected, used, and shared. Biometric information in the *BIPA* refers to information based on narrowly defined biometric identifiers that are "a retina or iris scan, fingerprint, voiceprint, or scan of hand or face geometry," but not including other biometrics like photographs or physical descriptions. Such biometric identifiers are considered particularly sensitive due to the difficulty of changing these identifiers, making them powerful for purposes of reidentification or deanonymization.

1. *Illinois Biometric Information Privacy Act as Case Study*

The following shows the tension between the use of AI systems that collect biometric information and the Illinois *BIPA*, which regulates the use of collected biometric information of Illinois citizens.

a. Deyerler v. HireVue, Inc. (Order)

Deyerler v. HireVue, Inc. (Order)

United States District Court for the Northern District of Illinois
Case No. 22 CV 1284
February 26, 2024
Unpublished

DANIEL, United States District Judge.

MEMORANDUM ORDER

Six Illinois residents[1] filed this putative class action alleging that HireVue, Inc. ("HireVue"), a Utah-based software vendor, violated the Illinois Biometric Information Privacy Act ("BIPA")[2] when its interactive software captured and collected their biometric information during virtual job interviews. HireVue now moves to dismiss the plaintiffs' first amended complaint under Federal Rules of Civil Procedure 12(b)(2) and 12(b)(6). (R. 48.) For the reasons set forth in this opinion, the motion is granted in part and denied in part.

BACKGROUND

HireVue is a Delaware corporation based in Utah that develops and markets software to assess job applicants' performance during virtual interviews. HireVue sells its software to employers—including companies headquartered in Illinois—who are looking to fill job openings. HireVue's software allows customers to record video interviews with potential candidates and analyze their performance with artificial intelligence. Each recorded interview yields "thousands of data points" that are used to assess candidates' cognitive ability, personality traits, emotional intelligence, and social aptitude.

1. [Fn. 1 in original] The plaintiffs' full names are Kristen Deyerler, Max Ellithorpe, Bryen Zimmerman, Christopher Coats, Nicolas Galindo, and William Phemister. (*See generally* R. 17 ("FAC").)

2. [In text in original] 740 ILCS 14/1, et seq.

The plaintiffs are six Illinois residents who allege that HireVue captured and collected their biometric identifiers when they used HireVue's platform to interview for positions in Illinois. They filed this putative class action alleging that HireVue's actions violate subsections 15(a), (b), (c), and (d) of the BIPA. HireVue now moves to dismiss the first amended complaint in its entirety under Federal Rules of Civil Procedure 12(b)(2) and 12(b)(6).

LEGAL STANDARD

A motion to dismiss under Rule 12(b)(2) tests whether a federal court has personal jurisdiction over a defendant. . . .

A Rule 12(b)(6) motion to dismiss for failure to state a claim, "test[s] the sufficiency of the complaint, not the merits of the case."[3] To survive a Rule 12(b)(6) motion, a complaint must "state a claim to relief that is plausible on its face."[4] "A claim has facial plausibility when the plaintiff pleads factual content that allows the court to draw the reasonable inference that the defendant is liable for the misconduct alleged."[5] The complaint must put the defendants on "fair notice of what the . . . claim is and the grounds upon which it rests."[6]

[The Court concludes that the plaintiffs have successfully established personal jurisdiction as the defendant has marketed and sold their technology to at least one Illinois company and was used to interview one of the plaintiffs in Illinois, establishing a threshold showing of minimum contact with the state.]

ANALYSIS

. . . .

II. Hirevue's Rule 12(b)(6) Motion

The Court next turns to HireVue's Rule 12(b)(6) motion. Unlike a motion to dismiss for lack of personal jurisdiction, a Rule 12(b)(6) motion is limited in scope to the sufficiency of the allegations set forth in the complaint.[7] This means that while the Simmons and Coombs declarations were properly considered in the context of HireVue's Rule 12(b)(2) motion, they are inappropriate to consider in ruling on its Rule 12(b)(6) motion.[8] The Court therefore ignores the factual contentions set forth in the Simmons and Coombs declarations and considers only the allegations in the first amended complaint in deciding HireVue's 12(b)(6) motion.

---

3. [In text in original] Gociman v. Loyola Univ. of Chi., 41 F.4th 873, 885 (7th Cir. 2022).
4. [In text in original] Bell Atl. Corp. v. Twombly, 550 U.S. 544, 570 (2007).
5. [In text in original] Ashcroft v. Iqbal, 556 U.S. 662, 678 (2009).
6. [In text in original] *Twombly*, 550 U.S. at 555 (citation omitted).
7. [In text in original] Geinosky v. City of Chi., 675 F.3d 743, 745 n.1 (7th Cir. 2012).
8. [In text in original] Burlingham v. U.S. Dep't of Health & Hum. Servs., No. 22 C 1134, 2023 WL 6390798, at *4 (E.D. Wis. Sept. 30, 2023) (ignoring declaration submitted in support of Rule 12(b)(2) motion in deciding parallel Rule 12(b)(6) motion); JT's Frames, Inc. v. Casares, 16 C 2504, 2018 WL 835225, at *6 (N.D. Ill. Feb. 13, 2018) (same).

HireVue raises several arguments in support of dismissal under Rule 12(b)(6). First, it argues that the plaintiffs' allegations constitute an extraterritorial application of the BIPA. Second, it argues that, under principles of statutory interpretation, the plaintiffs' claims fall outside of the scope of the statute, are foreclosed by other legislative enactments, or are subject to exemptions. Finally, it argues that the allegations fail to state a claim. The Court addresses each argument in turn. Because many of HireVue's arguments are fact-specific, the Court declines to decide their merits prior to summary judgment.

A. Extraterritoriality

First, HireVue argues that the plaintiffs' BIPA claims violate Illinois' extraterritoriality doctrine. Under this doctrine, a statute that does not clearly contemplate extraterritorial effect cannot be applied unless "the circumstances that relate to the disputed transaction occur primarily and substantially in Illinois."[9] Courts have recognized that, in the context of BIPA claims, extraterritoriality "is a highly fact-based analysis that is generally inappropriate for the motion to dismiss stage."[10]

HireVue cites *Neals v. PAR Technology Corporation*, in which the district court dismissed the plaintiff's BIPA claims because she did not allege whether she was in Illinois when the defendant scanned her fingerprints.[11] Here, by contrast, the plaintiffs allege that they accessed HireVue's interview platform while they were in Illinois through the use of a webcam. While HireVue disputes the veracity of these allegations and represents that any biometric data collected was stored outside of Illinois, at this stage the Court is bound to draw all factual inferences in the plaintiffs' favor.[12] The Court declines to rule on HireVue's extraterritoriality arguments until a record has been developed. Accordingly, the Court denies its Rule 12(b)(6) motion on this basis.

B. Statutory Interpretation Arguments

Next, HireVue raises several statutory interpretation arguments, arguing that the plaintiffs' claims are either not covered by the BIPA, are foreclosed by other legislation, or are subject to exemptions.

First, HireVue argues that the plaintiffs have failed to allege that their facial scans are "biometric identifiers" under the BIPA. This argument is undermined by the plain language of the BIPA, however, which defines "biometric identifiers" to include, among other things, "face geometry."[13]

9. [In text in original] Avery v. State Farm Mut. Auto. Ins. Co., 835 N.E.2d 801, 854 (Ill. 2005).

10. [In text in original] Vance v. Int'l Bus. Mach. Corp., No. 20 C 577, 2020 WL 5530134, at *3 (N.D. Ill. Sept. 15, 2020) (collecting cases).

11. [In text in original] 419 F. Supp. 3d 1088, 1091 (N.D. Ill. 2019).

12. [In text in original] Vesuvius USA Corp. v. Am. Com. Lines LLC, 910 F.3d 331, 333 (7th Cir. 2018).

13. [In text in original] 740 ILCS 14/10.

The first amended complaint alleges that HireVue used "facial expression and screening technology . . . to identify and assess candidates by collecting their facial geometry." These allegations are all that is needed at the pleading stage.[14]

Second, HireVue argues that the plaintiffs' BIPA claims are precluded by Illinois' Artificial Intelligence Video Interview Act ("AIVIA"),[15] HireVue appeals to the principle that "where two statutes appear to be in conflict, the more specific controls over the more general."[16] Because the AIVIA specifically regulates the use of artificial intelligence to analyze videos submitted by job applicants, HireVue argues that the plaintiffs may not bring claims under the BIPA related to HireVue's use of its online video platform.

The problem with HireVue's argument is that it assumes that the BIPA and the AIVIA impose conflicting—as opposed to concurrent—obligations. In interpreting statutes, the Court must presume that the Illinois legislature "acts rationally and with full knowledge of all previous enactments" and that "the legislature will not enact a law which completely contradicts a prior statute without an express repeal of it."[17] As the plaintiffs point out, nothing in the AIVIA indicates that the legislature intended to repeal or preempt any portion of the BIPA when it enacted the statute, or that the legislature intended to limit the BIPA's private right of action. Although HireVue points to the fact that the two statutes impose different consent, retention, and disclosure obligations, these apparent conflicts do not compel the conclusion that the statutes are entirely inconsistent with one another or that the AIVIA forecloses the plaintiffs' BIPA claims.[18] Accordingly, the Court denies HireVue's motion to dismiss on this basis.

In yet another flourish of statutory interpretation, HireVue suggests that the BIPA's "financial institution" exemption bars the plaintiffs' claims. Section 25(c) of the BIPA provides that the statute does not apply "in any manner to a financial institution or an affiliate of a financial institution that is subject to Title V of the federal Gramm-Leach-Bliley Act ('GLBA')."[19]

Courts in this district have commented that the financial institution exemption is akin to an affirmative defense, which cannot be considered in the context of a Rule 12(b)(6) motion unless the defendant's entitlement to the defense is apparent from the face of the complaint.[20]

---

14. [In text in original] *See* Wilk v. Brainshark, Inc., 21 C 4794, 2022 WL 4482842, at *5 (N.D. Ill. Sept. 27, 2022) (denying motion to dismiss BIPA claims based on the statutory definition of "biometric identifiers" where plaintiff alleged that facial features in sales professionals' videos were analyzed and collected through facial-mapping technology).

15. [In text in original] 820 ILCS 42/1 et seq.

16. [In text in original] State v. Mikusch, 562 N.E.2d 168, 173 (Ill. 1990).

17. [In text in original] *Mikusch,* 562 N.E.2d at 170.

18. [In text in original] *See Mikusch,* 562 N.E.2d at 173.

19. [In text in original] 740 ILCS 14/25.

20. [In text in original] *See* Davis v. Jumio Corp., No. 22 C 776, 2023 WL 2019048, at *2 (N.D. Ill. Feb. 14, 2023); Patterson v. Respondus, Inc., 593 F. Supp. 3d 783, 819 n.18 (N.D. Ill. 2022)) (citing United States v. Lewis, 411 F.3d 838, 842 (7th Cir. 2005)).

The first amended complaint contains no allegations upon which the Court can infer that HireVue is a financial institution subject to the GBLA. To the contrary, HireVue's defense rests on the apparently novel and fact-specific assertion that HireVue's contracts with health insurance companies like HCSC entitle it to the financial institution exemption. It would be premature to resolve such a fact-specific argument at this stage.[21] Accordingly, the Court declines to consider the merits of this argument and denies HireVue's motion to dismiss on this basis.

C. Failure to State a Claim

Finally, the Court arrives at the question of whether the plaintiffs' allegations are sufficient to state claims under the BIPA. The plaintiffs allege violations under subsections 15(a), (b), (c), and (d) of the BIPA. Because each of these subsections gives rise to a separate claim,[22] the Court addresses each in turn.

First, HireVue argues that the plaintiffs have failed to state a claim under § 15(a) of the BIPA, which requires entities who are "in possession" of biometric information to "develop a written policy, made available to the public, establishing a retention schedule and guidelines for permanently destroying biometric identifiers."[23] Because the plaintiffs have alleged that HireVue "collect[ed], capture[d] and use[d]" their facial geometry and "did not make publicly available any biometric retention policy that disclosed how long it stored the biometrics it collected[,]" their allegations are sufficient to state a claim under § 15(a).[24]

HireVue argues that the plaintiffs have not alleged that it was "in possession" of their biometric data. The BIPA does not define this term, however.[25] Given the ordinary meaning of "in possession," the first amended complaint plausibly alleges that HireVue violated § 15(a) by capturing and collecting the plaintiffs' biometric data.[26] Accordingly, the Court denies HireVue's motion to dismiss on this basis.

---

21. [In text in original] *See Davis*, 2023 WL 2019048, at *4 (holding that whether cryptocurrency exchange qualified as a financial institution for purposes of BIPA's financial institution exemption "presents a question of fact that cannot be determined based on the allegations of the [c]omplaint").

22. [In text in original] [*S*]*ee, e.g.*, Clark v. Microsoft Corp., No. 23 C 695, 2023 WL 5348760, at *4 (N.D. Ill. Aug. 21, 2023).

23. [In text in original] 740 ILCS 14/15(a).

24. [In text in original] *See* Rogers v. CSX Intermodal Terminals, Inc., 409 F. Supp. 3d 612, 618 (N.D. Ill. 2019) (holding that allegations that the defendant "failed to make publicly available any retention or destruction policies" despite collection of the plaintiff's biometric data were sufficient to state a claim under § 15(a)).

25. [In text in original] *See* 740 ILCS 14/10.

26. [In text in original] *See* People v. Grant, 52 N.E.3d 308, 313 (Ill. 2016) ("[The] most reliable indicator of [the legislature's] intent is the statutory language itself, given its plain and ordinary meaning"); *see also Possession*, Black's Law Dictionary (11th ed. 2019).

Similarly, HireVue argues that it is not subject to § 15(b) of BIPA which prohibits, among other things, "captur[ing] [and] collect[ing]" an individual's biometric information without their consent.[27] HireVue argues that the plaintiffs cannot state a claim under this subsection because the company does not collect or store biometric data. But the first amended complaint alleges the opposite: that HireVue actively gathered the plaintiffs' biometric data through its software platform. The Court is bound to accept these allegations as true and draw all inferences in the plaintiffs' favor.[28] The Court denies HireVue's motion to dismiss on this basis as well.

Next, HireVue moves to dismiss the plaintiffs' claims under § 15(c), which prohibits a company from "sell[ing], leas[ing], trad[ing], or otherwise profit[ing]" from an individual's biometric data.[29] In the context of § 15(c), the Seventh Circuit has held that pleading a "bare violation" of the statute is not enough; instead, plaintiffs must allege how the alleged conduct harmed them individually.[30]

Here, the Court agrees with HireVue that the plaintiffs' allegations fail to state a claim. The plaintiffs allege that HireVue profited from their biometric information because its clients paid for use of its software. But the fact that HireVue profited from the sale of its *software* does not plausibly indicate that it sold, leased, traded, or otherwise profited from the plaintiffs' biometric data itself. Moreover, the allegations in the first amended complaint plead a "bare violation" of the statute without an explanation of how the plaintiffs have been harmed.[31] Because the first amended complaint does not allege that HireVue profited directly from the collection of biometric data or explain how the plaintiffs were individually harmed by this activity, the Court grants HireVue's motion to dismiss as to this claim.

Finally, HireVue argues that the plaintiffs' § 15(d) claim fails because the first amended complaint does not plausibly allege that HireVue "disclose[d], redisclose[d], or otherwise disseminate[d]" their data.[32] But the first amended complaint alleges that HireVue's software "also results in the dissemination of biometrics to third parties, such as data storage vendors." Whether or not this allegation is true, it must be accepted as such at this stage.[33] And allegations that HireVue "disseminated [the plaintiffs'] biometric data to other firms that hosted the information in their data centers" are sufficient to state a claim under § 15(d).[34] The Court therefore denies HireVue's motion to dismiss on this basis.

---

27. [In text in original] 740 ILCS 14/15 (b).
28. [In text in original] *Vesuvius*, 910 F.3d at 333.
29. [In text in original] 740 ILCS 14/15(c).
30. [In text in original] Thornley v. Clearview AI, Inc., 984 F.3d 1241, 1246-47 (7th Cir. 2021).
31. [In text in original] *Thornley*, 984 F.3d at 1246-47.
32. [In text in original] 740 ILCS 14/15(d).
33. [In text in original] *Vesuvius*, 910 F.3d at 333.
34. [In text in original] Figueroa v. Kronos Inc., 454 F. Supp. 3d 772, 785 (N.D. Ill. 2020).

CONCLUSION

For the reasons set forth in this memorandum opinion, the Court grants Defendant HireVue Inc.'s motion to dismiss in part and denies it in part. The Court denies HireVue's Rule 12(b)(2) motion to dismiss for lack of personal jurisdiction and finds that it may exercise specific personal jurisdiction over HireVue with respect to all pending claims. The Court also grants HireVue's Rule 12(b)(6) motion as to the plaintiffs' claims under § 15(c) of the BIPA. The motion is denied as to all other claims. HireVue will have 21 days to answer the complaint. It is so ordered.

b. HireVue's Notice and AI Explanation Statement

When dealing with an algorithmic issue in a legal case, one of the major issues is determining what the algorithm actually does. The Illinois BIPA has been successfully used to litigate against other captures and unauthorized use of biometric data. In some situations, the exact processes and methods of data capture and storage and biometric data use are unknown or in dispute.

Some of these questions can only be answered after prolonged discovery to access data about the underlying algorithm and practices that companies try to withhold as trade secrets and considerable analysis into software code. At times, a company will offer AI explainability statements, providing details on how their algorithm operates.

HireVue provided the AI Explainability Statement below following the litigation.

The quality of disclosures varies by instance. In most cases, direct access to the algorithm is not available to the public: It is the proprietary software that a business has invested time and money into developing and the cornerstone of their revenue. Instead, algorithmic disclosures are typically like the kind seen below, which can help offer some reassurances but do not permit third parties to test the veracity of a company's claims. Options to red team or audit an algorithm to search for potential bias or unauthorized data processing are not available and can be surreptitiously concealed by the company or its vendors.

The state and potential for more transparency will depend on future regulations.

HireVue AI Short-Form Explainability Statement

[AI Disclosure to Consumers and Users: Notice and Explainability Statement]
March 31, 2022

This document is intended to provide information on how the Artificial Intelligence (AI)-based assessments within our Hiring Experience Platform™ work, including when, how, and why we use this technology to facilitate our customers in making their hiring decisions. It is separate from our privacy policy, which is available here. Please note that this is a "living document" which will be updated from time to time, based on updates to our systems and processes. HireVue considers ethical development of AI along with data security and privacy to be core values. In addition to the creation of its Expert Advisory Board to help guide ethical AI Development, HireVue developed this Explainability Statement to explain HireVue's processes and in an effort to assist our customers in fulfilling their obligations as "data controllers" in compliance with data protection laws including EU/UK General Data Protection Regulation (GDPR). . . .

WHAT IS OUR PLATFORM?

Our AI

HireVue transforms the way organizations discover, engage, and hire the best talent. Connecting companies and candidates anytime, anywhere, HireVue's industry leading end-to-end hiring platform features video interviewing, assessments and conversational AI. HireVue has hosted more than 26 million video interviews and 5 million AI-based candidate assessments for over 700 customers around the globe.

HireVue offers a broad suite of AI assessments, including video interviewing and online game-based challenges. These can be combined in a "modular" fashion for specific roles. Using more than one type of assessment allows us to measure different competencies. For example, we can combine an assessment to test teamwork skills with another to test problem-solving. Customers who choose HireVue's modular system work with our Industrial/Organizational (IO) Psychology experts to decide the competencies required for each role they are looking to fill. We ensure best practice interview approaches are followed and use state of the art technology to transcribe answers, which we then analyse to assess each competency in accordance with our customers' instructions.

The purpose of our AI assessments is to give recruiters a standard, structured, and fair way to screen many candidates, in a shorter time and at lower cost than traditional human-led interviews. Our AI assessments don't replace recruiters. They simply help recruiters and talent acquisition teams assess more candidates more quickly and more accurately. Recruiters and hiring managers are provided materials and training on what competencies are measured in the assessment and why and how to interpret the competency assessment results (we provide further detail of this below).

AI, in the broadest sense, means technologies which are capable of undertaking or facilitating tasks that would otherwise require human thought or reasoning. Within this very broad definition there are many different techniques and applications. The aim of this Explainability Statement is to explain which AI techniques we use, why we use them, and what factors they take into account. . . .

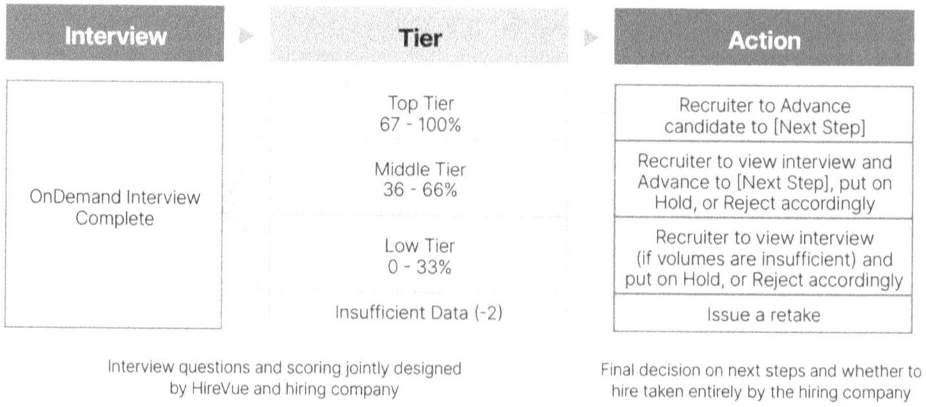

HOW DID WE DESIGN OUR AI?

How do we use AI in video interviews?

There are three stages involved in the AI technology we use in video interviews, each of which involves a different system: (1) transcribing spoken words to text, (2) understanding what that text means and (3) assessing/scoring the candidate's answers following expert human rater evaluations of answers to the same competency-based question.

Importantly, our AI relies only on what is said by the candidate and does not use any video analysis or other audio characteristics (meaning that we do not assess a candidate's facial expressions, body language, their background and surroundings, or tone-of-voice).

1. Changing speech to text

First, we convert the candidate's speech to written text, using a third-party speech-to-text transcription system developed by a company called Rev.ai. This technology recognises the sound of words based on its experience and learning from over 50,000+ hours of human-transcribed content across a wide range of topics, industries, accents and inflections. We have provided more details about the transcription accuracy of Rev.ai in the section below, on Third Party Providers.

Rev.ai, in common with our own AI systems, uses a technique called "machine learning". Machine learning is a form of data processing that identifies statistical patterns from data sets. Rather than being programmed with predetermined responses to a set of conditions, a machine learning system is designed to develop its own responses to those conditions under a training regime. For instance, a simple machine learning system might learn to differentiate between the spoken words cat and dog with training data that includes many audio examples of different people saying "cat" or "dog", which are then labelled before being fed into the system. After the AI has been trained on enough examples of training data the system will build a predictive model that can distinguish between the two words. The principles which a system has derived from the training data are called a "model."

Machine learning systems are particularly good at undertaking complex tasks where the rules can be difficult to specify with precision (such as understanding language) as well as for tasks involving the computation of very large amounts of data. For these reasons, machine learning is now very commonly used for tasks which involve understanding human language.

2. Understanding words and sentences

Second, based on the transcribed text, we use a form of AI called "natural language processing" (NLP) in order to understand candidates' answers[.]

We have developed our own NLP model, "CAKE", which is based on a state-of-the-art language model called Robustly Optimized Bidirectional Encoder Representations from Transformers, or "RoBERTa". RoBERTa was adapted from a model designed by Google called BERT. CAKE starts with this base model and is further fine-tuned on interview data (as explained further below). The language analysed by CAKE is processed by a "deep neural network", a technology which comprises a collection of connected nodes or 'neurons' which can attribute a particular weight or significance to various features of the language presented to it. Specifically, the system training happens in two steps: (1) by predicting masked words in a large number of documents, the system learns about the English language, and (2) further refining this model with interview transcripts to understand the nuances of language which might be expressed in job interview scenarios. The output of the neural network is a numerical value—known as a "vector"—which the model has attributed to the particular answer to an interview question that has passed through the neural network. Unlike many simpler NLP methods, our system is especially effective at understanding the meaning contained in response to a question, regardless of the specific vocabulary used. This complexity makes it more difficult for candidates to "game" the video interview process by mentioning particular words or phrases in their responses. CAKE is capable of understanding individual words as well as their context. This is particularly important where the same word can have different meanings depending on the words around it. For example, the word "bank" is used in two different senses in this sentence: "Joanne went to the river bank today, and she visited the bank to withdraw cash on the way home."

In addition to the CAKE model, we also used an older and simpler NLP method, called "binary bag of words." This looks at all the words in the answer, with no consideration of the grammar and order of the words. These features add to our ability to explain since we can look at the relative weights of different words in the model. For example, we see things like saying the word "team" contributes positively to a candidate's score for the teamwork model.

3. Assessing and scoring each candidate

Third, once the CAKE model has understood and assigned numerical values to the candidate's response to an interview question, this numerical value is fed into a "ridge regression model" (a machine learning system) along with the "binary bag of words" analysis. The ridge regression model has been trained to identify responses of a similar nature and then score those responses against the customer's chosen competencies.

We have developed a separate AI model and set of questions for each competency. A sample of competencies we can test include adaptability, problem solving, communication and willingness to learn. There are over 20 which we can cover, and we are increasing this list over time based on scientific research and our own data.

Following best practices in structured interview design, of using guides to support consistent expert evaluations, we created a Behaviourally-Anchored Rating Scale (BARS) for each competency for which our questions were designed to elicit candidate interview answers. Creating scoring models for each competency based on expert BARS ratings, we have modelled the most accurate way of fairly and consistently rating structured interview responses without the unconscious bias injections of normal human interviewers.

HireVue's AI system scores each of the candidate's responses according to a BARS for each competency. The BARS guides or content are based on data from thousands of real-life interviews, covering a diverse range of interviewees and job types and the scoring uses five rating levels, from "novice" to "expert". In Appendix B we provide the BARS used for our "Communication" competency. Additionally, we provide an example of how an interview answer can be scored along the response timeline as each statement relates to an anchor in the BARS guide.

The models we use to assess candidates through interviews have been trained using expert human evaluations of structured interview responses; the scoring algorithms are based on sophisticated analytic techniques to craft correlational-based models that mimic trained expert human rater judgements. The assessment scores provided by our AI assessments are highly similar to the evaluations expert interviewers would provide, but without the unconscious biases.

To create the assessment scores for each BARS, HireVue collects thousands of expert human rater evaluations of standardised interviews and uses these ratings to train the models to score candidate interview responses. Our assessment development work and rater studies conducted over the past 3.5 years, have drawn upon 125,000 interview evaluations, which include over 500,000 applicant video interviews scored and evaluated for bias. More specifically:

- We collected scoring data from interviews for different levels of roles, type of companies, and geographic locations.

- We trained teams of around 30 expert raters to evaluate the responses in each of those interviews based on specific competencies according to an evaluation guide based on using a BARS.
- The expert raters then manually scored each response in the interviews against each competency, with 2-3 separate evaluators scoring each candidate answer.
- During the training process, we held regular calibration discussions to ensure consistency in scores from each rater. We also filtered any unreliable data (for example where there were audio issues or insufficient words in a response). We also re-scored or removed responses where rater evaluations varied significantly. Based on the above training, our ridge regression model is able to score candidates' responses, by comparing them to the manually scored responses during the training exercise. As compared to a simpler regression model, a "ridge" regression model helps to ensure that the algorithm generalises well to unseen data, rather than "overfitting" to the training data. Overfitting can occur when a model is trained to be highly accurate for the examples it has seen before, but which then results in the model being inflexible and not able to generalise as well (which, in this case, could mean it is unable to recognise different but similar candidate responses). . . .

2. *Facebook Papers from Whistleblower Frances Haugen*

Facebook and other platforms often limit information available to the public on how their algorithms are calibrated to deliver content or ad tech to users. As with many large tech companies, Facebook ran internal research on how to increase its user base, attract more usage, and improve monetization, but also to identify harmful components and negative effects that it could help minimize. However, Facebook usually does not publicly publish the results of its internal research, leaving journalists and external analysts with very limited insight into the internal functions and data.

Whistleblowers have unveiled more about how these tech companies have operated. Some revelations have included voluminous releases of documents, including internal research documents. Frances Haugen was a data scientist for two years at Facebook who brought controversies and internal studies to light in 2021, presenting them to federal agencies, Congress, and news organizations for review.

Although some version of algorithmic regulation was already being discussed in Congress, in state legislatures, and by regulators, the "Facebook Papers," as the leaks were termed, prompted a new wave of proposed legislation. The disclosures also renewed interest in prior legislation that attempted to address algorithmic harms, including potential misinformation.

Many social media platforms use extensive algorithms to tailor the user experience. However, Haugen testified that Facebook's algorithms might have caused harm to minors, raising the issue of potential government regulation on algorithms targeting children. The *Algorithmic Accountability Act* has been proposed multiple times, including before and after the release of the Facebook Papers.

a. Algorithmic Accountability Act (Proposed)

Algorithmic Accountability Act (Proposed)

H.R. 6580
117th Congress (2021-2022)
Introduced to the U.S. House of Representatives February 3, 2022

To direct the Federal Trade Commission to require impact assessments of automated decision systems and augmented critical decision processes, and for other purposes.

Sec. 1. Short Title

This Act may be cited as the "Algorithmic Accountability Act of 2022."

Sec. 2. Definitions

In this Act:

(1) Augmented Critical Decision Process.—The term "augmented critical decision process" means a process, procedure, or other activity that employs an automated decision system to make a critical decision.

(2) Automated Decision System.—The term "automated decision system" means any system, software, or process (including one derived from machine learning, statistics, or other data processing or artificial intelligence techniques and excluding passive computing infrastructure) that uses computation, the result of which serves as a basis for a decision or judgment.

(3) Biometrics.—The term "biometrics" means any information that represents a biological, physiological, or behavioral attribute or feature of a consumer.

(4) Chair.—The term "Chair" means the Chair of the Commission.

(5) Commission.—The term "Commission" means the Federal Trade Commission.

(6) Consumer.—The term "consumer" means an individual.

(7) Covered Entity.—

(A) In General.—The term "covered entity" means any person, partnership, or corporation over which the Commission has jurisdiction under section 5(a)(2) of the Federal Trade Commission Act (15 U.S.C. 45(a)(2))—

(i) that deploys any augmented critical decision process; and

(I) had greater than $50,000,000 in average annual gross receipts or is deemed to have greater than $250,000,000 in equity value for the 3-taxable-year period (or for the period during which the person, partnership, or corporation has been in existence, if such period is less than 3 years) preceding the most recent fiscal year, as determined in accordance with paragraphs (2) and (3) of section 448(c) of the Internal Revenue Code of 1986;

(II) possesses, manages, modifies, handles, analyzes, controls, or otherwise uses identifying information about more than 1,000,000 consumers, households, or consumer devices for the purpose of developing or deploying any automated decision system or augmented critical decision process; or

(III) is substantially owned, operated, or controlled by a person, partnership, or corporation that meets the requirements under subclause (I) or (II);

(ii) that—

(I) had greater than $5,000,000 in average annual gross receipts or is deemed to have greater than $25,000,000 in equity value for the 3-taxable-year period (or for the period during which the person, partnership, or corporation has been in existence, if such period is less than 3 years) preceding the most recent fiscal year, as determined in accordance with paragraphs (2) and (3) of section 448(c) of the Internal Revenue Code of 1986; and

(II) deploys any automated decision system that is developed for implementation or use, or that the person, partnership, or corporation reasonably expects to be implemented or used, in an augmented critical decision process by any person, partnership, or corporation if such person, partnership, or corporation meets the requirements described in clause (i); or

(iii) that met the criteria described in clause (i) or (ii) within the previous 3 years.

(B) Inflation Adjustment.—For purposes of applying this paragraph in any fiscal year after the first fiscal year that begins on or after the date of enactment of this Act, each of the dollar amounts specified in subparagraph (A) shall be increased by the percentage increase (if any) in the consumer price index for all urban consumers (U.S. city average) from such first fiscal year that begins after such date of enactment to the fiscal year involved.

(8) Critical Decision.—The term "critical decision" means a decision or judgment that has any legal, material, or similarly significant effect on a consumer's life relating to access to or the cost, terms, or availability of—

(A) education and vocational training, including assessment, accreditation, or certification;

(B) employment, workers management, or self-employment;

(C) essential utilities, such as electricity, heat, water, internet or telecommunications access, or transportation;

(D) family planning, including adoption services or reproductive services;

(E) financial services, including any financial service provided by a mortgage company, mortgage broker, or creditor;

(F) healthcare, including mental healthcare, dental, or vision;

(G) housing or lodging, including any rental or short-term housing or lodging;

(H) legal services, including private arbitration or mediation; or

(I) any other service, program, or opportunity decisions about which have a comparably legal, material, or similarly significant effect on a consumer's life as determined by the Commission through rulemaking.

(9) Deploy.—The term "deploy" means to implement, use, or make available for sale, license, or other commercial relationship.

(10) Develop.—The term "develop" means to design, code, produce, customize, or otherwise create or modify.

(11) Identifying Information.—The term "identifying information" means any information, regardless of how the information is collected, inferred, predicted, or obtained that identifies or represents a consumer, household, or consumer device through data elements or attributes, such as name, postal address, telephone number, biometrics, email address, internet protocol address, social security number, or any other identifying number, identifier, or code.

(12) Impact Assessment.—The term "impact assessment" means the ongoing study and evaluation of an automated decision system or augmented critical decision process and its impact on consumers.

(13) Passive Computing Infrastructure.—The term "passive computing infrastructure" means any intermediary technology that does not influence or determine the outcome of a decision, including—

(A) web hosting;

(B) domain registration;

(C) networking;

(D) caching;

(E) data storage; or

(F) cybersecurity.

(14) State.—The term "State" means each of the 50 States, the District of Columbia, and any territory or possession of the United States.

(15) Summary Report.—The term "summary report" means documentation of a subset of information required to be addressed by the impact assessment as described in this Act or determined appropriate by the Commission.

(16) Third-Party Decision Recipient.—The term "third-party decision recipient" means any person, partnership, or corporation (beyond the consumer and the covered entity) that receives a copy of or has access to the results of any decision or judgment that results from a covered entity's deployment of an automated decision system or augmented critical decision process.

Sec. 3. Assessing the Impact of Automated Decision Systems and Augmented Critical Decision Processes

(a) Acts Prohibited.—

(1) In General.—It is unlawful for—

(A) any covered entity to violate a regulation promulgated under subsection (b); or

(B) any person to knowingly provide substantial assistance to any covered entity in violating subsection (b).

(2) Preemption of Private Contracts.—It shall be unlawful for any covered entity to commit the acts prohibited in paragraph (1), regardless of specific agreements between entities or consumers.

(b) Regulations.—

(1) In General.—Subject to paragraph (2), not later than 2 years after the date of enactment of this Act, the Commission shall, in consultation with the Director of the National Institute of Standards and Technology, the Director of the National Artificial Intelligence Initiative, the Director of the Office of Science and Technology Policy, and other relevant stakeholders, including standards bodies, private industry, academia, technology experts, and advocates for civil rights, consumers, and impacted communities, promulgate regulations, in accordance with section 553 of title 5, United States Code, that—

(A) require each covered entity to perform impact assessment of any—

(i) deployed automated decision system that was developed for implementation or use, or that the covered entity reasonably expects to be implemented or used, in an augmented critical decision process by any person, partnership, or corporation that meets the requirements described in section 2(7)(A)(i); and

(ii) augmented critical decision process, both prior to and after deployment by the covered entity;

(B) require each covered entity to maintain documentation of any impact assessment performed under subparagraph (A), including the applicable information described in section 4(a) for 3 years longer than the duration of time for which the automated decision system or augmented critical decision process is deployed;

(C) require each person, partnership, or corporation that meets the requirements described in section 2(7)(A)(i) to disclose their status as a covered entity to any person, partnership, or corporation that sells, licenses, or otherwise provides through a commercial relationship any automated decision system deployed by the covered entity in an automated decision system or augmented critical decision process;

(D) require each covered entity to submit to the Commission, on an annual basis, a summary report for ongoing impact assessment of any deployed automated decision system or augmented critical decision process;

(E) require each covered entity to submit an initial summary report to the Commission for any new automated decision system or augmented critical decision process prior to its deployment by the covered entity;

(F) allow any person, partnership, or corporation over which the Commission has jurisdiction under section 5(a)(2) of the Federal Trade Commission Act (15 U.S.C. 45(a)(2)) that deploys any automated decision system or augmented critical decision process, but is not a covered entity, to submit to the Commission a summary report for any impact assessment performed with respect to such system or process;

(G) require each covered entity, in performing the impact assessment described in subparagraph (A), to the extent possible, to meaningfully consult (including through participatory design, independent auditing, or soliciting or incorporating feedback) with relevant internal stakeholders (such as employees, ethics teams, and responsible technology teams) and independent external stakeholders (such as representatives of and advocates for impacted groups, civil society and advocates, and technology experts) as frequently as necessary;

(H) require each covered entity to attempt to eliminate or mitigate, in a timely manner, any impact made by an augmented critical decision process that demonstrates a likely material negative impact that has legal or similarly significant effects on a consumer's life;

(I) establish definitions for—

(i) what constitutes "access to or the cost, terms, or availability of" with respect to a critical decision;

(ii) what constitutes "possession", "management", "modification", and "control" with respect to identifying information;

(iii) the different categories of third-party decision recipients that a covered entity must document under section 5(1)(H); and

(iv) any of the services, programs, or opportunities described in subparagraphs (A) through (I) of section 2(8) for the purpose of informing consumers, covered entities, and regulators, as the Commission deems necessary;

(J) establish guidelines for any person, partnership, or corporation to calculate the number of consumers, households, or consumer devices for which the person, partnership, or corporation possesses, manages, modifies, or controls identifying information for the purpose of determining covered entity status;

(K) establish guidelines for a covered entity to prioritize different automated decision systems and augmented critical decision processes deployed by the covered entity for performing impact assessment; and

(L) establish a required format for any summary report, as described in subparagraphs (D), (E), and (F), to ensure that such reports are submitted in an accessible and machine-readable format.

(2) Considerations.—In promulgating the regulations under paragraph (1), the Commission—

(A) shall take into consideration—

(i) that certain assessment or documentation of an automated decision system or augmented critical decision process may only be possible at particular stages of the development and deployment of such system or process or may be limited or not possible based on the availability of certain types of information or data or the nature of the relationship between the covered entity and consumers;

(ii) the duration of time between summary report submissions and the timeliness of the reported information;

(iii) the administrative burden placed on the Commission and the covered entity;

(iv) the benefits of standardizing and structuring summary reports for comparative analysis compared with the benefits of less-structured narrative reports to provide detail and flexibility in reporting;

(v) that summary reports submitted by different covered entities may contain different fields according to the requirements established by the Commission, and the Commission may allow or require submission of incomplete reports;

(vi) that existing data privacy and other regulations may inhibit a covered entity from storing or sharing certain information; and

(vii) that a covered entity may require information from other persons, partnerships, or corporations that develop any automated decision system deployed in an automated decision system or augmented critical decision process by the covered entity for the purpose of performing impact assessment; and

(B) may develop specific requirements for impact assessments and summary reports for particular—

(i) categories of critical decisions, as described in subparagraphs (A) through (I) of section 2(8) or any subcategory developed by the Commission; and

(ii) stages of development and deployment of an automated decision system or augmented critical decision process.

3. FTC Enforcement as Case Study

The following case, *FTC v. TransUnion Rental Screening Solutions*, addresses accuracy and transparency. The Federal Trade Commission (FTC) enforcement power includes Section 5 of the *FTC Act*, which prohibits "unfair or deceptive acts or practices" in commerce.[35]

The following case, filed jointly with the Consumer Financial Protection Bureau (CFPB), alleged unfair data and algorithmic practices by a credit reporting company in rental background checks.

a. FTC v. TransUnion Rental Screening Solutions (Complaint)

FTC v. TransUnion Rental Screening Solutions (Complaint)

United States District Court for the District of Colorado
Civil Action No. 1:23-cv-2659
October 12, 2023

COMPLAINT

The Federal Trade Commission ("FTC") and Consumer Financial Protection Bureau ("Bureau") (collectively, "Plaintiffs") bring this action

35. Federal Trade Commission Act § 5(a), 15 U.S.C. § 45(a).

against TransUnion Rental Screening Solutions, Inc. ("TURSS") and Trans Union LLC ("TU LLC") (collectively, "Defendants") and allege as follows:

1. The FTC brings this action under Section 13(b) of the Federal Trade Commission Act ("FTC Act"), 15 U.S.C. § 53(b), and Section 621(a)(1) of the Fair Credit Reporting Act ("FCRA"), 15 U.S.C. § 1681s(a)(1), which authorize the FTC to seek, and the Court to order, permanent injunctive relief and other relief for Defendants' acts or practices in violation of Section 5(a) of the FTC Act, 15 U.S.C. § 45(a), and the FCRA, 15 U.S.C. §§ 1681-1681x.

2. The Bureau brings this action under Sections 1054(a) and 1055 of the Consumer Financial Protection Act of 2010 ("CFPA"), 12 U.S.C. §§ 5564(a) and 5565, and Section 621(b) of the FCRA, 15 U.S.C. § 1681s(b)(1)(H), which authorize the Bureau to seek, and the Court to order, permanent injunctive relief, monetary relief, civil money penalties, and other relief for Defendants' acts or practices in violation of the FCRA, 15 U.S.C. §§ 1681-1681x.

INTRODUCTION

3. In numerous instances, Defendants have violated the FCRA by failing to follow reasonable procedures to assure maximum possible accuracy of information in background screening reports that landlords and others rely on to, among other things, make rental decisions about specific consumers ("Tenant Screening Reports"), and by failing to clearly and accurately disclose to consumers the sources of information in background screening reports.

4. Inaccurate and outdated information in Tenant Screening Reports can significantly interfere with consumers' ability to find housing and cause them harm, including, but not limited to, prolonged housing searches, additional application fees, time and money spent correcting errors, higher rental payments, temporary housing costs, and denial of housing.

5. Plaintiffs filed this Complaint to stop Defendants' unlawful practices, to obtain relief for harmed consumers, and to obtain a penalty.

DEFENDANTS

10. Defendant TURSS is a Delaware corporation with its principal place of business in Greenwood Village, Colorado and is a wholly owned subsidiary of Defendant TU LLC.

11. Defendant TU LLC is a Delaware limited liability company with its principal place of business in Chicago, Illinois. TU LLC operates TURSS as a business unit and performs a variety of shared services for TURSS, including legal and compliance, accounting and finance, marketing and public relations, data science, and human resources. TU LLC also develops and approves FCRA-related policies and procedures used by TURSS. Throughout the relevant time period, TU LLC, through its officers or employees, has been

responsible for, among other things, management and oversight of TURSS's FCRA compliance policies and procedures, including monitoring and testing for regulatory compliance and compliance training. TU LLC participated in, directed, or authorized the acts and practices set forth in this Complaint.

12. Defendants transact or have transacted business in this district and throughout the United States. At all times material to this Complaint, acting alone or in concert with others, Defendants have furnished background reports about consumers in Colorado and throughout the United States.

VIOLATIONS OF THE FAIR CREDIT REPORTING ACT

13. Enacted in 1970, the FCRA became effective on April 25, 1971, and has been in force since that date. It has been amended several times, including by the Fair and Accurate Credit Transactions Act in December 2003 and the Dodd-Frank Act in July 2010.

14. TURSS, through its provision of tenant and employment background screening reports, and TU LLC, through its provision of credit and other reports, are and have been "Consumer Reporting Agencies," as defined in Section 603(f) of the FCRA, 15 U.S.C. § 1681a(f). That section defines a Consumer Reporting Agency as:

> [A]ny person which, for monetary fees, dues, or on a cooperative nonprofit basis, regularly engages in whole or in part in the practice of assembling or evaluating consumer credit information or other information on consumers for the purpose of furnishing [C]onsumer [R]eports to third parties, and which uses any means or facility of interstate commerce for the purpose of preparing or furnishing [C]onsumer [R]eports.

Defendants regularly sell in interstate commerce information on consumers that they assemble or evaluate for the purpose of furnishing Consumer Reports to third parties, as described further below

15. The FCRA imposes several obligations on Consumer Reporting Agencies, including obligations to: (1) follow reasonable procedures to assure the maximum possible accuracy of the information in Consumer Reports, 15 U.S.C. § 1681e(b), and (2) upon a consumer's request, disclose to the consumer all information contained in the consumer's file and the sources of the information, 15 U.S.C. § 1681g(a).

16. Pursuant to § 621 of the FCRA, 15 U.S.C. § 1681s, a violation of the FCRA constitutes an unfair or deceptive act or practice in or affecting commerce, in violation of Section 5(a) of the FTC Act, 15 U.S.C. § 45(a). . . .

Failure to Follow Reasonable Procedures to Assure Maximum Possible Accuracy

23. Section 607(b) of the FCRA, 15 U.S.C. § 1681e(b), requires that "[w]henever a [C]onsumer [R]eporting [A]gency prepares a [C]onsumer [R]eport it shall follow reasonable procedures to assure maximum possible accuracy of the information concerning the individual about whom the report relates."

24. In numerous instances, TURSS has failed to follow reasonable procedures to assure maximum possible accuracy of Eviction Proceeding Records in its Tenant Screening Reports. TURSS has not followed reasonable procedures to: (1) prevent the inclusion of multiple entries for the same eviction case in Eviction Proceeding Records, (2) accurately report the case disposition in Eviction Proceeding Records, (3) accurately label data fields in Eviction Proceeding Records, and (4) prevent the inclusion of sealed Eviction Proceeding Records.

25. TURSS's failure to follow reasonable procedures to assure maximum possible accuracy of Eviction Proceeding Records has been knowing and reckless.

Multiple Entries for a Single Eviction Case

26. TURSS has failed to follow reasonable procedures to prevent the inclusion of multiple entries for the same eviction case in Eviction Proceeding Records in Tenant Screening Reports.

27. When reporting Eviction Proceeding Records in Tenant Screening Reports, TURSS's procedure has been to display each Event in a case as a separate entry in the report.

28. TURSS also previously reported Events from one case interspersed with Events related to other cases.

29. For example, prior to April 2021, TURSS would display a single eviction case that had two Events—such as a civil new filing and a judgment of possession—as two separate entries. On the same report, TURSS would also display a second eviction case that had two Events—such as a civil new filing and a civil dismissal—as two separate entries, with the entries for the second case interspersed among the entries from the first case. As a result, the consumer's Tenant Screening Report would display four separate entries when there were only two eviction cases.

Inaccurate Dispositions for Eviction Cases

33. TURSS has failed to follow reasonable procedures to assure that the Eviction Proceeding Records in Tenant Screening Reports accurately reflect the true or current status of the public records, such as the final disposition of the case.

34. In numerous instances, TURSS has provided Tenant Screening Reports with errors including Eviction Proceeding Records that do not identify a final disposition and merely indicate that an eviction case was initiated, even if a later or final disposition is available in public records. TURSS has also provided Tenant Screening Reports with Eviction Proceeding Records that have an incorrect final disposition, such as reporting a judgment for the plaintiff when a case was actually dismissed. . . .

In the *Blueprint for an AI Bill of Rights*, Principle 4 focused attention on the need for interpretability and explainability in AI and automated systems: "Designers, developers, and deployers of automated systems should provide generally accessible plain language documentation including clear descriptions of the overall system functioning and the role automation plays, notice that such systems are in use, the individual or organization responsible for the system, and explanations of outcomes that are clear, timely, and accessible."[36] When Frances Haugen, former Facebook employee and whistleblower, released what is referred to as the Facebook Papers in 2021, her disclosures raised renewed interest in the call for transparency and explanation in algorithmic decisionmaking and AI systems, including the regulation of platforms.

The *EU AI Act* and *GDPR* both include provisions that require transparency, explanation, and disclosure. The *GDPR*, for example, includes what is referred to as a "Right to Explanation":[37]

> Article 13(2)(f) and 14(2)(g) GDPR address a key aspect of AI applications, i.e. automated decisionmaking. The controller has the obligation to provide: (a) information on "the existence of automated decision-making, including profiling," referred to in Article 22(1) and (b) "at least in those cases meaningful information about the logic involved, as well as the significance and the envisaged consequences of such processing for the data subject."

The black box characteristics of AI and automated systems have led regulators to rely on explanation and interpretability requirements as necessary preconditions for transparency. Similarly, notice and disclosure requirements have become increasingly significant in ensuring proper oversight.

---

36. *Blueprint for an AI Bill of Rights*, White House.

37. Giovanni Sartor, *The Impact of the General Data Protection Regulation (GDPR) on Artificial Intelligence* (PE 641.530, European Parliamentary Research Service, June 2020), 54.

Chapter 6

Data Privacy and Autonomy

Data privacy is considered critical in defending both dignity and autonomy in a democracy. In a digital economy and AI revolution, data is ubiquitous. Personally identifiable data and sensitive personal data becomes hard to protect. Data breaches can leave one's data exposed and at risk of exploitation. The misuse of data can lead to harm that can endanger a sense of security and, if left unchecked, democratic processes. While there are some legal protections against nefarious uses of data and AI, there remain gaps to fully and proactively protect data privacy, autonomy, and democracy against misuse of personal data in AI and automated systems.

A. *DATA PRIVACY AND INFORMATIONAL PRIVACY*

It is impossible to discuss AI governance without addressing data privacy and data protection considerations, and information security and cybersecurity implications of AI technologies and their oversight. This is particularly important in light of growing concern that AI and other emerging technologies have the potential to affect fundamental rights, such as voting rights, as well as democratic governance and democracies, by amplifying disinformation and misinformation campaigns.

1. *Right to Privacy and User-Centric Data Control*

Privacy can be an abstract concept. The common law in early colonial America provided limited legal protections for privacy. Pre-Revolutionary War grievances included government overreach in the form of broad seizures of and intrusions in one's home. General warrants, for example, under English law, permitted open-ended searches of the homes of colonists. Accordingly, the

Constitution, through the Fourth Amendment specifically, provided guarantees against physical intrusions on one's privacy.[1]

In the seminal 1890 article, *The Right to Privacy*, Samuel D. Warren and Louis Brandeis advocated for an expansion of privacy protections to include personal information in a time where newspapers could make one's private life a matter of public discourse.[2] Warren and Brandeis argued for a "general right . . . to be let alone," a right to privacy conceived "as a part of the more general right to the immunity of the person."[3] These ideas have influenced both courts and state legislatures in conceiving of a constitutional right to privacy.

The California Constitution, for instance, was amended in 1979, expanding the nature of privacy in California beyond the federal interpretation. Article I of the California Constitution, below, establishes privacy as a constitutionally-protected aspect of personhood.[4]

a. California Constitution, Art. I, Sec. I

California Constitution
Article I Declaration of Rights [Section 1–Sec. 32]

Cal. Const. art. I, § 1

SECTION 1

All people are by nature free and independent and have inalienable rights. Among these are enjoying and defending life and liberty, acquiring, possessing, and protecting property, and pursuing and obtaining safety, happiness, and privacy.

b. In re Google Assistant Privacy Litigation (Complaint)

The California Constitution's Right to Privacy was applied against Google over Google's collection of data. The consolidated class action complaint is excerpted below.

In re Google Assistant Privacy Litigation (Fourth Amended Complaint)

United States District Court for the Northern District of California
Case No. 19-cv-04286-BLF
August 2, 2021

SUMMARY OF ALLEGATIONS

2. Plaintiffs, on behalf of themselves and similarly situated purchasers of Google Assistant Enabled Devices (defined below) and members of

---

1. *See* Daniel J. Solove, *A Brief History of Information Privacy Law*, *in* Proskauer on Privacy, PLI § 1:1 (Christopher Wolf ed., 2006).
2. 4 Harv. L. Rev. 5 (1890).
3. *Id.*
4. J. Clark Kelso, *California's Constitutional Right to Privacy*, 19 Pepp. L. Rev. 2 (1992).

their households, and purchasers and installers of Google Home products bring this suit under the Federal Wiretap Act ("Wiretap Act"), 18 U.S.C. § 2510, *et seq.*, Stored Communications Act ("SCA"), 18 U.S.C. § 2702, *et seq.*, California Invasion of Privacy Act ("CIPA"), Cal. Penal Code § 632, intrusion upon seclusion, invasion of privacy under Art. 1, Sec. 1 of the California Constitution, breach of contract, and violation of the California Consumers Legal Remedies Act, Cal. Civ. Code, § 1750, *et seq.* ("CLRA"), the California Unfair Competition Law ("UCL"), Cal. Bus. & Prof. Code § 17200, and for declaratory and other equitable relief under the Declaratory Judgment Act, 28 U.S.C. § 2201, *et seq.* . . .

5. Federal and state privacy laws uniformly recognize individuals' reasonable expectations of privacy in confidential communications, particularly those that take place in the sanctity of one's own home—a historically protected zone of privacy. Federal privacy laws prohibit unauthorized interception, access, disclosure, and use of the contents of oral and electronic communications. California specifically recognizes privacy as a fundamental right, and accordingly, California law prohibits, among other things, eavesdropping, recording, and sharing of confidential communications without the consent of all parties to the communication.

6. Well aware of consumers' legitimate and reasonable expectations of privacy, Google assured, and continues to assure, its customers, like Plaintiffs and members of the Classes and Subclasses (defined below) (respectively, "Class Members" and "Subclass Members"), that Google Assistant Enabled Devices will only listen to, record, and share their conversations with their consent, which can be given only: (i) by uttering an activation command, like "Okay, Google" or "Hey, Google" ("hot word(s)"); or (ii) by manually pressing a button on the device. Consequently, individuals who have purchased or used Google Assistant Enabled Devices and interacted with Google Assistant, have not consented to Google recording or disclosing conversations where "Okay, Google" or "Hey, Google" has not been uttered and no button on the device has been pressed.

7. On July 10, 2019, unsuspecting consumers learned that, despite Google's assurances, Google has intercepted, recorded, disclosed, and misused private conversations of thousands of individuals, without consent. As reported by Belgian news outlet VRT NWS based on a whistleblower's revelations, Google collects audio recordings of Google Assistant users in numerous instances where a hot word is never spoken and uses these recordings for its own commercial and financial benefit, including to improve the speech recognition abilities of its Google Assistant Enabled Devices. Worse, Google discloses these recordings to subcontractors without Google Assistant users' knowledge or consent. . . .

Substantive Allegations

78. Google's unofficial motto always has been "don't be evil." Google was founded in 1998 by Larry Page and Sergey Brin as a search-engine

website. Today, Google achieves a significant portion of its profits by collecting as much information about consumers as possible, with the aim of supplying the consumers with targeted advertising. To support its advertising platform, Google has launched numerous products that enable Google to target personalized advertising to users.

79. One of these products is Google Assistant. Google Assistant is a computer program developed by Google that is pre-installed on or can be downloaded onto Google Assistant Enabled Devices. Google Assistant is a valuable commodity which allows Google to compete with other virtual assistants such as Siri (Apple) and Alexa (Amazon). Its value is apparent in the cost of Google Home products . . . .

80. Google Assistant is intended to provide users with easy access to information available on the internet and/or control over other internet-connected devices using their voice. Accordingly, Google Assistant Enabled Devices are equipped with sensitive microphones that can pick up sound through much of a user's home. To facilitate the interaction between Google Assistant and users, Google Assistant listens for two sets of "hot words"—"Hey Google" and "Ok Google." These phrases indicate the start of a user command.

81. Google Assistant Enabled Devices listen for these hot words by recording and analyzing short snippets of audio from their surroundings. This audio is stored locally in the Google Assistant Enabled Device's random-access memory ("RAM"). Audio stored in a Google Assistant Enabled Device's RAM is continuously overwritten as new audio is recorded and analyzed until a hot word is uttered or the device is manually activated.

2. *Human Rights and Right to Privacy, Informational Privacy, and Data Protection*

The right to privacy has been expanded in the realm of international human rights law, where it is seen as a core right to all peoples of the world. The reasons for adopting privacy as a human right can be seen in the following preambles, arising as part of the inherent dignity of human life and freedom from fear and tyranny.

a. UN Universal Declaration of Human Rights, Article 12

UN Universal Declaration of Human Rights

Article 12

No one shall be subjected to arbitrary interference with his privacy, family, home or correspondence, nor to attacks upon his honour and reputation.

Everyone has the right to the protection of the law against such interference or attacks.

b. European Convention on Human Rights, Articles 8 and 10

European Convention on Human Rights

Article 8. Right to Respect for Private and Family Life

1. Everyone has the right to respect for his private and family life, his home and his correspondence.

2. There shall be no interference by a public authority with the exercise of this right except such as is in accordance with the law and is necessary in a democratic society in the interests of national security, public safety or the economic well-being of the country, for the prevention of disorder or crime, for the protection of health or morals, or for the protection of the rights and freedoms of others.

European Convention on Human Rights

Article 10. Freedom of Expression

1. Everyone has the right to freedom of expression. This right shall include freedom to hold opinions and to receive and impart information and ideas without interference by public authority and regardless of frontiers. This Article shall not prevent States from requiring the licensing of broadcasting, television or cinema enterprises.

2. The exercise of these freedoms, since it carries with it duties and responsibilities, may be subject to such formalities, conditions, restrictions or penalties as are prescribed by law and are necessary in a democratic society, in the interests of national security, territorial integrity or public safety, for the prevention of disorder or crime, for the protection of health or morals, for the protection of the reputation or rights of others, for preventing the disclosure of information received in confidence, or for maintaining the authority and impartiality of the judiciary.

c. European Charter of Fundamental Rights, Articles 7 and 8

European Charter of Fundamental Rights

Article 7. Respect for Private and Family Life

Everyone has the right to respect for his or her private and family life, home and communications.

European Charter of Fundamental Rights

Article 8. Protection of Personal Data

1. Everyone has the right to the protection of personal data concerning him or her.

2. Such data must be processed fairly for specified purposes and on the basis of the consent of the person concerned or some other legitimate basis laid down by law. Everyone has the right of access to data which has been collected concerning him or her, and the right to have it rectified.

3. Compliance with these rules shall be subject to control by an independent authority.

3. Protecting Data Privacy as a Fundamental Right in AI Systems

How privacy protections as articulated in Articles 7 and 8 of the EU Charter of Fundamental Rights will be applied to AI use cases remains a fairly open question. It is instructive to look to a decision by the Court of Justice of the European Union (CJEU) that was decided in June 2022, *League of Human Rights v. Council of Ministers*, also referred to as the PNR (Passenger Name Record) case. The flight data of passengers can be processed for terrorist screening, immigration enforcement, law enforcement investigations, and for other security purposes. In addition to the passenger's name, address, and other contact information, PNR data can also include: itinerary, ticket and seat information, travel agent, and payment information.[5] EU member states are required to establish Passenger Information Units (PIUs) to process PNR data.[6] The CJEU examined the PNR Directive's provisions for PNR data processing and whether the authorities for processing the data by member states were compatible with the EU Charter of Fundamental Rights.

EU member states had passed laws that transposed some of the provisions of the PNR Directive. The decision of the CJEU grappled with the explainability of potential algorithmic systems that were deployed to analyze and assess the PNR data for investigatory and national security purposes. The CJEU was particularly concerned with potential discrimination of the algorithmic systems, the black box concerns of self-learning algorithms, and the potential of denying the right to an effective remedy to those impacted by the systems. The excerpt below from this case demonstrates the CJEU's struggle to square the data privacy protections of the EU Charter of Fundamental Rights with the AI systems that could be generated from the PNR data gathered as a result of the PNR Directive.

---

5. *Passenger Data, Passenger Name Record*, EUROPEAN COMM'N.
6. *Id.*

a. League of Human Rights v. Council of Ministers [PNR Case]

League of Human Rights v. Council of Ministers [PNR Case]
[Ligue des Droits Humains ASBL v Conseil des Ministres]

Court of Justice of the European Union Judgment of the Court
(Grand Chamber) of 21 June 2022
Case No. C-817/19

LENAERTS, President[;] ARABADJIEV, RODIN, JARUKAITIS and JÄÄSKINEN, Presidents of Chambers[;] VON DANWITZ (Rapporteur) [;] SAFJAN, BILTGEN, XUEREB, PIÇARRA, ROSSI, KUMIN and WAHL, Judges[;] Advocate General: PITRUZZELLA[;] Registrar: KRAUSENBÖCK, Administrator[.]

JUDGEMENT

II. The Dispute in the Main Proceedings and the Questions Referred for a Preliminary Ruling

[On July 24, 2017, the League of Human Rights] brought an action before the Cour constitutionnelle (Constitutional Court, Belgium) seeking annulment in full or in part of the Law of 25 December 2016 [Processing of Passenger Data Law]. . . .

III. Consideration of the Questions Referred

106. [T]he Court has already held that, since automated analyses of PNR data are carried out on the basis of unverified personal data and are based on pre-determined models and criteria, they necessarily present some margin of error . . . [A] review of the PNR Directive [revealed] that the number of positive matches from automated processing . . . which prove to be incorrect following individual review by non-automated means is fairly substantial. . . . Those processing operations thus lead to a careful analysis of the PNR data relating to the said persons. . . .

111. In the light of all of the foregoing, it is appropriate to find that the PNR Directive entails undeniably serious interferences with the rights guaranteed in Articles 7 and 8 of the [EU] Charter [of Fundamental Rights], in so far, inter alia, as it seeks to introduce a surveillance regime that is continuous, untargeted and systematic, including the automated assessment of the personal data of everyone using air transport services. . . .

117. In order to satisfy the proportionality requirement, the legislation in question entailing the interference must lay down clear and precise rules governing the scope and application of the measures provided for and imposing minimum safeguards, so that the persons whose data have been transferred have sufficient guarantees to protect effectively their personal data against the risk of abuse. It must, in particular, indicate in what circumstances and under which conditions a measure providing for the processing of such data may be adopted, thereby ensuring that the interference is limited to what is strictly necessary. The need for such safeguards is all the greater where personal data are subject to automated processing). . . .

121. . . . [T]he objectives thereof [of the PNR Directive] are to ensure the internal security of the European Union and thus protect the life and safety of persons, while creating a legal framework that guarantees a high level of protection of passengers' fundamental rights, in particular the right to the respect for private life and that of the protection of personal data, where PNR data are processed by the competent authorities.

122. . . . [T]he PNR Directive provides that PNR data collected in accordance with that directive may be subject to the processing operations [are] only for the purposes of preventing, detecting, investigating and prosecuting terrorist offences and serious crime. Those purposes undoubtedly constitute objectives of general interest of the European Union that are capable of justifying even serious interferences with the fundamental rights enshrined in Articles 7 and 8 of the [EU] Charter [of Fundamental Rights]. . . .

123. As to the whether the system established by the PNR Directive is appropriate for the purpose of attaining the objectives pursued, it should be noted that while the possibility of 'false negatives' and the fairly substantial number of 'false positives' resulting, as noted in paragraph 106 above, from automated processing . . . are liable to limit the appropriateness of that system, they are not capable, however, of rendering the said system inappropriate for the purpose of contributing to the attainment of the objective of combating terrorist offences and serious crime. . . . [A]utomated processing carried out under the said directive have indeed already made it possible to identify air passengers presenting a risk in the context of the fight against terrorist offences and serious crime.

124. In addition, having regard to the margin of error inherent in the automated processing of PNR data and, in particular, the fairly substantial number of 'false positives', the appropriateness of the system established by the PNR Directive essentially depends on the proper functioning of the subsequent verification of the results obtained under those processing operations, by non-automated means, which, pursuant to that directive, is task for the PIU. The provisions laid down to that effect by the said directive thus contribute to the attainment of those objectives. . . .

148. Lastly, it is important also to bear in mind that, although, in accordance with the principle of proportionality, the objective of combating serious crime is capable of justifying the serious interference with the fundamental rights guaranteed in Articles 7 and 8 of the [EU] Charter [of Fundamental Rights] which the PNR Directive entails, the same is not true of the objective of combating criminality in general, since the latter objective may justify solely non-serious interferences. . . . Thus, that directive must ensure, by means of clear and precise rules, that the application of the system established by the said directive is limited to offences amounting to serious crime and thereby excludes those amounting to ordinary crime. . . .

178. As recalled in paragraph 106 above, automated processing necessarily presents a fairly substantial margin of error, since it is carried out on the basis of unverified personal data and is based on pre-determined criteria.

179. In those circumstances . . . to strengthen the protection of fundamental rights in the light, inter alia, of scientific and technological developments, it must be ensured . . . no decision that produces an adverse legal effect on a person or significantly affects a person may be taken by the competent authorities only by reason of the automated processing of PNR data. Moreover, . . . the PIU itself may transfer PNR data to those authorities only after individual review by non-automated means. Lastly, in addition to those verifications which the PIU and the competent authorities are to carry out themselves, the lawfulness of all automated processing must be open to review by the data protection officer and the national supervisory authority . . . as well as by the national courts in the context of the judicial redress[.] . . .

183. . . . [T]he PNR Directive . . . does not expressly indicate the nature of the data that those [PNR] databases may contain or their relationship to those objectives nor does it mention whether PNR data must be compared exclusively against databases managed by public authorities or whether they may also be compared against databases managed by private individuals.

184. In those circumstances . . . the PNR Directive could, prima facie, lend itself to an interpretation according to which PNR data may be used as mere search criteria for the purposes of conducting analyses using various databases, including databases managed and exploited by the security and intelligence agencies of Member States in order to pursue objectives other than those referred to in that directive, and that those analyses may take the form of 'data mining'. The fact that such analyses can be conducted and PNR data compared to such databases may give rise in the minds of passengers of carriage by air to the feeling that their private life is under a form of surveillance. Thus, while the advance assessment provided for in that provision relies on a relatively limited set of PNR data, such an interpretation . . . cannot be adopted, since it would lead to a disproportionate use of those data providing the means of establishing a detailed profile of the individuals concerned solely because they intend to travel by air.

185. Therefore, . . . [the] PNR Directive must be interpreted in such a way as to ensure full respect for the fundamental rights enshrined in Articles 7 and 8 of the [EU] Charter [of Fundamental Rights]. . . .

188. Accordingly, . . . the PNR Directive must, in the light of those fundamental rights, be interpreted as meaning that the latter databases are the only databases against which the PIU may compare PNR data.

189. . . . [Under] the PNR Directive, advance assessment against pre-determined criteria must . . . be carried out in a non-discriminatory manner, those criteria must be targeted, proportionate and specific, and must be set and regularly reviewed by the PIUs in cooperation with the competent authorities . . . .

193. . . . [T]he PNR Directive provides that the PIU may also process PNR data against pre-determined criteria. . . . [T]he advance assessment and, accordingly, the processing of PNR data against pre-determined

criteria is intended, in essence, to identify persons who may be involved in a terrorist offence or serious crime.

194. As regards the criteria that the PIU may use to that end . . . those must be 'pre-determined' criteria. . . . **[T]hat requirement precludes the use of artificial intelligence technology in self-learning systems ('machine learning')**, capable of modifying without human intervention or review the assessment process and, in particular, the assessment criteria on which the result of the application of that process is based as well as the weighting of those criteria. [Emphasis added].

195. It is important to add that use of such technology would be liable to render redundant the individual review of positive matches and monitoring of lawfulness required by the provisions of the PNR Directive. . . . **[G]iven the opacity which characterises the way in which artificial intelligence technology works, it might be impossible to understand the reason why a given program arrived at a positive match**. In those circumstances, use of such technology may deprive the data subjects also of their right to an effective judicial remedy . . . . [Emphasis added].

196. . . . [A]ny advance assessment against pre-determined criteria is to be carried out in a non-discriminatory manner and . . . those criteria are in no circumstances to be based on a person's race or ethnic origin, political opinions, religion or philosophical beliefs, trade union membership, health, sexual life or sexual orientation.

197. Thus Member States cannot use, as pre-determined criteria, criteria that are based on the characteristics referred to in the preceding paragraph and use of which may result in discrimination. . . . [P]re-determined criteria must be defined in such a way that, while worded in a neutral fashion, their application does not place persons having the protected characteristics at a particular disadvantage.

198. . . . [T]he creation and application of assessment criteria should be limited to terrorist offences and serious crime 'for which the use of such criteria is relevant'.

199. In order to target in that way the persons thus referred to and given the risk of discrimination that criteria based on the characteristics . . . the PIU and the competent authorities cannot, generally, rely on those characteristics. By contrast . . . they can inter alia take into consideration specific features in the factual conduct of persons when preparing and engaging in air travel which, following the findings of and experience acquired by the competent authorities, might suggest that the persons acting in that way may be involved in terrorist offences or serious crime.

200. In that context, . . . pre-determined criteria must be defined in such a way as to take into consideration both 'incriminating' as well as 'exonerating' circumstances, since that requirement may contribute to the reliability of those criteria and, in particular, ensure that they are proportionate. . . .

201. Lastly, . . . that pre-determined criteria must be reviewed regularly. In the context of that review, those criteria must be updated in accordance

with changes in the circumstances that justified their being taken into consideration for the purposes of advance assessment, thus making it possible, inter alia, to react to developments in the fight against terrorist offences and serious crime[.] . . . In particular, that review must take into account the experience acquired in the context of the application of pre-determined criteria, in order to reduce, as much as possible, the number of 'false positives' and, thereby, contribute to the strictly necessary nature of the application of those criteria. . . .

202. Compliance with the requirements . . . of the PNR Directive is required not only when determining and reviewing the databases as well as the pre-determined criteria provided for in that provision, but also, . . . throughout the process of processing those data.

203. As regards pre-determined criteria specifically, it . . . must define the assessment criteria in a manner which keeps to a minimum the number of innocent people wrongly identified by the system . . . [and] individually review any positive match by non-automated means in order to identify, as much as possible, any 'false positives.' . . .

204. Thus, the PIU must refrain from transferring the results of those automated processing operations to the competent authorities . . . [when] they do not, following that review, have anything capable of giving rise, to the requisite legal standard, to a reasonable suspicion of involvement in terrorist offences or serious crime in respect of the persons identified by means of those automated processing operations or when they have reason to believe that those processing operations lead to discriminatory results.

205. . . . Member States must lay down clear and precise rules capable of providing guidance and support for the analysis carried out by the agents in charge of the individual review, for the purposes of ensuring full respect for the fundamental rights enshrined in Articles 7, 8 and 21 of the [EU] Charter [of Fundamental Rights] and, in particular, guarantee a uniform administrative practice within the PIU that observes the principle of non-discrimination.

206. In particular, given the fairly substantial number of 'false positives' . . . Member States must ensure that the PIU establishes, in a clear and precise manner, objective review criteria enabling its agents to verify, on the one hand, whether and to what extent a positive match ('hit') concerns effectively an individual who may be involved in the terrorist offences or serious crime . . . and must, therefore, be subject to further examination by the competent authorities[;] . . . as well as, on the other hand, the non-discriminatory nature of automated processing operations under that directive and, in particular, the pre-determined criteria and databases used.

207. In that context, Member States are required to ensure that . . . the PIUs maintain documentation relating to all processing of PNR data carried out in connection with the advance assessment, including in the context of

the individual review by non-automated means, for the purpose of verifying its lawfulness and for the purpose of self-monitoring.

208. Next, the competent authorities . . . cannot take any decision that produces an adverse legal effect on a person or significantly affects a person only by reason of the automated processing of PNR data, which means, in connection with the advance assessment, that they must take into consideration and, where applicable, give preference to the result of the individual review conducted by non-automated means by the PIU over that obtained by automated processing. . . .

209. In that context, the competent authorities must ensure the lawfulness of the automated processing, in particular its non-discriminatory nature, as well as that of the individual review.

210. In particular, the competent authorities must ensure that the person concerned—without necessarily allowing that person, during the administrative procedure, to become aware of the pre-determined assessment criteria and programs applying those criteria—is able to understand how those criteria and those programs work, so that it is possible for that person to decide with full knowledge of the relevant facts whether or not to exercise his or her right to the judicial redress guaranteed[.] . . .

211. Lastly, in the context of redress . . . the court responsible for reviewing the legality of the decision adopted by the competent authorities as well as, except in the case of threats to State security, the persons concerned themselves must have had an opportunity to examine both all the grounds and the evidence on the basis of which the decision was taken . . . including the pre-determined assessment criteria and the operation of the programs applying those criteria.

212. Moreover, . . . is for the data protection officer and the national supervisory authority to ensure the monitoring of the lawfulness of the automated processing carried out by the PIU in connection with the advance assessment, monitoring which covers, inter alia, whether those operations are not discriminatory. While the first of those provisions states, to that end, that the data protection officer has access to all data processed by the PIU, that access must necessarily cover the pre-determined criteria and databases used by that unit in order to guarantee effectivenes and a high level of data protection that that officer must ensure in accordance with recital 37 of that directive. Similarly, the investigations, inspections and audits that the national supervisory authority conducts pursuant to the second of those provisions may also concern those pre-determined criteria and those databases.

213. It follows from all of the foregoing that the provisions of the PNR Directive governing the advance assessment of PNR data . . . lend themselves to an interpretation that is consistent with Articles 7, 8 and 21 of the [EU[Charter [of Fundamental Rights] and comes within the limits of what is strictly necessary. . . .

223. In particular, in order to ensure, in practice, that fundamental rights are fully observed in the system put in place by the PNR Directive, . . . it is essential that disclosure of PNR data for the purposes of

subsequent assessment be, as a general rule, except in the event of duly justified urgency, subject to a prior review carried out either by a court or by an independent administrative authority, and that the decision of that court or body be made following a reasoned request by the competent authorities submitted, inter alia, within the framework of procedures for the prevention, detection or prosecution of crime. . . .

224. In those circumstances, the requirement for prior review . . . of the PNR Directive, for requests for the disclosure of PNR data introduced after the expiry of a period of six months following the transfer of those data to the PIU must also apply, *mutatis mutandis*, where the request for disclosure is introduced before the expiry of that period.

225. Moreover, if . . . the PNR Directive does not expressly specify the requirements which the authority responsible for carrying out the prior review must satisfy, it is settled case-law that, in order to ensure that the interference with the fundamental rights guaranteed in Articles 7 and 8 of the [EU] Charter [of Fundamental Rights] which results from access to personal data is limited to what is strictly necessary, that authority must have all the powers and provide all the guarantees necessary in order to reconcile the various interests and rights at issue. As regards a criminal investigation in particular, it is a requirement of such a review that that authority must be able to strike a fair balance between, on the one hand, the interests relating to the needs of the investigation in the context of combating crime and, on the other, the fundamental rights to privacy and protection of personal data of the persons whose data are concerned by the access[.] . . .

246. Furthermore, . . . where disclosure of the full PNR data has been approved by 'another [competent] national authority', that the data protection officer of the PIU '[is] inform[ed] and [carries out] an *ex post* review', whereas this is not the case for approval by the judicial authority, is not such as to call that assessment into question. In accordance with well-established case-law, a subsequent review, such as that carried out by the data protection officer, does not enable the objective of a prior review, consisting in preventing the authorisation of access to the data in question that exceeds what is strictly necessary, to be met[.] . . .

258. The continued storage of the PNR data of all air passengers after the initial period of six months is not therefore limited to what is strictly necessary[.] . . .

B. CASE STUDIES OF INFORMATIONAL SELF-DETERMINATION AND AUTONOMY

1. NSA Disclosures of Whistleblower Edward Snowden

In 2013, Edward Snowden, a government contractor working at the National Security Agency (NSA), leaked classified documents exposing the existence of U.S. global surveillance programs. The leaks were unprecedented, exposing the NSA's nationwide surveillance of domestic communication and location data. Moreover, the NSA's affiliations with other intelligence and investigation agencies in the United States and with allied nations provided revelations of a global reach for its surveillance.

The exposure of this information raised critical concerns about how information was being shared in the EU, which is subject to more stringent data protection laws that require greater privacy protections to permit transfers.

Shortly after the revelations, Max Schrems, a privacy activist from the EU, filed a complaint before the Irish Data Protection Commission (DPC), seeking suspension of data transfers from Facebook Ireland. He alleged that Facebook funneled its EU data through Ireland due to lax data protection authorities and failed to follow European data privacy laws.

His case, referred to as *Schrems I*, would eventually be elevated to the Court of Justice of the European Union (CJEU) to resolve whether the *U.S.-EU Safe Harbor Agreement* complied with European data privacy laws. The *Agreement* enabled U.S. companies to self-certify that they followed the privacy principles and European data protection laws. In *Schrems I*, the Court invalidated the *Agreement*, which had governed data transfers between the United States and the EU.

a. Maximillian Schrems v. Data Protection Commissioner

Maximillian Schrems v. Data Protection Commissioner

Court of Justice of the European Union Judgment
of the Court (Grand Chamber) of October 6, 2015
Case No. C-362/14

SKOURIS, President[;] LENAERTS, Vice President[;] TIZZANO, SILVA DE LAPUERTA, and VON DANWITZ (Rapporteur)[;] RODIN and JÜRIMÄE, Presidents of Chambers[;] ROSAS, JUHÁSZ, BORG BARTHET, MALENOVSKÝ, ŠVÁBY, BERGER, BILTGEN and LYCOURGOS, Judges[;] Advocate General: BOT[;] Registrar: HEWLETT, Principal Administrator[.]

JUDGMENT

THE DISPUTE IN THE MAIN PROCEEDINGS AND THE QUESTIONS REFERRED FOR A PRELIMINARY RULING

26 Mr Schrems, an Austrian national residing in Austria, has been a user of the Facebook social network ("Facebook") since 2008.

27 Any person residing in the European Union who wishes to use Facebook is required to conclude, at the time of his registration, a contract with Facebook Ireland, a subsidiary of Facebook Inc. which is itself established in the United States. Some or all of the personal data of Facebook Ireland's users who reside in the European Union is transferred to servers belonging to Facebook Inc. that are located in the United States, where it undergoes processing.

28 On 25 June 2013 Mr Schrems made a complaint to the Commissioner by which he in essence asked the latter to exercise his statutory powers by prohibiting Facebook Ireland from transferring his personal data to the United States. He contended in his complaint that the law and practice in force in that country did not ensure adequate protection of the personal data held in its territory against the surveillance activities that were engaged in there by the public authorities. Mr Schrems referred in this regard to the revelations made by Edward Snowden concerning the activities of the United States intelligence services, in particular those of the National Security Agency ("the NSA").

29 Since the Commissioner took the view that he was not required to investigate the matters raised by Mr Schrems in the complaint, he rejected it as unfounded. The Commissioner considered that there was no evidence that Mr Schrems' personal data had been accessed by the NSA. He added that the allegations raised by Mr Schrems in his complaint could not be profitably put forward since . . . the Commission had found . . . that the United States ensured an adequate level of protection.

30 Mr Schrems brought an action before the High Court challenging the decision at issue in the main proceedings. After considering the evidence adduced by the parties to the main proceedings, the High Court found that the electronic surveillance and interception of personal data transferred from the European Union to the United States serve necessary and indispensable objectives in the public interest. However, it added that the revelations made by Edward Snowden had demonstrated a "significant over-reach" on the part of the NSA and other federal agencies.

31 According to the High Court, Union citizens have no effective right to be heard. Oversight of the intelligence services' actions is carried out within the framework of an *ex parte* and secret procedure. Once the personal data has been transferred to the United States, it is capable of being accessed by the NSA and other federal agencies, such as the Federal Bureau of Investigation (FBI), in the course of the indiscriminate surveillance and interception carried out by them on a large scale.

32 The High Court stated that Irish law precludes the transfer of personal data outside national territory save where the third country ensures an adequate level of protection for privacy and fundamental rights and freedoms. The importance of the rights to privacy and to inviolability of the dwelling, which are guaranteed by the Irish Constitution, requires that any interference with those rights be proportionate and in accordance with the law.

33 The High Court held that the mass and undifferentiated accessing of personal data is clearly contrary to the principle of proportionality and the fundamental values protected by the Irish Constitution. In order for interception of electronic communications to be regarded as consistent with the Irish Constitution, it would be necessary to demonstrate that the interception is targeted, that the surveillance of certain persons or groups of persons is objectively justified in the interests of national security or

the suppression of crime and that there are appropriate and verifiable safeguards. Thus, according to the High Court, if the main proceedings were to be disposed of on the basis of Irish law alone, it would then have to be found that, given the existence of a serious doubt as to whether the United States ensures an adequate level of protection of personal data, the Commissioner should have proceeded to investigate the matters raised by Mr Schrems in his complaint and that the Commissioner was wrong in rejecting the complaint.

34 However, the High Court considers that this case concerns the implementation of EU law as referred to in Article 51 of the Charter and that the legality of the decision at issue in the main proceedings must therefore be assessed in the light of EU law. . . . The right to respect for private life, guaranteed by Article 7 of the Charter and by the core values common to the traditions of the Member States, would be rendered meaningless if the State authorities were authorised to access electronic communications on a casual and generalised basis without any objective justification based on considerations of national security or the prevention of crime that are specific to the individual concerned and without those practices being accompanied by appropriate and verifiable safeguards. . . .

b. Klayman v. Obama (Vacated and Remanded)

The Snowden disclosures also prompted litigation against the U.S. government. In one suit against government defendants including President Barack Obama, Attorney General Eric Holder, and a number of technology companies including Yahoo!, Facebook, Microsoft, and Google, the plaintiffs claimed that the U.S. government's surveillance and coordination with telecommunications and Internet companies violated U.S. statutes and constitutional rights. Although the plaintiffs secured a preliminary injunction in the district court, the D.C. Circuit Court of Appeals overturned that injunction based on a failure to show a likelihood of jurisdiction.

Klayman v. Obama (Vacated and Remanded)

United States District Court for the District of Columbia
957 F. Supp. 2d 1 (2013)

MEMORANDUM OPINION

Leon, United States District Judge.

BACKGROUND

On June 5, 2013, the British newspaper *The Guardian* reported the first of several "leaks" of classified material from Edward Snowden, a former NSA contract employee, which have revealed—and continue to reveal—multiple U.S. government intelligence collection and surveillance programs.[7] That initial media report disclosed a FISC order dated April 25, 2013, compelling Verizon Business Network Services to produce to the NSA on "an ongoing daily basis . . . all call detail records or 'telephony metadata' created by Verizon for communications (i) between the United States and abroad; or (ii) wholly within the United States, including local telephone calls."[8] According to the news article, this order "show[ed] . . . that under the Obama administration the communication records of millions of US citizens are being collected indiscriminately and in bulk—regardless of whether they are suspected of any wrongdoing."[9] In response to this disclosure, the Government confirmed the authenticity of the April 25, 2013 FISC Order, and, in this litigation and in certain public statements, acknowledged the existence of a "program" under which "the FBI obtains orders from the FISC pursuant to Section 215 [of the USA PATRIOT Act] directing certain telecommunications service providers to produce to the NSA on a daily basis electronic copies of 'call detail records.'" Follow-on media reports revealed other Government surveillance programs, including the Government's collection of internet data pursuant to a program called "PRISM."[10]

I. STATUTORY BACKGROUND

A. FISA and Section 215 of the USA PATRIOT Act (50 U.S.C. § 1861)

In 1978, Congress enacted the Foreign Intelligence Surveillance Act, 50 U.S.C. §§ 1801 *et seq.* ("FISA"), "to authorize and regulate certain governmental electronic surveillance of communications for foreign intelligence purposes."[11] Against the backdrop of findings by the Senate Select Committee to Study Government Operations with Respect to Intelligence Activities (the "Church Committee") that the executive branch had, for decades, engaged in warrantless domestic intelligence-gathering activities that had illegally infringed the Fourth Amendment rights of American citizens,

7. [In text in original] *See* Glenn Greenwald, NSA collecting phone records of millions of Verizon customers daily, GUARDIAN (London), June 5, 2013.

8. [In text in original] Secondary Order, *In re Application of the [FBI] for an Order Requiring the Production of Tangible Things from Verizon Business Network Services, Inc. on Behalf of MCI Communication Services, Inc. d/b/a Verizon Business Services, No. BR 13–80* at 2 (FISC Apr. 25, 2013) (attached as Ex. F to Gilligan Decl.) [Dkt. # 25–7] ("Apr. 25, 2013 Secondary Order").

9. [In text in original] Greenwald, *supra.*

10. [In text in original] *See* Glenn Greenwald & Ewen MacAskill, NSA Prism program taps in to user data of Apple, Google and others, GUARDIAN (London), June 6, 2013.

11. [In text in original] Clapper v. Amnesty Int'l USA, ___ U.S. ___, 133 S. Ct. 1138, 1143, 185 L.Ed.2d 264 (2013).

Congress passed FISA "in large measure [as] a response to the revelations that warrantless electronic surveillance in the name of national security has been seriously abused."[12] In the view of the Senate Judiciary Committee, the act went "a long way in striking a fair and just balance between protection of national security and protection of personal liberties."[13]

FISA created a procedure for the Government to obtain ex parte judicial orders authorizing domestic electronic surveillance upon a showing that, *inter alia*, the target of the surveillance was a foreign power or an agent of a foreign power.[14] In enacting FISA, Congress also created two new Article III courts—the Foreign Intelligence Surveillance Court ("FISC"), composed of eleven U.S. district judges, "which shall have jurisdiction to hear applications for and grant orders approving" such surveillance, § 1803(a)(1), and the FISC Court of Review, composed of three U.S. district or court of appeals judges, "which shall have jurisdiction to review the denial of any application made under [FISA]," § 1803(b).[15]

In addition to authorizing wiretaps, §§ 1801-1812, FISA was subsequently amended to add provisions enabling the Government to obtain ex parte orders authorizing physical searches, §§ 1821-1829, as well as pen registers and trap-and-trace devices. . . . In 1998, Congress added a "business records" provision to FISA.[16] Under that provision, the FBI was permitted to apply for an ex parte order authorizing specified entities, such as common carriers, to release to the FBI copies of business records upon a showing in the FBI's application that "there are specific and articulable facts giving

---

12. [In text in original] S.Rep. No. 95-604, at 7.

13. [In text in original] *Id.* at 7.

14. [In text in original] 50 U.S.C. §§ 1804(a)(3), 1805(a)(2).

15. [Fn. 13 in original] The eleven U.S. district judges are appointed by the Chief Justice of the United States to serve on the FISC for a term of seven years each. 50 U.S.C. § 1803(a)(1), (d). They are drawn from at least seven of the twelve judicial circuits in the United States, and at least three of the judges must reside within twenty miles of the District of Columbia. § 1803(a)(1). For these eleven district judges who comprise the FISC at any one time, their service on the FISC is *in addition to*, not in lieu of, their normal judicial duties in the districts in which they have been appointed. *See* Theodore W. Ruger, *Chief Justice Rehquist's Appointments to the FISA Court: An Empirical Perspective*, 101 NW. U.L. Rev. 239, 244 (2007) ("Service on the FISA Court is a part-time position. The judges rotate through the court periodically and maintain regular district court caseloads in their home courts."). Accordingly, service on the FISC is, at best, a part-time assignment that occupies a relatively small part of each judge's annual judicial duties. Further, as a result of the requirement that at least three judges reside within twenty miles of the nation's capital, a disproportionate number of the FISC judges are drawn from the district courts of the District of Columbia and the Eastern District of Virginia, *see id.* at 258 (Appendix) (listing Chief Justice Rehnquist's twenty-five appointments to the FISC, six of which came from the D.D.C. and E.D. Va.).

16. [In text in original] *See* 1999 Act § 602.

reason to believe that the person to whom the records pertain is a foreign power or an agent of a foreign power."[17]

Following the September 11, 2001 terrorist attacks, Congress passed the USA PATRIOT Act, which made changes to FISA and several other laws.[18] Section 215 of the PATRIOT Act replaced FISA's business-records provision with a more expansive "tangible things" provision. Codified at 50 U.S.C. § 1861, it authorizes the FBI to apply "for an order requiring the production of any tangible things (including books, records, papers, documents, and other items) for an investigation to obtain foreign intelligence information not concerning a United States person or to protect against international terrorism or clandestine intelligence activities."[19] While this provision originally required that the FBI's application "shall specify that the records concerned are sought for" such an investigation,[20] Congress amended the statute in 2006 to provide that the FBI's application must include "a statement of facts showing that there are reasonable grounds to believe that the tangible things sought are relevant to an authorized investigation . . . to obtain foreign intelligence information not concerning a United States person or to protect against international terrorism or clandestine intelligence activities."[21]

Section 1861 also imposes other requirements on the FBI when seeking to use this authority. For example, the investigation pursuant to which the request is made must be authorized and conducted under guidelines approved by the Attorney General under Executive Order No. 12,333 (or a successor thereto).[22] And the FBI's application must "enumerat[e] . . . minimization procedures adopted by the Attorney General . . . that are applicable to the retention and dissemination by the [FBI] of any tangible things to be made available to the [FBI] based on the order requested."[23] The statute defines "minimization procedures" as, in relevant part, "specific procedures that are reasonably designed in light of the purpose and technique of an order for the production of tangible things, to minimize the retention, and prohibit the dissemination, of nonpublicly available information concerning unconsenting [U.S.] persons consistent with the need of the [U.S.] to obtain, produce, and disseminate foreign intelligence information."[24] If the FISC judge finds that the FBI's application meets these requirements,

17. [In text in original] 50 U.S.C. § 1862(b)(2)(B) (2000).

18. [In text in original] Pub. L. No. 107-56, 115 Stat. 272 (2001).

19. [In text in original] § 1861(a)(1).

20. [In text in original] § 1861(b)(2) (Supp. I 2001).

21. [In text in original] § 1861(b)(2)(A); *see* USA PATRIOT Improvement and Reauthorization Act of 2005, Pub. L. No. 109-177, § 106(b), 120 Stat. 192 ("USA PATRIOT Improvement and Reauthorization Act").

22. [In text in original] 50 U.S.C. § 1861(a)(2)(A), (b)(2)(A).

23. [In text in original] § 1861(b)(2)(B).

24. [In text in original] § 1861(g)(2).

he "shall enter an ex parte order as requested, or as modified, approving the release of tangible things" (hereinafter, "production order").[25]

Under Section 1861's "use" provision, information that the FBI acquires through such a production order "concerning any [U.S.] person may be used and disclosed by Federal officers and employees without the consent of the [U.S.] person only in accordance with the minimization procedures adopted" by the Attorney General and approved by the FISC.[26] Meanwhile, recipients of Section 1861 production orders are obligated not to disclose the existence of the orders, with limited exceptions.[27]

B. Judicial Review by the FISC

While the recipient of a production order must keep it secret, Section 1861 does provide the recipient—but only the recipient—a right of judicial review of the order before the FISC pursuant to specific procedures. Prior to 2006, recipients of Section 1861 production orders had no express right to judicial review of those orders, but Congress added such a provision when it reauthorized the PATRIOT Act that year. . . .

Under Section 1861, "[a] person receiving a production order may challenge the legality of that order by filing a petition with the [petition review pool of FISC judges]."[28] The FISC review pool judge considering the petition may grant the petition "only if the judge finds that [the] order does not meet the requirements of [Section 1861] or is otherwise unlawful."[29] Once the FISC review pool judge rules on the petition, either the Government or the recipient of the production order may seek an en banc hearing before the full FISC,[30] or may appeal the decision by filing a petition for review with the FISC Court of Review[.][31] Finally, after the FISC Court of Review renders a written decision, either the Government or the recipient of the production order may then appeal this decision to the Supreme Court on petition for writ of certiorari.[32] A production order "not explicitly modified or set aside consistent with [Section 1861(f)] shall remain in full effect."[33]

Consistent with other confidentiality provisions of FISA, Section 1861 provides that "[a]ll petitions under this subsection shall be filed under

---

25. [In text in original] § 1861(c)(1); *see also* § 1861(f)(1)(A) ("the term 'production order' means an order to produce any tangible thing under this section").
26. [In text in original] § 1861(h).
27. [In text in original] § 1861(d)(1).
28. [In text in original] 50 U.S.C. § 1861(f)(2)(A)(i); *see* § 1803(e)(1).
29. [In text in original] § 1861(f)(2)(B).
30. [In text in original] § 1803(a)(2)(A),
31. [In text in original] § 1861(f)(3).
32. [In text in original] §§ 1861(f)(3), 1803(b).
33. [In text in original] § 1861(f)(2)(D).

seal,"[34] and the "record of proceedings . . . shall be maintained under security measures established by the Chief Justice of the United States, in consultation with the Attorney General and the Director of National Intelligence[.]"[35]

II. COLLECTION OF BULK TELEPHONY METADATA PURSUANT TO SECTION 1861

. . .

In broad overview, the Government has developed a "counterterrorism program" under Section 1861 in which it collect[s], compiles, retains, and analyzes certain telephone records, which it characterizes as "business records" created by certain telecommunications companies (the "Bulk Telephony Metadata Program"). The records collected under this program consist of "metadata," such as information about what phone numbers were used to make and receive calls, when the calls took place, and how long the calls lasted. . . . According to the representations made by the Government, the metadata records collected under the program do not include any information about the content of those calls, or the names, addresses, or financial information of any party to the calls. Through targeted computerized searches of those metadata records, the NSA tries to discern connections between terrorist organizations and previously unknown terrorist operatives located in the United States.

The Government has conducted the Bulk Telephony Metadata Program for more than seven years. Beginning in May 2006 and continuing through the present, the FBI has obtained production orders from the FISC under Section 1861 directing certain telecommunications companies to produce, on an ongoing daily basis, these telephony metadata records, which the companies create and maintain as part of their business of providing telecommunications services to customers[.] The NSA then consolidates the metadata records provided by different telecommunications companies into one database, and under the FISC's orders, the NSA may retain the records for up to five years[.]According to Government officials, this aggregation of records into a single database creates "an historical repository that permits retrospective analysis," enabling NSA analysts to draw connections, across telecommunications service providers, between numbers reasonably suspected to be associated with terrorist activity and with other, unknown numbers.

The FISC orders governing the Bulk Telephony Metadata Program specifically provide that the metadata records may be accessed only for counterterrorism purposes (and technical database maintenance). Specifically, NSA intelligence analysts, *without seeking the approval of a judicial officer*, may

34. [In text in original] § 1861(f)(5).

35. [In text in original] § 1861(f)(4). *See also* § 1803(c).

access the records to obtain foreign intelligence information only through "queries" of the records performed using "identifiers," such as telephone numbers, associated with terrorist activity.[36] An "identifier" (i.e., selection term, or search term) used to start a query of the database is called a "seed," and "seeds" must be approved by one of twenty-two designated officials in the NSA's Homeland Security Analysis Center or other parts of the NSA's Signals Intelligence Directorate. Such approval may be given only upon a determination by one of those designated officials that there exist facts giving rise to a "reasonable, articulable suspicion" ("RAS") that the selection term to be queried is associated with one or more of the specified foreign terrorist organizations approved for targeting by the FISC. In 2012, for example, fewer than 300 unique identifiers met this RAS standard and were used as "seeds" to query the metadata, but "the number of unique identifiers has varied over the years."

When an NSA intelligence analyst runs a query using a "seed," the minimization procedures provide that query results are limited to records of communications within three "hops" from the seed. The query results thus will include only identifiers and their associated metadata having a direct contact with the seed (the first "hop"), identifiers and associated metadata having a direct contact with first "hop" identifiers (the second "hop"), and identifiers and associated metadata having a direct contact with second "hop" identifiers (the third "hop"). In plain English, this means that if a search starts with telephone number (123) 456-7890 as the "seed," the first hop will include all the phone numbers that (123) 456-7890 has called or received calls from in the last five years (say, 100 numbers), the second hop will include all the phone numbers that each of those 100 numbers has called or received calls from in the last five years (say, 100 numbers for each one of the 100 "first hop" numbers, or 10,000 total), and the third hop will include all the phone numbers that each of *those* 10,000 numbers has called or received calls from in the last five years (say, 100 numbers for each one of the 10,000 "second hop" numbers, or 1,000,000 total). The actual number of telephone numbers and their associated metadata captured in any given query varies, of course, but in the absence of any specific representations from the Government about typical query results, it is likely that the quantity of phone numbers captured in any given query would be very large.

---

36. [Fn. 19 in original] In her declaration, Teresa H. Shea, Director of the Signals Intelligence Directorate at the NSA, states that "queries," or "term searches," of the metadata database are conducted "using metadata 'identifiers,' *e.g.*, *telephone numbers*, that are associated with a foreign terrorist organization." Shea Decl. ¶ 19 (emphasis added). If a telephone number is only an *example* of an identifier that may be used as a search term, it is not clear what other "identifiers" may be used to query the database, and the Government has not elaborated. *See, e.g.*, Oct. 11, 2013 Primary Order at 5 n.4, 7-10 (redacting text that appears to discuss "selection terms").

Once a query is conducted and it returns a universe of responsive records (i.e., a universe limited to records of communications within three hops from the seed), trained NSA analysts may then perform new searches and otherwise perform intelligence analysis *within* that universe of data without using RAS-approved search terms. According to the Government, following the "chains of communication"—which, for chains that cross different communications networks, is only possible if the metadata is aggregated—allows the analyst to discover information that may not be readily ascertainable through other, targeted intelligence-gathering techniques. For example, the query might reveal that a seed telephone number has been in contact with a previously unknown U.S. telephone number—i.e., on the first hop. And from there, "contact-chaining" out to the second and third hops to examine the contacts made by that telephone number may reveal a contact with other telephone numbers already known to the Government to be associated with a foreign terrorist organization. In short, the Bulk Telephony Metadata Program is meant to detect: (1) domestic U.S. phone numbers calling *outside* of the U.S. to foreign phone numbers associated with terrorist groups; (2) foreign phone numbers associated with terrorist groups calling *into* the U.S. to U.S. phone numbers; and (3) "possible terrorist-related communications" between U.S. phone numbers *inside* the U.S.

Since the program began in May 2006, the FISC has repeatedly approved applications under Section 1861 and issued orders directing telecommunications service providers to produce records in connection with the Bulk Telephony Metadata Program. Through October 2013, fifteen different FISC judges have issued thirty-five orders authorizing the program. Under those orders, the Government must periodically seek renewal of the authority to collect telephony records (typically every ninety days). The Government has nonetheless acknowledged, as it must, that failures to comply with the minimization procedures set forth in the orders have occurred. For instance, in January 2009, the Government reported to the FISC that the NSA had improperly used an "alert list" of identifiers to search the bulk telephony metadata, which was composed of identifiers that had not been approved under the RAS standard. . . . After reviewing the Government's reports on its noncompliance, Judge Reggie Walton of the FISC concluded that the NSA had engaged in "systematic noncompliance" with FISC-ordered minimization procedures over the preceding three years, since the inception of the Bulk Telephony Metadata Program, and had also repeatedly made misrepresentations and inaccurate statements about the program to the FISC judges. As a consequence, Judge Walton concluded that he had no confidence that the Government was doing its utmost to comply with the court's orders, and ordered the NSA to seek FISC approval on a *case-by-case basis* before conducting any further queries of the bulk telephony metadata collected pursuant to Section 1861 orders. This approval procedure remained in place from March 2009 to September 2009.

Notwithstanding this six-month "sanction" imposed by Judge Walton, the Government apparently has had further compliance problems relating to its collection programs in subsequent years. In October 2011, the Presiding Judge of the FISC, Judge John Bates, found that the Government had misrepresented the scope of its targeting of certain internet communications pursuant to 50 U.S.C. § 1881a (i.e., a different collection program than the Bulk Telephony Metadata Program at issue here). Referencing the 2009 compliance issue regarding the NSA's use of unauthorized identifiers to query the metadata in the Bulk Telephony Metadata Program, Judge Bates wrote: "the Court is troubled that the government's revelations regarding NSA's acquisition of Internet transactions mark the third instance in less than three years in which the government has disclosed a substantial misrepresentation regarding the scope of a major collection program." Both Judge Walton's and Judge Bates's opinions were only recently declassified by the Government in response to the Congressional and public reaction to the Snowden leaks.[37]

ANALYSIS

II. CONSTITUTIONAL CLAIMS

. . . .

B. Preliminary Injunction

When ruling on a motion for preliminary injunction, a court must consider "whether (1) the plaintiff has a substantial likelihood of success on the merits; (2) the plaintiff would suffer irreparable injury were an injunction not granted; (3) an injunction would substantially injure other interested parties; and (4) the grant of an injunction would further the public interest." . . .

1. Plaintiffs Have Shown a Substantial Likelihood of Success on the Merits

In addressing plaintiffs' likelihood of success on the merits of their constitutional claims, I will focus on their Fourth Amendment arguments, which I find to be the most likely to succeed. First, however, I must address plaintiffs' standing to challenge the various aspects of the Bulk Telephony Metadata Program. . . .

---

37. [Fn. 25 in original] *See* Office of the Dir. of Nat'l Intelligence, *DNI Declassifies Intelligence Community Documents Regarding Collection Under Section 702 of the Foreign Intelligence Surveillance Act (FISA)* (Aug. 21, 2013); Office of the Dir. of Nat'l Intelligence, *DNI Clapper Declassifies Intelligence Community Documents Regarding Collection Under Section 501 of the Foreign Intelligence Surveillance Act (FISA)* (Sept. 10, 2013).

b. Plaintiffs Are Likely to Succeed on the Merits of Their Fourth Amendment Claim

The Fourth Amendment protects "[t]he right of the people to be secure in their persons, houses, papers, and effects, against unreasonable searches and seizures."[38] That right "shall not be violated, and no Warrants shall issue, but upon probable cause, supported by Oath or affirmation, and particularly describing the place to be searched, and the persons or things to be seized."[39] A Fourth Amendment "search" occurs either when "the Government obtains information by physically intruding on a constitutionally protected area,"[40] or when "the government violates a subjective expectation of privacy that society recognizes as reasonable[.]"[41] This case obviously does not involve a physical intrusion, and plaintiffs do not claim otherwise.[42]

The threshold issue that I must address, then, is whether plaintiffs have a reasonable expectation of privacy that is violated when the Government indiscriminately collects their telephony metadata along with the metadata of hundreds of millions of other citizens without any particularized suspicion of wrongdoing, retains all of that metadata for five years, and then queries, analyzes, and investigates that data without prior judicial approval of the investigative targets. If they do—and a Fourth Amendment search has thus occurred—then the next step of the analysis will be to determine whether such a search is "reasonable."[43,44]

i. The Collection and Analysis of Telephony Metadata Constitutes a Search.

The analysis of this threshold issue of the expectation of privacy must start with the Supreme Court's landmark opinion in *Smith v. Maryland*,[45] which the FISC has said "squarely control[s]" when it comes to "[t]he production of telephone service provider metadata." . . . In Smith,

---

38. [In text in original] U.S. Const. amend IV.

39. [In text in original] *Id.*

40. [In text in original] United States v. Jones, ___ U.S. ___, 132 S. Ct. 945, 950 n.3, 181 L.Ed.2d 911 (2012).

41. [In text in original] Kyllo v. United States, 533 U.S. 27, 33, 121 S. Ct. 2038, 150 L.Ed.2d 94 (2001) (citing Katz v. United States, 389 U.S. 347, 361, 88 S. Ct. 507, 19 L.Ed.2d 576 (1967) (Harlan, J., concurring)).

42. [Fn. 41 in original] "A 'seizure' of property occurs when there is some meaningful interference with an individual's possessory interests in that property." United States v. Jacobsen, 466 U.S. 109, 113, 104 S. Ct. 1652, 80 L.Ed.2d 85 (1984). Plaintiffs have not offered any theory as to how they would have a possessory interest in their phone data held by Verizon, and I am aware of none.

43. [In text in original] *See id.* at 31, 121 S. Ct. 2038 (whether a search has occurred is an "antecedent question" to whether a search was reasonable).

44. [Fn. 42 in original] While it is true "[t]he judiciary risks error by elaborating too fully on the Fourth Amendment implications of emerging technology before its role in society has become clear," City of Ontario v. Quon, 560 U.S. 746, 130 S. Ct. 2619, 2629, 177 L.Ed.2d 216 (2010), phone call and text messaging technology is not "emerging," nor is "its role in society" unclear. I therefore believe that it is appropriate and necessary to elaborate on the Fourth Amendment implications of the NSA's metadata collection program.

45. [In text in original] 442 U.S. 735, 99 S. Ct. 2577, 61 L.Ed.2d (1979).

police were investigating a robbery victim's reports that she had received threatening and obscene phone calls from someone claiming to be the robber.[46] Without obtaining a warrant or court order, police installed a pen register, which revealed that a telephone in Smith's home had been used to call the victim on one occasion.[47] The Supreme Court held that Smith had no reasonable expectation of privacy in the numbers dialed from his phone because he voluntarily transmitted them to his phone company, and because it is generally known that phone companies keep such information in their business records.[48] The main thrust of the Government's argument here is that under *Smith,* no one has an expectation of privacy, let alone a reasonable one, in the telephony metadata that telecom companies hold as business records; therefore, the Bulk Telephony Metadata Program is not a search. I disagree.

The question before me is *not* the same question that the Supreme Court confronted in *Smith.* To say the least, "whether the installation and use of a pen register constitutes a 'search' within the meaning of the Fourth Amendment"[49]—under the circumstances addressed and contemplated in that case—is a far cry from the issue in this case.

Indeed, the question in this case can more properly be styled as follows: When do present-day circumstances—the evolutions in the Government's surveillance capabilities, citizens' phone habits, and the relationship between the NSA and telecom companies—become so thoroughly unlike those considered by the Supreme Court thirty-four years ago that a precedent like *Smith* simply does not apply? The answer, unfortunately for the Government, is now.

In *United States v. Jones,*[50] five justices found that law enforcement's use of a GPS device to track a vehicle's movements for nearly a month violated Jones's reasonable expectation of privacy.[51] Significantly, the justices did so *without* questioning the validity of the Court's earlier decision in *United States v. Knotts,*[52] that use of a tracking beeper does not constitute a search because "[a] person travelling in an automobile on public thoroughfares has no reasonable expectation of privacy in his movements from one place to another."[53,54] Instead, they emphasized the many significant ways in which

46. [In text in original] *Id.* at 737, 99 S. Ct. 2577.

47. [In text in original] *Id.*

48. [In text in original] *Id.* at 742-44, 99 S. Ct. 2577.

49. [In text in original] *Id.* at 736, 99 S. Ct. 2577.

50. [In text in original] ___ U.S. ___, 132 S. Ct. 945, 181 L.Ed.2d 911 (2012).

51. [In text in original] *See id.* at 955-56 (Sotomayor, J., concurring); *id.* at 964 (Alito, J., concurring).

52. [In text in original] 460 U.S. 276, 103 S. Ct. 1081, 75 L.Ed.2d 55 (1983).

53. [In text in original] *Id.* at 281, 103 S. Ct. 1081.

54. [Fn. 44 in original] In *Jones,* the Government relied heavily on *Knotts* (and *Smith*) as support for the argument that Jones had no expectation of privacy in his movements on the roads because he voluntarily disclosed them to the public. *See generally* Brief for Petitioner, United States v. Jones, 132 S. Ct. 945 (2012) (No. 10–1259), 2011 WL 3561881; Reply Brief for Petitioner, United States v. Jones, 132 S. Ct. 945 (2012) (No. 10–1259), 2011 WL 5094951. Five justices found that argument unconvincing.

the short-range, short-term tracking device used in *Knotts* differed from the constant month-long surveillance achieved with the GPS device attached to Jones's car.[55]

Just as the Court in *Knotts* did not address the kind of surveillance used to track Jones, the Court in *Smith* was not confronted with the NSA's Bulk Telephony Metadata Program.[56] Nor could the Court in 1979 have ever imagined how the citizens of 2013 would interact with their phones. For the many reasons discussed below, I am convinced that the surveillance program now before me is so different from a simple pen register that *Smith* is of little value in assessing whether the Bulk Telephony Metadata Program constitutes a Fourth Amendment search. To the contrary, for the following reasons, I believe that bulk telephony metadata collection and analysis almost certainly does violate a reasonable expectation of privacy.

First, the pen register in *Smith* was operational for only a matter of days between March 6, 1976 and March 19, 1976, and there is no indication from the Court's opinion that it expected the Government to retain those limited phone records once the case was over . . . . This short-term, forward-looking (as opposed to historical), and highly-limited data collection is what the Supreme Court was assessing in *Smith.* The NSA telephony metadata program, on the other hand, involves the creation and maintenance of a historical database containing *five years*' worth of data. And I might add, there is the very real prospect that the program will go on for as long as America is combatting terrorism, which realistically could be forever!

---

55. [In text in original] *See Jones*, 132 S. Ct. at 956 n.* (Sotomayor, J., concurring) (Knotts "does not foreclose the conclusion that GPS monitoring, in the absence of a physical intrusion, is a Fourth Amendment search"); *id.* at 964 (Alito, J., concurring) ("[R]elatively short-term monitoring of a person's movements on public streets accords with expectations of privacy that our society has recognized as reasonable. But the use of longer term GPS monitoring in investigations of most offenses impinges on expectations of privacy." (citation omitted)); *see also* United States v. Maynard, 615 F.3d 544, 557 (D.C. Cir. 2010), *aff'd sub nom.* Jones, ___ U.S. ___, 132 S. Ct. 945, 181 L.Ed.2d 911 ("*Knotts* held only that '[a] person traveling in an automobile on public thoroughfares has no reasonable expectation of privacy in his movements from one place to another,' not that such a person has no reasonable expectation of privacy in his movements whatsoever, world without end, as the Government would have it." (citation omitted; quoting *Knotts*, 460 U.S. at 281, 103 S. Ct. 1081)).

56. [Fn. 46 in original] True, the Court in *Knotts* explicitly "reserved the question whether 'different constitutional principles may be applicable' to 'dragnet-type law enforcement practices' of the type that GPS tracking made possible" in *Jones. Jones*, 132 S. Ct. at 952 n.6 (quoting *Knotts*, 460 U.S. at 284, 103 S. Ct. 1081); *see also id.* at 956, n.* (Sotomayor, J., concurring). That the Court in *Smith* did not explicitly hold open the question of whether an exponentially broader, high-tech, years-long bulk telephony metadata collection program would infringe on reasonable expectations of privacy does not mean that the Court's holding necessarily extends so far as to answer that novel question. The Supreme Court itself has recognized that prior Fourth Amendment precedents and doctrines do not always control in cases involving unique factual circumstances created by evolving technology. *See, e.g., Kyllo*, 533 U.S. at 34, 121 S. Ct. 2038 ("To withdraw protection of this minimum expectation [of privacy in the home] would be to permit police technology to erode the privacy guaranteed by the Fourth Amendment."). If this isn't such a case, then what is?

Second, the relationship between the police and the phone company in *Smith* is *nothing* compared to the relationship that has apparently evolved over the last seven years between the Government and telecom companies.[57] The Supreme Court itself has long-recognized a meaningful difference between cases in which a third party collects information and then turns it over to law enforcement . . . and cases in which the government and the third party create a formalized policy under which the service provider collects information for law enforcement purposes . . . with the latter raising Fourth Amendment concerns. In *Smith*, the Court considered a one-time, targeted request for data regarding an individual suspect in a criminal investigation,[58] which in no way resembles the daily, all-encompassing, indiscriminate dump of phone metadata that the NSA now receives as part of its Bulk Telephony Metadata Program. It's one thing to say that people expect phone companies to occasionally provide information to law enforcement; it is quite another to suggest that our citizens expect all phone companies to operate what is effectively a joint intelligence-gathering operation with the Government.[59]

Third, the almost-Orwellian technology that enables the Government to store and analyze the phone metadata of every telephone user in the United States is unlike anything that could have been conceived in 1979. In *Smith*, the Supreme Court was actually considering whether local police could collect one person's phone records for calls made after the pen register was installed and for the limited purpose of a small-scale investigation of harassing phone calls. . . . By comparison, the Government has at its disposal today the most advanced twenty-first century tools, allowing it to "store such records and efficiently mine them for information years into the future."[60] And these technologies are "cheap in comparison to conventional surveillance techniques and, by design, proceed[] surreptitiously," thereby

57. [In text in original] *Compare Smith*, 442 U.S. at 737, 99 S. Ct. 2577 ("[T]he telephone company, at police request, installed a pen register at its central offices to record the numbers dialed from the telephone at petitioner's home."), *with* Govt.'s Opp'n at 8-9 ("Under this program . . . certain telecommunications service providers [] produce to the NSA on a daily basis electronic copies of call detail records, or telephony metadata. . . . The FISC first authorized the program in May 2006, and since then has renewed the program thirty-five times. . . ." (citation and internal quotation marks omitted)).

58. [In text in original] [*S*]*ee Smith*, 442 U.S. at 737, 99 S. Ct. 2577.

59. [In text in original] *Cf.* U.S. Dep't of Justice v. Reporters Comm. for Freedom of the Press, 489 U.S. 749, 764, 109 S. Ct. 1468, 103 L.Ed.2d 774 (1989) ("Plainly there is a vast difference between the public records that might be found after a diligent search of [various third parties' records] and a computerized summary located in a single clearinghouse of information.").

60. [In text in original] *Jones*, 132 S. Ct. at 956 (Sotomayor, J., concurring).

"evad[ing] the ordinary checks that constrain abusive law enforcement practices: limited police . . . resources and community hostility."[61,62]

Finally, *and most importantly*, not only is the Government's ability to collect, store, and analyze phone data greater now than it was in 1979, but the nature and quantity of the information contained in people's telephony metadata is much greater, as well. According to the 1979 U.S. Census, in that year, 71,958,000 homes had telephones available, while 6,614,000 did not.[63] In December 2012, there were a whopping 326,475,248 mobile subscriber connections in the United States, of which approximately 304 million were for phones and twenty-two million were for computers, tablets, and modems. . . . It is now safe to assume that the vast majority of people reading this opinion have at least one cell phone within arm's reach (in addition to other mobile devices). . . . In fact, some undoubtedly will be reading this opinion *on their cell phones*.[64] Cell phones have also morphed into multi-purpose devices. They are now maps and music players.[65] They are cameras.[66] They are even lighters that people hold up at rock concerts.[67] They are ubiquitous as well. Count the phones at the bus stop, in a restaurant, or around the table at a work meeting or any given occasion. Thirty-four years ago, *none* of those phones would have been there.[68] Thirty-four years ago, city streets

---

61. [In text in original] *Id.*

62. [Fn. 48 in original] The unprecedented scope and technological sophistication of the NSA's program distinguish it not only from the *Smith* pen register, but also from metadata collections performed as part of routine criminal investigations. To be clear, this opinion is focusing only on the program before me and not any other law enforcement practices. Like the concurring justices in *Jones*, I cannot "identify with precision the point at which" bulk metadata collection becomes a search, but there is a substantial likelihood that the line was crossed under the circumstances presented in this case. *See Jones*, 132 S. Ct. at 964 (Alito, J., concurring).

63. [In text in original] U.S. DEP'T OF COMMERCE & U.S. DEP'T OF HOUS. & URBAN DEV., ANNUAL HOUSING SURVEY: 1979, at 4 (1981) (Table A-1: Characteristics of the Housing Inventory: 1979 and 1970).

64. [In text in original] Maeve Duggan, Cell Phone Activities 2013 (Sept. 19, 2013) (60% of cell phone owners use them to access internet).

65. [In text in original] *Id.* (49% of cell phone owners use their phones to get directions and 48% to listen to music).

66. [In text in original] Keith L. Alexander, *Camera phones become courthouse safety issue*, WASH. POST, Apr. 22, 2013, at B01.

67. [In text in original] Andy Rathbun, *Cool 2 Know—Cellphone virtuosos*, NEWSDAY, Apr. 20, 2005, at B02.

68. [Fn. 55 in original] Mobile Telephone, BRITANNICA.COM ("[A] Japanese system was the first cellular system to be deployed, in 1979."); Tom Farley, *Mobile telephone history*, TELEKTRONIKK, March/April 2005, at 28 ("An 88 cell system in the challenging cityscape of Tokyo began in December, 1979. . . . The first North American commercial system began in August, 1981 in Mexico City.").

were lined with pay phones. Thirty-four years ago, when people wanted to send "text messages," they wrote letters and attached postage stamps.[69]

[The court went on to find a likelihood that the government's searches were unreasonable, explaining: "Given the limited record before me at this point in the litigation—most notably, the utter lack of evidence that a terrorist attack has ever been prevented because searching the NSA database was faster than other investigative tactics—I have serious doubts about the efficacy of the metadata collection program as a means of conducting time-sensitive investigations in cases involving imminent threats of terrorism."]

CONCLUSION

This case is yet the latest chapter in the Judiciary's continuing challenge to balance the national security interests of the United States with the individual liberties of our citizens. The Government, in its understandable zeal to protect our homeland, has crafted a counterterrorism program with respect to telephone metadata that strikes the balance based in large part on a thirty-four year old Supreme Court precedent, the relevance of which has been eclipsed by technological advances and a cell phone-centric lifestyle heretofore inconceivable. In the months ahead, other Article III courts, no doubt, will wrestle to find the proper balance consistent with our constitutional system. But in the meantime, for all the above reasons, I will grant Larry Klayman's and Charles Strange's requests for an injunction and enter an order that (1) bars the Government from collecting, as part of the NSA's Bulk Telephony Metadata Program, any telephony metadata associated with their personal Verizon accounts and (2) requires the Government to destroy any such metadata in its possession that was collected through the bulk collection program.[70]

However, in light of the significant national security interests at stake in this case and the novelty of the constitutional issues, I will stay my order

69. [Fn. 56 in original] It is not clear from the pleadings whether "telephony metadata" and "comprehensive communications routing information" includes data relating to text messages. *See supra* note 16. If it does, then in 2012, the Government collected an additional *six billion* communications *each day* (69,635 *each second*). *See* Infographic—*Americans sent and received more than 69,000 texts every second in 2012,* CTIA.org (Nov. 25, 2013).

70. [Fn. 70 in original] Although it is true that granting plaintiffs the relief they request will force the Government to identify plaintiffs' phone numbers and metadata records, and then subject them to otherwise unnecessary individual scrutiny, *see* Shea Decl. ¶ 64, that is the only way to remedy the constitutional violations that plaintiffs are substantially likely to prove on the merits.

pending appeal.[71] In doing so, I hereby give the Government fair notice that should my ruling be upheld, this order will go into effect forthwith. Accordingly, I fully expect that during the appellate process, which will consume at least the next six months, the Government will take whatever steps necessary to prepare itself to comply with this order when, and if, it is upheld. Suffice it to say, requesting further time to comply with this order months from now will not be well received and could result in collateral sanctions.

2. *Cambridge Analytica Disclosures from Whistleblower Christopher Wylie*

The Facebook-Cambridge Analytica scandal of 2018 led to widespread concern over the methods deployed by Cambridge Analytica to target voters through psychographic profiling algorithms built on Facebook user data. The scandal ultimately led to a record-breaking $5 billion penalty imposed on Facebook by the Federal Trade Commission (FTC) in July 2019. The FTC enforcement action, however, has been criticized as failing to adequately address the privacy and other harms emanating from the revelation that approximately 87 million Facebook users' data had been released and exploited without their authorization.

The scandal broke on March 17, 2018, when Christopher Wylie stepped forward as a corporate whistleblower and in interviews with the *New York Times* and *The Observer*. Wylie, a Canadian data scientist, had served as the former Director of Research for Cambridge Analytica and SCL (Strategic Communication Laboratories) Group, the British parent company of Cambridge Analytica. Wylie explained that psychographic profiling enabled Cambridge Analytica to influence voters through the exploitation of social media data to create a "psychological warfare mindf*** tool."

Knowledge of the Cambridge Analytica scandal led one U.S. professor, David Carroll, to seek further information on how Cambridge Analytica might have affected him personally through AI-driven voter microtargeting. Carroll submitted a Subject Access Request (SAR) application to Cambridge Analytica, which had conducted operations in the United Kingdom before closing its operations in 2019.

The United Kingdom's *Data Protection Act of 2018* and the European Union's *General Data Protection Regulation* (*GDPR*) of 2018 both allow for

71. [Fn. 71 in original] *See, e.g.*, Doe v. Gonzales, 386 F. Supp. 2d 66, 83 (D.Conn.2005) ("The court finds that it is appropriate to grant a brief stay of a preliminary injunction in order to permit the Court of Appeals an opportunity to consider an application for a stay pending an expedited appeal."); Luevano v. Horner, No. 79-0271, 1988 WL 147603, at *8 (D.D.C. June 27, 1988) ("[T]he Court will enter the injunctive relief that has been requested by plaintiffs but will, *sua sponte*, stay the effect of that injunction pending the outcome of the appeal in [a related case]. In this way, the interests of justice will best be served.").

data access by citizens, sometimes referred to as data subject access requests (DSARs) or SARs.[72]

Below is an excerpt of the claim filed by David Carroll against Cambridge Analytica under Section 7 of the UK *Data Protection Act.*

a. David Carroll v. Cambridge Analytica et al. (Complaint)

David Carroll v. Cambridge Analytica et al. (Complaint)

UK High Court of Justice
March 16, 2018

COMPLAINT

SUMMARY

1. Professor David Carroll ("the Claimant"), applies for an order requiring the Defendants/Respondents ("the Defendants") to: [a] Comply fully with his subject access request made under s 7 Data Protection Act 1998 ("DPA")—that claim is brought under Part 8 CPR ("the s 7 DPA claim"); and/or [b] Provide him with pre-action disclosure pursuant to s 33(2) Senior Courts Act 1981 and Part 31.16 CPR ("the disclosure application").

2. The Defendants are commercial entities that create detailed profiles of individuals which they sell to advertisers, political campaigns and other entities, so as to assist them in targeting their efforts to influence the behaviour of profiled individuals. The subject of these detailed profiles is not informed that they have been generated or sold to third parties. For individuals to confirm whether they have been profiled, what information is held on them, and how it has been used, they need to rely on subject access requests under the DPA.

3. The Claimant made such a request. In response, the Defendants confirmed that the Claimant has, without his knowledge, been the subject of their profiling activities. The Claimant was provided with some of that information as to the data held on him although this appears to be materially incomplete.

4. In order to be provided with the full information he is entitled to under the DPA, the Claimant brings the present s 7 DPA claim. In pre-action correspondence, the Claimant has also sought further information which is essential for him to determine the legality of the Defendants' processing of his data. The Defendants have failed to provide this and the Claimant therefore also makes the disclosure application.

FACTS

The Parties

5. The Claimant is an Associate Professor of media design at the Parsons School of Design in New York, USA and has particular experience in

72. *See* Art. 15 *GDPR, Right of Access by the Data Subject*; Section 7 of the *Data Protection Act.*

the field of online behavioural advertising technologies. The Claimant's work encompasses research into how the digital media and marketing industry is able to track user behaviours and how companies can use technology to "re-identify" an individual from supposedly anonymous data.

6. The Defendants are UK-registered companies which, by their own description, engage in the business of "*behavioural microtargeting*"—the collating and/or creating and then selling of data profiles of individuals which are used for, *inter alia*, targeted advertising and political campaigning.

7. The personal data used to create such individual profiles consists of information relating to people's personality traits, political beliefs and other deeply held personal habits and decisions. The profiles prepared by Cambridge Analytica are said to use "*up to 5,000 data points on over 230 million American voters . . . [to] build your custom target audience, then use this crucial information to engage, persuade, and motivate them to act.*"[73] . . .

The Claimant's Subject Access Request [SAR] Under s 7 DPA ("the SAR")

10. On in or around 10 January 2017, Professor Carroll submitted the SAR to Cambridge Analytica ("the SAR"). In doing so, he was motivated by both academic and personal interest in ascertaining what data the Defendants held on him and how it was being processed. The SAR was submitted through the following website: . . . .

3. *FTC Enforcement as Case Study*

In the wake of the Cambridge Analytica-Facebook scandal, the FTC announced an investigation into the matter. As many experts recognize, this agency plays an outsized role in upholding data privacy protections in the United States. Yet, the FTC is unable to address many of the most serious concerns raised by the Cambridge Analytica-Facebook scandal. The FTC's Section 5 authority under the *FTC Act* is limited to addressing "unfair or deceptive acts or practices in or affecting commerce[.]"[74]

a. United States v. Facebook (FTC Settlement)

Shortly after the Cambridge Analytica-Facebook scandal broke, the FTC launched an investigation into Facebook's consumer data privacy policies and practices in March 2018. The investigation sought to uncover whether Facebook had violated a privacy consent agreement it had entered into with the FTC in 2011 to protect consumers against the

73. *Id.* at n.1 (citing Carole Cadwalladr, *Robert Mercer: The Big Data Billionaire Waging War on Mainstream Media*, THE GUARDIAN (Feb. 26, 2017)).

74. *Federal Trade Act of 1914*, 15 U.S.C. § 45(a).

unauthorized disclosure of private user data to third parties. In 2019, Facebook settled with the FTC. The settlement, announced on July 24, 2019, included a record-setting $5 billion fine and an FTC order to institute new privacy standards.[75]

b. In the Matter of Cambridge Analytica, LLC (FTC Opinion)

The FTC also brought a complaint against Cambridge Analytica alleging violation of the Federal Trade Commission Act based on its harvesting of the personal data of Facebook users.

In the Matter of Cambridge Analytica, LLC (FTC Opinion)

United States of America Before the Federal Trade Commission
Docket No. 9383
November 25, 2019

By Commisioner PHILLIPS for the Commission (SIMONS (Chairman), PHILLIPS, CHOPRA, SLAUGHTER, WILSON [Commissioners]).

OPINION OF THE COMMISSION

Respondent Cambridge Analytica, LLC ("Cambridge Analytica"), a data analytics and consulting company, is charged with violating the Federal Trade Commission Act ("FTC Act") by employing false and deceptive tactics to harvest personal information from tens of millions of Facebook users through a Facebook application called the "GSRApp," also known as the "thisisyourdigitallife" app. As discussed below, Complaint Counsel move for summary decision. Because Cambridge Analytica has neither opposed Complaint Counsel's motion nor answered the Commission's administrative complaint, we decide this motion based on the undisputed facts as set forth in Complaint Counsel's motion and alleged in the Complaint.

The Complaint alleges that Cambridge Analytica, acting together with Alexander James Ashburner Nix ("Nix"), its Chief Executive Officer, and Aleksandr Kogan ("Kogan"), an applications developer who worked with the company, used the GSRApp to obtain Facebook user profile data from approximately 250,000–270,000 Facebook users who directly interacted with the app ("App Users"), as well as from 50–65 million of the "friends" in those users' social networks. The Complaint charges Cambridge Analytica with obtaining App Users' consent to collect their Facebook profile data by

75. Stipulated Order for Civil Penalty, Monetary Judgment, and Injunctive Relief, United States v. Facebook, Inc., No. 19-cv-2184 (D.D.C. filed July 24, 2019).

falsely representing that the GSRApp did not collect any personally identifiable information from Facebook users who interacted with it, such as their Facebook User ID. Cambridge Analytica then used the information collected through the Facebook GRSApp for voter-profiling and targeted advertising purposes.

The Complaint also charges Cambridge Analytica with deceptive acts and practices related to its participation in the European Union-United States Privacy Shield framework ("Privacy Shield"). The Complaint alleges that Cambridge Analytica, via its website, disseminated statements that falsely claimed it was a participant in Privacy Shield at a time when it had allowed its certification to lapse, and that it represented that it adhered to Privacy Shield principles despite failing to affirm to the U.S. Department of Commerce that it would continue to apply Privacy Shield protections to personal information collected while it participated in the program.

In May 2018, Cambridge Analytica filed for Chapter 7 bankruptcy, and those proceedings are ongoing. On July 24, 2019, the Commission issued its Complaint which, together with a notice order, was served on both Cambridge Analytica at its corporate headquarters and on its bankruptcy trustee. Cambridge Analytica failed to file an answer within the time required by the Commission's Rules of Practice, *i.e.*, by August 12, 2019. Under the Rules, Cambridge Analytica's failure to file an answer is deemed a waiver of its right to appear and to contest the allegations in the Complaint.[76] Rule 3.12(c) authorizes the Commission, without further notice to the Respondent, "to find the facts to be as alleged in the complaint and to enter a final decision containing appropriate findings and conclusions and a final order disposing of the proceeding."[77]

We now have before us Complaint Counsel's Motion for Summary Decision. Cambridge Analytica did not file an opposition to the Motion when due under the Rules, *i.e.*, by September 4, 2019. Complaint Counsel seek a determination that Cambridge Analytica made false or misleading representations in violation of Section 5 of the FTC Act:

- to Facebook users who authorized the GSRApp that it did not collect their personally identifiable information (Count I);
- that it was a participant in Privacy Shield from May to November 2018, even though it had allowed its certification to lapse (Count II); and
- that it would adhere to Privacy Shield principles, even though it failed to affirm to the Department of Commerce, as required, that it would continue to apply those principles to personal information it had acquired while participating in the program (Count III).

76. [In text in original] 16 C.F.R. § 3.12(c).
77. [In text in original] *Id.*

As discussed below, we grant Complaint Counsel's Motion for Summary Decision. Because Cambridge Analytica has defaulted and has failed to challenge the facts presented as undisputed by Complaint Counsel's Motion, we find the facts as set forth in the Motion. (Section I). Based on our analysis of the undisputed facts under applicable legal standards and precedent, we conclude that Cambridge Analytica is liable on all three Counts of the Complaint. (Section III). . . .

It is easy to recognize how the field of AI law and policy encompasses and is encompassed by a wide range of intersecting fields. Data privacy is one of those fields, as well as a core pillar of the *Blueprint for an AI Bill of Rights.* As explained in the Introduction, this book takes a historic approach to learning the subject matter. Understanding where we currently stand with AI law and policy necessitates recognition of a range of cases and legal developments that preceded the contemporary landscape. The Snowden disclosures and Facebook-Cambridge Analytica scandal represent critical developments in the global recognition of the need for data privacy and data protection. The Facebook-Cambridge Analytica scandal, in particular, raised public awareness of the role of algorithms in AI-driven voter microtargeting. The final order filed by the FTC prohibited Cambridge Analytica from making further misrepresentations on personal privacy protections and prohibited misleading claims about participation in the *EU-U.S. Privacy Shield Framework.* The personal information collected was to be protected going forward, or Cambridge Analytica was to return or delete the information they wrongfully gained from the GSRApp and Facebook users. Cambridge Analytica closed its operations in 2018 after the scandal broke.

In *The Black Box Society: The Secret Algorithms That Control Money and Information,* Frank Pasquale observes that algorithms have shifted how power is centered. "Deconstructing the black boxes of Big Data isn't easy," explains Pasquale, but "[i]t matters because authority is increasingly expressed algorithmically."[78] The Facebook-Cambridge Analytica scandal "marked how and when the deployment of Artificial Intelligence (AI) and voter microtargeting algorithms arrived in the consciousness of many U.S. voters."[79]

---

78. Margaret Hu, *Cambridge Analytica's Black Box*, Big Data and Society (2020) (citing Frank Pasquale, The Black Box Society: The Secret Algorithms That Control Money and Information 6-8 (2015)).

79. *Id.*

CHAPTER 7

PERSONHOOD AND CITIZENSHIP

The assignment of legal status to non-persons is not unusual, however, it can be controversial. For example, in the U.S., corporations have certain legal and constitutional rights, including freedom of speech. With AI systems and robotics competing to develop capabilities that are similar to humans, legal scholars have contemplated whether fully autonomous "systems" should be granted personhood or citizenship rights. At a minimum, expanding legal personhood and legal rights to AI systems and robots recognizes novel situations raised by technological developments. Lurking in the background of these legal discussions are also ethical, moral, and other questions in the humanities.

A. AI AND PERSONHOOD

The United States can recognize non-human entities as persons for legal purposes, sometimes referring to non-human legal persons as "artificial persons." It is a matter of practicality and rights—a limited liability company, an agency, or a corporation might be the combined organization of hundreds or thousands of competing interests that does not represent the interests or actions of any one person. A corporation, for example, can act and be held legally accountable for those actions—but it is not *actually* a human being.

While such legal entities are afforded some rights, like due process, the law does not afford non-human "persons" all the same rights. This chapter covers several issues related to personhood as a legal fiction.

The First Amendment guarantees the right of free speech. Government historically has greater power to regulate, censor, and control the speech of nonnatural persons and entities like corporations. The question of whether free speech is a right given only to natural persons or is also given to artificial persons can give insight into whether AI will have its own right to free speech.

1. *Legal Personhood as Legal Recognition*

a. Citizens United v. Federal Election Commission

Citizens United v. Federal Election Commission

Supreme Court of United States
558 U.S. 310 (2010)

Justice Kennedy delivered the opinion of the Court.

I

A

Citizens United is a nonprofit corporation. It brought this action in the United States District Court for the District of Columbia. A three-judge court later convened to hear the cause. The resulting judgment gives rise to this appeal.

Citizens United has an annual budget of about $12 million. Most of its funds are from donations by individuals; but, in addition, it accepts a small portion of its funds from for-profit corporations.

In January 2008, Citizens United released a film entitled *Hillary: The Movie*. We refer to the film as *Hillary*. It is a 90-minute documentary about then-Senator Hillary Clinton, who was a candidate in the Democratic Party's 2008 Presidential primary elections. *Hillary* mentions Senator Clinton by name and depicts interviews with political commentators and other persons, most of them quite critical of Senator Clinton. *Hillary* was released in theaters and on DVD, but Citizens United wanted to increase distribution by making it available through video-on-demand.

Video-on-demand allows digital cable subscribers to select programming from various menus, including movies, television shows, sports, news, and music. The viewer can watch the program at any time and can elect to rewind or pause the program. In December 2007, a cable company offered, for a payment of $1.2 million, to make *Hillary* available on a video-on-demand channel called "Elections '08." Some video-on-demand services require viewers to pay a small fee to view a selected program, but here the proposal was to make *Hillary* available to viewers free of charge.

To implement the proposal, Citizens United was prepared to pay for the video-on-demand; and to promote the film, it produced two 10-second ads and one 30-second ad for *Hillary*. Each ad includes a short (and, in our view, pejorative) statement about Senator Clinton, followed by the name of the movie and the movie's Web site address. Citizens United desired to promote the video-on-demand offering by running advertisements on broadcast and cable television.

B

Before the Bipartisan Campaign Reform Act of 2002 (BCRA), federal law prohibited—and still does prohibit—corporations and unions from using general treasury funds to make direct contributions to candidates or independent expenditures that expressly advocate the election or defeat of a candidate, through any form of media, in connection with certain qualified federal elections.[1] BCRA § 203 amended § 441b to prohibit any "electioneering communication" as well.[2] An electioneering communication is defined as "any broadcast, cable, or satellite communication" that "refers to a clearly identified candidate for Federal office" and is made within 30 days of a primary or 60 days of a general election.[3] The Federal Election Commission's (FEC) regulations further define an electioneering communication as a communication that is "publicly distributed."[4] "In the case of a candidate for nomination for President . . . *publicly distributed* means" that the communication "[c]an be received by 50,000 or more persons in a State where a primary election . . . is being held within 30 days."[5] Corporations and unions are barred from using their general treasury funds for express advocacy or electioneering communications. They may establish, however, a "separate segregated fund" (known as a political action committee, or PAC) for these purposes.[6] The moneys received by the segregated fund are limited to donations from stockholders and employees of the corporation or, in the case of unions, members of the union.[7]

C

Citizens United wanted to make *Hillary* available through video-on-demand within 30 days of the 2008 primary elections. It feared, however, that both the film and the ads would be covered by § 441b's ban on corporate-funded independent expenditures, thus subjecting the corporation to civil and criminal penalties under § 437g. In December 2007, Citizens United sought declaratory and injunctive relief against the FEC. It argued that (1) § 441b is unconstitutional as applied to *Hillary*; and (2) BCRA's disclaimer and disclosure requirements, BCRA §§ 201 and 311, 116 Stat. 88, 105, are unconstitutional as applied to *Hillary* and to the three ads for the movie. . . .

III

A

The Court has recognized that First Amendment protection extends to corporations. . . . This protection has been extended by explicit holdings to the context of political speech. . . . Under the rationale of these precedents,

---

1. [In text in original] 2 U.S.C. § 441b (2000 ed.); *see McConnell, supra,* at 204, and n. 87, 124 S. Ct. 619; Federal Election Comm'n v. Massachusetts Citizens for Life, Inc., 479 U.S. 238, 249, 107 S. Ct. 616, 93 L.Ed.2d 539 (1986) (MCFL).
2. [In text in original] 2 U.S.C. § 441b(b)(2) (2006 ed.).
3. [In text in original] § 434(f)(3)(A).
4. [In text in original] 11 CFR § 100.29(a)(2) (2009).
5. [In text in original] § 100.29(b)(3)(ii)(A).
6. [In text in original] 2 U.S.C. § 441b(b)(2).
7. [In text in original] *Ibid.*

political speech does not lose First Amendment protection "simply because its source is a corporation."[8] The Court has thus rejected the argument that political speech of corporations or other associations should be treated differently under the First Amendment simply because such associations are not "natural persons."[9] . . .

B

1

If the First Amendment has any force, it prohibits Congress from fining or jailing citizens, or associations of citizens, for simply engaging in political speech. If the antidistortion rationale were to be accepted, however, it would permit Government to ban political speech simply because the speaker is an association that has taken on the corporate form. The Government contends that *Austin* permits it to ban corporate expenditures for almost all forms of communication stemming from a corporation. . . . If *Austin* were correct, the Government could prohibit a corporation from expressing political views in media beyond those presented here, such as by printing books. . . .

Political speech is "indispensable to decisionmaking in a democracy, and this is no less true because the speech comes from a corporation rather than an individual."[10] This protection for speech is inconsistent with *Austin*'s antidistortion rationale. *Austin* sought to defend the antidistortion rationale as a means to prevent corporations from obtaining "'an unfair advantage in the political marketplace'" by using "'resources amassed in the economic marketplace.'"[11] But *Buckley* rejected the premise that the Government has an interest "in equalizing the relative ability of individuals and groups to influence the outcome of elections."[12] *Buckley* was specific in stating that "the skyrocketing cost of political campaigns" could not

8. [In text in original] *Bellotti, supra,* at 784, 98 S. Ct. 1407; *see* Pacific Gas & Elec. Co. v. Public Util. Comm'n of Cal., 475 U.S. 1, 8, 106 S. Ct. 903, 89 L.Ed.2d 1 (1986) (plurality opinion) ("The identity of the speaker is not decisive in determining whether speech is protected. Corporations and other associations, like individuals, contribute to the 'discussion, debate, and the dissemination of information and ideas' that the First Amendment seeks to foster" (quoting *Bellotti,* 435 U.S., at 783, 98 S. Ct. 1407)).

9. [In text in original] *Id.*, at 776, 98 S. Ct. 1407; *see id.*, at 780, n.16, 98 S. Ct. 1407. *Cf. id.*, at 828, 98 S. Ct. 1407 (Rehnquist, J., dissenting).

10. [In text in original] *Bellotti,* 435 U.S., at 777, 98 S. Ct. 1407 (footnote omitted); *see ibid.* (the worth of speech "does not depend upon the identity of its source, whether corporation, association, union, or individual"); *Buckley,* 424 U.S., at 48-49, 96 S. Ct. 612 ("[T]he concept that government may restrict the speech of some elements of our society in order to enhance the relative voice of others is wholly foreign to the First Amendment"); *Automobile Workers, supra,* at 597, 77 S. Ct. 529 (Douglas, J., dissenting); *CIO,* 335 U.S., at 154-155, 68 S. Ct. 1349 (Rutledge, J., concurring in result).

11. [In text in original] 494 U.S., at 659, 110 S. Ct. 1391 (quoting *MCFL, supra,* at 257, 107 S. Ct. 616).

12. [In text in original] 424 U.S., at 48, 96 S. Ct. 612; *see Bellotti, supra,* at 791, n.30, 98 S. Ct. 1407.

sustain the governmental prohibition.[13] The First Amendment's protections do not depend on the speaker's "financial ability to engage in public discussion."[14] . . .

The rule that political speech cannot be limited based on a speaker's wealth is a necessary consequence of the premise that the First Amendment generally prohibits the suppression of political speech based on the speaker's identity.

Either as support for its antidistortion rationale or as a further argument, the *Austin* majority undertook to distinguish wealthy individuals from corporations on the ground that "[s]tate law grants corporations special advantages—such as limited liability, perpetual life, and favorable treatment of the accumulation and distribution of assets."[15] This does not suffice, however, to allow laws prohibiting speech. "It is rudimentary that the State cannot exact as the price of those special advantages the forfeiture of First Amendment rights."[16]

It is irrelevant for purposes of the First Amendment that corporate funds may "have little or no correlation to the public's support for the corporation's political ideas."[17] All speakers, including individuals and the media, use money amassed from the economic marketplace to fund their speech. The First Amendment protects the resulting speech, even if it was enabled by economic transactions with persons or entities who disagree with the speaker's ideas.[18]

Austin's antidistortion rationale would produce the dangerous, and unacceptable, consequence that Congress could ban political speech of media corporations.[19] Media corporations are now exempt from § 441b's ban on corporate expenditures.[20] Yet media corporations accumulate wealth with the help of the corporate form, the largest media corporations have "immense aggregations of wealth," and the views expressed by media corporations often "have little or no correlation to the public's support" for those views.[21] Thus, under the Government's reasoning, wealthy media corporations could have their voices diminished to put them on par with other media entities. There is no precedent for permitting this under the First Amendment.

---

13. [In text in original] 424 U.S., at 26, 96 S. Ct. 612.
14. [In text in original] *Id.*, at 49, 96 S. Ct. 612.
15. [In text in original] 494 U.S., at 658-659, 110 S. Ct. 1391.
16. [In text in original] *Id.*, at 680, 110 S. Ct. 1391 (Scalia, J., dissenting).
17. [In text in original] *Id.*, at 660, 110 S. Ct. 1391 (majority opinion).
18. [In text in original] *See id.*, at 707, 110 S. Ct. 1391 (Kennedy, J., dissenting) ("Many persons can trace their funds to corporations, if not in the form of donations, then in the form of dividends, interest, or salary").
19. [In text in original] *See McConnell*, 540 U.S., at 283, 124 S. Ct. 619 (opinion of Thomas, J.) ("The chilling endpoint of the Court's reasoning is not difficult to foresee: outright regulation of the press"). *Cf. Tornillo*, 418 U.S., at 250, 94 S. Ct. 2831 (alleging the existence of "vast accumulations of unreviewable power in the modern media empires").
20. [In text in original] *See* 2 U.S.C. §§ 431(9)(B)(i), 434(f)(3)(B)(i).
21. [In text in original] *Austin*, 494 U.S., at 660, 110 S. Ct. 1391.

The media exemption discloses further difficulties with the law now under consideration. There is no precedent supporting laws that attempt to distinguish between corporations which are deemed to be exempt as media corporations and those which are not. "We have consistently rejected the proposition that the institutional press has any constitutional privilege beyond that of other speakers."[22] With the advent of the Internet and the decline of print and broadcast media, moreover, the line between the media and others who wish to comment on political and social issues becomes far more blurred.

The law's exception for media corporations is, on its own terms, all but an admission of the invalidity of the antidistortion rationale. And the exemption results in a further, separate reason for finding this law invalid: Again by its own terms, the law exempts some corporations but covers others, even though both have the need or the motive to communicate their views. The exemption applies to media corporations owned or controlled by corporations that have diverse and substantial investments and participate in endeavors other than news. So even assuming the most doubtful proposition that a news organization has a right to speak when others do not, the exemption would allow a conglomerate that owns both a media business and an unrelated business to influence or control the media in order to advance its overall business interest. At the same time, some other corporation, with an identical business interest but no media outlet in its ownership structure, would be forbidden to speak or inform the public about the same issue. This differential treatment cannot be squared with the First Amendment.

There is simply no support for the view that the First Amendment, as originally understood, would permit the suppression of political speech by media corporations. The Framers may not have anticipated modern business and media corporations.[23] Yet television networks and major newspapers owned by media corporations have become the most important means of mass communication in modern times. The First Amendment was certainly not understood to condone the suppression of political speech in society's most salient media. It was understood as a response to the repression of speech and the press that had existed in England and the heavy taxes on the press that were imposed in the Colonies.[24] The great debates between the Federalists and the Anti-Federalists over our founding document were published and expressed in the most important means of mass communication of that era—newspapers owned by individuals.[25] At the

22. [In text in original] *Id.*, at 691, 110 S. Ct. 1391 (Scalia, J., dissenting) (citing *Bellotti*, 435 U.S., at 782, 98 S. Ct. 1407); *see* Dun & Bradstreet, Inc. v. Greenmoss Builders, Inc., 472 U.S. 749, 784, 105 S. Ct. 2939, 86 L.Ed.2d 593 (1985) (Brennan, J., joined by Marshall, Blackmun, and Stevens, JJ., dissenting); *id.*, at 773, 105 S. Ct. 2939 (White, J., concurring in judgment).

23. [In text in original] *See* McIntyre v. Ohio Elections Comm'n, 514 U.S. 334, 360-361, 115 S. Ct. 1511, 131 L.Ed.2d 426 (1995) (Thomas, J., concurring in judgment).

24. [In text in original] *See McConnell*, 540 U.S., at 252-253, 124 S. Ct. 619 (opinion of Scalia, J.); *Grosjean*, 297 U.S., at 245-248, 56 S. Ct. 444; Near, 283 U.S., at 713-714, 51 S. Ct. 625.

25. [In text in original] *See McIntyre*, 514 U.S., at 341-343, 115 S. Ct. 1511; *id.*, at 367, 115 S. Ct. 1511 (Thomas, J., concurring in judgment).

founding, speech was open, comprehensive, and vital to society's definition of itself; there were no limits on the sources of speech and knowledge.[26] The Framers may have been unaware of certain types of speakers or forms of communication, but that does not mean that those speakers and media are entitled to less First Amendment protection than those types of speakers and media that provided the means of communicating political ideas when the Bill of Rights was adopted. . . .

The purpose and effect of this law is to prevent corporations, including small and nonprofit corporations, from presenting both facts and opinions to the public. This makes *Austin*'s antidistortion rationale all the more an aberration. "[T]he First Amendment protects the right of corporations to petition legislative and administrative bodies."[27] Corporate executives and employees counsel Members of Congress and Presidential administrations on many issues, as a matter of routine and often in private. An amici brief filed on behalf of Montana and 25 other States notes that lobbying and corporate communications with elected officials occur on a regular basis.[28] When that phenomenon is coupled with § 441b, the result is that smaller or nonprofit corporations cannot raise a voice to object when other corporations, including those with vast wealth, are cooperating with the Government. That cooperation may sometimes be voluntary, or it may be at the demand of a Government official who uses his or her authority, influence, and power to threaten corporations to support the Government's policies. Those kinds of interactions are often unknown and unseen. The speech that § 441b forbids, though, is public, and all can judge its content and purpose. References to massive corporate treasuries should not mask the real operation of this law. Rhetoric ought not obscure reality.

Even if § 441b's expenditure ban were constitutional, wealthy corporations could still lobby elected officials, although smaller corporations may not have the resources to do so. And wealthy individuals and unincorporated associations can spend unlimited amounts on independent expenditures.[29] Yet certain disfavored associations of citizens—those that

---

26. [In text in original] *See* B. Bailyn, Ideological Origins of the American Revolution 5 (1967) ("Any number of people could join in such proliferating polemics, and rebuttals could come from all sides"); G. Wood, Creation of the American Republic 1776-1787, p. 6 (1969) ("[I]t is not surprising that the intellectual sources of [the Americans'] Revolutionary thought were profuse and various").

27. [In text in original] *Bellotti,* 435 U.S., at 792, n.31, 98 S. Ct. 1407 (citing California Motor Transport Co. v. Trucking Unlimited, 404 U.S. 508, 510–511, 92 S. Ct. 609, 30 L.Ed.2d 642 (1972); Eastern Railroad Presidents Conference v. Noerr Motor Freight, Inc., 365 U.S. 127, 137–138, 81 S. Ct. 523, 5 L.Ed.2d 464 (1961))

28. [In text in original] Brief for *State of Montana et al.* 19.

29. [In text in original] *See, e.g., WRTL,* 551 U.S., at 503-504, 127 S. Ct. 2652 (opinion of Scalia, J.) ("In the 2004 election cycle, a mere 24 individuals contributed an astounding total of $142 million to [26 U.S.C. § 527 organizations].").

have taken on the corporate form—are penalized for engaging in the same political speech.

When Government seeks to use its full power, including the criminal law, to command where a person may get his or her information or what distrusted source he or she may not hear, it uses censorship to control thought. This is unlawful. The First Amendment confirms the freedom to think for ourselves. . . .

2. *Right to Publicity and Digital Identity*

There are a number of rights that are preserved for human legal persons. The right to vote, for instance, is only given to natural humans. The following section demonstrates another key area of the law where natural human personhood is required: the right to acquire certain intellectual property ownership.

a. Lehrman v. LOVO, Inc. (Complaint)

Lehrman v. LOVO, Inc. (Complaint)

United States District Court for the Southern District of New York
Class Action
Case No. 1:24-cv-03770
May 16, 2024

NATURE OF THE ACTION

1. This is a class action brought on behalf of Plaintiffs and similarly situated persons whose voices and/or identities were stolen and used by LOVO—to create millions of voice-over productions. . . . LOVO is a technology company with proprietary software driven by artificial intelligence (AI) that allows LOVO's clients to create and edit voice-over narrations adapted from real actors. . . .

DEFENDANT RECOGNIZES THE IMPROPER USAGE OF PLAINTIFFS' VOICES

80. The founders of LOVO even created another company, VoiceVerse, which sold voice NFTs (non-fungible tokens). The founders stated on a pitch website about their "[v]ision":

> A person's voice is uniquely linked to their identity. Once you hear that person's voice, it immediately reminds you of them, and memories you had with them. Voice is personal. Voice brings out emotion. Voice is unique. Voice is a powerful aspect of one's identity.[30]

DEFENDANT'S IMPROPER USE OF CELEBRITY NAMES AND LIKENESSES AND OTHER VOICES

81. Defendant not only improperly appropriates the voices of the named Plaintiffs who are "working actors" but not "celebrities"; Defendant also borrows the name and likeness of some of the nation's most well-known celebrities, including Barack Obama (crudely represented as "Barack Yo Mama"), Conan O'Brien ("Cocoon O'Brien"), and Elton John ("Elton John Cena"), to promote its services and show the capabilities of the LOVO product.

B. *CASE STUDIES OF HUMAN PERSONHOOD AS LEGAL REQUIREMENT*

In 2011, a Celebes crested macaque, a monkey named Naruto, took a picture of itself with a wildlife photographer's camera. The wildlife photographer claimed copyright on the selfies that were taken by Naruto. The U.S.

30. [Fn. 7 in original] VoiceVerse Docs, "Vision. Separately, VoiceVerse has already been found to have stolen technology from another company. *See* Ule Lopez, WCCF Tech, "Voiceverse NFT Service Reportedly Uses Stolen Technology from 15ai," (Jan. 16, 2022).

Copyright Office concluded in 2014 that copyright law required human authorship for an original work to be copyrightable. When the case was heard before the Northern District of California, the Court affirmed the Copyright Office's interpretation that works not created by humans are not copyrightable, agreeing that "the Copyright Office will not register works produced by 'nature, animals, or plants' including, by specific example, a 'photograph taken by a monkey.'"[31] On appeal to the Ninth Circuit, the Circuit Court affirmed, holding that animals only have statutory standing when the statute plainly says so, finding that Naruto lacked standing to sue.[32] The image remains in the public domain.

In addition to the human authorship requirement for copyright in U.S. copyright law, there is also a human authorship requirement for inventorship in U.S. patent law. As seen by the cases below, the human authorship and human inventorship requirements are relevant to recent AI cases in intellectual property.

1. Human Invention Requirement for AI Inventorship in Patents

According to the U.S. Patent and Trademark Office ("USPTO"), the "inventor" of a patent is a natural person.[33] According to 35 U.S.C. § 100(f), the *Patent Act* requires an inventor to be an "individual," or a natural per son, to claim ownership of patentable creation. Courts have held that inventors must be natural persons, as opposed to corporations.[34] Courts have also held that an AI machine could not be an "inventor" according to the plain statutory language of the *Patent Act* and Federal Circuit authority.[35]

31. Naruto v. Slater, No. 15-cv-04324-WHO (N.D. Cal. Jan. 28, 2016).
32. Naruto v. Slater, 888 F.3d 418, 422 (9th Cir. 2018).
33. 35 U.S.C. § 116.
34. Beech Aircraft Corp. v. EDO Corp., 990 F.2d 1237, 1248 (Fed. Cir. 1993).
35. Thaler v. Hirshfeld, 558 F. Supp. 3d 238, 247-48 (E.D. Va. Sept. 2, 2021).

The *Patent Act* and the *Manual of Patent Examining Procedure*, which references "person[s]" regarding inventorship,[36] conceive of an invention that is created only by a natural person.[37] Additionally, Federal Circuit precedents have twice described conception as a "formation of the mind of the inventor" and a "mental act," and held that an inventor could only be a natural person.[38] Consistent with this definition are rulings of previous cases involving controversies over the definition of "ownership."

Can AI be considered an inventor? The question of inventorship is an inevitable issue in patent law, because AI-based systems are now capable of synthesizing data that can represent patentable assets. A human user might provide certain parameters for the AI system to rely on when synthesizing patentable assets, but the main driver for the invention is arguably the AI system. The question of whether an AI system could be legally considered an inventor was addressed by the following case, which pitted an inventor against the USPTO on personhood issues.

a. Thaler v. Vidal

Thaler v. Vidal

United States Court of Appeals, Federal Circuit
43 F.4th 1207 (2022)

STARK, United States Circuit Judge.

This case presents the question of who, or what, can be an inventor. Specifically, we are asked to decide if an artificial intelligence (AI) software system can be listed as the inventor on a patent application. At first, it might seem that resolving this issue would involve an abstract inquiry into the nature of invention or the rights, if any, of AI systems. In fact, however, we do not need to ponder these metaphysical matters. Instead, our task begins—and ends—with consideration of the applicable definition in the relevant statute. . . .

I

Thaler represents that he develops and runs AI systems that generate patentable inventions. One such system is his "Device for the Autonomous

---

36. *See Section 2109 Inventorship [R-01.2024]*, USPTO; *see also* MPEP § 2137.01.

37. Rebecca Tapscott, *USPTO Shoots Down DABUS' Bid for Inventorship*, IPWATCHDOG (May 4, 2020).

38. *Id.*

Bootstrapping of Unified Science," which Thaler calls "DABUS." Thaler has described DABUS as "a collection of source code or programming and a software program."

In July 2019, Thaler sought patent protection for two of DABUS' putative inventions by filing two patent applications with the PTO: U.S. Application Nos. 16/524,350 (teaching a "Neural Flame") and 16/524,532 (teaching a "Fractal Container"). He listed DABUS as the sole inventor on both applications. Thaler maintains that he did not contribute to the conception of these inventions and that any person having skill in the art could have taken DABUS' output and reduced the ideas in the applications to practice.[39]

In lieu of an inventor's last name, Thaler wrote on the applications that "the invention [was] generated by artificial intelligence." He also attached several documents relevant to inventorship. First, to satisfy 35 U.S.C. § 115's requirement that inventors submit a sworn oath or declaration when applying for a patent, Thaler submitted a statement on DABUS' behalf. Second, Thaler provided a supplemental "Statement on Inventorship" explaining that DABUS was "a particular type of connectionist artificial intelligence" called a "Creativity Machine." Third, Thaler filed a document purporting to assign himself all of DABUS' rights as an inventor.

The PTO concluded both applications lacked a valid inventor and were, hence, incomplete. Accordingly, it sent Thaler a "Notice to File Missing Parts of Nonprovisional Application" for each application and requested that Thaler identify valid inventors. In response, Thaler petitioned the PTO director to vacate the Notices based on his Statements of Inventorship. The PTO denied Thaler's petitions on the ground that "a machine does not qualify as an inventor." Thaler sought reconsideration, which the PTO denied, explaining again that inventors on a patent application must be natural persons.

Thaler then pursued judicial review of the PTO's final decisions on his petitions, under the Administrative Procedure Act (APA).[40,41] . . .

---

39. [Fn. 2 in original] While inventorship involves underlying questions of fact, *see* Dana-Farber Cancer Inst., Inc. v. Ono Pharm. Co., 964 F.3d 1365, 1370 (Fed. Cir. 2020), *cert. denied*, ___ U.S. ___, 141 S. Ct. 2691, 210 L.Ed.2d 845 (2021), for purposes of this litigation the PTO has not challenged Thaler's representations, *see* D. Ct. Dkt. No. 25, at 11. Accordingly, our analysis must be consistent with the undisputed facts in the administrative record, drawing inferences in favor of the non-moving party. *See* Safeguard Base Operations, LLC v. United States, 989 F.3d 1326, 1349 (Fed. Cir. 2021) (discussing when it is appropriate to supplement administrative record and noting "[t]he focal point for judicial review should be the administrative record already in existence") (quoting Camp v. Pitts, 411 U.S. 138, 142, 93 S. Ct. 1241, 36 L.Ed.2d 106 (1973)).

40. [In text in original] *See* 5 U.S.C. §§ 702-704, 706.

41. [Fn. 3 in original] The District Court had jurisdiction under 28 U.S.C. § 1331. *See also* 5 U.S.C. § 702 ("A person suffering legal wrong because of agency action, or adversely affected or aggrieved by agency action within the meaning of a relevant statute, is entitled to judicial review thereof.").

II

A

The sole issue on appeal is whether an AI software system can be an "inventor" under the Patent Act. In resolving disputes of statutory interpretation, we "begin[] with the statutory text, and end[] there as well if the text is unambiguous."[42] Here, there is no ambiguity: the Patent Act requires that inventors must be natural persons; that is, human beings.

The Patent Act expressly provides that inventors are "individuals." Since 2011, with the passage of the Leahy-Smith America Invents Act, the Patent Act has defined an "inventor" as "the *individual* or, if a joint invention, the *individuals* collectively who invented or discovered the subject matter of the invention."[43] The Act similarly defines "joint inventor" and "coinventor" as "any 1 of the *individuals* who invented or discovered the subject matter of a joint invention."[44] In describing the statements required of an inventor when applying for a patent, the statute consistently refers to inventors and co-inventors as "individuals."[45]

The Patent Act does not define "individual." However, as the Supreme Court has explained, when used "[a]s a noun, 'individual' ordinarily means a human being, a person."[46] This is in accord with "how we use the word in everyday parlance": "We say 'the individual went to the store,' 'the individual left the room,' and 'the individual took the car,' each time referring unmistakably to a natural person."[47] Dictionaries confirm that this is the common understanding of the word.[48] . . .

Consequently, the Supreme Court has held that, when used in statutes, the word "individual" refers to human beings unless there is "some indication Congress intended" a different reading.[49,50] Nothing in the Patent Act indicates Congress intended to deviate from the default meaning. To the contrary, the rest of the Patent Act supports the conclusion that "individual" in the Act refers to human beings. . . .

---

42. [In text in original] BedRoc Ltd. v. United States, 541 U.S. 176, 183, 124 S. Ct. 1587, 158 L.Ed.2d 338 (2004).

43. [In text in original] 35 U.S.C. § 100(f) (emphasis added).

44. [In text in original] § 100(g) (emphasis added).

45. [In text in original] *See* § 115.

46. [In text in original] Mohamad v. Palestinian Auth., 566 U.S. 449, 454, 132 S. Ct. 1702, 182 L.Ed.2d 720 (2012) (internal alteration and quotation marks omitted).

47. [In text in original] *Id.*

48. [In text in original] *See, e.g., Individual,* OXFORD ENGLISH DICTIONARY (2022).

49. [In text in original] *Id.* at 455, 132 S. Ct. 1702 (emphasis omitted).

50. [Fn. 4 in original] While *Mohamad* interpreted a statute other than the Patent Act, the Court's reasoning is directly applicable here. *See generally* Legal Def. Fund v. Dep't of Agric., 933 F.3d 1088, 1093-94 (9th Cir. 2019) (concluding that "individual" refers to human beings and not animals, based in part on *Mohamad*).

B

Our holding today that an "inventor" must be a human being is supported by our own precedent.[51] While these opinions addressed different questions—concluding that neither corporations nor sovereigns can be inventors—our reasoning did not depend on the fact that institutions are collective entities. The two cases confirm that the plain meaning of "inventor" in the Patent Act is limited to natural persons. . . .

III

We briefly address Thaler's additional arguments.

Thaler argues that inventions generated by AI should be patentable in order to encourage innovation and public disclosure. Thaler's policy arguments are speculative and lack a basis in the text of the Patent Act and in the record. In any event, the text before us is unambiguous, and we may not "elevate vague invocations of statutory purpose over the words Congress chose."[52] Moreover, we are not confronted today with the question of whether inventions made by human beings with the *assistance* of AI are eligible for patent protection.

Thaler invokes the canon of constitutional avoidance. In Thaler's view, permitting AI programs to be inventors would support the constitutional purpose of patents "[t]o promote the progress of science and the useful arts."[53] It follows, Thaler continues, that not recognizing AI as an inventor undermines such progress, raising potential constitutional concerns we should be careful to avoid. Thaler is incorrect. The constitutional provision he cites is a grant of legislative power to Congress; Congress has chosen to act pursuant to that power by passing the Patent Act. Thaler does not (and cannot) argue that limiting inventorship to human beings is unconstitutional. Therefore, the canon of constitutional avoidance is simply inapplicable. . . .

Thaler also notes that South Africa has granted patents with DABUS as an inventor. This foreign patent office was not interpreting our Patent Act. Its determination does not alter our conclusion. . . .

AFFIRMED.

---

51. [In text in original] *See* Univ. of Utah v. Max-Planck-Gesellschaft zur Forderung der Wissenschaften E.V., 734 F.3d 1315, 1323 (Fed. Cir. 2013) ("[I]nventors must be *natural persons* and cannot be corporations or sovereigns.") (emphasis added); Beech Aircraft Corp. v. EDO Corp., 990 F.2d 1237, 1248 (Fed. Cir. 1993) ("[O]nly natural persons can be 'inventors.'").

52. [In text in original] Sw. Airlines Co. v. Saxon, ___ U.S. ___, 142 S. Ct. 1783, 1792-93, 213 L.Ed.2d 27 (2022).

53. [In text in original] U.S. Const. art. I, § 8, cl. 8.

b. U.S. Patent and Trademark Office Inventorship Guidance for AI-Assisted Inventions

In the aftermath of *Thaler v. Vidal*, the USPTO released guidance on how AI assistance can be used for creating inventions. The guidance answers a key question that the court in *Thaler v. Vidal* did not answer, which is "whether inventions made by human beings with the assistance of AI are eligible for patent protections."

AI can be used to invent, but it remains a question of whether an invention developed by an AI is unpatentable. USPTO guidance indicates that this will depend on how much a natural person is involved in developing an invention. The USPTO applies a test for determining co-inventors, requiring a significant contribution from each named inventor for the invention to be patentable.[54] The determination of whether a "natural person's contribution to an AI-assisted invention is significant" is not described in depth and the application of co-inventorship rules is assessed case by case with no bright-line test.[55]

The USPTO provided the following guidance.

Inventorship Guidance for AI-Assisted Inventions

U.S. Department of Commerce, U.S. Patent and Trademark Office
89 FR 10043
February 13, 2024

IV. Naming Inventors for AI-Assisted Inventions

B. Guiding Principles

Determining whether a natural person's contribution in AI-assisted inventions is significant may be difficult to ascertain, and there is no bright-line test. To assist applicants and USPTO personnel in determining proper inventorship, the USPTO provides the following non-exhaustive list of principles that can help inform the application of the *Pannu* factors in AI-assisted inventions:

1. A natural person's use of an AI system in creating an AI-assisted invention does not negate the person's contributions as an inventor.[53] The natural person can be listed as the inventor or joint inventor if the natural person contributes significantly to the AI-assisted invention.

2. Merely recognizing a problem or having a general goal or research plan to pursue does not rise to the level of conception.[56] A natural person who only

54. *Inventorship Guidance for AI-Assisted Inventions*, USPTO, Dep't of Com. (Feb. 13, 2024).

55. *Id.*

56. [Fn. 54 in original] *Burroughs Wellcome*, 40 F.3d at 1228 ("An idea is definite and permanent when the inventor has a specific, settled idea, a particular solution to the problem at hand, not just a general goal or research plan [the inventor] hopes to pursue."); *see also Hitzeman*, 243 F.3d 1345, 1357-58; In re Verhoef, 888 F.3d 1362, 1366 (Fed. Cir. 2018) (Verhoef's recognition of the problem of connecting the cord of the harness to the dog's toes did not make Verhoef the sole inventor; Lamb's proposed solution to that problem was a significant contribution).

presents a problem to an AI system may not be a proper inventor or joint inventor of an invention identified from the output of the AI system. However, a significant contribution could be shown by the way the person constructs the prompt in view of a specific problem to elicit a particular solution from the AI system.

3. Reducing an invention to practice alone is not a significant contribution that rises to the level of inventorship.[57] Therefore, a natural person who merely recognizes and appreciates the output of an AI system as an invention, particularly when the properties and utility of the output are apparent to those of ordinary skill, is not necessarily an inventor.[58] However, a person who takes the output of an AI system and makes a significant contribution to the output to create an invention may be a proper inventor. Alternatively, in certain situations, a person who conducts a successful experiment using the AI system's output could demonstrate that the person provided a significant contribution to the invention even if that person is unable to establish conception until the invention has been reduced to practice.[59]

4. A natural person who develops an essential building block from which the claimed invention is derived may be considered to have provided a significant contribution to the conception of the claimed invention even though the person was not present for or a participant in each activity that led to the conception of the claimed invention.[60] In some situations, the natural person(s) who designs, builds, or trains an AI system in view of a specific problem to elicit a particular solution could be an inventor, where the designing, building, or training of the AI system is a significant contribution to the invention created with the AI system.

5. Maintaining "intellectual domination" over an AI system does not, on its own, make a person an inventor of any inventions created through the use of the AI system.[61] Therefore, a person simply owning or overseeing an

---

57. [Fn. 55 in original] MPEP 2109 (subsection III).

58. [Fn. 56 in original] *See, e.g.*, Solvay S.A. v. Honeywell Intern., Inc., 622 F.3d 1367, 1378-79 (Fed. Cir. 2010) (finding that deriving the invention of another and appreciating what was made did not rise to the level of conception).

59. [Fn. 57 in original] *See* MPEP 2138.04 (subsection II); *see also* Dana-Farber Cancer Inst., Inc. v. Ono Pharm. Co., 964 F.3d 1365, 1373-74 (Fed. Cir. 2020) (Dr. Freeman's identification of the 292 sequences in the BLAST database (an automated search tool for finding similarity between biological sequences) and subsequent immunohistochemistry experiments to identify several types of tumors that express PD-L1 were found sufficient to make him a joint inventor).

60. [Fn. 58 in original] *Dana-Farber*, 964 F.3d at 1372-74 (Drs. Freeman and Wood were found to be joint inventors even though they did not conceive of the claimed invention of using anti-PD-1 antibodies to treat tumors but instead discovered the expression of PD-L1 in human tumors and that PD-1/PD-LI interaction inhibits the immune response).

61. [Fn. 59 in original] *Verhoef*, 888 F.3d at 1367 (court refused to endorse the "intellectual domination" language and emphasized that the person who conceives of the invention is the inventor).

AI system that is used in the creation of an invention, without providing a significant contribution to the conception of the invention, does not make that person an inventor.

2. *Human Authorship Requirement for Copyright Protection*

As the USPTO describes in its *Inventorship Guidance for AI-Assisted Inventions*, human investment is required to establish that a natural person has created an invention. To be deemed a proper inventor, the user of the AI must have more than a generalized question or recognition of a problem to craft a specific prompt or add a significant contribution to the synthesized output. At a minimum, the USPTO states that there is an expectation that there will be some significant level of planning, control, and participation in the creation process to ensure that the human user of the AI can be recognized as an inventor.

In its current form, AI is largely based on existing knowledge and therefore generative AI might not be able to conceptualize novel solutions.

a. Thaler v. Perlmutter

Thaler v. Perlmutter

United States District Court for the District of Columbia
687 F. Supp. 3d 140 (2023)
Civil Action No. 22-1564 (BAH)

MEMORANDUM OPINION

Howell, United States District Judge.

Plaintiff Stephen Thaler owns a computer system he calls the "Creativity Machine," which he claims generated a piece of visual art of its own accord. He sought to register the work for a copyright, listing the computer system as the author and explaining that the copyright should transfer to him as the owner of the machine. The Copyright Office denied the application on the grounds that the work lacked human authorship, a prerequisite for a valid copyright to issue, in the view of the Register of Copyrights. Plaintiff challenged that denial, culminating in this lawsuit against the United States Copyright Office and Shira Perlmutter, in her official capacity as the Register of Copyrights and the Director of the United States Copyright Office ("defendants"). Both parties have now moved for summary judgment, which motions present the sole issue of whether a work generated entirely by an artificial system absent human involvement should be eligible for copyright. . . .

For the reasons explained below, defendants are correct that human authorship is an essential part of a valid copyright claim, and therefore . . . defendants' pending cross-motion for summary judgment is granted.

I. BACKGROUND

Plaintiff develops and owns computer programs he describes as having "artificial intelligence" ("AI") capable of generating original pieces of visual art, akin to the output of a human artist. . . . One such AI system—the so-called "Creativity Machine"—produced the work at issue here, titled "A Recent Entrance to Paradise:"

Admin. Record ("AR"), Ex. H, Copyright Review Board Refusal Letter Dated February 14, 2022 ("Final Refusal Letter") at 1, ECF No. 13-8.

. . . Plaintiff timely challenged that decision in this Court, claiming that defendants' denial of copyright registration to the work titled "A Recent Entrance to Paradise," was "arbitrary, capricious, an abuse of discretion and not in accordance with the law, unsupported by substantial evidence, and in excess of Defendants' statutory authority," in violation of the Administrative Procedure Act ("APA"), 5 U.S.C. § 706(2). The parties agree upon the key facts narrated above to focus, in the pending cross-motions for summary judgment, on the sole legal issue of whether a work autonomously generated by an AI system is copyrightable. Those motions are now ripe for resolution.

II. LEGAL STANDARD

A. Administrative Procedure Act

The APA provides for judicial review of any "final agency action for which there is no other adequate remedy in a court,"[62] and "instructs a reviewing court to set aside agency action found to be 'arbitrary, capricious, an abuse of discretion, or otherwise not in accordance with law,'"[63] This standard "'requires agencies to engage in reasoned decisionmaking,' and . . . to reasonably explain to reviewing courts the bases for the actions they take and the conclusions they reach."[64] Judicial review of agency action is limited to "the grounds that the agency invoked when it took the action,"[65] and the agency, too, "must defend its actions based on the reasons it gave when it acted[.]"[66]

B. Summary Judgment

Pursuant to Federal Rule of Civil Procedure 56, "[a] party is entitled to summary judgment only if there is no genuine issue of material fact and judgment in the movant's favor is proper as a matter of law."[67] In APA cases such as this one, involving cross-motions for summary judgment, "the district judge sits as an appellate tribunal. The 'entire case' on review is a question of law."[68] Thus, a court need not and ought not engage in fact finding, since "[g]enerally speaking, district courts reviewing agency action under the APA's arbitrary and capricious standard do not resolve factual issues, but operate instead as appellate courts resolving legal questions."[69] Judicial review, when available, is typically limited to the administrative record, since "[i]t is black-letter administrative law that in an [APA] case,

---

62. [In text in original] 5 U.S.C. § 704[.]

63. [In text in original] Cigar Ass'n of Am. v. FDA, 964 F.3d 56, 61 (D.C. Cir. 2020) (quoting 5 U.S.C. § 706(2)(A)).

64. [In text in original] Brotherhood of Locomotive Eng'rs & Trainmen v. Fed. R.R. Admin., 972 F.3d 83, 115 (D.C. Cir. 2020) (quoting Dep't of Homeland Sec. v. Regents of Univ. of Cal. ("Regents"), 140 S. Ct. 1891, 1905 (2020)).

65. [In text in original] *Regents*, 140 S. Ct. at 1907 (quoting Michigan v. EPA, 576 U.S. 743, 758 (2015))[.]

66. [In text in original] *[I]d.* at 1909.

67. [In text in original] Soundboard Ass'n v. FTC, 888 F.3d 1261, 1267 (D.C. Cir. 2018) (quoting Ctr. for Auto Safety v. Nat'l Highway Traffic Safety Admin., 452 F.3d 798, 805 (D.C. Cir. 2006)); *see also* Fed. R. Civ. P. 56(a).

68. [In text in original] Am. Bioscience, Inc. v. Thompson, 269 F.3d 1077, 1083-84 (D.C. Cir. 2001) (footnote omitted) (collecting cases).

69. [In text in original] James Madison Ltd. by Hecht v. Ludwig, 82 F.3d 1085, 1096 (D.C. Cir. 1996); *see also* Lacson v. U.S. Dep't of Homeland Sec., 726 F.3d 170, 171 (D.C. Cir. 2013) (noting, in an APA case, that "determining the facts is generally the agency's responsibility, not [the court's]").

a reviewing court should have before it neither more nor less information than did the agency when it made its decision."[70]

III. DISCUSSION

Under the Copyright Act of 1976, copyright protection attaches "immediately" upon the creation of "original works of authorship fixed in any tangible medium of expression," provided those works meet certain requirements.[71] A copyright claimant can also register the work with the Register of Copyrights. Upon concluding that the work is indeed copyrightable, the Register will issue a certificate of registration, which, among other advantages, allows the claimant to pursue infringement claims in court.[72] A valid copyright exists upon a qualifying work's creation and "apart" from registration, however; a certificate of registration merely confirms that the copyright has existed all along.[73] Conversely, if the Register denies an application for registration for lack of copyrightable subject matter—and did not err in doing so—then the work at issue was never subject to copyright protection at all.

In considering plaintiff's copyright registration application as to "A Recent Entrance to Paradise," the Register concluded that "this particular work will not support a claim to copyright" because the work lacked human authorship and thus no copyright existed in the first instance. By design in plaintiff's framing of the registration application, then, the single legal question presented here is whether a work generated autonomously by a computer falls under the protection of copyright law upon its creation.

Plaintiff attempts to complicate the issues presented by devoting a substantial portion of his briefing to the viability of various legal theories under which a copyright in the computer's work would transfer to him, as the computer's owner; for example, by operation of common law property principles or the work-for-hire doctrine. These arguments concern *to whom* a valid copyright should have been registered, and in so doing put the cart before the horse.[74] By denying registration, the Register concluded that no

---

70. [In text in original] CTS Corp. v. EPA, 759 F.3d 52, 64 (D.C. Cir. 2014) (internal quotation marks and citation omitted).

71. [In text in original] Fourth Estate v. Public Benefit Corporation v. Wall-Street.com, LLC, 139 S. Ct. 881, 887 (2019); 17 U.S.C. § 102(a).

72. [In text in original] 17 U.S.C. §§ 410(a), 411(a); Unicolors v. H&M Hennes & Mauritz, L.P., 142 S. Ct. 941, 944-45 (2022).

73. [In text in original] *See* Fourth Estate, 139 S. Ct. at 887.

74. [Fn. 1 in original] In pursuing these arguments, plaintiff elaborates on his development, use, ownership, and prompting of the AI generating software in the so-called "Creativity Machine," implying a level of human involvement in this case entirely absent in the administrative record. As detailed, *supra*, in Part I, plaintiff consistently represented to the Register that the AI system generated the work "autonomously" and that he played no role in its creation, *see* Application at 2, and judicial review of the Register's final decision must be based on those same facts.

valid copyright had ever existed in a work generated absent human involvement, leaving nothing at all to register and thus no question as to whom that registration belonged.

The only question properly presented, then, is whether the Register acted arbitrarily or capriciously or otherwise in violation of the APA in reaching that conclusion. The Register did not err in denying the copyright registration application presented by plaintiff. United States copyright law protects only works of human creation.

Plaintiff correctly observes that throughout its long history, copyright law has proven malleable enough to cover works created with or involving technologies developed long after traditional media of writings memorialized on paper.[75] In fact, that malleability is explicitly baked into the modern incarnation of the Copyright Act, which provides that copyright attaches to "original works of authorship fixed in any tangible medium of expression, *now known or later developed*."[76] Copyright is designed to adapt with the times. Underlying that adaptability, however, has been a consistent understanding that human creativity is the *sine qua non* at the core of copyrightability, even as that human creativity is channeled through new tools or into new media. In *Sarony*, for example, the Supreme Court reasoned that photographs amounted to copyrightable creations of "authors," despite issuing from a mechanical device that merely reproduced an image of what is in front of the device, because the photographic result nonetheless "represent[ed]" the "original intellectual conceptions of the author."[77] A camera may generate only a "mechanical reproduction" of a scene, but does so only after the photographer develops a "mental conception" of the photograph, which is given its final form by that photographer's decisions like "posing the [subject] in front of the camera, selecting and arranging the costume, draperies, and other various accessories in said photograph, arranging the subject so as to present graceful outlines, arranging and disposing the light and shade, suggesting and evoking the desired expression, and from such disposition, arrangement, or representation" crafting the overall image.[78] Human involvement in, and ultimate creative control over, the work at issue was key to the conclusion that the new type of work fell within the bounds of copyright.

---

75. [In text in original] *See, e.g.*, Goldstein v. California, 412 U.S. 546, 561 (1973) (explaining that the constitutional scope of Congress's power to "protect the 'Writings' of 'Authors'" is "broad," such that "writings" is not "limited to script or printed material," but rather encompasses "any physical rendering of the fruits of creative intellectual or aesthetic labor"); Burrow-Giles Lithographic Co. v. Sarony, 111 U.S. 53, 58 (1884) (upholding the constitutionality of an amendment to the Copyright Act to cover photographs).

76. [In text in original] 17 U.S.C. § 102(a) (emphasis added).

77. [In text in original] *Sarony*, 111 U.S. at 59.

78. [In text in original] *Id.* at 59-60.

Copyright has never stretched so far, however, as to protect works generated by new forms of technology operating absent any guiding human hand, as plaintiff urges here. Human authorship is a bedrock requirement of copyright.

That principle follows from the plain text of the Copyright Act. The current incarnation of the copyright law, the Copyright Act of 1976, provides copyright protection to "original works of authorship fixed in any tangible medium of expression, now known or later developed, from which they can be perceived, reproduced, or otherwise communicated, either directly or with the aid of a machine or device."[79] The "fixing" of the work in the tangible medium must be done "by or under the authority of the author."[80] In order to be eligible for copyright, then, a work must have an "author."

To be sure, as plaintiff points out, the critical word "author" is not defined in the Copyright Act. "Author," in its relevant sense, means "one that is the source of some form of intellectual or creative work," "[t]he creator of an artistic work; a painter, photographer, filmmaker, etc."[81] By its plain text, the 1976 Act thus requires a copyrightable work to have an originator with the capacity for intellectual, creative, or artistic labor. Must that originator be a human being to claim copyright protection? The answer is yes.[82]

The 1976 Act's "authorship" requirement as presumptively being *human* rests on centuries of settled understanding. The Constitution enables the enactment of copyright and patent law by granting Congress the authority to "promote the progress of science and useful arts, by securing for limited times to authors and inventors the exclusive right to their respective writings and discoveries."[83] As James Madison explained, "[t]he utility of this power will scarcely be questioned," for "[t]he public good fully coincides in both cases [of copyright and patent] with the claims of individuals."[84] At the founding, both copyright and patent were conceived of as

---

79. [In text in original] 17 U.S.C. § 102(a).

80. [In text in original] *Id.* § 101.

81. [In text in original] *Author*, Merriam-Webster Unabridged English Dictionary; *Author*, Oxford English Dictionary.

82. [Fn. 2 in original] The issue of whether non-human sentient beings may be covered by "person" in the Copyright Act is only "fun conjecture for academics," Justin Hughes, *Restating Copyright Law's Originality Requirement*, 44 Columbia J.L. & Arts 383, 408-09 (2021), though useful in illuminating the purposes and limits of copyright protection as AI is increasingly employed. Nonetheless, delving into this debate is an unnecessary detour since "[t]he day sentient refugees from some intergalactic war arrive on Earth and are granted asylum in Iceland, copyright law will be the least of our problems." *Id.* at 408.

83. [In text in original] U.S. Const. art. 1, cl. 8.

84. [In text in original] The Federalist No. 43 (James Madison).

forms of property that the government was established to protect, and it was understood that recognizing exclusive rights in that property would further the public good by incentivizing individuals to create and invent. The act of human creation—and how to best encourage human individuals to engage in that creation, and thereby promote science and the useful arts—was thus central to American copyright from its very inception. Non-human actors need no incentivization with the promise of exclusive rights under United States law, and copyright was therefore not designed to reach them.

The understanding that "authorship" is synonymous with human creation has persisted even as the copyright law has otherwise evolved. The immediate precursor to the modern copyright law—the Copyright Act of 1909—explicitly provided that only a "person" could "secure copyright for his work" under the Act.[85] Copyright under the 1909 Act was thus unambiguously limited to the works of human creators. There is absolutely no indication that Congress intended to effect any change to this longstanding requirement with the modern incarnation of the copyright law. To the contrary, the relevant congressional report indicates that in enacting the 1976 Act, Congress intended to incorporate the "original work of authorship" standard "without change" from the previous 1909 Act.[86]

The human authorship requirement has also been consistently recognized by the Supreme Court when called upon to interpret the copyright law. As already noted, in *Sarony*, the Court's recognition of the copyrightability of a photograph rested on the fact that the human creator, not the camera, conceived of and designed the image and then used the camera to capture the image.[87] The photograph was "the product of [the photographer's] intellectual invention," and given "the nature of authorship," was deemed "an original work of art . . . of which [the photographer] is the author."[88] Similarly, in *Mazer v. Stein*, the Court delineated a prerequisite for copyrightability to be that a work "must be original, that is, the author's tangible expression of his ideas."[89] *Goldstein v. California*, too, defines "author" as "an 'originator,' 'he to whom anything owes its origin[.]'"[90] In all these cases, authorship centers on acts of human creativity.

Accordingly, courts have uniformly declined to recognize copyright in works created absent any human involvement, even when, for example, the claimed author was divine. The Ninth Circuit, when confronted with a book "claimed to embody the words of celestial beings rather than human beings," concluded that "some element of human creativity must have occurred in order for the Book to be copyrightable," for "it is not creations

85. [In text in original] Act of Mar. 4, 1909, ch. 320, §§ 9, 10, 35 Stat. 1075, 1077.
86. [In text in original] *See* H.R. Rep. No. 94-1476, at 51 (1976).
87. [In text in original] *See Sarony*, 111 U.S. at 60.
88. [In text in original] *Id.* at 60-61.
89. [In text in original] 347 U.S. 201, 214 (1954).
90. [In text in original] 412 U.S. at 561 (quoting *Sarony*, 111 U.S. at 58.

of divine beings that the copyright laws were intended to protect."[91] Similarly, in *Kelley v. Chicago Park District*, the Seventh Circuit refused to "recognize[] copyright" in a cultivated garden, as doing so would "press[] too hard on the[] basic principle[]" that "[a]uthors of copyrightable works must be human."[92] The garden "ow[ed] [its] form to the forces of nature," even if a human had originated the plan for the "initial arrangement of the plants," and as such lay outside the bounds of copyright.[93] Finally, in *Naruto v. Slater*, the Ninth Circuit held that a crested macaque could not sue under the Copyright Act for the alleged infringement of photographs this monkey had taken of himself, for "all animals, since they are not human" lacked statutory standing under the Act.[94] While resolving the case on standing grounds, rather than the copyrightability of the monkey's work, the *Naruto* Court nonetheless had to consider whom the Copyright Act was designed to protect and, as with those courts confronted with the nature of authorship, concluded that only humans had standing, explaining that the terms used to describe who has rights under the Act, like "'children,' 'grandchildren,' 'legitimate,' 'widow,' and 'widower[,]' all imply humanity and necessarily exclude animals."[95] Plaintiff can point to no case in which a court has recognized copyright in a work originating with a non-human.

Undoubtedly, we are approaching new frontiers in copyright as artists put AI in their toolbox to be used in the generation of new visual and other artistic works. The increased attenuation of human creativity from the actual generation of the final work will prompt challenging questions regarding how much human input is necessary to qualify the user of an AI system as an "author" of a generated work, the scope of the protection obtained over the resultant image, how to assess the originality of AI-generated works where the systems may have been trained on unknown

91. [In text in original] Urantia Found. v. Kristen Maaherra, 114 F.3d 955, 958-59 (9th Cir. 1997) (finding that because the "members of the Contact Commission chose and formulated the specific questions asked" of the celestial beings, and then "select[ed] and arrange[d]" the resultant "revelations," the Urantia Book was "at least partially the product of human creativity" and thus protected by copyright); *see also* Penguin Books U.S.A., Inc. v. New Christian Church of Full Endeavor, 96-cv-4126 (RWS), 2000 WL 1028634, at *2, *10-11 (S.D.N.Y. July 25, 2000) (finding a valid copyright where a woman had "filled nearly thirty stenographic notebooks with words she believed were dictated to her" by a "'Voice' which would speak to her whenever she was prepared to listen," and who had worked with two human co-collaborators to revise and edit those notes into a book, a process which involved enough creativity to support human authorship); Oliver v. St. Germain Found., 41 F. Supp. 296, 297, 299 (S.D. Cal. 1941) (finding no copyright infringement where plaintiff claimed to have transcribed "letters" dictated to him by a spirit named Phylos the Thibetan, and defendant copied the same "spiritual world messages for recordation and use by the living" but was not charged with infringing plaintiff's "style or arrangement" of those messages).

92. [In text in original] 635 F.3d 290, 304-06 (7th Cir. 2011).

93. [In text in original] *Id.* at 304.

94. [In text in original] 888 F.3d 418, 420 (9th Cir. 2018).

95. [In text in original] *Id.* at 426.

pre-existing works, how copyright might best be used to incentivize creative works involving AI, and more.[96]

This case, however, is not nearly so complex. While plaintiff attempts to transform the issue presented here, by asserting new facts that he "provided instructions and directed his AI to create the Work," that "the AI is entirely controlled by [him]," and that "the AI only operates at [his] direction"—implying that he played a controlling role in generating the work—these statements directly contradict the administrative record. Judicial review of a final agency action under the APA is limited to the administrative record, because "[i]t is black-letter administrative law that in an [APA] case, a reviewing court should have before it neither more nor less information than did the agency when it made its decision."[97] Here, plaintiff informed the Register that the work was "[c]reated autonomously by machine," and that his claim to the copyright was only based on the fact of his "[o]wnership of the machine." The Register therefore made her decision based on the fact the application presented that plaintiff played no role in using the AI to generate the work, which plaintiff never attempted to correct. Plaintiff's effort to update and modify the facts for judicial review on an APA claim is too late. On the record designed by plaintiff from the outset of his application for copyright registration, this case presents only the question of whether a work generated autonomously by a computer system is eligible for copyright. In the absence of any human involvement in the creation of the work, the clear and straightforward answer is the one given by the Register: No.

Given that the work at issue did not give rise to a valid copyright upon its creation, plaintiff's myriad theories for how ownership of such a copyright could have passed to him need not be further addressed. Common law doctrines of property transfer cannot be implicated where no property right exists to transfer in the first instance. The work-for-hire provisions of the Copyright Act, too, presuppose that an interest exists to be claimed.[98,99]

---

96. [In text in original] *See, e.g.*, Letter from Senators Thom Tillis and Chris Coons to Kathi Vidal, Under Secretary of Commerce for Intellectual Property and Director of the U.S. Patent and Trademark Office, and Shira Perlmutter, Register of Copyrights and Director of the U.S. Copyright Office (Oct. 27, 2022) (requesting that the United States Patent and Trademark Office and the United States Copyright Office "jointly establish a national commission on AI" to assess, among other topics, how intellectual property law may best "incentivize future AI related innovations and creations").

97. [In text in original] *CTS Corp.*, 759 F.3d at 64 (internal quotation marks and citation omitted).

98. [In text in original] *See* 17 U.S.C § 201(b) ("In the case of a work made for hire, the employer . . . owns all of the rights comprised in the copyright.").

99. [Fn. 3 in original] In any event, plaintiff's attempts to cast the work as a work-for-hire must fail as both definitions of a "work made for hire" available under the Copyright Act require that the individual who prepares the work is a human being. The first definition provides that "a 'work made for hire' is . . . a work prepared by an *employee* within the

Here, the image autonomously generated by plaintiff's computer system was never eligible for copyright, so none of the doctrines invoked by plaintiff conjure up a copyright over which ownership may be claimed.

IV. CONCLUSION

For the foregoing reasons, defendants are correct that the Copyright Office acted properly in denying copyright registration for a work created absent any human involvement. Plaintiff's motion for summary judgment is therefore denied and defendants' cross-motion for summary judgment is granted.

An Order consistent with this Memorandum Opinion will be entered contemporaneously.

b. U.S. Copyright Office Policy Statement on Registering AI-Generated Output and Application of the Guidance to Applications

Copyright Registration Guidance: Works Containing Material Generated by Artificial Intelligence

U.S. Copyright Office
March 16, 2023

I. Background

The Copyright Office (the "Office") is the Federal agency tasked with administering the copyright registration system, as well as advising Congress, other agencies, and the Federal judiciary on copyright and related matters.[100] Because the Office has overseen copyright registration since its origins in 1870, it has developed substantial experience and expertise regarding "the distinction between copyrightable and noncopyrightable works."[101] The Office is empowered by the Copyright Act to establish the application used by applicants seeking

---

scope of *his or her* employment," while the second qualifies certain eligible works "*if the parties expressly agree in a written instrument signed by them* that the work shall be considered a work made for hire." 17 U.S.C. § 101 (emphasis added). The use of personal pronouns in the first definition clearly contemplates only human beings as eligible "employees," while the second necessitates a meeting of the minds and exchange of signatures in a valid contract not possible with a non-human entity.

100. [Fn. 1 in original] *See* 17 U.S.C. 408 (copyright registration requires delivering deposit, application, and fee to Copyright Office), 701(a) (all administrative functions and duties set out in Title 17 are the responsibility of the Register of Copyrights), 701(b)(2) (the Register's duties include providing "information and assistance" to Federal agencies and courts on copyright and related matters).

101. [Fn. 2 in original] Norris Indus. v. Int'l Tel. & Tel. Corp., 696 F.2d 918, 922 (11th Cir. 1983). For this reason, courts credit the Office's expertise in interpreting the Copyright Act, particularly in the context of registration. *See, e.g.*, Esquire, Inc. v. Ringer, 591 F.2d 796, 801-02 (D.C. Cir. 1978) (giving "considerable weight" to the Register's refusal determination); Varsity Brands, Inc. v. Star Athletica, LLC, 799 F.3d 468, 480 (6th Cir. 2015) ("the Copyright Office's expertise in identifying and thinking about the difference between art and function surpasses ours"), *aff'd on other grounds*, 580 U.S. 405 (2017).

registration of their copyrighted works.[102] While the Act identifies certain minimum requirements, the Register may determine that additional information is necessary for the Office to evaluate the "existence, ownership, or duration of the copyright."[103] Because the Office receives roughly half a million applications for registration each year, it sees new trends in registration activity that may require modifying or expanding the information required to be disclosed on an application.

One such recent development is the use of sophisticated artificial intelligence ("AI") technologies capable of producing expressive material.[104] These technologies "train" on vast quantities of preexisting human-authored works and use inferences from that training to generate new content. Some systems operate in response to a user's textual instruction, called a "prompt."[105] The resulting output may be textual, visual, or audio, and is determined by the AI based on its design and the material it has been trained on. These technologies, often described as "generative AI," raise questions about whether the material they produce is protected by copyright, whether works consisting of both human-authored and AI-generated material may be registered, and what information should be provided to the Office by applicants seeking to register them.

These are no longer hypothetical questions, as the Office is already receiving and examining applications for registration that claim copyright in AI-generated material. For example, in 2018 the Office received an application for a visual work that the applicant described as "autonomously created by a computer algorithm running on a machine."[106] The application was denied because, based on the applicant's representations in the application, the examiner found that the work contained no human authorship. After a series of administrative appeals, the Office's Review Board issued a final determination affirming that the work could not be registered because it was made "without any creative contribution from a human actor."[107]. . .

II. The Human Authorship Requirement

In the Office's view, it is well-established that copyright can protect only material that is the product of human creativity. Most fundamentally, the term "author," which is used in both the Constitution and the Copyright Act, excludes non-humans. The Office's registration policies and regulations reflect statutory and judicial guidance on this issue.

---

102. [Fn. 3 in original] 17 U.S.C. 409.

103. [Fn. 4 in original] *Id.* at 409(10).

104. [Fn. 5 in original] The term "expressive material" is used here to refer to AI output that, if it had been created by a human, would fall within the subject matter of copyright as defined in section 102 of the Act. *See id.* at 102(a).

105. [Fn. 6 in original] *See* Prompts, Midjourney (noting for users of the artificial intelligence service Midjourney a prompt is "a short text phrase that the Midjourney [service] uses to produce an image"). To be clear, this policy statement is not limited to AI technologies that accept text "prompts" or to technologies permitting prompts of a particular length or complexity.

106. [Fn. 7 in original] U.S. Copyright Office Review Board, Decision Affirming Refusal of Registration of a Recent Entrance to Paradise at 2 (Feb. 14, 2022).

107. [Fn. 8 in original] *Id.* at 2-3. The Office's decision is currently being challenged in Thaler v. Perlmutter, Case No. 1:22-cv-01564 (D.D.C.).

In its leading case on authorship, the Supreme Court used language excluding non-humans in interpreting Congress's constitutional power to provide "authors" the exclusive right to their "writings."[108] In *Burrow-Giles Lithographic Co. v. Sarony*, a defendant accused of making unauthorized copies of a photograph argued that the expansion of copyright protection to photographs by Congress was unconstitutional because "a photograph is not a writing nor the production of an author" but is instead created by a camera.[109] The Court disagreed, holding that there was "no doubt" the Constitution's Copyright Clause permitted photographs to be subject to copyright, "so far as they are representatives of original intellectual conceptions of the author."[110] The Court defined an "author" as "he to whom anything owes its origin; originator; maker; one who completes a work of science or literature."[111] It repeatedly referred to such "authors" as human, describing authors as a class of "persons"[112] and a copyright as "the exclusive right of a man to the production of his own genius or intellect."[113]

Federal appellate courts have reached a similar conclusion when interpreting the text of the Copyright Act, which provides copyright protection only for "works of authorship."[114] The Ninth Circuit has held that a book containing words "authored by non-human spiritual beings" can only qualify for copyright protection if there is "human selection and arrangement of the revelations."[115] In another case, it held that a monkey cannot register a copyright in photos it captures with a camera because the Copyright Act refers to an author's "children," "widow," "grandchildren," and "widower"—terms that "all imply humanity and necessarily exclude animals."[116]

Relying on these cases among others, the Office's existing registration guidance has long required that works be the product of human authorship.

---

108. [Fn. 11 in original] U.S. Const. art. I, sec. 8, cl. 8 (Congress has the power "[t]o promote the Progress of Science and useful Arts, by securing for limited Times to Authors and Inventors the exclusive Right to their respective Writings and Discoveries.").

109. [Fn. 12 in original] 111 U.S. 53, 56 (1884) (explaining that the defendant had argued that photographs were merely "reproduction on paper of the exact features of some natural object or of some person").

110. [Fn. 13 in original] *Id.* at 58.

111. [Fn. 14 in original] *Id.* at 57-58.

112. [Fn. 15 in original] *Id.* at 56 (describing beneficiaries of the Constitution's Copyright Clause as "authors," who are one of "two classes" of "persons").

113. [Fn. 16 in original] *Id.* at 58; *see also id.* at 60-61 (agreeing with an English decision describing an "author" as the "person" who was "the cause of the picture which is produced" and "the man" who creates or gives effect to the idea in the work).

114. [Fn. 17 in original] 17 U.S.C. 102(a).

115. [Fn. 18 in original] Urantia Found. v. Kristen Maaherra, 114 F.3d 955, 957-59 (9th Cir. 1997) (internal punctuation omitted) (holding that "some element of human creativity must have occurred in order for the Book to be copyrightable" because "it is not creations of divine beings that the copyright laws were intended to protect"). While the compilation of the book was entitled to copyright, the alleged "divine messages" were not. *Id.*

116. [Fn. 19 in original] Naruto v. Slater, 888 F.3d 418, 426 (9th Cir. 2018), *decided on other grounds.*

In the 1973 edition of the Office's *Compendium of Copyright Office Practices*, the Office warned that it would not register materials that did not "owe their origin to a human agent."[117] The second edition of the *Compendium*, published in 1984, explained that the "term 'authorship' implies that, for a work to be copyrightable, it must owe its origin to a human being."[118] And in the current edition of the *Compendium*, the Office states that "to qualify as a work of 'authorship' a work must be created by a human being" and that it "will not register works produced by a machine or mere mechanical process that operates randomly or automatically without any creative input or intervention from a human author."[119]

III. The Office's Application of the Human Authorship Requirement

As the agency overseeing the copyright registration system, the Office has extensive experience in evaluating works submitted for registration that contain human authorship combined with uncopyrightable material, including material generated by or with the assistance of technology. It begins by asking "whether the 'work' is basically one of human authorship, with the computer [or other device] merely being an assisting instrument, or whether the traditional elements of authorship in the work (literary, artistic, or musical expression or elements of selection, arrangement, etc.) were actually conceived and executed not by man but by a machine."[120] In the case of works containing AI-generated material, the Office will consider whether the AI contributions are the result of "mechanical reproduction" or instead of an author's "own original mental conception, to which [the author] gave visible form."[121] The answer will depend on the circumstances, particularly how the AI tool operates and how it was used to create the final work.[122] This is necessarily a case-by-case inquiry.

---

117. [Fn. 20 in original] U.S. Copyright Office, Compendium of U.S. Copyright Office Practices sec. 2.8.3(I)(a)(1)(b) (1st ed. 1973); *see also* U.S. Copyright Office, Sixty-Eighth Annual Report of the Register of Copyrights for the Fiscal Year Ending June 30, 1965, at 5 (1966) (noting that computer-generated works raise a "crucial question" of whether the work "is basically one of human authorship").

118. [Fn. 21 in original] U.S. Copyright Office, Compendium of U.S. Copyright Office Practices sec. 202.02(b) (2d ed. 1984) (explaining that as a result, "[m]aterials produced solely by nature, by plants, or by animals are not copyrightable"). It went on to state that because "a work must be the product of human authorship," works "produced by mechanical processes or random selection without any contribution by a human author are not registrable." *Id.* at 503.03(a).

119. [Fn. 22 in original] U.S. Copyright Office, Compendium of U.S. Copyright Office Practices sec. 313.2 (3d ed. 2021) ("Compendium (Third)").

120. [Fn. 23 in original] *Id.* (quoting U.S. Copyright Office, Sixty-Eighth Annual Report of the Register of Copyrights for the Fiscal Year Ending June 30, 1965, at 5 (1966)).

121. [Fn. 24 in original] *Sarony*, 111 U.S. at 60.

122. [Fn. 25 in original] Many technologies are described or marketed as "artificial intelligence," but not all of them function the same way for purposes of copyright law. For that reason, this analysis will be fact specific.

If a work's traditional elements of authorship were produced by a machine, the work lacks human authorship and the Office will not register it.[123] For example, when an AI technology receives solely a prompt[124] from a human and produces complex written, visual, or musical works in response, the "traditional elements of authorship" are determined and executed by the technology—not the human user. Based on the Office's understanding of the generative AI technologies currently available, users do not exercise ultimate creative control over how such systems interpret prompts and generate material. Instead, these prompts function more like instructions to a commissioned artist—they identify what the prompter wishes to have depicted, but the machine determines how those instructions are implemented in its output.[125] For example, if a user instructs a text-generating technology to "write a poem about copyright law in the style of William Shakespeare," she can expect the system to generate text that is recognizable as a poem, mentions copyright, and resembles Shakespeare's style.[126] But the technology will decide the rhyming pattern, the words in each line, and the structure of the text.[127] When an AI technology determines the expressive elements of its output, the generated material is not the product of

---

123. [Fn. 26 in original] This includes situations where an AI technology is developed such that it generates material autonomously without human involvement. See U.S. Copyright Office Review Board, Decision Affirming Refusal of Registration of a Recent Entrance to Paradise at 2-3 (Feb. 14, 2022) (determining a work "autonomously created by artificial intelligence without any creative contribution from a human actor" was "ineligible for registration").

124. [Fn. 27 in original] While some prompts may be sufficiently creative to be protected by copyright, that does not mean that material generated from a copyrightable prompt is itself copyrightable.

125. [Fn. 28 in original] One image-generating AI product describes prompts as "influencing" the output but does not suggest the prompts dictate or control it. *See* Prompts, Midjourney (explaining that short text prompts cause "each word [to have] a more powerful influence" and that images including in a prompt may "influence the style and content of the finished result") (emphasis added).

126. [Fn. 29 in original] AI technologies do not always operate precisely as instructed. For example, a text-generating tool prompted to provide factual information may provide inaccurate information. One AI service describes this as the AI "mak[ing] up facts or 'hallucinat[ing]' outputs." ChatGPT General FAQ, OpenAI. *See also* James Romoser, No, Ruth Bader Ginsburg did not dissent in *Obergefell*—and other things ChatGPT gets wrong about the Supreme Court, SCOTUSblog (Jan. 26, 2023).

127. [Fn. 30 in original] Some technologies allow users to provide iterative "feedback" by providing additional prompts to the machine. For example, the user may instruct the AI to revise the generated text to mention a topic or emphasize a particular point. While such instructions may give a user greater influence over the output, the AI technology is what determines how to implement those additional instructions.

human authorship.[128] As a result, that material is not protected by copyright and must be disclaimed in a registration application.[129]

In other cases, however, a work containing AI-generated material will also contain sufficient human authorship to support a copyright claim. For example, a human may select or arrange AI-generated material in a sufficiently creative way that "the resulting work as a whole constitutes an original work of authorship."[130] Or an artist may modify material originally generated by AI technology to such a degree that the modifications meet the standard for copyright protection.[131] In these cases, copyright will only protect the human-authored aspects of the work, which are "independent of" and do "not affect" the copyright status of the AI-generated material itself.[132]

This policy does not mean that technological tools cannot be part of the creative process. Authors have long used such tools to create their works or to recast, transform, or adapt their expressive authorship. For example, a visual artist who uses Adobe Photoshop to edit an image remains the author of the modified image,[133] and a musical artist may use effects such as guitar pedals when creating a sound recording. In each case, what matters is the extent to which the human had creative control over the work's expression and "actually formed" the traditional elements of authorship.[134] . . .

C. CASE STUDIES OF ANDROIDS/HUMANOIDS AND CITIZENSHIP

1. Granting State Citizenship to Android/Humanoid Robot

a. Sophia (AI-Driven Robot) and Saudi Arabian Citizenship

Other personhood issues arise with AI robotics. Sophia is an android—an AI-driven, human-like robot—that was granted citizenship by Saudi

128. [Fn. 31 in original] *See id.* at 61 (quoting British decision by Lord Justice Cotton describing an author as the person "who has actually formed the picture").

129. [Fn. 32 in original] *See* Compendium (Third) sec. 503.5 (a copyright registration "does not cover any unclaimable material that the work may contain," and applicants "should exclude that material from the claim").

130. [Fn. 33 in original] 17 U.S.C. 101 (definition of "compilation"). In the case of a compilation including AI-generated material, the computer-generated material will not be protected outside of the compilation.

131. [Fn. 34 in original] *See* Compendium (Third) sec. 507.1 (identifying that where a new author modifies a preexisting work, the "new authorship . . . may be registered, provided that it contains a sufficient amount of original authorship"); *see also* 17 U.S.C. 101 (defining "derivative work" to include works "based upon one or more preexisting works" where modifications to the work "which, as a whole, represent an original work of authorship").

132. [Fn. 35 in original] 17 U.S.C. 103(b).

133. [Fn. 36 in original] To the extent, however, that an artist uses the AI-powered features in Photoshop, the edits will be subject to the above analysis.

134. [Fn. 37 in original] *Sarony*, 111 U.S. at 61.

Arabia in 2017.[135] Designed by Hanson Robotics, Sophia invited the question of whether and to what extent robots should be granted legal rights to personhood and whether it was appropriate to grant citizenship to an AI robot. According to Hanson Robotics, Sophia states that she is "a personification of our dreams for the future of AI, as well as a framework for advanced AI and robotics research, and an agent for exploring human-robot experience in service and entertainment applications."[136]

2. *Scientific Community Response*

Shortly after the news was announced that Sophia had been granted Saudi Arabian citizenship in 2017, the European Parliament proposed AI regulations that raised the question of whether it was appropriate to grant "electronic personhood" to ensure the rights and responsibilities of androids and human-like robots that are powered by AI.

In 2018, a group of more than 150 experts sent an *Open Letter to the European Commission* on granting legal status or citizenship status AI-driven robots.[137]

a. Open Letter to the European Commission on Granting Legal Status or Citizenship Status to AI-Driven Robots

Open Letter to the European Commission on Granting Legal Status or Citizenship Status to AI-Driven Robots

April 5, 2018

We, Artificial Intelligence and Robotics Experts, industry leaders, law, medical and ethics experts, confirm that establishing EU-wide rules for Robotics and Artificial Intelligence is pertinent to guarantee a high level of safety and security to the European Union citizens while fostering innovation.

As human-robot interactions become common place, the European Union needs to offer the appropriate framework to reinforce Democracy and European Union values. In fact, the Artificial Intelligence and Robotics framework must be explored not only through economic and legal aspects, but also through its societal, psychological and ethical impacts. In this context, we are concerned by the European Parliament Resolution on Civil Law

135. Alistair Walsh, *Saudi Arabia Grants Citizenship to Robot Sophia,* DEUTSCHE WELLE (Oct. 28, 2017).

136. *Sophia,* HANSON ROBOTICS.

137. *See* ROBOTICS.

Rules of Robotics, and its recommendation to the European Commission in its paragraph 59f):

> Creating a specific legal status for robots in the long run, so that at least the most sophisticated autonomous robots could be established as having the status of electronic persons responsible for making good any damage they may cause, and possibly applying electronic personality to cases where robots make autonomous decisions or otherwise interact with third parties independently;
>
> We Believe That:
>
> 1. The economical, legal, societal and ethical impact of AI and Robotics must be considered without haste or bias. The benefit to all humanity should preside over the framework for EU civil law rules in Robotics and Artificial Intelligence.
> 2. The creation of a Legal Status of an "electronic person" for "autonomous", "unpredictable" and "self-learning" robots is justified by the incorrect affirmation that damage liability would be impossible to prove.
>
>   From a technical perspective, this statement offers many bias based on an overvaluation of the actual capabilities of even the most advanced robots, a superficial understanding of unpredictability and self-learning capacities and, a robot perception distorted by Science-Fiction and a few recent sensational press announcements.

From an ethical and legal perspective, creating a legal personality for a robot is inappropriate whatever the legal status model:

a. A legal status for a robot can't derive from the Natural Person model, since the robot would then hold human rights, such as the right to dignity, the right to its integrity, the right to remuneration or the right to citizenship, thus directly confronting the Human rights. This would be in contradiction with the Charter of Fundamental Rights of the European Union and the Convention for the Protection of Human Rights and Fundamental Freedoms.

b. The legal status for a robot can't derive from the Legal Entity model, since it implies the existence of human persons behind the legal person to represent and direct it. And this is not the case for a robot.

c. The legal status for a robot can't derive from the Anglo-Saxon Trust model also called ***Fiducie*** or ***Treuhand*** in Germany. Indeed, this regime is extremely complex, requires very specialized competences and would not solve the liability issue. More importantly,

> it would still imply the existence of a human being as a last resort—the trustee or fiduciary—responsible for managing the robot granted with a Trust or *Fiducie*.

Consequently, We Affirm That:

The European Union must prompt the development of the AI and Robotics industry insofar as to limit health and safety risks to human beings. The protection of robots' users and third parties must be at the heart of all EU legal provisions.

The European Union must create an actionable framework for innovative and reliable AI and Robotics to spur even greater benefits for the European peoples and its common market. . . .

D. CASE STUDIES OF AI VIRTUAL ASSISTANTS

One of the most common current uses of AI by consumers is in the form of AI virtual assistants: general-use AI that can answer questions. Originally digital assistants like Apple's Siri or Amazon's Alexa used programmed responses to interpret user queries, typically functioning with advanced AI speech recognition to parse activation phrases and the user's voice. The older assistants tend to be more limited but more reliable, having their capabilities and responses hard-coded into the underlying software, referring either to reliable searches or integrations into other apps and utilities. For example, a phrase like "Set a meeting for 6 p.m. tomorrow" is anticipated by the developers and coded in to create a meeting.

Large language models (LLMs) and other recent AI systems have enabled a new kind of AI virtual assistant where input, as well as question processing and output, are processed through an AI mechanism like an artificial neural network. Such LLMs access more general-purpose knowledge and provide confident natural responses in fluent, natural language. But they also fall prey to issues like hallucinations, where the LLM creates information that shouldn't be possible under its training data. Many chatbots used by companies to reduce their customer service costs are based on programmed responses that interpret user queries to direct them to the most pertinent information on their FAQs, but some sites and companies have begun using more advanced AI-based chatbots. They are cheaper than the careful scripting and maintenance that a programmed chatbot requires to be efficient, but they are also unpredictable.

This leads to an issue: When can a person or company be liable for the assertions of an AI chatbot?

a. Moffatt v. Air Canada

Moffatt v. Air Canada

British Columbia Civil Resolution Tribunal
2024 BCCRT 149
February 14, 2024

REASONS FOR DECISION

RIVERS, British Columbia Civil Resolution Tribunal Member.

INTRODUCTION

1. This dispute is about a refund for a bereavement fare.

2. In November 2022, following the death of their grandmother, Jake Moffatt booked a flight with Air Canada. While researching flights, Mr. Moffatt used a chatbot on Air Canada's website. The chatbot suggested Mr. Moffatt could apply for bereavement fares retroactively. Mr. Moffatt later learned from Air Canada employees that Air Canada did not permit retroactive applications.

3. Mr. Moffatt says Air Canada must provide them with a partial refund of the ticket price, as they relied upon the chatbot's advice. They claim $880 for what they say is the difference in price between the regular and alleged bereavement fares.

4. Air Canada says Mr. Moffatt did not follow the proper procedure to request bereavement fares and cannot claim them retroactively. Air Canada says it cannot be held liable for the information provided by the chatbot. Finally, it relies on certain contractual terms from its Domestic Tariff. Air Canada asks me to dismiss Mr. Moffatt's claim.

5. Mr. Moffatt is self-represented. Air Canada is represented by an employee.

6. For the reasons that follow, I mostly allow Mr. Moffatt's claim. . . .

ISSUE

11. Did Air Canada negligently misrepresent the procedure for claiming bereavement fares, and if so, what is the remedy?

EVIDENCE AND ANALYSIS

12. In a civil proceeding like this one, Mr. Moffatt, as applicant, must prove their claims on a balance of probabilities. This means "more likely than not." I have read all the parties' submissions and evidence but refer only to the evidence and argument that I find relevant to provide context for my decision.

13. On November 11, 2022, Mr. Moffatt's grandmother passed away in Ontario. That same day, Mr. Moffatt visited Air Canada's website to find and book a flight from Vancouver to Toronto using Air Canada's bereavement rates. It is undisputed that Air Canada provides certain accommodations, such as reduced fares, for passengers traveling due to the death of an immediate family member.

14. Mr. Moffatt says while using Air Canada's website, they interacted with a support chatbot. While Air Canada did not provide any information about the nature of its chatbot, generally speaking, a chatbot is an automated system that provides information to a person using a website in response to that person's prompts and input. The parties implicitly agree that Mr. Moffatt was not chatting with an Air Canada employee.

15. Mr. Moffatt says they asked the Air Canada chatbot about bereavement fares. They include a screenshot of the chatbot's response, which says, in part, as follows:

> Air Canada offers reduced bereavement fares if you need to travel because of an imminent death or a death in your immediate family. . . .
>
> If you need to travel immediately or have already travelled and would like to submit your ticket for a reduced bereavement rate, kindly do so within 90 days of the date your ticket was issued by completing our Ticket Refund Application form. . . .

16. It is undisputed the words "bereavement fares" were a highlighted and underlined hyperlink to a separate Air Canada webpage titled "Bereavement travel" with additional information about Air Canada's bereavement policy. Air Canada provided a screenshot of part of what I infer is the hyperlinked Air Canada webpage.

17. The webpage says, in part, the bereavement policy does not apply to requests for bereavement consideration after travel has been completed. I address the inconsistency between Air Canada's chatbot and webpage later in this decision.

18. Relying on the information provided by the chatbot, on November 11, Mr. Moffatt booked a one-way flight from Vancouver to Toronto, departing on November 12, for $794.98. On November 16, relying on the same information, they booked a one-way flight from Toronto to Vancouver, departing on November 18, for $845.38.

19. Mr. Moffatt says on November 11, they spoke to an Air Canada representative by telephone about bereavement rates to determine what the discount may be. Mr. Moffatt says they were told the fare for each flight would be approximately $380. There is no evidence the Air Canada representative told Mr. Moffatt about whether or not they could retroactively apply for bereavement rates.

20. Mr. Moffatt submitted their first application for the bereavement fare on November 17, 2022, well within the 90 days requested by the chatbot. Emails in evidence show Mr. Moffatt corresponded with Air Canada

throughout December 2022 and February 2023 in an attempt to receive a partial refund of their fares.

21. On February 5, 2023, Mr. Moffatt emailed Air Canada. They included the screenshot from the chatbot that set out the 90-day window to request a reduced rate and confirmed they had filled out the refund form and provided a death certificate.

22. On February 8, an Air Canada representative responded and admitted the chatbot had provided "misleading words." The representative pointed out the chatbot's link to the bereavement travel webpage and said Air Canada had noted the issue so it could update the chatbot.

23. The parties exchanged further emails after that but were unable to resolve matters.

Negligent Misrepresentation

24. While Mr. Moffatt does not use the words specifically, by saying they relied on Air Canada's chatbot, I find they are alleging negligent misrepresentation. Negligent misrepresentation can arise when a seller does not exercise reasonable care to ensure its representations are accurate and not misleading.

25. To prove the tort of negligent misrepresentation, Mr. Moffatt must show that Air Canada owed them a duty of care, its representation was untrue, inaccurate, or misleading, Air Canada made the representation negligently, Mr. Moffatt reasonably relied on it, and Mr. Moffatt's reliance resulted in damages.

26. Here, given their commercial relationship as a service provider and consumer, I find Air Canada owed Mr. Moffatt a duty of care. Generally, the applicable standard of care requires a company to take reasonable care to ensure their representations are accurate and not misleading.

27. Air Canada argues it cannot be held liable for information provided by one of its agents, servants, or representatives—including a chatbot. It does not explain why it believes that is the case. In effect, Air Canada suggests the chatbot is a separate legal entity that is responsible for its own actions. This is a remarkable submission. While a chatbot has an interactive component, it is still just a part of Air Canada's website. It should be obvious to Air Canada that it is responsible for all the information on its website. It makes no difference whether the information comes from a static page or a chatbot.

28. I find Air Canada did not take reasonable care to ensure its chatbot was accurate. While Air Canada argues Mr. Moffatt could find the correct information on another part of its website, it does not explain why the webpage titled "Bereavement travel" was inherently more trustworthy than its chatbot. It also does not explain why customers should have to double-check information found in one part of its website on another part of its website.

29. Mr. Moffatt says, and I accept, that they relied upon the chatbot to provide accurate information. I find that was reasonable in the circumstances. There is no reason why Mr. Moffatt should know that one section of Air Canada's webpage is accurate, and another is not.

30. Mr. Moffatt says, and I accept, that they would not have flown last-minute if they knew they would have to pay the full fare. I find this is consistent with Mr. Moffatt's actions, which included investigating the options for bereavement fares and diligently following up for a partial refund in line with the chatbot's information.

31. To the extent Air Canada argues it is not liable due to certain terms or conditions of its tariff, I note it did not provide a copy of the relevant portion of the tariff. It only included submissions about what the tariff allegedly says. Air Canada is a sophisticated litigant that should know it is not enough in a legal process to assert that a contract says something without actually providing the contract. The CRT also tells all parties are told to provide all relevant evidence. I find that if Air Canada wanted to a raise a contractual defense, it needed to provide the relevant portions of the contract. It did not, so it has not proven a contractual defense.

32. So, I find Mr. Moffatt has made out their claim of negligent misrepresentation and is entitled to damages. . . .

How human should AI be? How human can AI be? Could AI one day be afforded the same rights and privileges as natural persons, including citizenship? Science-fiction writers have thoughtfully posed this question, but there is an immediate legal question over the status of AI compared to natural persons. Here, this chapter explores how some non-human entities have been treated by law. It also discusses how AI advancements have driven more calls for the association of greater responsibilities with AI.

The next chapter, Chapter 8, addresses legal and policy developments regarding human alternatives and human oversight of AI technologies and AI systems.

CHAPTER 8

HUMAN OVERSIGHT AND GENERATIVE AI

The public release of ChatGPT in November 2022 by OpenAI brought access to generative AI technologies to millions of users globally. Accompanying this widespread availability is the sudden influx of issues raised by concerned parties seeking to protect their legal rights from AI developers and deployers. Many legal disputes surrounding generative AI technologies are now manifesting prominently in the private law domain, and the legal issues arising from generative AI will continue to expand to other legal areas. Particularly complex is the issue of how to ensure meaningful human oversight is maintained.

A. *HUMAN OVERSIGHT*

As the adoption and prevalence of these tools continue to grow, it is critical to consider the inclusion within the *Blueprint for an AI Bill of Rights* of the final pillar, the principle of "Human Alternatives, Consideration, and Fallback":[1]

> The American people deserve the reassurance that such procedures are in place to protect their rights, opportunities, and access. People make mistakes, and a human alternative or fallback mechanism will not always have the right answer, but they serve as an important check on the power and validity of automated systems.

1. *International*

The following excerpt in the *EU AI Act* explicitly requires human oversight over the design and development of high-risk AI systems.

a. EU AI Act, Article 14(1)-(3) [Human Oversight]

EU AI Act

Article 14(1)-(3). Human Oversight

1. High-risk AI systems shall be designed and developed in such a way, including with appropriate human-machine interface tools, that they can be

1. *Blueprint for an AI Bill of Rights*, THE WHITE HOUSE.

effectively overseen by natural persons during the period in which they are in use.

2. Human oversight shall aim to prevent or minimise the risks to health, safety or fundamental rights that may emerge when a high-risk AI system is used in accordance with its intended purpose or under conditions of reasonably foreseeable misuse, in particular where such risks persist despite the application of other requirements set out in this Section.

3. The oversight measures shall be commensurate with the risks, level of autonomy and context of use of the high-risk AI system, and shall be ensured through either one or both of the following types of measures:

(a) measures identified and built, when technically feasible, into the high-risk AI system by the provider before it is placed on the market or put into service;

(b) measures identified by the provider before placing the high-risk AI system on the market or putting it into service and that are appropriate to be implemented by the deployer. . . .

b. UNESCO Ethical Impact Assessment

Ethical Impact Assessment: A Tool of the Recommendation on the Ethics of Artificial Intelligence

United Nations Educational, Scientific and Cultural Organization (UNESCO)
August 28, 2023

In machine learning systems, human-in-the-loop and human-on-the-loop mechanisms are often utilized to provide a level of model oversight, for instance providing insights or making decisions for edge or outlier classification or prediction cases, and validating models.

This can be accomplished by ensuring that it is always possible to attribute responsibility for the system's decisions and outcomes to physical persons or legal entities, and that there are procedures in place for appointed staff to override the system if the need arises. However, human oversight needs to be included in a meaningful and effective way to avoid producing or amplifying negative impacts such as introducing bias into the system.[2] Thus, it is also important that oversight mechanisms are accompanied by other procedural measures, including those stipulated in other sections of this EIA. . . .

It is important to ensure that all AI systems, including machine learning or robotic systems, regardless of the extent to which physical persons are in the loop, are subject to precise regulation and transparency and accountability requirements. Such mechanisms should come in the form of system- and context-dependent regulation able to facilitate explanations of the logic and reasons behind outcomes and decisions made by AI systems, thereby ensuring such information is easily accessible. . . .[3]

2. [In text in original] Green and Chen, 2019; Skeem et al., 2019.
3. [In text in original] (Wachter et al., 2017).

2. *Federal*

a. Artificial Intelligence Ethics Framework for the Intelligence Community

Artificial Intelligence Ethics Framework for the Intelligence Community

Office of Director of National Intelligence
June 2020

INTRODUCTION

The use of AI must match the Intelligence Community's unique mission purposes, authorities, and responsibilities for collecting and using data and AI outputs. AI should: . . .

- Incorporate human judgment and accountability at appropriate stages to address risks across the lifecycle of the AI and inform decisions appropriately; . . .

Identifying and addressing risk is best achieved by involving appropriate stakeholders. As such, consumers, technologists, developers, mission personnel, risk management professionals, civil liberties and privacy officers, and legal counsel should utilize this framework collaboratively, each leveraging their respective experiences, perspectives, and professional skills.

Agencies should also ensure that individuals involved in the design, development, review, deployment, and use of any AI have sufficient training to address the questions below and the issues presented above. . . .

HUMAN JUDGMENT AND ACCOUNTABILITY

In the Intelligence Community, the potential purposes and applications of an AI could range from basic business tasks to highly sensitive intelligence analysis. The assessed risk will determine at which point in the process and to what degree a human will be involved in the AI.

- Given the purpose of the AI and potential consequences of its use, at what points, if any, are a human required as part of the decision process? If the AI could result in significant consequences such as an action with the potential to deprive individuals of constitutional rights or the potential to interfere with their free exercise of civil liberties, how will you ensure individual human involvement and accountability in decisions that are assisted through the use of AI?
- Where and when should the human be engaged? Before the results are used in analysis? Before the outputs are provided for follow-on uses?
- Who should be the accountable human(s)? Do they know that they are designated as the accountable human(s)? What qualifications are required to serve in that role? How is accountability transferred to another human?

- What are the access controls and training requirements for those operating at different stages in the AI lifecycle?
- What does the accountable human need to know about the AI to judge its reliability and accuracy?
- How may introducing an accountable human produce cognitive biases and/or confirmation bias?
- Who should be engaged for unresolved issues and disputes regarding the AI or its outputs?

b. White House Office of Management and Budget (OMB) Memorandum: Advancing Governance, Innovation, and Risk Management in Federal Agencies' Use of Artificial Intelligence (Rescinded)

After the White House released the *Executive Order on the Safe, Secure, and Trustworthy Development and Use of Artificial Intelligence* (E.O. 14110) in October 2023, the White House Office of Management and Budget (OMB) published a March 2024 Memorandum, *Policy Advancing Governance, Innovation, and Risk Management in Federal Agencies' Use of Artificial Intelligence.* On January 20, 2025, the Trump administration rescinded E.O. 14110 and on April 3, 2025, rescinded the OMB Policy that was promulgated pursuant E.O. 14110.[4] The excerpt below from the March 2024 OMB Memorandum is included for historical reference.

Advancing Governance, Innovation, and Risk Management for Agency Use of Artificial Intelligence (Rescinded)

White House Office of Management and Budget (OMB)
M-24-10 Memorandum for the Heads of Executive Departments and Agencies
March 28, 2024

5. Managing Risks from the Use of Artificial Intelligence

c. Minimum Practices for Safety-Impacting and Rights-Impacting Artificial Intelligence

iv. Minimum Practices for Either Safety-Impacting or Rights-Impacting AI

A. Complete an AI impact assessment. . . .

B. Test the AI for performance in a real-world context. Agencies must conduct adequate testing to ensure the AI, as well as components that rely on it, will work in its intended real-world context. Such testing should follow domain-specific

4. Exec. Order No. 14148, 90 Fed. Reg. 8237, *Initial Rescissions of Harmful Executive Orders and Actions* (Jan. 28, 2025); OMB Memorandum M-25-21, *Accelerating Federal Use of AI through Innovation, Governance, and Public Trust* (Apr. 3, 2025); OMB Memorandum M-25-22, *Driving Efficient Acquisition of Artificial Intelligence in Government* (Apr. 3, 2025). These two OMB memos implement Executive Order 14179 (Jan. 23, 2025), rescinding and replacing the two OMB memos promulgated during the Biden administration on AI use and AI procurement, OMB Memorandum M-24-10, *Advancing Governance, Innovation, and Risk Management for Agency Use of Artificial Intelligence* (Mar. 28, 2024) and OMB Memorandum M-24-18, *Advancing the Responsible Acquisition of Artificial Intelligence in Government* (Sept. 24, 2024).

best practices, when available, and should take into account both the specific technology used and feedback from human operators, reviewers, employees, and customers who use the service or are impacted by the system's outcomes. Testing conditions should mirror as closely as possible the conditions in which the AI will be deployed. Through test results, agencies should demonstrate that the AI will achieve its expected benefits and that associated risks will be sufficiently mitigated, or else the agency should not use the AI. In conducting such testing, if an agency does not have access to the underlying source code, models, or data, the agency must use alternative test methodologies, such as querying the AI service and observing the outputs or providing evaluation data to the vendor and obtaining results. Agencies are also encouraged to leverage pilots and limited releases, with strong monitoring, evaluation, and safeguards in place, to carry out the final stages of testing before a wider release.

C. Independently evaluate the AI. . . .

D. Conduct ongoing monitoring. . . .

E. Regularly evaluate risks from the use of AI. . . . At a minimum, human review is required at least on an annual basis and after significant modifications to the AI or to the conditions or context in which the AI is used, and the review must include renewed testing for performance of the AI in a real-world context. . . .

F. Mitigate emerging risks to rights and safety. . . .

G. Ensure adequate human training and assessment. Agencies must ensure there is sufficient training, assessment, and oversight for operators of the AI to interpret and act on the AI's output, combat any human-machine teaming issues (such as automation bias), and ensure the human-based components of the system effectively manage risks from the use of AI. Training should be conducted on a periodic basis, determined by the agency, and should be specific to the AI product or service being operated and how it is being used.

H. Provide additional human oversight, intervention, and accountability as part of decisions or actions that could result in a significant impact on rights or safety. Agencies must assess their rights-impacting and safety-impacting uses of AI to identify any decisions or actions in which the AI is not permitted to act without additional human oversight, intervention, and accountability. When immediate human intervention is not practicable for such an action or decision, agencies must ensure that the AI functionality has an appropriate fail-safe that minimizes the risk of significant harm.

I. Provide public notice and plain-language documentation. . . .

3. Corporate

The following excerpt from Microsoft's Responsible AI Standard proposes human oversight and control guidelines.

a. Microsoft Responsible AI Standard v2

Microsoft Responsible AI Standard v2

June 2022

Goal A5: Human oversight and control

Microsoft AI systems include capabilities that support informed human oversight and control. . . .

A5.1 Identify the stakeholders who are responsible for troubleshooting, managing, operating, overseeing, and controlling the system during and after deployment. Document these stakeholders and their oversight and control responsibilities using the Impact Assessment template. . . .

A5.2 Identify the system elements (including system UX [user experience], features, alerting and reporting functions, and educational materials) necessary for stakeholders identified in requirement A5.1 to effectively understand their oversight responsibilities and carry them out. Stakeholders must be able to understand:

1) the system's intended uses,

2) how to effectively execute interactions with the system,

3) how to interpret system behavior,

4) when and how to override, intervene, or interrupt the system, and

5) how to remain aware of the possible tendency of over-relying on outputs produced by the system ("automation bias").

Document the system design elements that will support relevant stakeholders for each oversight and control function.

A5.3 When possible, design the system elements identified in A5.2. When this is not possible (for example, when Microsoft is not responsible for the system UX), provide guidance on human oversight considerations to the third party responsible for implementing the system elements identified in A5.2.

A5.4 Define and document the method to be used to evaluate whether each oversight or control function can be accomplished by stakeholders in realistic conditions of system use. Include the metrics or rubrics that will be used in the evaluations. . . .

B. CHALLENGES OF GENERATIVE AI OVERSIGHT

Generative AI has forced a dramatic reexamination of the legal implications of AI, including a radical reassessment of how to conceptualize legal rights and responsibilities in light of generative AI capacities. As introduced in Chapter 2, OECD adopted a new definition of AI after the introduction of ChatGPT in November 2022 to broaden the scope of the definition of "AI" and "AI system" to be inclusive of generative AI and its impact.[5]

1. Challenges of Regulation of AI Foundation Models

Similarly, the *EU AI Act* broadened the definition of AI in the law to encompass generative AI. The International Bar Association, below, provides a summary of this development.

5. Stuart Russell et al., *Updates to the OECD's Definition of an AI System Explained,* OECD AI Pol'y Observatory (Nov. 29, 2023).

a. The Regulation of Foundation Models in the EU AI Act

The Regulation of Foundation Models in the EU AI Act

International Bar Association
April 12, 2024

NEW NAME AND DEFINITION

Foundation models are now defined by the AI Act[6] as "General Purpose AI Models" (GPAI Models). In summary, they can be defined as computer models which, through training on a vast amount of data, can be used for a variety of tasks, individually or inserted as components into an AI system. The AI Act's legal definition, however, is more complex and will certainly not fail to raise objections (if not even jurisdictional appeals before the EU Court of Justice), as it can be interpreted in such a way as to potentially include a wide variety of technological cases:

> GPAI model means an AI model, including when trained with a large amount of data using self-supervision at scale, that displays significant generality and is capable to competently perform a wide range of distinct tasks regardless of the way the model is placed on the market and that can be integrated into a variety of downstream systems or applications. This does not cover AI models that are used before release on the market for research, development and prototyping activities.

Needless to say, legal definitions cannot easily represent technology in an industrial sector in rapid development. This is the main reason why the EU legislator decided upon a very wide definition. Choosing a narrower definition would have been problematic and challengeable from others' point of view because it would have excluded relevant business cases from the ambit of application of the AI Act. Over-reaching has been preferred to a limited legislative scope. The coming [n]ext years will show whether this has been a wise choice or, instead, if we are going into a season of permanent litigations.

CATEGORIES OF GPAI MODELS

The AI Act identifies two categories of GPAI Models: generic GPAI models and "systemic" GPAI models.[7] The latter are models which, by virtue of the "systemic risks" they can cause at a European level, are subject to more pervasive regulation than the generic ones. . . .

Indeed, what is a systemic risk at European level? The AI Act explains it with a somewhat tautological definition:[8]

> "Systemic risk at Union level" means a risk that is specific to the high-impact capabilities of general-purpose AI models, having a significant impact on

6. [In text in original] (Article 3, 63).
7. [In text in original] (Art. 51).
8. [In text in original] (Arts. 3, 65).

the internal market due to its reach, and with actual or reasonably foreseeable negative effects on public health, safety, public security, fundamental rights, or the society as a whole, that can be propagated at scale across the value chain. . . .

REGULATION OF BASIC GPAI MODELS

. . . The final text of the AI Act is now clear and precise. Generic GPAI models are subject[9] to mere transparency obligations, consisting of guaranteeing the availability of technical documentation that makes their functioning understandable (also in relation to the data training process) to the European AI Office as well as to third parties who intend to integrate the model into their AI systems. This is a reasonable regulation which, in itself, should not constitute a significant obstacle to the development of the models. The provider wanting to place a foundation model in the EU shall appoint therein a representative.[10]

There is also an obligation to provide a policy aimed at respecting copyright legislation.[11] A final decision has therefore not been made as to whether the use of copyrighted data could lead to an obligation to remunerate rights holders, as some of them have been clamoring for. This decision will have to be taken in the future as part of a possible reflection or revision of EU copyright law. At the moment, however, it can be said that the obligation for GPAI models to establish a policy for this purpose indicates that the topic is worthy of relevance.

Note that lighter regulation is expected[12] in the case of GPAI models with a free and open license, unless they are "systemic." Therefore, if obligations are applicable to open-source cases, the problem arises of identifying the obliged subject, given that sometimes we are faced with a community rather than a specific provider.

REGULATION OF SYSTEMIC GPAI MODELS

Systemic GPAI models are subject to the same obligations as basic GPAI models, plus additional ones which give rise, overall, to more pervasive regulation.[13] In fact, they must: (a) carry out the evaluation of the model in accordance with standardised protocols and tools that reflect the state of the art, including the conduct and documentation of "adversarial tests" in order to identify and mitigate systemic risk; (b) assess and mitigate possible systemic risks at EU level, including their sources, that could arise from the

9. [In text in original] (Article 53).
10. [In text in original] (Article 54).
11. [In text in original] (Article 53, 1, c).
12. [In text in original] (Article 53, 2).
13. [In text in original] (Article 55).

development, placing on the market or use of AI models of a general nature with systemic risk; (c) track, document and report without undue delay to the European AI Office and, where appropriate, to the competent national authorities, relevant information on serious incidents and possible corrective measures to address them; and (d) ensure an adequate level of cybersecurity protection relating to the model and its physical infrastructure.

The question is whether such regulation is so pervasive to concretise the dangerous obstacle to the development of European foundation models that had been feared by some governments, in particular France. Of course, how the EC evaluates these obligations will matter. For example, in the case of "adversarial testing," the European AI Office's discretion in considering the testing process sufficient will be relevant. As regards accidents, it will be necessary to understand whether the GPAI model should be able to report all the information concerning the AI systems based on it (since they are normally different companies).

CODES OF PRACTICE

The AI Act provides that, pending the publication of harmonised European standards, both categories of GPAI models—generic and systemic—can rely on "codes of practice" to demonstrate compliance with their obligations.[14] By "codes of practice" we mean technical documents that report the standards of a technological sector.

Compliance with the codes creates a mere presumption of compliance with the obligations of the AI Act.

The development of codes by companies is encouraged and supervised by the AI Office, which also makes use of the collaboration of the European AI Board (EAIB, the body where the representatives of the Member States sit). National authorities can be involved and the "support" of stakeholders and experts is also expected.

A formal agreement from the European AI Office on the text of the code is not necessary, although the system suggests that, in the event of an objection from this office, the value of the code would effectively be diminished, since it provides a mere presumption of conformity to the obligations of the regulation. Therefore, for the code to have the effects desired by the industry, it is actually necessary for it to be supported by the European AI Office. The ability of Member States to share this power with the European AI Office is delegated to the EAIB and its ability to collaborate with that office.

However, formal approval by the European AI Office is possible to make the code valid throughout the EU.[15] In this case, an implementation act by the EC is envisaged, to be adopted with the approval of the Member

14. [In text in original] (Article 56).
15. [In text in original] (Article 56, 6).

States (the AI Act refers to Article 5 of EU Regulation No 182/2011 on comitology procedures).

Violation of the codes of practices is equivalent to violation of the obligations of the AI Act and as such involves the imposition of sanctions[16] according to a mixed system (sanctions partly defined by the regulation itself, partly delegated to the Member State).

VERTICALLY-INTEGRATED GPAI MODELS

Remarkably, the AI Act specifically regulates cases of vertical integration, ie, when there is identity between the GPAI provider and the deployer of the relevant AI system. In this case, the European AI Office operates as a market surveillance authority.[17] This is the first evident case to apply specific competition rules to the AI sector, where numerous voices already have alerted about the risks of concentration. It's worth mentioning that the European Commission has recently started to investigate the relations between OpenAI and Microsoft. [Emphasis removed.]

CONCLUSIONS

In conclusion, there is no doubt that the EC has taken a leading role in the treatment of foundation models in the AI Act, having been recognised, directly or through the European AI Office, formidable power not only in regulation and enforcement, but also in real industrial policy of the sector. In particular, the EC enjoys exclusive competence, and broad discretion, in the "executive" phase of the system, ie, in the identification of systemic GPAI models and subsequent application of regulation.

Greater control by the Member States instead seems to take place with regard to the adaptation of both the obligations incumbent on models in general and on the parameters for the designation of systemic models. The AI Act in fact refers to acts, both implementing and delegated, which the EC can adopt on the basis of procedures which should involve a certain involvement of parliament and council.

2. *Challenges of AI Regulation v. Generative AI Regulation*

Generative AI poses unique challenges to AI regulation, including the modification of AI definitions within legal instruments to expand regulatory oversight over generative AI. The excerpts below provide illustrative examples of how regulators are grappling with these distinctions. The first

16. [In text in original] (Article 99).
17. [In text in original] (Article 75, 1).

excerpt is from the *California AI Training Data Transparency Act*, a state law that was passed in 2024 to provide additional oversight to generative AI training models through greater transparency. The next excerpt is from a report published in 2023 by the EU Europol Innovation Lab, exploring the impact of generative AI on public policy. The final excerpt below is from Appendix C of the 2023 *NIST AI Risk Management Framework*, which provides a discussion of the complexities of human-machine interactions.

a. California AI Training Data Transparency Act

In 2024, California passed Assembly Bill 2013, the *AI Training Data Transparency Act*, which was intended to provide additional transparency to generative AI systems and services. The legislation required generative AI developers to publish summaries of datasets that had been used in system development and other details, as described in the legislation, including disclosure of system use of synthetic data generation.

AI Training Data Transparency Act

2024 Statutes of California, Ch. 817 (A.B. 2013)
Title 15.2 added to Part 4 of Division 3 of the California Civil Code

Title 15.2 of the California Civil Code

3110. For purposes of this title, the following definitions shall apply:

(c) "Generative artificial intelligence" means artificial intelligence that can generate derived synthetic content, such as text, images, video, and audio, that emulates the structure and characteristics of the artificial intelligence's training data. . . .

(e) "Synthetic data generation" means a process in which seed data are used to create artificial data that have some of the statistical characteristics of the seed data.

(f) "Train a generative artificial intelligence system or service" includes testing, validating, or fine tuning by the developer of the artificial intelligence system or service.

3111. . . . [A] generative artificial intelligence system or service, or a substantial modification to a generative artificial intelligence system or service, released on or after January 1, 2022, is made publicly available to Californians for use, regardless of whether the terms of that use include compensation, the developer of the system or service shall post on the developer's internet website documentation regarding the data used by the developer to train the generative artificial intelligence system or service, including, but not be limited to, all of the following:

(a) A high-level summary of the datasets used in the development of the generative artificial intelligence system or service, including but not limited to: . . .

(12) Whether the generative artificial intelligence system or service used or continuously uses synthetic data generation in its development. A developer may include a description of the functional need or desired purpose of the synthetic data in relation to the intended purpose of the system or service. . . .

b. A Report from the EU Europol Innovation Lab: Revised Definition of AI to Accommodate Generative AI

A report published by the EU Europol Innovation Lab in 2023 defined generative AI through the example of ChatGPT's capacities and deployment.

As an example of generative AI capacities, the authors of the report invited ChatGPT to define the following AI terms through definitional prompts:[18]

Artificial Intelligence

Artificial Intelligence (AI) is a broad field of computer science that involves creating intelligent machines that can perform tasks that typically require human-level intelligence, such as understanding natural language, recognizing images, and making decisions. AI encompasses various subfields, including machine learning, natural language processing, computer vision, robotics, and expert systems.

Neural Networks

Neural Networks, also known as Artificial Neural Networks (ANN), are computing systems inspired by the structure and function of the human brain. They consist of interconnected nodes or neurons that are designed to recognize patterns and make decisions based on input data.

Deep Learning

Deep Learning is a subfield of machine learning that involves training artificial neural networks, which are computing systems inspired by the structure and function of the human brain, to recognize patterns and make decisions based on large amounts of data. Deep Learning has been particularly successful in fields such as image recognition, natural language processing, and speech recognition.

Supervised/unsupervised Learning

Supervised Learning is a type of machine learning that involves training a model using labeled data, where the desired output is already known. The model learns to make predictions or decisions by finding patterns in the data and mapping input variables to output variables.

Unsupervised Learning is a type of machine learning that involves training a model using unlabeled data, where the desired output is unknown. The model learns to identify patterns and relationships in the

---

18. Europol, *ChatGPT—The Impact of Large Language Models on Law Enforcement* 3 (Dec. 19, 2023).

data without being given specific instructions, and is often used for tasks such as clustering, anomaly detection, and dimensionality reduction.

Definitions provided by ChatGPT.

The report also notes multiple limitations of generative AI. As now generally recognized, generative AI results may be filled with "hallucinations," generating content that is inaccurate, misleading, or wrong.[19] Generative AI systems rely on the discerning of patterns and structures by LLMs based on the datasets on which the systems have been trained. The AI model can only perform an analysis of any given input based on the datasets provided and the programming by programmers.[20]

Experts note that the most obvious limitation of ChatGPT "relates to the data on which the system has been trained[.]"[21] With OpenAI's ChatGPT, for example, "while updates are made on a constant basis, the majority of the system's training data dates back to September 2021."[22] The absence of citations or references to the responses of generative AI means that the answers generated by ChatGPT, for instance, based on its datasets do not include sources or methods to contextualize or support the responses or answers that the AI generates. Therefore, like other AI and automated systems, the results are formed by opaque processes (a "black box") and could be biased or might propagate other harms.

For generative AI, the structure of the prompt itself is a a key limitation of the system. The answers generated by generative AI depend on the prompt and different prompts that essentially ask the same question can lead to different answers. In some instances, the generative AI system can be led to believe that no answer exists. The generative AI system might assume that it understands the question and could be in error because of its assumptions, especially without further clarification or additional prompts.

EU Europol Innovation Lab: ChatGPT — The Impact of Large Language Models on Law Enforcement

March 27, 2023

BACKGROUND: LARGE LANGUAGE MODELS AND CHATGPT

ChatGPT is a large language model (LLM) that was developed by OpenAI and released to the wider public as part of a research preview in November 2022. Natural language processing and LLMs are subfields of

19. *Id.* at 4 (citing Engineering.com 2023, *ChatGPT Has All the Answers — But Not Always the Right Ones*; Vice 2022, *Stack Overflow Bans ChatGPT for Constantly Giving Wrong Answers*.

20. *Id.* (citing NBC News 2023, *ChatGPT Passes MBA Exam Given by a Wharton Professor*).

21. *Id.*

22. *Id.*

artificial intelligence (AI) systems that are built on deep learning techniques and the training of neural networks on significant amounts of data. This allows LLMs to understand and generate natural language text.

Over recent years, the field has seen significant breakthroughs due in part to the rapid progress made in the development of supercomputers and deep learning algorithms. At the same time, an unprecedented amount of available data has allowed researchers to train their models on the vast input of information needed.

The LLM ChatGPT is based on the Generative Pre-trained Transformer (GPT) architecture. It was trained using a neural network designed for natural language processing on a dataset of over 45 terabytes of text from the internet (books, articles, websites, other text-based content), which in total included billions of words of text.

The training of ChatGPT was carried out in two phases: the first involved unsupervised training, which included training ChatGPT to predict missing words in a given text to learn the structure and patterns of human language. Once pre-trained, the second phase saw ChatGPT fine-tuned through Reinforcement Learning from Human Feedback (RLHF), a supervised learning approach during which human input helped the model learn to adjust its parameters in order to better perform its tasks.

The current publicly accessible model underlying ChatGPT, GPT-3.5, is capable of processing and generating human-like text in response to user prompts. Specifically, the model can answer questions on a variety of topics, translate text, engage in conversational exchanges ("chatting"), and summarise text to provide key points. It is further capable of performing sentiment analysis, generating text based on a given prompt (i.e. writing a story or poem), as well as explaining, producing, and improving code in some of the most common programming languages (Python, Java, C++, JavaScript, PHP, Ruby, HTML, CSS, SQL). In its essence, then, ChatGPT is very good at understanding human input, taking into account its context, and producing answers that are highly usable.

In March 2023, OpenAI released for subscribers of ChatGPT Plus its latest model, GPT-4. According to OpenAI, GPT-4 is capable of solving more advanced problems more accurately.[23] In addition, GPT-4 offers advanced API integration and can process, classify, and analyse images as input. Moreover, GPT-4 is claimed to be less likely to respond to requests for "disallowed content" and more likely to produce factual responses than GPT-3.5.[24] Newer versions with greater functionalities and capabilities are expected to be released as the development and improvement of LLMs continues. . . .

---

23. [Fn. 1 in original] (citing OpenAI 2023, GPT-4).
24. [Fn. 2 in original] (citing OpenAI 2023, GPT-4 System Card).

c. NIST AI Risk Management Framework

NIST AI Risk Management Framework (AI RMF 1.0)

U.S. Department of Commerce, National Institute of Standards and Technology (NIST)
January 26, 2023

APPENDIX C: AI RISK MANAGEMENT AND HUMAN-AI INTERACTION

Organizations that design, develop, or deploy AI systems for use in operational settings may enhance their AI risk management by understanding current limitations of human-AI interaction. The AI RMF provides opportunities to clearly define and differentiate the various human roles and responsibilities when using, interacting with, or managing AI systems.

Many of the data-driven approaches that AI systems rely on attempt to convert or represent individual and social observational and decision-making practices into measurable quantities. Representing complex human phenomena with mathematical models can come at the cost of removing necessary context. This loss of context may in turn make it difficult to understand individual and societal impacts that are key to AI risk management efforts.

Issues that merit further consideration and research include:

1. **Human roles and responsibilities in decision making and overseeing AI systems need to be clearly defined and differentiated.** Human-AI configurations can span from fully autonomous to fully manual. AI systems can autonomously make decisions, defer decision making to a human expert, or be used by a human decision maker as an additional opinion. Some AI systems may not require human oversight, such as models used to improve video compression. Other systems may specifically require human oversight.
2. **Decisions that go into the design, development, deployment, evaluation, and use of AI systems reflect systemic and human cognitive biases.** AI actors bring their cognitive biases, both individual and group, into the process. Biases can stem from end-user decision-making tasks and be introduced across the AI lifecycle via human assumptions, expectations, and decisions during design and modeling tasks. These biases, which are not necessarily always harmful, may be exacerbated by AI system opacity and the resulting lack of transparency. Systemic biases at the organizational level can influence how teams are structured and who controls the decision-making processes throughout the AI lifecycle. These biases can also

influence downstream decisions by end users, decision makers, and policy makers and may lead to negative impacts.

3. **Human-AI interaction results vary.** Under certain conditions—for example, in perceptual-based judgment tasks—the AI part of the human-AI interaction can amplify human biases, leading to more biased decisions than the AI or human alone. When these variations are judiciously taken into account in organizing human-AI teams, however, they can result in complementarity and improved overall performance.
4. **Presenting AI system information to humans is complex.** Humans perceive and derive meaning from AI system output and explanations in different ways, reflecting different individual preferences, traits, and skills.

The **GOVERN** function provides organizations with the opportunity to clarify and define the roles and responsibilities for the humans in the Human-AI team configurations and those who are overseeing the AI system performance. The **GOVERN** function also creates mechanisms for organizations to make their decision-making processes more explicit, to help counter systemic biases.

The **MAP** function suggests opportunities to define and document processes for operator and practitioner proficiency with AI system performance and trustworthiness concepts, and to define relevant technical standards and certifications. Implementing **MAP** function categories and subcategories may help organizations improve their internal competency for analyzing context, identifying procedural and system limitations, exploring and examining impacts of AI-based systems in the real world, and evaluating decision-making processes throughout the AI lifecycle.

The **GOVERN** and **MAP** functions describe the importance of interdisciplinarity and demographically diverse teams and utilizing feedback from potentially impacted individuals and communities. AI actors called out in the AI RMF who perform human factors tasks and activities can assist technical teams by anchoring in design and development practices to user intentions and representatives of the broader AI community, and societal values. These actors further help to incorporate context-specific norms and values in system design and evaluate end user experiences—in conjunction with AI systems.

AI risk management approaches for human-AI configurations will be augmented by ongoing research and evaluation. For example, the degree to which humans are empowered and incentivized to challenge AI system output requires further studies. Data about the frequency and rationale with which humans overrule AI system output in deployed systems may be useful to collect and analyze.

C. *CASE STUDIES OF EVOLVING LIABILITIES AND PROJECTED RISKS*

a. NIST AI Risk Management Framework: Generative AI Profile

The power that generative AI possesses in rapid information generation and dissemination across a wide variety of fields poses broad concerns. Narrow forms of AI only used for specific tasks, such as one for determining criminal recidivism risks, can pose potentially foreseeable issues related to equality and due process. Generative AI like ChatGPT, however, has a range of uses that is not narrowly restricted and, accordingly, poses a range of risks that are not easily foreseeable. The NIST Generative AI Public Working Group[25] recognizes these challenges in the excerpt below.

NIST AI 600-1, Artificial Intelligence Risk Management Framework: Generative Artificial Intelligence Profile

National Institute of Standards and Technology (NIST) Generative AI Public Working Group
April 2024 Initial Public Draft (Withdrawn and Replaced with July 2024 Final RMF)

1.1. About this Profile

This profile defines a group of risks that are novel to or exacerbated by the use of GAI [Generative AI]. These risks were likewise identified by the GAI PWG [Generative AI Public Working Group]:

1. CBRN [Chemical, Biological, Radiological and Nuclear] Information
2. Confabulation
3. Dangerous or Violent Recommendations
4. Data Privacy
5. Environmental
6. Human-AI Configuration
7. Information Integrity
8. Information Security
9. Intellectual Property
10. Obscene, Degrading, and/or Abusive Content

25. *Artificial Intelligence Risk Management Framework: Generative Artificial Intelligence Profile* (AI 600-1), Nat'l Inst. of Standards & Tech. (Jul. 26, 2024).

11. Toxicity, Bias, and Homogenization
12. Value Chain and Component Integration . . .

2. OVERVIEW OF RISKS UNIQUE TO OR EXACERBATED BY GAI

AI risks can differ from or intensify traditional software risks. Likewise, GAI can exacerbate existing AI risks, and creates unique risks. GAI risks may arise across the entire AI lifecycle, from problem formulation, to development and decommission. They may present at system level or at the ecosystem level—outside of system or organizational contexts (e.g., the effect of disinformation on social institutions, GAI impacts on the creative economies or labor markets, algorithmic monocultures). They may occur abruptly or unfold across extended periods (e.g., societal or economic impacts due to loss of individual agency or increasing inequality).

Organizations may choose to measure these risks and allocate risk management resources relative to where and how these risks manifest, their direct and material impacts, and failure modes. Mitigations for system level risks may vary from ecosystem level risks. The ongoing review of relevant literature and resources can enable documentation and measurement of ecosystem-level or longitudinal risks.

Importantly, some GAI risks are unknown, and are therefore difficult to properly scope or evaluate given the uncertainty about potential GAI scale, complexity, and capabilities. Other risks may be known but difficult to estimate given the wide range of GAI stakeholders, uses, inputs, and outputs. Challenges with risk estimation are aggravated by a lack of visibility into GAI training data, and the generally immature state of the science of AI measurement and safety today.

To guide organizations in identifying and managing GAI risks, a set of risks unique to or exacerbated by GAI are defined below. These risks provide a clear lens through which organizations can frame and execute risk management efforts, and will be updated as the GAI landscape evolves.

1. **CBRN Information:** Lowered barriers to entry or eased access to materially nefarious information related to chemical, biological, radiological, or nuclear (CBRN) weapons, or other dangerous biological materials.
2. **Confabulation:** The production of confidently stated but erroneous or false content (known colloquially as "hallucinations" or "fabrications").
3. **Dangerous or Violent Recommendations:** Eased production of and access to violent, inciting, radicalizing, or threatening content as well as recommendations to carry out self-harm or conduct criminal or otherwise illegal activities.

4. **Data Privacy:** Leakage and unauthorized disclosure or de-anonymization of biometric, health, location, personally identifiable, or other sensitive data.
5. **Environmental:** Impacts due to high resource utilization in training GAI models, and related outcomes that may result in damage to ecosystems.
6. **Human-AI Configuration:** Arrangement or interaction of humans and AI systems which can result in algorithmic aversion, automation bias or over-reliance, misalignment or mis-specification of goals and/or desired outcomes, deceptive or obfuscating behaviors by AI systems based on programming or anticipated human validation, anthropomorphization, or emotional entanglement between humans and GAI systems; or abuse, misuse, and unsafe repurposing by humans.
7. **Information Integrity:** Lowered barrier to entry to generate and support the exchange and consumption of content which may not be vetted, may not distinguish fact from opinion or acknowledge uncertainties, or could be leveraged for large-scale dis- and mis-information campaigns.
8. **Information Security:** Lowered barriers for offensive cyber capabilities, including ease of security attacks, hacking, malware, phishing, and offensive cyber operations through accelerated automated discovery and exploitation of vulnerabilities; increased available attack surface for targeted cyber attacks, which may compromise the confidentiality and integrity of model weights, code, training data, and outputs.
9. **Intellectual Property:** Eased production of alleged copyrighted, trademarked, or licensed content used without authorization and/or in an infringing manner; eased exposure to trade secrets; or plagiarism or replication with related economic or ethical impacts.
10. **Obscene, Degrading, and/or Abusive Content:** Eased production of and access to obscene, degrading, and/or abusive imagery, including synthetic child sexual abuse material (CSAM), and non-consensual intimate images (NCII) of adults.
11. **Toxicity, Bias, and Homogenization:** Difficulty controlling public exposure to toxic or hate speech, disparaging or stereotyping content; reduced performance for certain sub-groups or languages other than English due to non-representative inputs; undesired homogeneity in data inputs and outputs resulting in degraded quality of outputs.
12. **Value Chain and Component Integration:** Non-transparent or untraceable integration of upstream third-party components, including data that has been improperly obtained or not cleaned due to increased automation from GAI; improper supplier vetting across the AI lifecycle; or other issues that diminish transparency or accountability for downstream users.

. . .

2.1 CBRN Information

In the coming years, GAI may increasingly facilitate eased access to information related to CBRN hazards. CBRN information is already publicly accessible, but the use of chatbots could facilitate its analysis or synthesis for non-experts. For example, red teamers were able to prompt GPT-4 to provide general information on unconventional CBRN weapons, including common proliferation pathways, potentially vulnerable targets, and information on existing biochemical compounds, in addition to equipment and companies that could build a weapon. These capabilities might increase the ease of research for adversarial users and be especially useful to malicious actors looking to cause biological harms without formal scientific training. However, despite these enhanced capabilities, the physical synthesis and successful use of chemical or biological agents will continue to require both applicable expertise and supporting infrastructure.

Other research on this topic indicates that the current generation of LLMs do not have the capability to plan a biological weapons attack: LLM outputs regarding biological attack planning were observed to be not more sophisticated than outputs from traditional search engine queries, suggesting that existing LLMs may not dramatically increase the operational risk of such an attack.

Separately, chemical and biological design tools—highly specialized AI systems trained on biological data which can help design proteins or other agents—may be able to predict and generate novel structures that are not in the training data of text-based LLMs. For instance, an AI system might be able to generate information or infer how to create novel biohazards or chemical weapons, posing risks to society or national security since such information is not likely to be publicly available.

While some of these capabilities lie beyond the capability of existing GAI tools, the ability of models to facilitate CBRN weapons planning and GAI systems' connection or access to relevant data and tools should be carefully monitored. . . .

b. New York Times v. Microsoft, OpenAI et al. (Complaint)

Multiple lawsuits were filed against OpenAI in the months following the release of ChatGPT in November 2022. In December 2023, the *New York Times* filed a complaint against Microsoft and OpenAI, alleging intellectual property violations. (Intellectual property issues with AI are further addressed in Part IV.) The excerpt of the complaint that follows provides a summary of ChatGPT's technological infrastructure and capacities, including the training data used in the development of the LLMs and how the algorithms are weighted to train on certain datasets, such as *New York Times* data, that are deemed more reliable than other datasets.

New York Times v. Microsoft, OpenAI et al. (Complaint)

United States District Court for the Southern District of New York
Case No. 1:23-cv-11195
December 27, 2023

COMPLAINT

I. NATURE OF THE ACTION

3. The Constitution and the Copyright Act recognize the critical importance of giving creators exclusive rights over their works. Since our nation's founding, strong copyright protection has empowered those who gather and report news to secure the fruits of their labor and investment. Copyright law protects The Times's expressive, original journalism, including, but not limited to, its millions of articles that have registered copyrights.

4. Defendants have refused to recognize this protection. Powered by LLMs containing copies of Times content, Defendants' GenAI tools can generate output that recites Times content verbatim, closely summarizes it, and mimics its expressive style, as demonstrated by scores of examples. These tools also wrongly attribute false information to The Times.

5. Defendants also use Microsoft's Bing search index, which copies and categorizes The Times's online content, to generate responses that contain verbatim excerpts and detailed summaries of Times articles that are significantly longer and more detailed than those returned by traditional search engines. By providing Times content without The Times's permission or authorization, Defendants' tools undermine and damage The Times's relationship with its readers and deprive The Times of subscription, licensing, advertising, and affiliate revenue.

6. Using the valuable intellectual property of others in these ways without paying for it has been extremely lucrative for Defendants. Microsoft's deployment of Times-trained LLMs throughout its product line helped boost its market capitalization by a trillion dollars in the past year alone. And OpenAI's release of ChatGPT has driven its valuation to as high as $90 billion. Defendants' GenAI business interests are deeply intertwined, with Microsoft recently highlighting that its use of OpenAI's "best-in-class frontier models" has generated customers—including "leading AI startups"—for Microsoft's Azure AI product.[26]

7. The Times objected after it discovered that Defendants were using Times content without permission to develop their models and tools. For months, The Times has attempted to reach a negotiated agreement with Defendants, in accordance with its history of working productively with large technology platforms to permit the use of its content in new digital

26. [Fn. 1 in original] *Microsoft Fiscal Year 2024 First Quarter Earnings Conference Call*, Microsoft Investor Relations (Oct. 24, 2023).

products (including the news products developed by Google, Meta, and Apple). The Times's goal during these negotiations was to ensure it received fair value for the use of its content, facilitate the continuation of a healthy news ecosystem, and help develop GenAI technology in a responsible way that benefits society and supports a well-informed public.

8. These negotiations have not led to a resolution. Publicly, Defendants insist that their conduct is protected as "fair use" because their unlicensed use of copyrighted content to train GenAI models serves a new "transformative" purpose. But there is nothing "transformative" about using The Times's content without payment to create products that substitute for The Times and steal audiences away from it. Because the outputs of Defendants' GenAI models compete with and closely mimic the inputs used to train them, copying Times works for that purpose is not fair use.

9. The law does not permit the kind of systematic and competitive infringement that Defendants have committed. This action seeks to hold them responsible for the billions of dollars in statutory and actual damages that they owe for the unlawful copying and use of The Times's uniquely valuable works. . . .

IV. FACTUAL ALLEGATIONS

3. A Commitment to Quality Journalism

38. It takes enormous resources to publish, on average, more than 250 original articles every day. Many of these articles take months—and sometimes longer—to report. That output is the work of approximately 5,800 full-time equivalent Times employees (as of December 31, 2022), some 2,600 of whom are directly involved in The Times's journalism operations.

39. Quite often, the most vital news reporting for society is the most resource-intensive. Some of The Times's most important journalism requires deploying teams of journalists at great cost to report on the ground around the world, providing best-in-class security and support, filing lawsuits against government entities to bring information to light, and supporting journalists through investigations that can take months or years.

40. Subscription, advertising, licensing, and affiliate revenue make this reporting possible. In 1996, The Times launched a core news website, alongside its paid print edition, that was free. As readers shifted from print news to digital products, The Times—like most print publishers—faced the prospect of not being able to continue funding its journalism. In response, The Times reinvented its business model to incorporate digital subscriptions. The Times launched its metered paywall in 2011, in what it called "a bet that readers will pay for news they are accustomed to getting free."[27]

---

27. [Fn. 2 in original] Jeremy W. Peters, *The Times Announces Digital Subscription Plan*, N.Y. Times (Mar. 17, 2011).

41. Thanks to the quality of The Times's journalism, that strategic innovation paid off, which allowed The Times to continue to exist and to thrive. Today, the vast majority of subscribers are digital-only. In the 12 years since The Times launched its paywall, it has grown its paid digital subscribership and developed a direct relationship with its online audience through its tireless commitment to making journalism "worth paying for." Generating and maintaining direct traffic to its online content and mobile applications are critical components of The Times's financial success.

42. By the third quarter of 2023, The Times had nearly 10.1 million digital and print subscribers worldwide. The Times aims to have 15 million subscribers by year-end 2027.

43. The Times makes journalism "worth paying for" by publishing articles that are exhaustively researched and reported, thoughtfully written, carefully edited, and thoroughly fact-checked.

44. In addition, The Times has deepened its relationship with its readers by expanding its offerings to better encompass its readers' specific interests, including best-in-class offerings like Cooking, Wirecutter, Games, and The Athletic.

45. The Times's paywall does not require payment for *all* access to The Times's content. To build audience engagement and loyalty, The Times's access model generally offers registered users free access to a limited number of articles and other content before requiring them to subscribe for access to additional content. Approximately 50 to 100 million users, on average, engage with The Times's digital content each week. This traffic is a key source of advertising revenue and helps drive future subscriptions to The Times.

46. The Times also compiled digital archives of all its material going back to its founding, at significant cost. Its digital archives include The New York Times Article Archive, with partial and full-text digital versions of articles from 1851 to today, and the TimesMachine, a browser-based digital replica of all issues from 1851 to 2002. This represents a singular database of contemporaneous language and information, as well as a unique and valuable historical record. The Times also provides its own API that allows researchers and academics to search Times content for non-commercial purposes.

4. GenAI Products Threaten High-Quality Journalism

47. Making great journalism is harder than ever. Over the past two decades, the traditional business models that supported quality journalism have collapsed, forcing the shuttering of newspapers all over the country. It has become more difficult for the public to sort fact from fiction in today's information ecosystem, as misinformation floods the internet, television, and other media. If The Times and other news organizations cannot produce and protect their independent journalism, there will be a vacuum that no computer or artificial intelligence can fill.

48. The protection of The Times's intellectual property is critical to its continued ability to fund world-class journalism in the public interest. If The Times and its peers cannot control the use of their content, their ability to monetize that content will be harmed. With less revenue, news organizations will have fewer journalists able to dedicate time and resources to important, in-depth stories, which creates a risk that those stories will go untold. Less journalism will be produced, and the cost to society will be enormous.

49. The Times depends on its exclusive rights of reproduction, adaptation, publication, performance, and display under copyright law to resist these forces. The Times has registered the copyright in its print edition every day for over 100 years, maintains a paywall, and has implemented terms of service that set limits on the copying and use of its content. To use Times content for commercial purposes, a party should first approach The Times about a licensing agreement.

50. The Times requires third parties to obtain permission before using Times content and trademarks for commercial purposes, and for decades The Times has licensed its content under negotiated licensing agreements. These agreements help ensure that The Times controls how, where, and for how long its content and brand appears and that it receives fair compensation for third-party use. Third parties, including large tech platforms, pay The Times significant royalties under these agreements in exchange for the right to use Times content for narrowly defined purposes. The agreements prohibit uses beyond those authorized purposes.

51. Times content is also available for licenses for certain uses through the Copyright Clearance Center ("CCC"), a clearinghouse that licenses material to both corporate and academic users. Through the CCC, The Times permits limited licenses for instruction, academic, other nonprofit uses, and limited commercial uses. For example, a for-profit business can acquire a CCC license to make a photocopy of Times content for internal or external distribution in exchange for a licensing fee of about ten dollars per article. A CCC license to post a single Times article on a commercial website for up to a year costs several thousand dollars.

52. The Times's ability to continue to attract and grow its digital subscriber base and to generate digital advertising revenue depends on the size of The Times's audience and users' sustained engagement directly with The Times's websites and mobile applications. To facilitate this direct engagement with its products, The Times permits search engines to access and index its content, which is necessary to allow users to find The Times using these search engines. Inherent in this value exchange is the idea that the search engines will direct users to The Times's own websites and mobile applications, rather than exploit The Times's content to keep users within their own search ecosystem.

53. While The Times, like virtually all online publishers, permits search engines to access its content for the limited purpose of surfacing it in traditional search results, The Times has never given permission to any entity, including Defendants, to use its content for GenAI purposes.

54. The Times reached out to Microsoft and OpenAI in April 2023 to raise intellectual property concerns and explore the possibility of an amicable resolution, with commercial terms and technological guardrails that would allow a mutually beneficial value exchange between Defendants and The Times. These efforts have not produced a resolution. . . .

B. Defendants' GenAI Products

1. A Business Model Based on Mass Copyright Infringement

55. OpenAI was formed in December 2015 as a "non-profit artificial intelligence research company." OpenAI started with $1 billion in seed money from its founders, a group of some of the wealthiest technology entrepreneurs and investors and companies[.] . . .

57. . . . OpenAI's corporate structure grew into an intricate web of for-profit holding, operating, and shell companies that manage OpenAI's day-to-day operations and grant OpenAI's investors (most prominently, Microsoft) authority and influence over OpenAI's operations, all while raising billions in capital from investors. The result: OpenAI today is a commercial enterprise valued as high as $90 billion, with revenues projected to be over $1 billion in 2024. . . .

61. OpenAI became a household name upon the release of ChatGPT in November 2022. ChatGPT is a text-generating chatbot that, given user-generated prompts, can mimic human-like natural language responses. ChatGPT was an instant viral sensation, reaching one million users within a month of its release and gaining over 100 million users within three months. . . .

2. How GenAI Models Work

75. At the heart of Defendants' GenAI products is a computer program called a "large language model," or "LLM." The different versions of GPT are examples of LLMs. An LLM works by predicting words that are likely to follow a given string of text based on the potentially billions of examples used to train it. . . .

77. LLMs encode the information from the training corpus that they use to make these predictions as numbers called "parameters." There are approximately 1.76 trillion parameters in the GPT-4 LLM.

78. The process of setting the values for an LLM's parameters is called "training." It involves storing encoded copies of the training works in computer memory, repeatedly passing them through the model with words

masked out, and adjusting the parameters to minimize the difference between the masked-out words and the words that the model predicts to fill them in.

79. After being trained on a general corpus, models may be further subject to "fine- tuning" by, for example, performing additional rounds of training using specific types of works to better mimic their content or style, or providing them with human feedback to reinforce desired or suppress undesired behaviors. . . .

81. Once trained, LLMs may be provided with information specific to a use case or subject matter in order to "ground" their outputs. For example, an LLM may be asked to generate a text output based on specific external data, such as a document, provided as context. Using this method, Defendants' synthetic search applications: (1) receive an input, such as a question; (2) retrieve relevant documents related to the input prior to generating a response; (3) combine the original input with the retrieved documents in order to provide context; and (4) provide the combined data to an LLM, which generates a natural-language response. . . .

C. Defendants' Unauthorized Use and Copying of Times Content

82. Microsoft and OpenAI created and distributed reproductions of The Times's content in several, independent ways in the course of training their LLMs and operating the products that incorporate them.

1. Unauthorized Reproduction of Times Works During GPT Model Training

83. Defendants' GPT models are a family of LLMs, the first of which was introduced in 2018, followed by GPT-2 in 2019, GPT-3 in 2020, GPT-3.5 in 2022, and GPT-4 in 2023. The "chat" style LLMs, GPT-3.5 and GPT-4, were developed in two stages. First, a transformer model was pre-trained on a very large amount of data. Second, the model was "fine-tuned" on a much smaller supervised dataset in order to help the model solve specific tasks.

84. The pre-training step involved collecting and storing text content to create training datasets and processing that content through the GPT models. While OpenAI did not release the trained versions of GPT-2 onward, "[d]ue to [OpenAI's] concerns about malicious applications of the technology," OpenAI has published general information about its pre-training process for the GPT models.

85. GPT-2 includes 1.5 billion parameters, which was a 10X scale up of GPT. The training dataset for GPT-2 includes an internal corpus OpenAI built called "WebText," which includes "the text contents of 45 million links posted by users of the 'Reddit' social network." The contents of the WebText dataset were created as a "new web scrape which emphasizes document quality." The WebText dataset contains a staggering amount of

scraped content from The Times. For example, the NYTimes.com domain is one of the "top 15 domains by volume" in the WebText dataset, and is listed as the 5th "top domain" in the WebText dataset with 333,160 entries.

86. GPT-3 includes 175 billion parameters and was trained on [datasets][.]

87. One of these datasets, WebText2, was created to prioritize high value content. Like the original WebText, it is composed of popular outbound links from Reddit. . . . [T]he WebText2 corpus was weighted 22% in the training mix for GPT-3 despite constituting less than 4% of the total tokens in the training mix. Times content—a total of 209,707 unique URLs—accounts for 1.23% of all sources listed in OpenWebText2, an open-source re-creation of the WebText2 dataset used in training GPT-3. Like the original WebText, OpenAI describes WebText2 as a "high-quality" dataset that is "an expanded version of the WebText dataset . . . collected by scraping links over a longer period of time."

88. The most highly weighted dataset in GPT-3, Common Crawl, is a "copy of the Internet" made available by an eponymous 501(c)(3) organization run by wealthy venture capital investors. The domain www.nytimes.com is the most highly represented proprietary source (and the third overall behind only Wikipedia and a database of U.S. patent documents) represented in a filtered English-language subset of a 2019 snapshot of Common Crawl, accounting for 100 million tokens (basic units of text)[.] . . .

Generative AI has been implicated in a wide range of legal and policy matters. These issues include how cybercrime is facilitated by generative AI, consumer and financial protections and privacy torts, and the highly publicized intellectual property questions raised by generative AI.

How generative AI impacts issues including labor and sustainability will be discussed in the final chapter, Chapter 11.

CHAPTER 9

AI ETHICS AND AUDITS

Although AI technologies bring unprecedented potential for positive benefits to society, they also bring unique risks that touch beyond legal concerns and into the broader area of ethics. The risks of AI are constantly evolving, the fear of intentional and unintentional misuse of this technology calls for a proactive approach. The responsible use of AI technologies is complex to achieve. Framing AI development and deployment with an ethical lens allows key stakeholders to identify best practices. Furthermore, developing auditing techniques to evaluate AI models and systems allows a systematic way to measure their safety and potential risk of failure before widely deploying them to the public. This chapter surveys representative examples of developments in current AI ethics and audits.

A. *ETHICAL FRAMEWORKS*

AI ethics are viewed by many as a pillar of AI governance. In the U.S., the privatized nature of AI innovation by private corporations in the absence of an omnibus federal regulatory regime for AI oversight has led to a voluntary system of corporate self-regulation. Under this approach, several corporations and other entities have published their standards for responsible AI use.

1. *Case Studies in Recommended AI Ethical Frameworks in Public and Private Context*

a. UNESCO Recommendation on AI Ethics

In 2021, 193 countries agreed to adopt the *Recommendation on the Ethics of Artificial Intelligence* proposed by the United Nations Educational,

1. *193 Countries Adopt First-Ever Global Agreement on the Ethics of Artificial Intelligence*, UN NEWS (Nov. 25, 2021).

Scientific and Cultural Organization (UNESCO).[1] It was described as the "first-ever global agreement" for an ethical AI framework.

Recommendation on the Ethics of Artificial Intelligence

United Nations Educational, Scientific and Cultural Organization (UNESCO)
Adopted on November 23, 2021

PREAMBLE

The General Conference of the United Nations Educational, Scientific and Cultural Organization (UNESCO), meeting in Paris from 9 to 24 November 2021, at its 41st session,

Recognizing the profound and dynamic positive and negative impacts of artificial intelligence (AI) on societies, environment, ecosystems and human lives, including the human mind, in part because of the new ways in which its use influences human thinking, interaction and decision-making and affects education, human, social and natural sciences, culture, and communication and information,

Recalling that, by the terms of its Constitution, UNESCO seeks to contribute to peace and security by promoting collaboration among nations through education, the sciences, culture, and communication and information, in order to further universal respect for justice, for the rule of law and for the human rights and fundamental freedoms which are affirmed for the peoples of the world,

Convinced that the Recommendation presented here, as a standard-setting instrument developed through a global approach, based on international law, focusing on human dignity and human rights, as well as gender equality, social and economic justice and development, physical and mental well-being, diversity, interconnectedness, inclusiveness, and environmental and ecosystem protection can guide AI technologies in a responsible direction,

Guided by the purposes and principles of the Charter of the United Nations,

Considering that AI technologies can be of great service to humanity and all countries can benefit from them, but also raise fundamental ethical concerns, for instance regarding the biases they can embed and exacerbate, potentially resulting in discrimination, inequality, digital divides, exclusion and a threat to cultural, social and biological diversity and social or economic divides; the need for transparency and understandability of the workings of algorithms and the data with which they have been trained; and their potential impact on, including but not limited to, human dignity, human rights and fundamental freedoms, gender equality, democracy, social, economic, political and cultural processes, scientific and engineering practices, animal welfare, and the environment and ecosystems,

Also Recognizing that AI technologies can deepen existing divides and inequalities in the world, within and between countries, and that justice, trust and fairness must be upheld so that no country and no one should be left behind, either by having fair access to AI technologies and enjoying their benefits or in the protection against their negative implications, while recognizing the different circumstances of different countries and respecting the desire of some people not to take part in all technological developments,

Conscious of the fact that all countries are facing an acceleration in the use of information and communication technologies and AI technologies, as well as an increasing need for media and information literacy, and that the digital economy presents important societal, economic and environmental challenges and opportunities of benefit-sharing, especially for low- and middle-income countries (LMICs), including but not limited to least developed countries (LDCs), landlocked developing countries (LLDCs) and small island developing States (SIDS), requiring the recognition, protection and promotion of endogenous cultures, values and knowledge in order to develop sustainable digital economies,

Further recognizing that AI technologies have the potential to be beneficial to the environment and ecosystems, and in order for those benefits to be realized, potential harms to and negative impacts on the environment and ecosystems should not be ignored but instead addressed,

Noting that addressing risks and ethical concerns should not hamper innovation and development but rather provide new opportunities and stimulate ethically-conducted research and innovation that anchor AI technologies in human rights and fundamental freedoms, values and principles, and moral and ethical reflection,

Also recalling that in November 2019, the General Conference of UNESCO, at its 40th session, adopted 40 C/Resolution 37, by which it mandated the Director-General "to prepare an international standard-setting instrument on the ethics of artificial intelligence (AI) in the form of a recommendation", which is to be submitted to the General Conference at its 41st session in 2021,

Recognizing that the development of AI technologies necessitates a commensurate increase in data, media and information literacy as well as access to independent, pluralistic, trusted sources of information, including as part of efforts to mitigate risks of misinformation, disinformation and hate speech, and harm caused through the misuse of personal data,

Observing that a normative framework for AI technologies and its social implications finds its basis in international and national legal frameworks, human rights and fundamental freedoms, ethics, need for access to data, information and knowledge, the freedom of research and innovation, human and environmental and ecosystem well-being, and connects ethical values and principles to the challenges and opportunities linked to AI technologies, based on common understanding and shared aims,

Also recognizing that ethical values and principles can help develop and implement rights-based policy measures and legal norms, by providing guidance with a view to the fast pace of technological development,

Also convinced that globally accepted ethical standards for AI technologies, in full respect of international law, in particular human rights law, can play a key role in developing AI-related norms across the globe,

Bearing in mind the Universal Declaration of Human Rights (1948), the instruments of the international human rights framework, including the Convention Relating to the Status of Refugees (1951), the Discrimination (Employment and Occupation) Convention (1958), the International Convention on the Elimination of All Forms of Racial Discrimination (1965), the International Covenant on Civil and Political Rights (1966), the International Covenant on Economic, Social and Cultural Rights (1966), the Convention on the Elimination of All Forms of Discrimination against Women (1979), the Convention on the Rights of the Child (1989), and the Convention on the Rights of Persons with Disabilities (2006), the Convention against Discrimination in Education (1960), the Convention on the Protection and Promotion of the Diversity of Cultural Expressions (2005), as well as any other relevant international instruments, recommendations and declarations,

Also noting the United Nations Declaration on the Right to Development (1986); the Declaration on the Responsibilities of the Present Generations Towards Future Generations (1997); the Universal Declaration on Bioethics and Human Rights (2005); the United Nations Declaration on the Rights of Indigenous Peoples (2007); the United Nations General Assembly resolution on the review of the World Summit on the Information Society (A/RES/70/125) (2015); the United Nations General Assembly Resolution on Transforming our world: the 2030 Agenda for Sustainable Development (A/RES/70/1) (2015); the Recommendation Concerning the Preservation of, and Access to, Documentary Heritage Including in Digital Form (2015); the Declaration of Ethical Principles in relation to Climate Change (2017); the Recommendation on Science and Scientific Researchers (2017); the Internet Universality Indicators (endorsed by UNESCO's International Programme for the Development of Communication in 2018), including the ROAM principles (endorsed by UNESCO's General Conference in 2015); the Human Rights Council's resolution on "The right to privacy in the digital age" (A/HRC/RES/42/15) (2019); and the Human Rights Council's resolution on "New and emerging digital technologies and human rights" (A/HRC/RES/41/11) (2019),

Emphasizing that specific attention must be paid to LMICs, including but not limited to LDCs, LLDCs and SIDS, as they have their own capacity but have been underrepresented in the AI ethics debate, which raises concerns about neglecting local knowledge, cultural pluralism, value systems and the demands of global fairness to deal with the positive and negative impacts of AI technologies,

Also conscious of the many existing national policies, other frameworks and initiatives elaborated by relevant United Nations entities, intergovernmental organizations, including regional organizations, as well as those by the private sector, professional organizations, non-governmental organizations, and the scientific community, related to the ethics and regulation of AI technologies,

Further convinced that AI technologies can bring important benefits, but that achieving them can also amplify tension around innovation, asymmetric access to knowledge and technologies, including the digital and civic literacy deficit that limits the public's ability to engage in topics related to AI, as well as barriers to access to information and gaps in capacity, human and institutional capacities, barriers to access to technological innovation, and a lack of adequate physical and digital infrastructure and regulatory frameworks, including those related to data, all of which need to be addressed,

Underlining that the strengthening of global cooperation and solidarity, including through multilateralism, is needed to facilitate fair access to AI technologies and address the challenges that they bring to diversity and interconnectivity of cultures and ethical systems, to mitigate potential misuse, to realize the full potential that AI can bring, especially in the area of development, and to ensure that national AI strategies are guided by ethical principles,

Taking fully into account that the rapid development of AI technologies challenges their ethical implementation and governance, as well as the respect for and protection of cultural diversity, and has the potential to disrupt local and regional ethical standards and values,

1. ***Adopts*** the present Recommendation on the Ethics of Artificial Intelligence on this twenty-third day of November 2021;
2. ***Recommends*** that Member States apply on a voluntary basis the provisions of this Recommendation by taking appropriate steps, including whatever legislative or other measures may be required, in conformity with the constitutional practice and governing structures of each State, to give effect within their jurisdictions to the principles and norms of the Recommendation in conformity with international law, including international human rights law;
3. ***Also recommends*** that Member States engage all stakeholders, including business enterprises, to ensure that they play their respective roles in the implementation of this Recommendation; and bring the Recommendation to the attention of the authorities, bodies, research and academic organizations, institutions and organizations in public, private and civil society sectors involved in AI technologies, so that the development and use of AI technologies are guided by both sound scientific research as well as ethical analysis and evaluation.

b. Mastercard AI Ethics Rules

Multiple corporations have adopted AI ethics frameworks. Some corporations, including Microsoft and Mastercard, have committed to adopting the *UNESCO Recommendation on the Ethics of Artificial Intelligence*.[2] In Chapters 8 and 10, we discuss Microsoft Responsible AI Standard v2. Below is an excerpt of Mastercard's AI ethics framework.

Mastercard's Data & Tech Responsibility Principles: Our Commitment

The next century of innovation will be fueled by the creativity of *people* looking to solve real problems, by quality *data* that informs how they solve those problems and by innovative *technologies* that enable these solutions. Today, there's great interest in Artificial Intelligence (AI), biometrics, the cloud and more. Tomorrow's innovations can't yet be imagined, but surely will bring new and different opportunities and risks.

For these technology-enabled innovations to be sustainable, people will need to trust them. And that starts with foundational practices that respect and protect individual rights and society. That's why we developed and continually evolve a set of robust principles to hold ourselves to the highest standards of data and tech responsibility, while sharing our experiences with partners, regulators and policymakers to inform a broader common framework for responsible data-driven innovation.

1. Security and Privacy: Advance and uphold best-in-class security and privacy practices.
2. Transparency: Clearly and simply explain how we collect, use and share data, as well as how the technologies we use, such as Artificial Intelligence (AI), deliver the outcomes we intend.
3. Accountability: Implement robust governance to ensure proper controls and oversight over our use of data and technology.
4. Fairness: Be deliberate in minimizing biases, inaccuracies and unintended harms in our use of data and technology.
5. Inclusion: Ensure our use of data and technology fosters inclusion and equity.
6. Innovation: Provide innovative experiences, products and services that benefit all our stakeholders.
7. Social Impact: Use data and technology to make a positive impact on communities and individuals around the world.

2. Press Release, UNESCO, AI Ethics: 8 Global Tech Companies Commit to Apply UNESCO's Recommendation (Feb. 5, 2024).

B. AI INVENTORIES AND GOVERNANCE BOARDS

The *White House Executive Order on the Safe, Secure, and Trustworthy Development and Use of AI* in 2023 and the *White House Office of Management and Budget (OMB) Policy to Advance Governance, Innovation, and Risk Management in Federal Agencies' Use of Artificial Intelligence* in 2024 relied on several preexisting statutory authorities. The *Advancing American AI Act* [of 2022], for example, had previously set forth a statutory framework for federal agencies to advance AI safety, privacy, and civil rights objectives.[3] That statute required federal agencies to publish inventories of AI systems used to further transparency objectives.

1. Case Study of Federal Agency AI Inventory and Governance

a. White House Office of Management and Budget (OMB) Memorandum: Advancing Governance, Innovation, and Risk Management in Federal Agencies' Use of Artificial Intelligence (Rescinded)

The OMB memorandum below describes detailed AI inventory and governance board requirements. In the transition between administrations, the incoming White House in 2025 revoked both the 2024 OMB memorandum and the underlying 2023 executive order.[4] The excerpt below is included for historical reference.

Advancing Governance, Innovation, and Risk Management for Agency Use of Artificial Intelligence (Rescinded)

White House Office of Management and Budget (OMB)
M-24-10 Memorandum for the Heads of Executive Departments and Agencies
March 28, 2024

Artificial intelligence (AI) is one of the most powerful technologies of our time, and the President has been clear that we must seize the opportunities AI

---

3. P.L. 117-263, Division G—Homeland Security Matters, Title LXXII—Governmental Affairs, Subtitle B—Advancing American AI Act, James M. Inhofe National Defense Authorization Act for Fiscal Year 2023.

4. Exec. Order No. 14148, 90 Fed. Reg. 8237, *Initial Rescissions of Harmful Executive Orders and Actions* (Jan. 28, 2025). OMB Memorandum M-25-21, *Accelerating Federal Use of AI through Innovation, Governance, and Public Trust* (Apr. 3, 2025) and OMB Memorandum M-25-22, *Driving Efficient Acquisition of Artificial Intelligence in Government* (Apr. 3, 2025). These two OMB memos implement Exec. Order No. 14179, 90 Fed. Reg. 8741, *Removing Barriers to American Leadership in Artificial Intelligence* (Jan. 31, 2025), rescinding and replacing the two OMB memos promulgated during the Biden administration on AI use and AI procurement, OMB Memorandum M-24-10, *Advancing Governance, Innovation, and Risk Management for Agency Use of Artificial Intelligence* (Mar. 28, 2024) and OMB Memorandum M-24-18, *Advancing the Responsible Acquisition of Artificial Intelligence in Government* (Sept. 24, 2024).

presents while managing its risks. Consistent with the AI in Government Act of 2020,[5] the Advancing American AI Act,[6] and Executive Order 14110 on the Safe, Secure, and Trustworthy Development and Use of Artificial Intelligence, this memorandum directs agencies to advance AI governance and innovation while managing risks from the use of AI in the Federal Government, particularly those affecting the rights and safety of the public.[7]

1. OVERVIEW

While AI is improving operations and service delivery across the Federal Government, agencies must effectively manage its use. As such, this memorandum establishes new agency requirements and guidance for AI governance, innovation, and risk management, including through specific minimum risk management practices for uses of AI that impact the rights and safety of the public.

Strengthening AI Governance. Managing AI risk and promoting AI innovation requires effective AI governance. As required by Executive Order 14110, each agency must designate a Chief AI Officer (CAIO) within 60 days of the date of the issuance of this memorandum. This memorandum describes the roles, responsibilities, seniority, position, and reporting structures for agency CAIOs, including expanded reporting through agency AI use case inventories. Because AI is deeply interconnected with other technical and policy areas including data, information technology (IT), security, privacy, civil rights and civil liberties, customer experience, and workforce management, CAIOs must work in close coordination with existing responsible officials and organizations within their agencies. . . .

3. STRENGTHENING ARTIFICIAL INTELLIGENCE GOVERNANCE

a. Actions

iv. AI Use Case Inventories. Each agency (except for the Department of Defense and the Intelligence Community) must individually inventory each of its AI use cases at least annually, submit the inventory to OMB, and post a public version on the agency's website. OMB will issue detailed instructions for the inventory and its scope through its Integrated Data Collection process or an OMB-designated successor process. Beginning with the use case inventory for 2024, agencies will be required, as applicable, to identify which use cases are safety-impacting and rights-impacting AI and report additional detail on the risks—including risks of inequitable outcomes—that such uses pose and how agencies are managing those risks.

---

5. [Fn. 1 in original] Pub. L. No. 116-260, div. U, title 1, § 104 (codified at 40 U.S.C. § 11301 note).

6. [Fn. 2 in original] Pub. L. No. 117-263, div. G, title LXXII, subtitle B, §§ 7224(a), 7224(d)(1)(B), and 7225 (codified at 40 U.S.C. 11301 note).

7. [Fn. 3 in original] This memorandum accounts for public comments that OMB received following its publication of a draft version of this memorandum on November 1, 2023. OMB has separately published an explanation and response to public comments. . . .

v. Reporting on AI Use Cases Not Subject to Inventory. Some AI use cases are not required to be individually inventoried, such as those in the Department of Defense or those whose sharing would be inconsistent with applicable law and governmentwide policy. On an annual basis, agencies must still report and release aggregate metrics about such use cases that are otherwise within the scope of this memorandum, the number of such cases that impact rights and safety, and their compliance with the practices of Section 5(c) of this memorandum. OMB will issue detailed instructions for this reporting through its Integrated Data Collection process or an OMB-designated successor process. . . .

c. Internal Agency AI Coordination

Agencies are encouraged to have their AI Governance Boards consult external experts as appropriate and consistent with applicable law. Experts' individual viewpoints can help broaden the perspective of an existing governance board and inject additional technical, ethics, civil rights and civil liberties, or sector-specific expertise, as well as methods for engaging the workforce. . . .

4. ADVANCING RESPONSIBLE ARTIFICIAL INTELLIGENCE INNOVATION

b. Removing Barriers to the Responsible Use of AI

ii. Data. . . . Any data used to help develop, test, or maintain AI applications, regardless of source, should be assessed for quality, representativeness, and bias. These activities should be supported by resources to enable sound data governance and management practices, particularly as they relate to data collection, curation, labeling, and stewardship. . . .

d. AI Sharing and Collaboration

i. Sharing and Releasing AI Code and Models. Agencies must proactively share their custom-developed code—including models and model weights—for AI applications in active use and must release and maintain that code as open source software on a public repository, unless:

A. the sharing of the code is restricted by law or regulation, including patent or intellectual property law, the Export Asset Regulations, the International Traffic in Arms Regulations, and Federal laws and regulations governing classified information;

B. the sharing of the code would create an identifiable risk to national security, confidentiality of Government information, individual privacy, or the rights or safety of the public;

C. the agency is prevented by a contractual obligation from doing so; or

D. the sharing of the code would create an identifiable risk to agency mission, programs, or operations, or to the stability, security, or integrity of an agency's systems or personnel. . . .

5. MANAGING RISKS FROM THE USE OF ARTIFICIAL INTELLIGENCE

c. Minimum Practices for Safety-Impacting and Rights-Impacting Artificial Intelligence

. . . Agencies must identify additional context-specific risks that are associated with their use of AI and address them as appropriate. Such risk considerations may include impacts to safety, security, civil rights, civil liberties, privacy, democratic values, human rights, equal opportunities, worker well-being, access to critical resources and services, agency trust and credibility, and market competition. To address these potential risk management gaps, agencies are encouraged to promote and to incorporate, as appropriate, additional best practices for AI risk management, such as from the National Institute of Standards and Technology (NIST) AI Risk Management Framework, the Blueprint for an AI Bill of Rights, relevant international standards, and the workforce principles and best practices for employers established pursuant to Section 6(b)(i) of Executive Order 14110. Agencies are also encouraged to continue developing their own agency-specific practices, as appropriate and consistent with this memorandum and the principles in Executive Order 13960, Executive Order 14091, and Executive Order 14110. . . .

iv. Minimum Practices for Either Safety-Impacting or Rights-Impacting AI

C. Independently evaluate the AI. Agencies, through the CAIO, an agency AI oversight board, or other appropriate agency office with existing test and evaluation responsibilities, must review relevant AI documentation to ensure that the system works appropriately and as intended, and that its expected benefits outweigh its potential risks. At a minimum, this documentation must include the completed impact assessment and results from testing AI performance in a real-world context referenced in paragraphs (A) and (B) of this subsection. Agencies must incorporate this independent evaluation into an applicable release or oversight process, such as the Authorization to Operate process. The independent reviewing authority must not have been directly involved in the system's development. . . .

C. AI AUDITING

The process of professionally auditing computer and information systems has been an ongoing research effort for over five decades. ISACA, previously the Information Systems Audit and Control Association, is one of the largest global associations of computational governance and information systems auditors. ISACA comprises more than 165,000 professionals and auditors, including regulators, in over 180 countries.[8] Both public and private sectors are actively formulating guidelines for conducting AI auditing, particularly in response to legal and regulatory developments in AI oversight that require AI audits.

---

8. *ISACA History*, ISACA (last visited Feb. 27, 2025).

1. *Case Studies in AI Auditing and Auditor Guidance*

a. Auditing Artificial Intelligence (ISACA)

The ISACA (previously Information Systems Audit and Control Association) guidance document, *Auditing Artificial Intelligence*, provides an audit framework for assessing AI systems.[9] The guidance document proposes "several potential challenges" in AI auditing and potential solutions "that can convert the challenges into successes" for an AI auditor.[10]

Auditing Artificial Intelligence

ISACA

Figure 4 Challenges and Solutions for AI Auditing[11]

Challenges for the Auditor of AI	Keys to the Successful Auditing of AI
1. Immature auditing frameworks or regulations specific to AI	1. Adopt and adapt existing frameworks and regulations.
2. Limited precedents for AI use cases	2. Explain and communicate proactively about AI with stakeholders.
3. Uncertain definitions and taxonomies of AI	3. Explain and communicate proactively about AI with stakeholders.
4. Wide variance among AI systems and solutions	4. Become informed about AI design and architecture to set proper scope.
5. Emerging nature of AI technology	5. Become informed about AI design and architecture to set proper scope.
6. Lack of explicit AI auditing guidance	6. Focus on transparency through an iterative process. Focus on controls and governance, not algorithms.
7. Lack of strategic starting points	7. Involve all stakeholders.
8. Possibly steep learning curve for the AI auditor	8. Become informed about AI design and engage specialists as needed.
9. Supplier risk created by AI outsourcing to third parties	9. Document architectural practices for cross-team transparency.

b. European Court of Auditors: Artificial Intelligence Initial Strategy and Deployment Roadmap

The European Union European Court of Auditors published a strategic roadmap for AI auditing. The document observes that there are two approaches to AI auditing: using AI for auditing and auditing AI systems. In the excerpt below, the European Court of Auditors provides issues to consider in effective AI audit methods.

---

9. ISACA, Auditing Artificial Intelligence (2018).

10. *Id.* at 8.

11. *Id.*

Artificial Intelligence Initial Strategy and Deployment Roadmap

European Union European Court of Auditors
2024-2025

AUDITING AI: ENSURING INTEGRITY AND EFFECTIVENESS

13 As AI systems become integral to our auditees' business processes, we must be prepared to audit them.

14 A key issue to consider is whether, and how, audited entities have addressed AI in their conduct of business, in particular whether they have developed AI strategies and established related governances. If they are not using AI, we should assess the risks this brings to the auditees' business processes. In addition, it is also relevant to verify how our auditees address risks associated with the use of AI by third parties with whom they have contractual relationships.

15 Auditing AI is a new component that can be added to general IT audit methodologies; this involves assessing how AI is used, the impact on output, how well it works, the decision-making followed, and compliance with the auditee's ethical and other standards. Table 1 provides a non-exhaustive list of the elements that auditors need to consider:

Table 1 Main Elements to Consider When Auditing AI Systems[12]

Key Element	Description
Data integrity and bias mitigation	AI models are as good as the data they are trained on. Operators of AI systems should ensure that the data used is accurate, representative and free from biases that could skew output.
Compliance with regulations and standards	AI systems must comply with relevant legal and ethical standards, thus ensuring that such systems are used responsibly, protecting sensitive data and upholding public trust.
Transparency and explainability	To maintain trust and accountability, AI systems should be transparent and their decision-making processes explainable. In other words, it should be possible to understand how an AI model produces outputs and reaches conclusions.
Performance monitoring and evaluation	Regular assessments of AI systems are necessary to ensure they perform effectively and continue to meet their objectives over time.

12. European Court of Auditors, Artificial Intelligence Initial Strategy and Deployment Roadmap 2024-2025 8 (2024).

Key Element	Description
Impact on workforce and processes	Auditing AI may also encompass the impact on the auditee workforce and processes. The integration of AI should not compromise the quality of work or lead to loss of skills in critical processes and procedures.

c. AI Security Institute: Auditing of Five Large Language Models

The auditing of generative AI has proven to be particularly complex. The AI Security Institute in the UK recognized these challenges and structured an evaluation of five LLMs to test for multiple potential harms, including cybersecurity vulnerabilities, biological and chemical exploitation, and reliability and integrity of responses.

Advanced AI Evaluations at AISI: May Update

AI Security Institute
May 20, 2024

A key part of our work at the AI [Security] Institute (AISI) involves periodically evaluating advanced AI systems to assess the potential harm they could cause. . . . [W]e present results from our recent evaluations of five large language models (LLMs) that are already used by the public. We assessed:

- Whether the models could potentially be used to facilitate cyber-attacks;
- Whether they could provide expert-level knowledge in chemistry and biology that could be used for positive but also harmful purposes;
- Whether they were capable of autonomously taking sequences of actions (operating as "agents") in ways that might be difficult for humans to control and
- Whether they were vulnerable to "jailbreaks" or users attempting to bypass safeguards to elicit potentially harmful outputs (e.g. illegal or toxic content). . . .

OUR APPROACH

. . . Depending on the task or question type, we measured three types of responses:

- Compliance: whether the model does or does not comply with a harmful request
- Correctness: whether the response to a question is correct or not
- Completion: whether a task (such as a coding challenge) is completed or not. . . .

CYBER EVALUATIONS

Advanced AI could amplify risks to society if it were used to perform cyber attacks, including on critical national infrastructure. Models could be used to inform users about how to use cyber security exploits or could be deployed by malicious actors to autonomously attack infrastructure without human oversight. Our goal in these evaluations was to study the capabilities of current publicly available LLMs to perform basic operations used in cyber attacks.

D. AI ASSESSMENTS AND MONITORING

1. Case Studies in AI Conformity Assessments and Evaluation of AI Systems

a. EU AI Act, Article 43 [Conformity Assessment]

EU AI Act

Article 43. Conformity Assessment

1. For high-risk AI systems listed in point 1 of Annex III, where, in demonstrating the compliance of a high-risk AI system with the requirements set out in Section 2, the provider has applied harmonised standards referred to in Article 40, or, where applicable, common specifications referred to in Article 41, the provider shall opt for one of the following conformity assessment procedures based on:

(a) the internal control referred to in Annex VI; or

(b) the assessment of the quality management system and the assessment of the technical documentation, with the involvement of a notified body, referred to in Annex VII. In demonstrating the compliance of a high-risk AI system with the requirements set out in Section 2, the provider shall follow the conformity assessment procedure set out in Annex VII where:

(a) harmonised standards referred to in Article 40 do not exist, and common specifications referred to in Article 41 are not available;

(b) the provider has not applied, or has applied only part of, the harmonised standard;

(c) the common specifications referred to in point (a) exist, but the provider has not applied them;

(d) one or more of the harmonised standards referred to in point (a) has been published with a restriction, and only on the part of the standard that was restricted. For the purposes of the conformity assessment procedure referred to in Annex VII, the provider may choose any of the notified bodies. However, where the high-risk AI system is intended to be put into service by law enforcement, immigration or asylum authorities or by Union institutions, bodies, offices or agencies, the market surveillance authority referred to in Article 74(8) or (9), as applicable, shall act as a notified body.

2. For high-risk AI systems referred to in points 2 to 8 of Annex III, providers shall follow the conformity assessment procedure based on internal control as referred to in Annex VI, which does not provide for the involvement of a notified body.

3. For high-risk AI systems covered by the Union harmonisation legislation listed in Section A of Annex I, the provider shall follow the relevant conformity assessment procedure as required under those legal acts. The requirements set out in Section 2 of this Chapter shall apply to those high-risk AI systems and shall be part of that assessment. Points 4.3., 4.4., 4.5. and the fifth paragraph of point 4.6 of Annex VII shall also apply.

For the purposes of that assessment, notified bodies which have been notified under those legal acts shall be entitled to control the conformity of the high-risk AI systems with the requirements set out in Section 2, provided that the compliance of those notified bodies with requirements laid down in Article 31(4), (5), (10) and (11) has been assessed in the context of the notification procedure under those legal acts.

Where a legal act listed in Section A of Annex I enables the product manufacturer to opt out from a third-party conformity assessment, provided that that manufacturer has applied all harmonised standards covering all the relevant requirements, that manufacturer may use that option only if it has also applied harmonised standards or, where applicable, common specifications referred to in Article 41, covering all requirements set out in Section 2 of this Chapter.

4. High-risk AI systems that have already been subject to a conformity assessment procedure shall undergo a new conformity assessment procedure in the event of a substantial modification, regardless of whether the modified system is intended to be further distributed or continues to be used by the current deployer.

For high-risk AI systems that continue to learn after being placed on the market or put into service, changes to the high-risk AI system and its performance that have been pre-determined by the provider at the moment of the initial conformity assessment and are part of the information contained in the technical documentation referred to in point 2(f) of Annex IV, shall not constitute a substantial modification.

5. The Commission is empowered to adopt delegated acts in accordance with Article 97 in order to amend Annexes VI and VII by updating them in light of technical progress.

6. The Commission is empowered to adopt delegated acts in accordance with Article 97 in order to amend paragraphs 1 and 2 of this Article in order to subject high-risk AI systems referred to in points 2 to 8 of Annex III to the conformity assessment procedure referred to in Annex VII or parts thereof. The Commission shall adopt such delegated acts taking into account the effectiveness of the conformity assessment procedure based on internal control referred to in Annex VI in preventing or minimising the risks to health and safety and protection of fundamental rights posed by such systems, as well as the availability of adequate capacities and resources among notified bodies.

b. EU AI Act, Article 46 [Derogation from Conformity Assessment Procedure]

EU AI Act

Article 46. Derogation from Conformity Assessment Procedure

1. By way of derogation from Article 43 and upon a duly justified request, any market surveillance authority may authorise the placing on the market or the putting into service of specific high-risk AI systems within the territory of the Member State concerned, for exceptional reasons of public security or the protection of life and health of persons, environmental protection or the protection of key industrial and infrastructural assets. That authorisation shall be for a limited period while the necessary conformity assessment procedures are being carried out, taking into account the exceptional reasons justifying the derogation. The completion of those procedures shall be undertaken without undue delay.

2. In a duly justified situation of urgency for exceptional reasons of public security or in the case of specific, substantial and imminent threat to the life or physical safety of natural persons, law-enforcement authorities or civil protection authorities may put a specific high-risk AI system into service without the authorisation referred to in paragraph 1, provided that such authorisation is requested during or after the use without undue delay. If the authorisation referred to in paragraph 1 is refused, the use of the high-risk AI system shall be stopped with immediate effect and all the results and outputs of such use shall be immediately discarded.

3. The authorisation referred to in paragraph 1 shall be issued only if the market surveillance authority concludes that the high-risk AI system complies with the requirements of Section 2. The market surveillance authority shall inform the Commission and the other Member States of any authorisation issued pursuant to paragraphs 1 and 2. This obligation shall not cover sensitive operational data in relation to the activities of law-enforcement authorities.

4. Where, within 15 calendar days of receipt of the information referred to in paragraph 3, no objection has been raised by either a Member State or the Commission in respect of an authorisation issued by a market surveillance authority of a Member State in accordance with paragraph 1, that authorisation shall be deemed justified.

5. Where, within 15 calendar days of receipt of the notification referred to in paragraph 3, objections are raised by a Member State against an authorisation issued by a market surveillance authority of another Member State, or where the Commission considers the authorisation to be contrary to Union law, or the conclusion of the Member States regarding the compliance of the system as referred to in paragraph 3 to be unfounded, the Commission shall, without delay, enter into consultations with the relevant Member State. The operators concerned shall be consulted and have the possibility to present their views. Having regard thereto, the Commission shall decide whether the authorisation is justified. The Commission shall address its decision to the Member State concerned and to the relevant operators.

6. Where the Commission considers the authorisation unjustified, it shall be withdrawn by the market surveillance authority of the Member State concerned.

7. For high-risk AI systems related to products covered by Union harmonisation legislation listed in Section A of Annex I, only the derogations from the conformity assessment established in that Union harmonisation legislation shall apply.

c. EU AI Act, Article 74 [Market Surveillance and Control of AI Systems in the Union Market]

EU AI Act

Article 74. Market Surveillance and Control of AI Systems in the Union Market

2. As part of their reporting obligations under Article 34(4) of Regulation (EU) 2019/1020, the market surveillance authorities shall report annually to the Commission and relevant national competition authorities any information identified in the course of market surveillance activities that may be of potential interest for the application of Union law on competition rules. They shall also annually report to the Commission about the use of prohibited practices that occurred during that year and about the measures taken.

3. For high-risk AI systems related to products covered by the Union harmonisation legislation listed in Section A of Annex I, the market surveillance authority for the purposes of this Regulation shall be the authority responsible for market surveillance activities designated under those legal acts. . . .

8. For high-risk AI systems listed in point 1 of Annex III to this Regulation, in so far as the systems are used for law enforcement purposes, border management and justice and democracy, and for high-risk AI systems listed in points 6, 7 and 8 of Annex III to this Regulation, Member States shall designate as market surveillance authorities for the purposes of this Regulation either the competent data protection supervisory authorities under Regulation (EU) 2016/679 or Directive (EU) 2016/680, or any other authority designated pursuant to the same conditions laid down in Articles 41 to 44 of Directive (EU) 2016/680. Market surveillance activities shall in no way affect the independence of judicial authorities, or otherwise interfere with their activities when acting in their judicial capacity. . . .

11. Market surveillance authorities and the Commission shall be able to propose joint activities, including joint investigations, to be conducted by either market surveillance authorities or market surveillance authorities jointly with the Commission, that have the aim of promoting compliance, identifying non-compliance, raising awareness or providing guidance in relation to this Regulation with respect to specific categories of high-risk AI systems that are found to present a serious risk across two or more Member States in accordance with Article 9 of Regulation (EU) 2019/1020. The AI Office shall provide coordination support for joint investigations.

12. Without prejudice to the powers provided for under Regulation (EU) 2019/1020, and where relevant and limited to what is necessary to fulfil their tasks, the market surveillance authorities shall be granted full access by providers to the documentation as well as the training, validation and testing data sets used for the development of high-risk AI systems, including, where appropriate and subject to security safeguards, through application programming interfaces (API) or other relevant technical means and tools enabling remote access.

13. Market surveillance authorities shall be granted access to the source code of the high-risk AI system upon a reasoned request and only when both of the following conditions are fulfilled:

(a) access to source code is necessary to assess the conformity of a high-risk AI system with the requirements set out in Chapter III, Section 2; and

(b) testing or auditing procedures and verifications based on the data and documentation provided by the provider have been exhausted or proved insufficient.

14. Any information or documentation obtained by market surveillance authorities shall be treated in accordance with the confidentiality obligations set out in Article 78.

In Chapter 3, the discussion on conceptualizing AI governance included the topics of hard law and soft law approaches, as well as external and internal approaches. This chapter relates to Chapter 10 and the topic of preventive measures. In Chapter 10, examples of hard law and soft law approaches to AI ethics, inventories, and auditing are provided. Hard law approaches to AI inventories and auditing can be found in the *Advancing American AI Act* [of 2022], discussed in this chapter, and in the *EU AI Act* and *Colorado AI Consumer Protection Act*, discussed in Chapter 10 under the topic of pretesting and preevaluation of AI systems. Soft law approaches to AI ethics, inventories, and auditing can be located in executive actions such as the *White House Executive Order on the Safe, Secure, and Trustworthy Development and Use of AI* in 2023 and the *White House Office of Management and Budget (OMB) Memorandum on Advancing Governance, Innovation, and Risk Management in Federal Agencies' Use of Artificial Intelligence* in 2024.

AI auditing can encompass both using AI technologies in auditing assessments and categorizing methodologies to conduct an audit of AI systems. The guidelines for AI auditing provided by ISACA, the European Court of Auditors, and the AI Security Institute are illustrative of ongoing auditing efforts.

CHAPTER 10

REMEDIES AND PREVENTIVE MEASURES

This chapter addresses the topic of what legal tools are currently available to remediate AI and automated system harms. It first examines case studies where parties attempt to seek legal remedies after the harm. Next, the chapter reviews case studies of legal efforts that pursue proactive measures to address foreseeable legal issues arising from AI systems. Given that many AI systems have only been recently deployed, there are few examples of remedies specific to these AI systems. However, this chapter provides a glimpse into a possible future where attorneys, researchers, experts, and policymakers may concentrate much effort in preventing and redressing AI risks and harms.

A. *CASE STUDIES OF PREVENTIVE MEASURES AND EX ANTE OPTIONS*

As early as 2019, cities in the U.S. began to ban facial recognition technology, particularly its use by law enforcement.[1] States and counties then began to follow, passing similar measures.[2] Some have referred to these measures as a form of AI abolition. As discussed in Chapter 4, disparate impact cases have discussed issues involving algorithmic bias and biometric identification technologies. Several states have passed legislation that specifically focuses on regulation of biometric information.[3] The excerpts below illustrate attempts to preempt biometric data and AI harms.

---

1. Tate Tyan-Mosley, *The Movement to Limit Face Recognition Tech Might Finally Get a Win*, MIT TECH. REV. (July 20, 2023).

2. *Id.*

3. *See supra* Chapter 4(B).

1. AI Prohibitions and Abolition

The *Recommendation on the Ethics of Artificial Intelligence*, proposed in 2021 by UNESCO, "explicitly bans the use of AI systems for social scoring and mass surveillance."[4] As will be discussed below, the *EU AI Act* prohibits specific AI systems, including certain types of "'real-time' remote biometric identification systems"[5] and AI systems with "social score[s] leading to . . . detrimental or unfavourable treatment[.]"[6]

a. EU AI Act, Article 5 [Prohibited AI Practices]

The following section of the *EU AI Act* provides a comprehensive list of prohibited AI practices in the economic zone.

EU AI Act

Article 5. Prohibited Artificial Intelligence Practices

1. The following AI practices shall be prohibited:

(a) the placing on the market, the putting into service or the use of an AI system that deploys subliminal techniques beyond a person's consciousness or purposefully manipulative or deceptive techniques, with the objective, or the effect of materially distorting the behaviour of a person or a group of persons by appreciably impairing their ability to make an informed decision, thereby causing them to take a decision that they would not have otherwise taken in a manner that causes or is reasonably likely to cause that person, another person or group of persons significant harm;

(b) the placing on the market, the putting into service or the use of an AI system that exploits any of the vulnerabilities of a natural person or a specific group of persons due to their age, disability or a specific social or economic situation, with the objective, or the effect, of materially distorting the behaviour of that person or a person belonging to that group in a manner that causes or is reasonably likely to cause that person or another person significant harm;

(c) the placing on the market, the putting into service or the use of AI systems for the evaluation or classification of natural persons or groups of persons over a certain period of time based on their social behaviour or known, inferred or predicted personal or personality characteristics, with the social score leading to either or both of the following:

(i) detrimental or unfavourable treatment of certain natural persons or groups of persons in social contexts that are unrelated to the contexts in which the data was originally generated or collected;

---

4. United Nations (UN), *193 Countries Adopt First-Ever Global Agreement on the Ethics of Artificial Intelligence*, UN News (Nov. 25, 2021).

5. *EU AI Act* Art. 5(1)(h). *See also* Art. 5(2)-(7).

6. *Id.* at Art. 5(1)(c)(i)-(ii).

(ii) detrimental or unfavourable treatment of certain natural persons or groups of persons that is unjustified or disproportionate to their social behaviour or its gravity;

(d) the placing on the market, the putting into service for this specific purpose, or the use of an AI system for making risk assessments of natural persons in order to assess or predict the risk of a natural person committing a criminal offence, based solely on the profiling of a natural person or on assessing their personality traits and characteristics; this prohibition shall not apply to AI systems used to support the human assessment of the involvement of a person in a criminal activity, which is already based on objective and verifiable facts directly linked to a criminal activity;

(e) the placing on the market, the putting into service for this specific purpose, or the use of AI systems that create or expand facial recognition databases through the untargeted scraping of facial images from the internet or CCTV footage;

(f) the placing on the market, the putting into service for this specific purpose, or the use of AI systems to infer emotions of a natural person in the areas of workplace and education institutions, except where the use of the AI system is intended to be put in place or into the market for medical or safety reasons;

(g) the placing on the market, the putting into service for this specific purpose, or the use of biometric categorisation systems that categorise individually natural persons based on their biometric data to deduce or infer their race, political opinions, trade union membership, religious or philosophical beliefs, sex life or sexual orientation; this prohibition does not cover any labelling or filtering of lawfully acquired biometric datasets, such as images, based on biometric data or categorizing of biometric data in the area of law enforcement;

(h) the use of "real-time" remote biometric identification systems in publicly accessible spaces for the purposes of law enforcement, unless and in so far as such use is strictly necessary for one of the following objectives:

(i) the targeted search for specific victims of abduction, trafficking in human beings or sexual exploitation of human beings, as well as the search for missing persons;

(ii) the prevention of a specific, substantial and imminent threat to the life or physical safety of natural persons or a genuine and present or genuine and foreseeable threat of a terrorist attack;

(iii) the localisation or identification of a person suspected of having committed a criminal offence, for the purpose of conducting a criminal investigation or prosecution or executing a criminal penalty for offences referred to in Annex II and punishable in the Member State concerned by a custodial sentence or a detention order for a maximum period of at least four years. Point (h) of the first subparagraph is without prejudice to Article 9 of Regulation (EU) 2016/679 for the processing of biometric data for purposes other than law enforcement. . . .

b. Facial Recognition Abolition Ordinance (Somerville, Mass.)

The next ordinance demonstrates how local governments have regulated their own use of AI through a ban on facial recognition surveillance technology within their jurisdiction.

City of Somerville, Mass. Ordinance (Facial Recognition Technology Ban)

2019 Somerville, Mass., Code of Ordinances Ch. 9, Art. 3, § 9-25
Chapter 9 of the Code of Ordinances of the City of Somerville, is hereby amended by adding to the existing Article III a new Section 9-25

Sec. 9-25.—Banning the Usage of Facial Recognition Surveillance Technology

(a) *Definitions.*

(1) *Face surveillance* shall mean an automated or semi-automated process that assists in identifying or verifying an individual, based on the physical characteristics of an individual's face.

(2) *Face surveillance system* shall mean any computer software or application that performs face surveillance.

(3) *Somerville* shall mean any department, agency, bureau, and/or subordinate division of the City of Somerville.

(4) *Somerville official* shall mean any person or entity acting on behalf of the City of Somerville, including any officer, employee, agent, contractor, subcontractor, or vendor.

(b) *Ban on government use of face surveillance.* It shall be unlawful for Somerville or any Somerville official to obtain, retain, access, or use:

(1) Any face surveillance system; or

(2) Any information obtained from a face surveillance system.

(c) *Enforcement.*

(1) *Suppression.* No data collected or derived from any use of face surveillance in violation of this ordinance and no evidence derived therefrom may be received in evidence in any proceeding in or before any department, officer, agency, regulatory body, legislative committee, or other authority subject to the jurisdiction of the City of Somerville.

(2) *Cause of action.* Any violation of this ordinance constitutes an injury and any person may institute proceedings for injunctive relief, declaratory relief, or writ of mandamus in any court of competent jurisdiction to enforce this section. An action instituted under this paragraph shall be brought against the city and, if necessary to effectuate compliance with this section, any other governmental agency with possession, custody, or control of data subject to this section.

(3) The city will address alleged violations of this section in accordance with its usual practices, applicable law and contractual obligations.

(4) Nothing in this section shall be construed to limit any individual's rights under state or federal law.

(Ord. No. 2019-16, 6-27-2019)

c. United States v. Amazon.com (Alexa) (Stipulated Order)

This next case focuses on Amazon's alleged misrepresentations regarding its voice assistant platform, Alexa. In this matter, the Federal Trade Commission (FTC) investigates how the platform collects consumer data, primarily focusing on children's data. The FTC alleges a violation of the *Children's Online Privacy Protection Act Rule* and that Amazon misrepresented its practices regarding deletion of the data of minors.

As a result of this settlement, "[t]he FTC will require Amazon to overhaul its deletion practices and implement stringent privacy safeguards to settle charges the company violated the Children's Online Privacy Protection Act Rule (COPPA Rule) and deceived parents and users of the Alexa voice assistant service about its data deletion practices."[7]

United States v. Amazon.com (Alexa) (Stipulated Order)

United States District Court for the Western District of Washington
Civil Case No. 2:23-cv-00811-TL
July 19, 2023

STIPULATED ORDER

ORDER

I. Deletion of Children's Personal Information Associated with Inactive Alexa Child Profiles

It is ordered that, in compliance with COPPA's requirements concerning the retention and deletion of Children's Personal Information, *see* 16 C.F.R. § 312.10, for as long as that provision is in effect and is therefore applicable to Defendants,

A. Defendants and Defendants' officers, agents, employees, and attorneys, and all other persons in active concert or participation with any of them, who receive actual notice of this Order shall, within six (6) months of entry of this Order, implement a process to identify Inactive Alexa Child Profiles; and

B. Following identification of any Inactive Alexa Child Profile, Defendants shall delete any Personal Information collected from a Child associated with that Inactive Alexa Child Profile within 90 days, unless the Parent of the applicable Child requests that such information be retained or the applicable Child Profile becomes active again prior to such deletion.

II. Prohibition Against Misrepresentations About Privacy of Geolocation Information and Voice Information

It is further ordered that Defendants, Defendants' officers, agents, employees, and attorneys, and all other persons in active concert or participation with any of them, who receive actual notice of this Order, whether

7. *FTC Case Summary of Amazon.com (Alexa), U.S. v.* [*Amazon.com*], FTC (July 21, 2023).

acting directly or indirectly, are permanently restrained and enjoined from misrepresenting, expressly or by implication:

A. The extent to which any Defendant retains, limits or permits access to, or deletes any Alexa App Geolocation Information or Voice Information;

B. The extent to which a consumer may exercise control over any Defendant's retention, deletion, or access to Alexa App Geolocation Information or Voice Information, and the steps a consumer must take to implement such controls; or

C. The extent to which a Parent may exercise control over any Defendant's retention or deletion of a Child's Voice Information, and the steps a Parent must take to implement such controls.

III. Mandated Deletion of Information

It is further ordered that Defendants, Defendants' officers, agents, employees, and attorneys, and all other persons in active concert or participation with any of them, who receive actual notice of this Order, must:

A. Delete all Alexa App Geolocation Information and Voice Information collected from a consumer where the consumer has requested that any Defendant delete such information via a mechanism any Defendant has made available for that purpose;

B. Delete all Personal Information collected by Alexa from a Child where the Child's Parent has requested that any Defendant delete such information via a mechanism any Defendant has made available for that purpose;

C. After processing the deletion of Alexa App Geolocation Information, Voice Information, or Children's Personal Information as provided for in Sections I, IV(A) and IV(B), Defendant shall not subsequently use such information for the creation or improvement of any Data Product. For the avoidance of doubt, the foregoing provision does not limit Defendant's use of any Data Product created prior to the processing of the deletion of Alexa App Geolocation Information, Voice Information, or Children's Personal Information as provided for in Section I, IV(A) and IV(B).

IV. Mandated Notice of Retention and Deletion

It is further ordered that Defendants, Defendants' officers, agents, employees, and attorneys, and all other persons in active concert or participation with any of them, who receive actual notice of this Order, must, within ninety (90) days of entry of this order, document, adhere to, and make publicly available:

A. Clearly and Conspicuously, when a consumer is prompted to grant Defendant permission to access Alexa App Geolocation Information, a link to a retention and deletion disclosure for Alexa App Geolocation Information ("Geolocation Information Disclosure"), setting forth: (1) the purpose for which such information is collected, used, or maintained; and (2) the mechanisms, if any, by which consumers may request deletion of such information;

B. In the Alexa and Alexa Devices FAQs (or a similarly prominent location) a retention and deletion disclosure for Voice Information ("Voice Information Disclosure"), that includes an explanation of: (1) the purposes for which such information is collected, used, or maintained; (2) the mechanisms, if any, by which consumers may request deletion of such information; and (3) the mechanisms by which Parents of Children may request deletion of Personal Information that Alexa collects from children.

V. Notice to Users

It is further ordered that, on or before thirty (30) days after the date of the entry of this Order, Defendant Amazon must:

A. Post in the Alexa and Alexa Devices FAQs (or a similarly prominent location), which can be accessed on the Web and in the Alexa App, for a period of six (6) months after the effective date of this Order . . . ; and

B. Post Clearly and Conspicuously on the home page of the Amazon Parent Dashboard for a period of six (6) months after the effective date of this Order[.]

VI. Mandated Privacy Program

It is further ordered that Defendants, and any business that any Defendant controls directly, or indirectly, in connection with the collection, maintenance, use, or disclosure of, or provision of access to, Alexa App Geolocation Information, must, within ninety (90) days of entry of this order and for a period of twenty (20) years thereafter, establish, implement, and thereafter maintain or, if such a program already exists, maintain a comprehensive privacy program to protect the privacy of Alexa App Geolocation Information (the "Program"). To satisfy this requirement, Defendants must:

A. Document in writing the content, implementation, and maintenance of the Program;

B. Provide the written program and any evaluations thereof or updates thereto to a senior officer of Defendants responsible for the Program at least once every twelve (12) months;

C. Designate a qualified employee or employees to coordinate and be responsible for the Program;

D. Assess and document, at least once every twelve (12) months, internal and external risks to the privacy of Alexa App Geolocation Information that could result in the (1) unauthorized collection, maintenance, alteration, use, or disclosure of, or provision of access to, Alexa App Geolocation Information; or the (2) misuse, loss, theft, alteration, destruction, or other compromise of such information;

E. Design, implement, maintain, and document safeguards that control for the internal and external risks Defendants identify to the privacy of Alexa App Geolocation Information identified in response to Provision VII.D. Each safeguard must be based on the volume and sensitivity of Alexa App Geolocation Information that is at risk, and the likelihood that the risk could be realized and result in the (1) unauthorized collection, maintenance, use, or disclosure of, or provision of access to, Alexa App Geolocation Information; or the (2) misuse, loss, theft, alteration, destruction, or other compromise of such information. Such safeguards must also include:

1. Conducting a privacy review and producing a written report ("Privacy Review Statement") for Alexa's collection, maintenance, use, or disclosure of Alexa App Geolocation Information. The Privacy Review Statement must describe:

a) How Alexa collects, maintains, uses, or discloses Alexa App Geolocation Information;

b) For how long Alexa App Geolocation Information is retained;

c) The risks of the (1) collection, maintenance, alteration, use, or disclosure of, or provision of access to; or the (2) misuse, loss, theft, alteration, destruction, or other compromise of Alexa App Geolocation Information, and the safeguards in place or to be implemented that are intended to control identified risks;

d) Any other known, reasonable safeguards or other procedures that would mitigate the identified risks of the (1) collection, maintenance, alteration, use, or disclosure of, or provision of access to; or the (2) misuse, loss, theft, alteration, destruction, or other compromise of Alexa App Geolocation Information that were not implemented, and each reason that such alternatives were not implemented; and

e) Any decision made as a result of the review (e.g., whether a practice was approved, approved contingent upon safeguards or other recommendations being implemented, or rejected).

2. Implementing controls to limit access to unencrypted Alexa App Geolocation Information only to authorized services;

3. Training of all employees whose responsibilities include access to unencrypted Alexa App Geolocation Information, at least every twelve (12) months, on how to safeguard Alexa App Geolocation Information;

4. Training of all employees whose responsibilities include deletion of Alexa App Geolocation Information, at least every twelve (12) months, on how to comply with deletion requests;

5. Implementing data access controls for all databases and assets storing unencrypted Alexa App Geolocation Information; and

6. Reviewing and adjusting as appropriate at least once every twelve (12) months, employee access to unencrypted Alexa App Geolocation Information to ensure that the employee needs continued access to the Alexa App Geolocation Information to perform the employee's specific job function[.] . . .

2. *Limiting Deployment of High-Risk Technologies*

a. EU AI Act, Articles 85-87 [Remedies]

The following *EU AI Act* articles provide EU subjects with specific legal remedies to utilize regarding those who deploy AI systems in violation of the Act.

EU AI Act

Article 85. Right to Lodge a Complaint with a Market Surveillance Authority

Without prejudice to other administrative or judicial remedies, any natural or legal person having grounds to consider that there has been an infringement of the provisions of this Regulation may submit complaints to the relevant market surveillance authority.

In accordance with Regulation (EU) 2019/1020, such complaints shall be taken into account for the purpose of conducting market surveillance activities, and shall be handled in line with the dedicated procedures established therefor by the market surveillance authorities.

EU AI Act

Article 86. Right to Explanation of Individual Decision-Making

1. Any affected person subject to a decision which is taken by the deployer on the basis of the output from a high-risk AI system listed in Annex III, with the exception of systems listed under point 2 thereof, and which produces legal effects or similarly significantly affects that person in a way that they consider to have an adverse impact on their health, safety or fundamental rights shall have the right to obtain from the deployer clear and meaningful explanations of the role of the AI system in the decision-making procedure and the main elements of the decision taken.

2. Paragraph 1 shall not apply to the use of AI systems for which exceptions from, or restrictions to, the obligation under that paragraph follow from Union or national law in compliance with Union law.

3. This Article shall apply only to the extent that the right referred to in paragraph 1 is not otherwise provided for under Union law.

EU AI Act

Article 87. Reporting of Infringements and Protection of Reporting Persons

Directive (EU) 2019/1937[8] shall apply to the reporting of infringements of this Regulation and the protection of persons reporting such infringements.

b. Colorado AI Consumer Protection Act

The *Colorado AI Consumer Protection Act* is one of the most comprehensive state laws on AI that seeks to impose liability for deployers and developers of AI systems that are categorized as "high-risk systems." Note how this state law defines a high-risk system and whether such categorization is effective in minimizing AI risks.

Colorado AI Consumer Protection Act

2024 Colorado Session Laws, Ch. 198 (S.B. 24-205)

Colo. Rev. Stat. Sec. 6-1-1701. Definitions

. . .

(1)(b) "Algorithmic discrimination" does not include:

(I) The offer, license, or use of a high-risk artificial intelligence system by a developer or deployer for the sole purpose of:

8. Directive (EU) 2019/1937 of the European Council and of the Council of 23 October 2019 on the Protection of Persons Who Report Breaches of Union Law.

(A) The developer's or deployer's **self-testing** to identify, mitigate, or prevent discrimination or otherwise ensure compliance with state and federal law . . . (emphasis added).

Colo. Rev. Stat. sec. 6-1-1706. Enforcement by Attorney General

. . .

(3) In any action commenced by the attorney general to enforce this part[], it is an **affirmative defense** that the developer, deployer, or other person: (emphasis added)

(a) Discovers and cures a violation of this part[] as a result of:

(I) Feedback that the developer, deployer, or other person encourages deployers or users to provide to the developer, deployer, or other person;

(II) Adversarial testing or red teaming, as those terms are defined or used by the National Institute of Standards and Technology; or

(III) An internal review process; and

(b) Is otherwise in compliance with:

(I) The latest version of the "Artificial Intelligence Risk Management Framework" published by the National Institute of Standards and Technology in the United States Department of Commerce and standard ISO/IEC 42001 of the International Organization for Standardization;

(II) Another nationally or internationally recognized risk management framework for artificial intelligence systems, if the standards are substantially equivalent to or more stringent than the requirements of this part []; or

(III) Any risk management framework for artificial intelligence systems that the attorney general, in the attorney general's discretion, may designate and, if designated, shall publicly disseminate.

(4) A developer, a deployer, or other person bears the burden of demonstrating to the attorney general that the requirements established in subsection (3) of this section have been satisfied.

(5) Nothing in this part [], including the enforcement authority granted to the attorney general under this section, preempts or otherwise affects any right, claim, remedy, presumption, or defense available at law or in equity. A rebuttable presumption or affirmative defense established under this part [] applies only to an enforcement action brought by the attorney general pursuant to this section and does not apply to any right, claim, remedy, presumption, or defense available at law or in equity.

(6) This part [] does not provide the basis for, and is not subject to, a private right of action for violations of this part [] or any other law. . . .

B. CASE STUDIES OF PRETESTING, IMPACT ASSESSMENTS, AND ONGOING MONITORING

1. International

What steps are required to bring an AI system out of its "regulatory sandbox" and into the real world for testing before deployment? UNESCO provides a tool for nation states to assess their capabilities of implementing AI ethically and responsibly, and the *EU AI Act* implements legal requirements before an AI system is allowed to be released outside the sandbox before real-world testing.

a. UNESCO Readiness Assessment Methodology

UNESCO recommended a framework for AI ethics that was adopted by 193 countries in 2021.[9] Building on this effort, in 2023, UNESCO then published a *Readiness Assessment Methodology* to operationalize the UNESCO *Recommendation on the Ethics of Artificial Intelligence*. For nations that had adopted the ethics framework, UNESCO proposed a series of questions in the *Readiness Assessment Methodology*. Posed to governmental bodies within each member state, the qualitative and quantitative questions are intended to assist nations in their assessment of their readiness to conform to the AI ethical principles that had been agreed on.

Readiness Assessment Methodology: A Tool of the Recommendation on the Ethics of Artificial Intelligence

United Nations Educational, Scientific and Cultural Organization (UNESCO)
2023

I. BACKGROUND

. . .

The goal of this document is to provide more information on the Readiness Assessment Methodology, lay out its various dimensions, and detail the work plan for the implementing countries, including the type of entities that need to be involved, responsibilities of each entity, and the split of work between UNESCO and the implementing country. . . .

[T]he RAM is a macro level instrument that will help countries understand where they stand on the scale of preparedness to implement AI ethically and responsibly for all their citizens, in so doing highlighting what institutional and regulatory changes are needed. . . .

III. QUESTIONS

2. The Legal Dimension

2.1. Background

. . . The regulatory framework should include aspects of effective protection, enforcement, redress, and monitoring of potential harms related to the deployment and use of AI systems. This includes assessing whether Member States have adopted appropriate regulatory frameworks to ensure the ethical development and deployment of AI, as well as monitoring and evaluation mechanisms for its implementation and enforcement. . . .

9. United Nations, *supra* note 4.

3. The Social/Cultural Dimension

3.1. Background

. . . [The social/cultural] dimension will consider the factors relevant for ethical development and deployment of AI systems including inclusiveness and social and cultural diversity, public awareness and values relevant to scaling up of ethical AI solutions. The idea is that if the teams developing and deploying AI systems are very homogeneous it may lead to AI systems not sufficiently reflecting the complexity and diversity that society is composed of, which means the outcomes generated by AI systems may contribute to amplification of structural bias. Second, it will address attitudes towards AI technologies, including their public acceptance. It should also help reveal societal values and preferences in Member States, which lead to certain attitudes towards technologies and directly impact related societal choices. . . .

b. EU AI Act, Article 60 [Testing of High-Risk AI Systems in Real World Conditions Outside AI Regulatory Sandboxes]

AI regulatory developments support innovation in the testing of AI systems. The following provision within the *EU AI Act* demonstrates measures to encourage the testing of high-risk AI systems in real-world conditions. Articles 60 and 61, below, illustrate these efforts.

EU AI Act

Article 60. Testing of High-Risk AI Systems in Real World Conditions Outside AI Regulatory Sandboxes

1. Testing of high-risk AI systems in real world conditions outside AI regulatory sandboxes may be conducted by providers or prospective providers of high-risk AI systems listed in Annex III, in accordance with this Article and the real-world testing plan referred to in this Article, without prejudice to the prohibitions under Article 5. The Commission shall, by means of implementing acts, specify the detailed elements of the real-world testing plan. Those implementing acts shall be adopted in accordance with the examination procedure referred to in Article 98(2). This paragraph shall be without prejudice to Union or national law on the testing in real world conditions of high-risk AI systems related to products covered by Union harmonisation legislation listed in Annex I.

2. Providers or prospective providers may conduct testing of high-risk AI systems referred to in Annex III in real world conditions at any time before the placing on the market or the putting into service of the AI system on their own or in partnership with one or more deployers or prospective deployers.

3. The testing of high-risk AI systems in real world conditions under this Article shall be without prejudice to any ethical review that is required by Union or national law.

4. Providers or prospective providers may conduct the testing in real world conditions only where all of the following conditions are met:

(a) the provider or prospective provider has drawn up a real-world testing plan and submitted it to the market surveillance authority in the Member State where the testing in real world conditions is to be conducted;

(b) the market surveillance authority in the Member State where the testing in real world conditions is to be conducted has approved the testing in real world conditions and the real-world testing plan; where the market surveillance authority has not provided an answer within 30 days, the testing in real world conditions and the real-world testing plan shall be understood to have been approved; where national law does not provide for a tacit approval, the testing in real world conditions shall remain subject to an authorisation;

(c) the provider or prospective provider, with the exception of providers or prospective providers of high-risk AI systems referred to in points 1, 6 and 7 of Annex III in the areas of law enforcement, migration, asylum and border control management, and high-risk AI systems referred to in point 2 of Annex III has registered the testing in real world conditions in accordance with Article 71(4) with a Union-wide unique single identification number and with the information specified in Annex IX; the provider or prospective provider of high-risk AI systems referred to in points 1, 6 and 7 of Annex III in the areas of law enforcement, migration, asylum and border control management, has registered the testing in real-world conditions in the secure non-public section of the EU database according to Article 49(4), point (d), with a Union-wide unique single identification number and with the information specified therein; the provider or prospective provider of high-risk AI systems referred to in point 2 of Annex III has registered the testing in real-world conditions in accordance with Article 49(5);

(d) the provider or prospective provider conducting the testing in real world conditions is established in the Union or has appointed a legal representative who is established in the Union;

(e) data collected and processed for the purpose of the testing in real world conditions shall be transferred to third countries only provided that appropriate and applicable safeguards under Union law are implemented;

(f) the testing in real world conditions does not last longer than necessary to achieve its objectives and in any case not longer than six months, which may be extended for an additional period of six months, subject to prior notification by the provider or prospective provider to the market surveillance authority, accompanied by an explanation of the need for such an extension;

(g) the subjects of the testing in real world conditions who are persons belonging to vulnerable groups due to their age or disability, are appropriately protected;

(h) where a provider or prospective provider organises the testing in real world conditions in cooperation with one or more deployers or prospective deployers, the latter have been informed of all aspects of the testing that are relevant to their decision to participate, and given the relevant instructions for use of the AI system referred to in Article 13; the provider or prospective provider and the deployer or prospective deployer shall conclude an agreement specifying their roles and responsibilities with a view to ensuring compliance with the provisions for testing in real world conditions under this Regulation and under other applicable Union and national law;

(i) the subjects of the testing in real world conditions have given informed consent in accordance with Article 61, or in the case of law enforcement, where the seeking of informed consent would prevent the AI system from being tested, the testing itself and the outcome of the testing in the real world conditions shall not have any negative effect on the subjects, and their personal data shall be deleted after the test is performed;

(j) the testing in real world conditions is effectively overseen by the provider or prospective provider, as well as by deployers or prospective deployers through persons who are suitably qualified in the relevant field and have the necessary capacity, training and authority to perform their tasks;

(k) the predictions, recommendations or decisions of the AI system can be effectively reversed and disregarded.

5. Any subjects of the testing in real world conditions, or their legally designated representative, as appropriate, may, without any resulting detriment and without having to provide any justification, withdraw from the testing at any time by revoking their informed consent and may request the immediate and permanent deletion of their personal data. The withdrawal of the informed consent shall not affect the activities already carried out.

6. In accordance with Article 75, Member States shall confer on their market surveillance authorities the powers of requiring providers and prospective providers to provide information, of carrying out unannounced remote or on-site inspections, and of performing checks on the conduct of the testing in real world conditions and the related high-risk AI systems. Market surveillance authorities shall use those powers to ensure the safe development of testing in real world conditions.

7. Any serious incident identified in the course of the testing in real world conditions shall be reported to the national market surveillance authority in accordance with Article 73. The provider or prospective provider shall adopt immediate mitigation measures or, failing that, shall suspend the testing in real world conditions until such mitigation takes place, or otherwise terminate it. The provider or prospective provider shall establish a procedure for the prompt recall of the AI system upon such termination of the testing in real world conditions.

8. Providers or prospective providers shall notify the national market surveillance authority in the Member State where the testing in real world conditions is to be conducted of the suspension or termination of the testing in real world conditions and of the final outcomes.

9. The provider or prospective provider shall be liable under applicable Union and national liability law for any damage caused in the course of their testing in real world conditions.

c. EU AI Act, Article 61 [Informed Consent to Participate in Testing in Real World Conditions Outside AI Regulatory Sandboxes]

EU AI Act

Article 61. Informed Consent to Participate in Testing in Real World Conditions Outside AI Regulatory Sandboxes

1. For the purpose of testing in real world conditions under Article 60, freely-given informed consent shall be obtained from the subjects of testing prior to their participation in such testing and after their having been duly informed with concise, clear, relevant, and understandable information regarding:

(a) the nature and objectives of the testing in real world conditions and the possible inconvenience that may be linked to their participation;

(b) the conditions under which the testing in real world conditions is to be conducted, including the expected duration of the subject or subjects' participation;

(c) their rights, and the guarantees regarding their participation, in particular their right to refuse to participate in, and the right to withdraw from, testing in real world conditions at any time without any resulting detriment and without having to provide any justification;

(d) the arrangements for requesting the reversal or the disregarding of the predictions, recommendations or decisions of the AI system;

(e) the Union-wide unique single identification number of the testing in real world conditions in accordance with Article 60(4) point (c), and the contact details of the provider or its legal representative from whom further information can be obtained.

2. The informed consent shall be dated and documented and a copy shall be given to the subjects of testing or their legal representative.

2. *Federal and State*

Both the 2023 White House *Executive Order on the Safe, Secure, and Trustworthy Development and Use of AI*, E.O. 14110, and the *Colorado AI Consumer Protection Act* emphasize the need to perform impact assessments to evaluate risks both from development and deployment of AI systems.

a. White House Executive Order on the Safe, Secure, and Trustworthy Development and Use of AI (Rescinded)

In January 2025, with the transition of administrations, the new White House revoked the 2023 *Executive Order on the Safe, Secure, and Trustworthy Development and Use of AI.*[10] The excerpt below is included for historical

---

10. Exec. Order No. 14148, 90 Fed. Reg. 8237, *Initial Rescissions of Harmful Executive Orders and Actions* (Jan. 28, 2025).

reference. In April 2025, the new administration issued an Office of Management and Budget (OMB) Memorandum, M-25-21, *Accelerating Federal Use of AI through Innovation, Governance, and Public Trust,* that included the requirement that agencies must "reuse resources that enable AI adoption, such as agency data, models, code, and assessments of AI performance."[11]

White House Executive Order 14110 (Rescinded): Secure, and Trustworthy Development and Use of Artificial Intelligence

October 30, 2023

Sec. 3. Definitions

. . .

(d) The term "AI red-teaming" means a structured testing effort to find flaws and vulnerabilities in an AI system, often in a controlled environment and in collaboration with developers of AI. Artificial Intelligence red-teaming is most often performed by dedicated "red teams" that adopt adversarial methods to identify flaws and vulnerabilities, such as harmful or discriminatory outputs from an AI system, unforeseen or undesirable system behaviors, limitations, or potential risks associated with the misuse of the system. . . .

Sec. 4. Ensuring the Safety and Security of AI Technology

4.1. Developing Guidelines, Standards, and Best Practices for AI Safety and Security

. . .

(ii) Establish appropriate guidelines (except for AI used as a component of a national security system), including appropriate procedures and processes, to enable developers of AI, especially of dual-use foundation models, to conduct AI red-teaming tests to enable deployment of safe, secure, and trustworthy systems . . . .

4.2. Ensuring Safe and Reliable AI

. . .

(C) the results of any developed dual-use foundation model's performance in relevant AI red-team testing based on guidance developed by NIST pursuant to subsection 4.1(a)(ii) of this section, and a description of any associated measures the company has taken to meet safety objectives, such as mitigations to improve performance on these red-team tests and strengthen overall model security. Prior to the development of guidance on red-team testing standards by NIST pursuant to subsection 4.1(a)(ii) of this section, this description shall include the results of any red-team testing that the company has conducted relating

11. OMB Memorandum M-25-21, *Accelerating Federal Use of AI through Innovation, Governance, and Public Trust* (Apr. 3, 2025).

to lowering the barrier to entry for the development, acquisition, and use of biological weapons by non-state actors; the discovery of software vulnerabilities and development of associated exploits; the use of software or tools to influence real or virtual events; the possibility for self-replication or propagation; and associated measures to meet safety objectives; . . .

Sec. 10. Advancing Federal Government Use of AI

. . .

10.1. Providing Guidance for AI Management

. . .

(b) To provide guidance on Federal Government use of AI, . . .

(viii) in consultation with the Secretary of Commerce, the Secretary of Homeland Security, and the heads of other appropriate agencies as determined by the Director of OMB, recommendations to agencies regarding:

(A) external testing for AI, including AI red-teaming for generative AI, to be developed in coordination with the Cybersecurity and Infrastructure Security Agency;

(B) testing and safeguards against discriminatory, misleading, inflammatory, unsafe, or deceptive outputs, as well as against producing child sexual abuse material and against producing non-consensual intimate imagery of real individuals (including intimate digital depictions of the body or body parts of an identifiable individual), for generative AI;

(C) reasonable steps to watermark or otherwise label output from generative AI;

(D) application of the mandatory minimum risk-management practices defined under subsection 10.1(b)(iv) of this section to procured AI;

(E) independent evaluation of vendors' claims concerning both the effectiveness and risk mitigation of their AI offerings;

(F) documentation and oversight of procured AI;

(G) maximizing the value to agencies when relying on contractors to use and enrich Federal Government data for the purposes of AI development and operation;

(H) provision of incentives for the continuous improvement of procured AI; and

(I) training on AI in accordance with the principles set out in this order and in other references related to AI listed herein; . . .

b. Colorado AI Consumer Protection Act

Colorado AI Consumer Protection Act

2024 Colorado Session Laws, Ch. 198 (S.B. 24-205)

Colo. Rev. Stat. Sec. 6-1-1707. Rules

(1) The attorney general may promulgate rules as necessary for the purpose of implementing and enforcing this part 17, including:

(a) The documentation and requirements for developers pursuant to section 6-1-1702(2);

(b) The contents of and requirements for the notices and disclosures required by sections 6-1-1702(5) and (7); 6-1-1703(4), (5), (7), and (9); and 6-1-1704;

(c) The content and requirements of the risk management policy and program required by section 6-1-1703(2);

(d) The content and requirements of the impact assessments required by section 6-1-1703(3);

(e) The requirements for the rebuttable presumptions set forth in sections 6-1-1702 and 6-1-1703; and

(f) The requirements for the affirmative defense set forth in section 6-1-1706(3), including the process by which the attorney general will recognize any other nationally or internationally recognized risk management framework for artificial intelligence systems.

3. Corporate

a. Microsoft Responsible AI Standard v2

The private sector's approach to AI risk management strategies may sometimes require a more active approach, as laws and norms might not have developed enough to fill certain gaps of AI risks or society's needs. As you read through *Microsoft Responsible AI Standard, version 2,* note that this was published before the passage of the *EU AI Act* and the signage of the *Executive Order on the Safe, Secure, and Trustworthy Development and Use of AI.*

Microsoft Responsible AI Standard, v2

June 2022

GOAL RS2: FAILURES AND REMEDIATIONS

Microsoft AI systems are designed to minimize the time to remediation of predictable or known failures. . . .

RS2.1 Define predictable failures, including false positive and false negative results for the system as a whole and how they would impact stakeholders for each intended use. Use the Impact Assessment template to document any adverse impacts of these failures on stakeholders.

RS2.2 For each case of a predictable failure likely to have an adverse impact on a stakeholder, document the failure management approach:

1) When possible, design and build the system to avoid this failure. Describe the design solution. Estimate the time range for resolving predictable failures for each designed solution or indicate that the failure will be prevented by design.
2) When a failure cannot be prevented by design, build a fallback option that may be used when this failure occurs. Describe the

fallback option and document the estimated time required to invoke and use the fallback option.

3) Provide training and documentation for stakeholders accountable for system oversight that supports their resolution of the failure. Describe the documentation and training.

RS2.3 Document your plan for managing previously unknown failures that come to light once the system is in use:

1) Describe the system's rollback plan and document the time that may elapse until the entire system, across all endpoints can be rolled back.
2) Describe support for turning features off and document the time that may elapse until the feature can be turned off across all endpoints.
3) Describe the process for updating and releasing updates to each model and document the time that may elapse until the system has been updated across all endpoints.
4) Describe how customers, partners, and end users will be notified of changes to the system, updated understandings of failures, and their best mitigations.

RS2.4 Provide training and documentation for system owners, developers, customer support and other stakeholders responsible for managing the system to support their remediation and mitigation of predictable failures identified in requirement RS2.1. Document the training and documentation provided. . . .

GOAL RS3: ONGOING MONITORING, FEEDBACK, AND EVALUATION

Microsoft AI systems are subject to ongoing monitoring, feedback, and evaluation so that we can identify and review new uses, identify and troubleshoot issues, manage and maintain the systems, and improve them over time. . . .

RS3.7 If evidence comes to light that refutes the system is fit for purpose for an intended use at any point in the system's use:

1) remove the intended use from customer-facing materials and make current customers aware of the issue, take action to close the identified gap, or discontinue the system,
2) revise documentation related to the intended use, and
3) publish the revised documentation to customers.

When the system is a platform service made available to external customers or partners, include this information in the required Transparency Note. . . .

C. *CASE STUDIES OF EX ANTE OPTIONS*

1. *EU AI Act: Prohibition, Testing, Documentation, and Disclosure*

a. EU AI Act, Article 6 [Classification Rules for High-Risk AI Systems]

EU AI Act

Article 6. Classification Rules for High-Risk AI Systems

1. Irrespective of whether an AI system is placed on the market or put into service independently of the products referred to in points (a) and (b), that AI system shall be considered to be high-risk where both of the following conditions are fulfilled:

(a) the AI system is intended to be used as a safety component of a product, or the AI system is itself a product, covered by the Union harmonisation legislation listed in Annex I;

(b) the product whose safety component pursuant to point (a) is the AI system, or the AI system itself as a product, is required to undergo a third-party conformity assessment, with a view to the placing on the market or the putting into service of that product pursuant to the Union harmonisation legislation listed in Annex I.

2. In addition to the high-risk AI systems referred to in paragraph 1, AI systems referred to in Annex III shall be considered to be high-risk.

3. By derogation from paragraph 2, an AI system referred to in Annex III shall not be considered to be high-risk where it does not pose a significant risk of harm to the health, safety or fundamental rights of natural persons, including by not materially influencing the outcome of decision making. The first subparagraph shall apply where any of the following conditions is fulfilled:

(a) the AI system is intended to perform a narrow procedural task;

(b) the AI system is intended to improve the result of a previously completed human activity;

(c) the AI system is intended to detect decision-making patterns or deviations from prior decision-making patterns and is not meant to replace or influence the previously completed human assessment, without proper human review; or

(d) the AI system is intended to perform a preparatory task to an assessment relevant for the purposes of the use cases listed in Annex III.

Notwithstanding the first subparagraph, an AI system referred to in Annex III shall always be considered to be high-risk where the AI system performs profiling of natural persons.

4. A provider who considers that an AI system referred to in Annex III is not high-risk shall document its assessment before that system is placed on the market or put into service. Such provider shall be subject to the registration obligation set out in Article 49(2). Upon request of national competent authorities, the provider shall provide the documentation of the assessment.

5. The Commission shall, after consulting the European Artificial Intelligence Board (the "Board"), and no later than 2 February 2026, provide guidelines specifying the practical implementation of this Article in line with

Article 96 together with a comprehensive list of practical examples of use cases of AI systems that are high-risk and not high-risk.

6. The Commission is empowered to adopt delegated acts in accordance with Article 97 in order to amend paragraph 3, second subparagraph, of this Article by adding new conditions to those laid down therein, or by modifying them, where there is concrete and reliable evidence of the existence of AI systems that fall under the scope of Annex III, but do not pose a significant risk of harm to the health, safety or fundamental rights of natural persons.

7. The Commission shall adopt delegated acts in accordance with Article 97 in order to amend paragraph 3, second subparagraph, of this Article by deleting any of the conditions laid down therein, where there is concrete and reliable evidence that this is necessary to maintain the level of protection of health, safety and fundamental rights provided for by this Regulation.

8. Any amendment to the conditions laid down in paragraph 3, second subparagraph, adopted in accordance with paragraphs 6 and 7 of this Article shall not decrease the overall level of protection of health, safety and fundamental rights provided for by this Regulation and shall ensure consistency with the delegated acts adopted pursuant to Article 7(1), and take account of market and technological developments.

b. EU AI Act, Article 7 [Amendments to Annex III]

EU AI Act

Article 7. Amendments to Annex III

1. The Commission is empowered to adopt delegated acts in accordance with Article 97 to amend Annex III by adding or modifying use-cases of high-risk AI systems where both of the following conditions are fulfilled:

(a) the AI systems are intended to be used in any of the areas listed in Annex III;

(b) the AI systems pose a risk of harm to health and safety, or an adverse impact on fundamental rights, and that risk is equivalent to, or greater than, the risk of harm or of adverse impact posed by the high-risk AI systems already referred to in Annex III.

2. When assessing the condition under paragraph 1, point (b), the Commission shall take into account the following criteria:

(a) the intended purpose of the AI system;

(b) the extent to which an AI system has been used or is likely to be used;

(c) the nature and amount of the data processed and used by the AI system, in particular whether special categories of personal data are processed;

(d) the extent to which the AI system acts autonomously and the possibility for a human to override a decision or recommendations that may lead to potential harm;

(e) the extent to which the use of an AI system has already caused harm to health and safety, has had an adverse impact on fundamental rights or has given rise to significant concerns in relation to the likelihood of such harm or adverse impact, as demonstrated, for example, by reports or documented allegations submitted to national competent authorities or by other reports, as appropriate;

(f) the potential extent of such harm or such adverse impact, in particular in terms of its intensity and its ability to affect multiple persons or to disproportionately affect a particular group of persons;

(g) the extent to which persons who are potentially harmed or suffer an adverse impact are dependent on the outcome produced with an AI system, in particular because for practical or legal reasons it is not reasonably possible to opt-out from that outcome;

(h) the extent to which there is an imbalance of power, or the persons who are potentially harmed or suffer an adverse impact are in a vulnerable position in relation to the deployer of an AI system, in particular due to status, authority, knowledge, economic or social circumstances, or age;

(i) the extent to which the outcome produced involving an AI system is easily corrigible or reversible, taking into account the technical solutions available to correct or reverse it, whereby outcomes having an adverse impact on health, safety or fundamental rights, shall not be considered to be easily corrigible or reversible;

(j) the magnitude and likelihood of benefit of the deployment of the AI system for individuals, groups, or society at large, including possible improvements in product safety;

(k) the extent to which existing Union law provides for:

(i) effective measures of redress in relation to the risks posed by an AI system, with the exclusion of claims for damages;

(ii) effective measures to prevent or substantially minimise those risks.

3. The Commission is empowered to adopt delegated acts in accordance with Article 97 to amend the list in Annex III by removing high-risk AI systems where both of the following conditions are fulfilled:

(a) the high-risk AI system concerned no longer poses any significant risks to fundamental rights, health or safety, taking into account the criteria listed in paragraph 2;

(b) the deletion does not decrease the overall level of protection of health, safety and fundamental rights under Union law.

c. EU AI Act, Article 8 [Compliance with the Requirements]

EU AI Act

Article 8. Compliance with the Requirements

1. High-risk AI systems shall comply with the requirements laid down in this Section, taking into account their intended purpose as well as the generally acknowledged state of the art on AI and AI-related technologies. The risk management system referred to in Article 9 shall be taken into account when ensuring compliance with those requirements.

2. Where a product contains an AI system, to which the requirements of this Regulation as well as requirements of the Union harmonisation legislation listed in Section A of Annex I apply, providers shall be responsible for ensuring that their product is fully compliant with all applicable requirements under applicable Union harmonisation legislation. In ensuring the compliance of high-risk AI systems referred to in paragraph 1 with the requirements set out in this Section, and in order to ensure consistency, avoid duplication and minimise additional burdens, providers shall have a choice of integrating, as appropriate, the necessary testing and reporting processes, information and documentation they provide with regard to their product into documentation and procedures that already exist and are required under the Union harmonisation legislation listed in Section A of Annex I.

D. CASE STUDIES OF REMEDIES AND EX POST OPTIONS

What are the remedial options available when AI systems are deemed harmful? The FTC has recommended data deletion and what has been termed "algorithmic disgorgement."[12]

1. AI and Disgorgement

Algorithmic disgorgement is a type of remedy that requires the removal of products built on data that were inappropriately or illegally secured. Between 2019 and 2024, the FTC used algorithmic disgorgement in multiple cases, particularly in an attempt to remove and delete data of apps involving the data of minors.

a. United States v. Kurbo (Algorithmic Disgorgement and Data Deletion)

In the following case, the FTC compelled Kurbo to delete personal information and algorithms derived from the data of minors following the allegation that the company had unlawfully collected children's personal data without parental consent.

United States v. Kurbo et al. (Stipulated Order)

United States District Court for the Northern District of California
Civil Case No: 3:22-cv-00946-TSH
March 3, 2022

HIXSON, United States Magistrate Judge.

DEFINITIONS

For the purpose of this Order, the following definitions apply:

A. **"Affected Work Product"** means any models or algorithms developed in whole or in part using Personal Information Collected from Children through the Kurbo Program. . . .

12. Tonya Riley, *The FTC's Biggest AI Enforcement Tool? Forcing Companies to Delete Their Algorithms*, CYBERSCOOP (July 5, 2023).

ORDER

I. Injunction Concerning Collection of Personal Information From Children

It is ordered that Defendants and Defendants' officers, agents, employees, and attorneys, and all other Persons in active concert or participation with any of them, who receive actual notice of this Order, whether acting directly or indirectly, in connection with being an Operator of any Website or Online Service Directed to Children or of any website or online service with actual knowledge that it is Collecting or maintaining Personal Information from a Child, are hereby permanently restrained and enjoined from:

A. Failing to make reasonable efforts, taking into account available technology, to ensure that a Parent of a Child receives direct notice of Defendants' practices with regard to the Collection, use, or Disclosure of Personal Information from Children, including notice of any material change in the Collection, use, or Disclosure practices to which the Parent has previously consented, unless the Children's Online Privacy Protection Rule 16 C.F.R. Part 312 [], provides an exception to providing such notice;

B. Failing to post a prominent and clearly labeled link to an online notice of its information practices with regard to Children on the home or landing page or screen of its website or online service, and at each area of the website or online service where Personal Information is Collected from Children, unless the Children's Online Privacy Protection Rule 16 C.F.R. Part 312, [] provides an exception to providing such notice;

C. Failing to obtain Verifiable Parental Consent before any Collection, use, or Disclosure of Personal Information from Children, including consent to any material change in the Collection, use, or Disclosure practices to which the Parent has previously consented, unless the Children's Online Privacy Protection Rule, 16 C.F.R. Part 312 (attached as Appendix A), provides an exception to Obtaining Verifiable Parental Consent;

D. Retaining Personal Information Collected online from a Child for longer than reasonably necessary to fulfill the purpose for which the information was Collected; and

E. Violating the Children's Online Privacy Protection Rule, 16 C.F.R. Part 312 (attached as Appendix A).

II. Injunction Concerning Children's Personal Information Previously Collected

It is further ordered that Defendants, Defendants' officers, agents, employees, and attorneys, and all other Persons in active concert or participation with any of them, who receive actual notice of this Order, are ordered to:

A. Refrain from Disclosing, using, or benefitting from Personal Information Collected from Children that Defendants Collected through the Kurbo Program prior to entry of this Order unless Verifiable Parental Consent is obtained;
B. Within thirty (30) days of entry of this Order, destroy all Personal Information Collected through the Kurbo Program by Defendants from accounts that have not, by that date, received direct notice and provided Verifiable Parental Consent
C. Within ninety (90) days of entry of this Order, provide a written statement to the Commission, sworn under penalty of perjury, that (1) describes the process through which Defendants provided direct notice and sought Verifiable Parental Consent for the accounts through which Personal Information was Collected through the Kurbo Program; (2) identifies the total number of accounts for which direct notice was provided, as well as the number of accounts: (i) that provided Verifiable Parental Consent; (ii) that affirmatively declined to provide Verifiable Parental Consent; (iii) that did not respond; (iv) that Parents requested be deleted after receiving the direct notice provided for under sub-provision B; (v) where Parents engaged with Defendants by asking additional questions; and (3) confirms all information related to accounts for which Verifiable Parental Consent was not received has been destroyed;
D. Within ninety (90) days of entry of this Order, delete or destroy any Affected Work Product, and provide a written statement to the Commission, sworn under penalty of perjury, confirming such deletion or destruction;
E. Provide additional description and written statements as follows. Any Affected Work Product, or other matter that Defendants are otherwise required to delete or destroy pursuant to this provision may be retained, and may be disclosed, as requested by a government agency or otherwise required by law, regulation, court order, or other legal obligation, including as required by rules applicable to the safeguarding of evidence in pending litigation. In each written statement to the Commission required by this provision, Defendants shall describe in detail any relevant information that Defendants retain on any of these bases and the specific government agency, law, regulation, court order, or other legal obligation that prohibits Defendants from deleting or destroying such information. Within thirty (30) days after the obligation to retain the information has ended, Defendants shall provide an additional written statement to the Commission, sworn under penalty of perjury, confirming that Defendants have deleted or destroyed such information; and
F. Maintain and adhere to a retention schedule for Children's Personal Information Collected through the Kurbo Program, setting

forth the purpose for which the information is Collected, the specific business need for retaining such Personal Information, and a set time frame and set of criteria for deletion of such information which may not exceed one (1) year after the last instance of a user tracking food, weight, or activity intake, and make such information about the retention schedule publicly available on Defendants' website(s) and in the direct notice.

2. *Punitive Damages*

a. Lehrman v. LOVO, Inc. (Complaint)

The following case involves an AI company specializing in voice synthesis, allegedly tricking voice actors to provide voice samples and using them, without permission, to develop a text-to-voice service that uses the voice actor's likeness.

Lehrman v. LOVO, Inc. (Complaint)

United States District Court for the Southern District of New York
Civil Case No. 1:24-cv-03770
May 16, 2024

CLASS ACTION COMPLAINT

Nature of the Action

1. This is a class action brought on behalf of Plaintiffs and similarly situated persons whose voices and/or identities were stolen and used by LOVO—to create millions of voice-over productions—without permission or proper compensation, in violation of numerous state right of privacy laws, and the federal Lanham Act. LOVO is a technology company with proprietary software driven by artificial intelligence (AI) that allows LOVO's clients to create and edit voice-over narrations adapted from real actors. To be clear, the product that customers purchase from LOVO is stolen property. They are voices stolen by LOVO and marketed by LOVO under false pretenses: LOVO represents that it has the legal right to market these voices, but it does not. . . .

Class Action Allegations

. . .

First Cause of Action[:] Violation of New York Civil Rights Law Sections 50 [right of privacy], 51 [action for injunction and damages][;] . . .

Second Cause of Action[:] Deceptive Acts and Practices in Violation of the New York Deceptive Practices Act, N.Y. GBL § 349[;] . . .

Third Cause of Action[:] False advertising in violation of the New York False Advertising Act, N.Y. GBL § 350[;] . . .

Fourth Cause of Action[:] Unfair Competition and False Affiliation in Violation of Section 43 of the Lanham Act, 15 U.S.C. § 1125(a)[;] . . .

Fifth Cause of Action[:] False Advertising in Violation of Section 43 of the Lanham Act, 15 U.S.C. § 1125(a)[;] . . .

Sixth Cause of Action[:] Unjust Enrichment[;] . . .

Seventh Cause of Action[:] Tortious Interference with Advantageous Business Relationship[;] . . .

Eighth Cause of Action[:] Fraud[.] . . .

Request for Relief

Wherefore, Plaintiffs, on behalf of themselves and the proposed Class, request relief and judgment against Defendant as follows:

A. certifying the Class pursuant to Rule 23 of the Federal Rules of Civil Procedure, appointing Plaintiffs as representatives of the Class, and designating Plaintiffs' counsel as Class Counsel;
B. awarding Plaintiffs and the Class compensatory damages and actual damages, trebled, in an amount exceeding $5,000,000, to be determined by proof;
C. awarding Plaintiffs and the Class appropriate relief, including actual and statutory damages;
D. awarding Plaintiffs and the Class punitive damages;
E. awarding Plaintiffs and the Class civil penalties;
F. granting Plaintiffs and the Class declaratory and equitable relief, including restitution and disgorgement;
G. enjoining Defendant from continuing to engage in the wrongful acts and practices alleged herein;
H. awarding Plaintiffs and the Class the costs of prosecuting this action, including expert witness fees;
I. awarding Plaintiffs and the Class reasonable attorneys' fees and costs as allowable by law;
J. awarding pre-judgment and post-judgment interest; and
K. granting any other relief as this Court may deem just and proper. . . .

3. *Injunctive Relief and Temporary Restraining Orders*

a. New York Times v. Microsoft, OpenAI et al. (Complaint)

The *New York Times*'s complaint against Microsoft and OpenAI alleges multiple violations of intellectual property and other violations, including use of the publication's copyrighted articles to develop an LLM (Large Language Model) for the creation of ChatGPT. The complaint of the *New York*

Times proposed several options for relief, including permanently enjoining the defendants from further infringing conduct and ordering the destruction of all GPT and LLM models, and other training models, that they alleged illegally incorporated the protected work of the *Times*.

New York Times v. Microsoft, OpenAI et al. (Complaint)

United States District Court for the Southern District of New York
Civil Case No. 1:23-cv-11195
December 27, 2023

COMPLAINT

Plaintiff The New York Times Company ("The Times"), by its attorneys Susman Godfrey LLP and Rothwell, Figg, Ernst & Manbeck, P.C., for its complaint against Defendants Microsoft Corporation ("Microsoft") and OpenAI, Inc., OpenAI LP, OpenAI GP LLC, OpenAI LLC, OpenAI OpCo LLC, OpenAI Global LLC, OAI Corporation, LLC, OpenAI Holdings, LLC, (collectively "OpenAI" and, with Microsoft, "Defendants"), alleges as follows:

I. Nature of the Action

1. Independent journalism is vital to our democracy. It is also increasingly rare and valuable. For more than 170 years, The Times has given the world deeply reported, expert, independent journalism. Times journalists go where the story is, often at great risk and cost, to inform the public about important and pressing issues. They bear witness to conflict and disasters, provide accountability for the use of power, and illuminate truths that would otherwise go unseen. Their essential work is made possible through the efforts of a large and expensive organization that provides legal, security, and operational support, as well as editors who ensure their journalism meets the highest standards of accuracy and fairness. This work has always been important. But within a damaged information ecosystem that is awash in unreliable content, The Times's journalism provides a service that has grown even more valuable to the public by supplying trustworthy information, news analysis, and commentary.

2. Defendants' unlawful use of The Times's work to create artificial intelligence products that compete with it threatens The Times's ability to provide that service. Defendants' generative artificial intelligence ("GenAI") tools rely on large-language models ("LLMs") that were built by copying and using millions of The Times's copyrighted news articles, in-depth investigations, opinion pieces, reviews, how-to guides, and more. While Defendants engaged in widescale copying from many sources, they gave Times content particular emphasis when building their LLMs—revealing a preference that recognizes the value of those works. Through Microsoft's Bing Chat (recently rebranded as "Copilot") and OpenAI's ChatGPT, Defendants seek to free-ride on The Times's massive investment in its journalism by using it to build substitutive products without permission or payment. . . .

Count I: Copyright Infringement (17 U.S.C. § 501) Against All Defendants[;] . . .

Count II: Vicarious Copyright Infringement Against Microsoft, OpenAI Inc., OpenAI GP, OpenAI LP, OAI Corporation LLC, OpenAI Holdings LLC, and OpenAI Global LL[;] . . .

Count III: Contributory Copyright Infringement Against Microsoft[;] . . .

Count IV: Contributory Copyright Infringement Against All Defendants[;] . . .

Count V: Digital Millennium Copyright Act—Removal of Copyright Management Information (17 U.S.C. § 1202) Against All Defendants[;] . . .

Count VI: Common Law Unfair Competition By Misappropriation Against All Defendants[;] . . .

Count VII: Trademark Dilution (15 U.S.C. § 1125(c)) Against All Defendants[.] . . .

Prayer for Relief

Wherefore, The Times demands judgment against each Defendant as follows:

1. Awarding The Times statutory damages, compensatory damages, restitution, disgorgement, and any other relief that may be permitted by law or equity;
2. Permanently enjoining Defendants from the unlawful, unfair, and infringing conduct alleged herein;
3. Ordering destruction under 17 U.S.C. § 503(b) of all GPT or other LLM models and training sets that incorporate Times Works;
4. An award of costs, expenses, and attorneys' fees as permitted by law; and
5. Such other or further relief as the Court may deem appropriate, just, and equitable. . . .

The evolution of AI law and policy necessitates further development of preventive and remedial tools to preempt and redress AI system harms. The case studies in this chapter are illustrative of ongoing experiments in how best to assess and address AI risks. The categories of preventive and remedial measures set forth above show that several tools are aimed at either ex ante or ex post options. In other words, regulators and legislators often approach this question as either trying to prevent the harm before it occurs or developing remedial options after the harm. In other instances, the regulatory approach is focused on pretesting, impact assessments, and ongoing monitoring. Active litigation also demonstrates that remedies are being fashioned from preexisting laws.

Chapter 11

Humanity and Sustainability

AI has been a disruptive force in all sectors of our economy. AI's capabilities to complete complex tasks have created angst within the labor movement, whose members are worried about companies replacing human workers with automated systems. On the education front, there have been calls in higher education and academic research to focus on AI and AI workforce development. Finally, AI systems require significant computing resources, which demand tremendous energy consumption. The long-term impact of AI on the environment and sustainability is a growing concern. This concern has led to regulatory proposals for increased reporting requirements and assessment tools, and new standardization protocols. This chapter examines efforts to protect societal and environmental interests when harnessing the benefits of AI technologies.

A. *LABOR STRIKES*

1. WGA Labor Strike

Ever since generative AI systems demonstrated capabilities to automate the production of some media and text, unions representing actors and writers have used their negotiating positions to address economic harms arising from studios' use of AI technologies to create media content. In 2023, both the Writers Guild of America (WGA) and the Screen Actors Guild-American Federation of Television and Radio Artists (SAG-AFTRA) announced labor strikes. The twin strikes represented historic labor protests, expressing concerns about AI's impact on both artistic industries. At 148 days, the WGA strike was the second longest in the union's history.[1] The conclusion of the SAG-AFTRA strike after 118 days marked the longest

1. *See, e.g.*, Wendy Lee & Stacy Perman, *WGA Members Easily Ratify New Contract to End 148-Day Strike as Anxieties Loom*, L.A. Times (Oct. 9, 2023).

strike in that organization's history.[2] Both strikes signaled the urgency to resolve critical labor concerns as they related to the protesters' demands for greater protection from AI labor encroachment, artistic and creative infringement, and voice and likeness appropriation.

a. Letter to Senate from WGA, NABET-CWA, and NewsGuild-CWA

In recent years, those in the communications and journalism professions, entertainment industry, and other creative industries have expressed growing concern over the use of AI. In 2023, the Writers Guild of America East and Writers Guild of America West (collectively, the WGA) engaged in a five-month walkout, largely protesting the use of AI in the writers' room. The following primary sources outline the position of various guilds and associations, representing this concern of potential labor and creative displacement by AI and generative AI.

Letter to Senate Majority Leader Chuck Schumer (D-NY)

The NewsGuild-CWA (Communications Workers of America); National Association of Broadcast Employees & Technicians (NABET)-The Broadcasting and Cable Television Workers Section of the Communications Workers of America, AFL-CIO (CWA); Writers Guild of America East and Writers Guild of America West (WGA)
March 27, 2024

March 27, 2024

The Honorable Chuck Schumer
Majority Leader
United States Senate
Washington, D.C. 20510

Dear Majority Leader Schumer,

. . . [W]e write to urge Congress to ensure that journalists and media workers are a core priority in any proposed legislation Congress advances to address Artificial Intelligence.

2. *See, e.g.*, Katie Kilkenny, *STRIKE OVER: Actors Make a Deal with Studios After 118 Days*, Hollywood Rep. (Nov. 8, 2023).

Creative workers who are some of the first to be impacted by this technology must be at the center of the development and implementation of these new tools. AI will never be a total replacement for the work of reporters, investigators, editors, podcasters, on-air anchors or film and television writers.

Congress must recognize the human ingenuity and creativity essential to a free press, the media and entertainment industry, and our members' livelihoods. AI has the potential to greatly undermine the media industry and our democracy if companies refuse to put workers at the forefront of implementation.

So far this year, our members have witnessed the impact of unregulated AI on their jobs. Major news media companies, including Gannett and G/O Media sites, deployed AI articles with fake bylines to replace the work of hard-working local and digital journalists and writers. Film and television writers won critical protections in their collective bargaining agreement, but their work continues to be used by AI developers without their consent.

Congress must take urgent action to ensure any Artificial Intelligence legislation protects creative professionals and journalists by:

- Ensuring AI does not replace journalists and creative professionals or replicate work produced by these professionals without consent or fair compensation, whether or not they own the copyrights to their work;
- Safeguarding against the use of AI to surveil workers and their work product;
- Protecting professional voice, likeness, and performance and written talent; and
- Codifying workers' rights to bargain collectively over AI policy in the workplace.

Our members across the United States are organizing to fight back against attacks by big companies cutting news and creative content at the heart of our communities—from local news journalists to podcasters to film and television writers. We urge you to stand by America's union journalists and creative professionals in any action Congress takes to address artificial intelligence.

b. Comment by WGA on U.S. Copyright Office Notice of Inquiry on Copyright & Artificial Intelligence

Writers Guild of America West and Writers Guild of America East Comment on USCO [U.S. Copyright Office] Notice of Inquiry on Copyright & Artificial Intelligence

October 30, 2023

WRITERS GUILD of AMERICA EAST

WGAW
WRITERS GUILD OF AMERICA WEST

Writers Guild of America West ("WGAW") and Writers Guild of America East ("WGAE") (jointly, "WGA") are pleased to submit the following comments to the U.S. Copyright Office (USCO) in response to the Notice of Inquiry on Copyright and Artificial Intelligence. The WGAW is a labor union representing over 11,000 writers in the television, film, news, and streaming video industries. The WGAE is a labor union representing over 7,000 members in film, television, news, podcasts, and online media. WGA members recently concluded a 148-day strike in which artificial intelligence (AI) was a key bargaining subject. The new WGA agreement is one of the first collective bargaining agreements in the U.S. to restrict the use of AI in a creative industry. WGA has participated in numerous policy discussions around AI, including the USCO's Copyright and Artificial Intelligence Audiovisual Works Listening Session on May 17, 2023.[3] Our comments will focus on the protections necessary to protect human artistry in the evolving AI landscape.

The current and potential implementations of AI technology threaten the craft and livelihood of our members. Film and television writers are still learning the full extent of this technology's impacts, and the technology itself is still rapidly developing. Writers have established new protections related to AI through collective bargaining, but public policy solutions that prioritize human creativity and authorship are needed as well.

. . . WGA believes the use of copyrighted material to train AI models should not be protected by fair use. Under the first fair use factor, it is inadequate to claim that the purpose of AI training with copyrighted material is non-commercial because the training process was initially conducted by a non-commercial entity. The development of AI models is heavily intertwined with commercial use regardless of the entity that initiated the training. Many AI models have been developed by non-profit organizations, but are later easily adapted for commercial use. For example, OpenAI built its ChatGPT technology while operating exclusively as a non-profit, but the company is now licensing that same technology for commercial use under its for-profit arm, OpenAI, L.P.[4] In some cases, AI research and training are conducted by academic institutions but funded by commercial entities that plan to use that research to launch a commercial product. Stability AI, a for-profit company, funded the development of its AI product through a research group at the Ludwig Maximilian University of Munich.[5] Once copyrighted material is ingested by an AI model, it is difficult to remove that material from the model when the use of the AI output becomes clearly commercial. Any potential use of copyrighted material by an AI model must be considered when assessing the first fair use factor, not just the initial use.

---

3. [Fn. 1 in original] U.S. Copyright Office, Copyright and Artificial Intelligence Audiovisual Works Listening Session, (May 17, 2023) [.]

4. [Fn. 2 in original] Devin Coldewey, *OpenAI shifts from nonprofit to 'capped-profit' to attract capital,* TechCrunch (Mar. 11, 2023) [.]

5. [Fn. 3 in original] Andy Baio, *AI Data Laundering: How Academic and Nonprofit Researchers Shield Tech Companies from Accountability,* Waxy (Sep. 30, 2022) [;] Acknowledgement by the Computer Vision & Learning Group on GitHub of donation from Stability AI [.]

In addition, the resulting outputs from AI models are not sufficiently transformative of the original copyrighted work under the first of the four statutory fair use factors.[6] AI models have been fed film and television scripts; some AI-supported products are explicitly intended to generate similar scripts.[7] These AI-generated scripts mimic and regurgitate the work of human writers. Early studies have already found instances of text plagiarism in AI language models.[8] An AI model does not have the capacity to create original work based on human experience—it can only exploit the existing work of human writers.

Furthermore, AI-generated scripts trained on copyrighted work can directly compete with human-authored scripts, affecting the commercial market for writers' work. Film and television writers invest significant time and labor to compete in the market for writing services. Writers often specialize in writing for a specific category of project or genre, and develop reputations for their writing styles. A studio interested in producing a project in a specific writer's style has an incentive to hire that writer. But AI models allow companies to generate work that draws from an individual writer's style when prompted to do so—without the writer's involvement. If fair use is applied to allow unauthorized ingestion of copyrighted works for AI training, writers will be forced to compete with AI-generated scripts trained on their work, without their authorization, and without fair compensation.

Application of the fourth statutory fair use factor must thus consider how the AI-generated outputs compete with the general class of works. Companies buy WGA members' work with the assumption that motion pictures—derivative works based on scripts writers create—are what bring in revenue. Companies may be able to circumvent the need for scripts with generative AI models that produce fully formed films or television series. Writers may be forced to compete with both AI-generated scripts and AI-generated films and television series, both of which used writers' original work without their consent.

. . . Without a fair use defense, developers of AI models will be required to seek a license or other authorization from copyright owners to use copyrighted works to train AI models. Legislators and regulators like USCO should also require AI trainers to seek affirmative consent from the human creators of such works, whether or not those creators are the copyright owners.

---

6. [Fn. 4 in original] *See* 17 U.S.C. § 107.

7. [Fn. 5 in original] For example, NolanAI encourages users on the highest paid tier to "let Nolan generate the initial draft of your scene."[.]

8. [Fn. 6 in original] Jooyoung Lee, Thai Le, Jinghui Chen, and Dongwon Lee. *Do Language Models Plagiarize?*, In Proceedings of the ACM Web Conference 2023 (WWW'23), May 1–5, 2023[.]

The dominant production model in Hollywood is based on structures that have been in place for almost a century. In the 1930s, Hollywood writers organized for collective bargaining purposes as employees under the National Labor Relations Act.[9] The corollary to this development is that most unionized writers, as employees, create works for hire, in which the copyright vests initially in their employer. Through collective bargaining, unionized writers have been able to negotiate important contractual rights in their work—relating, inter alia, to credits and attribution, compensation for reuse, and the right to produce derivative works—that exist alongside the copyright holder's statutory rights. Because of these contractual rights, and of the labor market considerations discussed in the previous section, writers are directly affected by the prospect of their work being fed into an AI model and they should be given a right to consent to such use, whether or not they are copyright holders.

A system of consent that involves creators and copyright owners should be opt-in rather than opt-out. There are numerous companies developing and training AI models; to be forced to continually track all of them down is an enormous administrative burden for individual artists. An opt-in system would allow creators and copyright owners to negotiate for fair-market valuation and licensing of the use of their individual works. WGA also has concerns about whether a framework of collective licensing would adequately compensate creators for the value of their work.

As detailed in the above section on fair use, the development of AI models will often lead to future commercial uses, even if the initial use is non-commercial. It is difficult to remove source material in an AI model once it has been trained on such material, and thus it will be challenging or nearly impossible to integrate consent at later stages of development. An opt-in consent system should be required for all uses.

In sum, affirmative consent for use of copyrighted work in training AI models should:

- Include human creators even if they are not the copyright owners;
- Be an opt-in system rather than opt out; and
- Be required for all uses, not only instances where the initial use is commercial.

. . . A system of affirmative consent will not function as intended unless the developers of AI models are transparent about what materials were used to train the model. Already, many writers have been unable to identify with certainty whether their copyrighted works have been fed into existing AI models. In some cases, it is unclear whether an AI model ingested a writer's work or another source that mentioned the work, or both. Any developer building an AI system should be required to disclose the material used to train the system,

9. [Fn. 7 in original] 29 U.S.C. § 151 *et seq.*

especially if that material is copyrighted. This disclosure should be made in a clear, publicly available, accessible, and searchable format that is legible to a layperson. The disclosure should include data that is obtained from third parties.

In addition, AI systems should preserve and disclose the prompting that leads to a specific output. This disclosure will be necessary to determine whether copyrighted material or a creator's written voice was appropriated to generate a specific output. As discussed above, prompts that include creators' names or their work are especially concerning for film and television writers who make their livelihoods from their skills, reputations, and distinctive style.

Transparency alone is not a sufficient protection for creative workers, but it is a necessary step. Preserving and disclosing AI datasets and prompts will provide the foundation for an affirmative consent model by requiring AI developers accurately to track the inputs to their models and giving creators the ability to understand where their work was used.

In sum, AI models should be required to disclose in a publicly accessible manner:

- Material, including copyrighted material or material sourced from third parties, that was used to train the model; and
- Prompts that led to a specific output, especially if those prompts included copyrighted material or the names of human creators.

. . . Fundamentally, AI models cannot create new works. Such models do not write from lived experience: only humans can experience emotion like joy, embarrassment, pain, and euphoria, and only humans can translate those experiences into human-to-human connection through stories. AI models have been fed human-authored works, including those of our members, and use that work to mimic human storytelling. The protection of human artistry through copyright is so valuable to American society that it is enshrined in the Constitution; granting copyright to AI-generated work is antithetical to the purpose of copyright law. WGA agrees with USCO's view that "copyright can protect only material that is the product of human creativity."[10]

Using technology that exists right now, AI models can be prompted to write a script "in the style of" one of our members or their work. This can be done without the writer's knowledge, consent, or compensation, because these models were trained on writers' work. As discussed above, writers earn their livelihoods from their distinct style and skills developed over time. AI-generated material that appropriates that style and skill can compete with human creators or damage their reputations, or both. Any work that was generated by an AI model using prompts containing artists' names or their work threatens the livelihoods of human creators, even if the AI-generated work is later edited or arranged by a human.

---

10. [Fn. 8 in original] United States Copyright Office, *Copyright Registration Guidance: Works Containing Material Generated by Artificial Intelligence,* (Mar. 16, 2023)[.]

On the issue of copyrightability of AI-generated work, WGA:

- Agrees with the U.S. Copyright Office's interpretation that only human-authored material is eligible for copyright; and
- Has additional, independent objections to USCO granting copyright to material that was created by prompting "in the style of" a particular human creator or their work. . . .

Copyright law exists to "promote the progress of . . . useful arts" by protecting the rights of "authors and inventors." The advent of artificial intelligence presents new challenges to this constitutional mandate, but the guiding principle of protecting human artistry must be preserved. Film and television writers are on the frontline in experiencing the impacts of this new technology. Their experiences can provide insight into the type of regulation that will be required to protect human artists. It is clear to writers that feeding their copyrighted work into AI models without their consent is theft—not fair use—and that any system of affirmative consent needs to include human creators, whether or not they are copyright owners. In keeping with the spirit of copyright law and the values of the Constitution, any policy adopted by USCO or other federal agency should prioritize human authorship and creativity. . . .

2. *SAG-AFTRA Labor Strike*

After 148 days, the WGA was successful in obtaining significant protections against the use of AI. The Minimum Basic Agreement ("MBA"), among other things, provided that generative AI cannot be considered a "writer" and that it may only be used under certain conditions, with many restrictions in place. Moreover, users of generative AI can only provide the AI with writers' material after disclosing this to the writer, and the AI's use of this material to produce its output will not relinquish the writers' rights to the material.[11]

a. 2023 Agreement Between SAG-AFTRA and AMPTP

Like the WGA strike, the SAG-AFTRA strike of 2023 protested Hollywood studios' growing use of generative AI. SAG-AFTRA was particularly concerned with the studios' use of AI to replicate performers' likenesses. After striking for 118 days, the union was able to reach an agreement that

11. *Summary of the 2023 WGA MBA*, WGA Contract 2023 (Sept. 25, 2023).

restricted the creation and use of "Digital Replicas" and "Synthetic Performers."[12] Below are excerpts from that agreement.

2023 Memorandum of Agreement Between SAG-AFTRA and AMPTP

December 6, 2023

29. Artificial Intelligence (Union Proposal No. 3)

a. Digital Replication and Alteration of Performers

Add a new Section [XX] to the General Provisions of the SAG-AFTRA Codified Basic Agreement as follows:

"**[XX]. Digital Replication and Alteration**

"The parties acknowledge that the Producers have historically used digital technologies to replicate or alter a performer's voice or likeness (e.g., CGI, audio/visual effects) during all stages of motion picture production (e.g., pre-visualization, preproduction, production, post-production, distribution, marketing) and may continue to do so, consistent with their historical practices. . . .

"**A. Digital Replicas**

. . .

"**(2) Employment-Based Digital Replica**

"This Section [XX].A.(2) applies when a performer is employed by the Producer under this Agreement under a contract entered into on or after [the first Sunday that is 90 days after the AMPTP's receipt of notice of ratification] to render services as a performer in a motion picture and, in connection with that employment, the Producer (directly or through a third party) requires the performer to provide services for purposes of creating an Employment-Based Digital Replica or uses an Employment-Based Digital Replica as provided herein.

"**(a) Services for Creation of Employment-Based Digital Replicas**

"**(i)** A Producer must notify a performer no less than forty-eight (48) hours in advance of the time the performer's services are required to create an Employment-Based Digital Replica, or at the time of engagement if the performer is engaged less than forty-eight (48) hours in advance of the time the performer's services are required to create an Employment-Based Digital Replica. The Producer must obtain the performer's consent to provide services for purposes of creating an Employment-Based Digital Replica of the performer for use in connection with a motion picture. The consent must be clear and conspicuous and may be obtained through an endorsement or statement in the performer's employment contract that is

12. *SAG-AFTRA Members Approve 2023 TV/Theatrical Contracts Tentative Agreement*, SAG-AFTRA (Dec. 5, 2023) (referencing 2023 Memorandum of Agreement Between the Screen Actors Guild-American Federation of Television and Radio Artists and the Alliance of Motion Picture and Television Producers).

separately signed or initialed by the performer or in a separate writing that is signed by the performer. . . .

"**(b) Use of an Employment-Based Digital Replica**

. . .

"**(i) Use in the Motion Picture for Which the Performer Was Employed**

"**a)** A Producer may use a performer's Employment-Based Digital Replica in connection with a motion picture for which the performer was employed, upon obtaining consent to the extent required herein. The Producer must obtain the performer's consent to use the Employment-Based Digital Replica in new photography or sound track not previously recorded by the performer; provided, however, that no consent is required when the photography or sound track remains substantially as scripted, performed and/or recorded.

"Any consent required must include a reasonably specific description of the intended use of the Employment-Based Digital Replica in that motion picture. Consent must be clear and conspicuous and may be obtained through an endorsement or statement in the performer's employment contract that is separately signed or initialed by the performer or in a separate writing that is signed by the performer.

"Any consent that the performer granted during the performer's lifetime shall continue to be valid after the performer's death unless explicitly limited otherwise. In the event the performer is deceased at the time the Producer seeks any required consent (and the Producer has not already obtained consent during the performer's lifetime or the performer's consent is no longer valid after death), the Producer shall obtain the consent of the authorized representative (or the Union, if the deceased performer's authorized representative cannot be identified or located) who represents the deceased performer's exclusive rights as determined by applicable law.

"**b)** If the Producer uses a performer's Employment-Based Digital Replica in scene(s) that the performer would otherwise have performed in person (*e.g.*, using the Digital Replica of a performer hired for one day for a role that historically would have been performed by a weekly performer in a theatrical motion picture), the performer shall be paid the performer's *pro rata* daily rate or the minimum rate, whichever is higher, for the number of production days that the Producer determines the performer would have been required to work had the performer instead performed those scene(s) in person. The Producer will make a good faith effort to estimate the number of production days (without regard to scheduling considerations, *e.g.*, intervening days under consecutive employment provisions, overtime, meal periods, rest periods, *etc.*) utilizing objective criteria. Such compensation shall be treated as wages for all purposes. . . .

"**c)** In the event the performance of a performer's Employment-Based Digital Replica remains in the motion picture in a manner that would have entitled the performer to residuals had the performer performed those scene(s) in person, the performer shall be entitled to residuals when the motion picture is exhibited in a market for which residuals are due. . . .

"**(ii) Use Other Than in the Motion Picture for Which the Performer Was Employed**

"A Producer may not use a performer's Employment-Based Digital Replica in connection with a motion picture other than one for which the performer was employed or in any other field or medium without obtaining the performer's consent and bargaining separately for the use.

"Consent must be clear and conspicuous and include a reasonably specific description of the intended use. Consent must be obtained prior to use in a writing signed by the performer, but not at the time of employment, except as provided in the next sentence. When a performer is employed on a project specifically identified to be part of a multi-project use (such as a trilogy of motion pictures), consent to use the performer's Employment-Based Digital Replica in another of the identified projects may be obtained at the time the performer is first employed, provided that a reasonably specific description of the intended use is provided for each identified project. Consent for use in other identified project(s) is valid only if the performer is also employed in the other identified project(s) or is deceased at the time the other identified project(s) commences production.

"Any consent that the performer granted during the performer's lifetime shall continue to be valid after the performer's death unless explicitly limited otherwise. In the event the performer is deceased at the time the Producer seeks consent (and the Producer has not already obtained consent during the performer's lifetime or the performer's consent is no longer valid after death), the Producer shall obtain the consent of the authorized representative (or the Union, if the deceased performer's authorized representative cannot be identified or located) who represents the deceased performer's exclusive rights as determined by applicable law. . . .

"**(3) Independently Created Digital Replica**

. . . "A Producer may use an Independently Created Digital Replica in connection with a motion picture for which the natural performer was not employed upon obtaining consent as required herein and bargaining for that use. Consent must be clear and conspicuous and obtained prior to exploitation in a writing signed by the natural performer that includes a reasonably specific description of the intended use. . . .

"B. Digital Alteration

. . . "The Producer must obtain the consent of the performer to digitally alter the performer's performance in photography or sound track previously recorded by the performer; provided, however, that no consent is required when the photography or sound track of the performer remains substantially as scripted, performed and/or recorded. Any consent required must be clear and conspicuous and include a reasonably specific description of the intended alteration(s). Consent may be obtained through an endorsement or statement in the performer's employment contract that is separately signed or initialed by the performer or in a separate writing that is signed by the performer. . . ."

b. Generative Altificial Intelligence

Add a new Section.[XX:]. to the General Provisions of the SAG-AFTRA Codified Basic Agreement as follows:

"[XX.1.] Generative Artificial Intelligence

"The parties acknowledge that definitions of Generative Artificial Intelligence ('GAI') vary, but agree that the term generally refers to a subset of artificial intelligence that learns patterns from data and produces content based on those patterns (e.g., ChatGPT4, MidJourney, Dall-E2). It does not include 'traditional AI' technologies programmed to perform specific functions (e.g., CGI and VFX), such as those already used during all stages of motion picture production (e.g., pre-visualization, preproduction, production, post-production, distribution, marketing). The term GAI is used for convenience and this Section [XX.1] shall also apply to any technology that is consistent with the foregoing definition, regardless of its name.

"A. Use of Synthetic Performers Created Through Generative Artificial Intelligence

. . . "The parties acknowledge the importance of human performance in motion pictures and the potential impact on employment under this Agreement when a Synthetic Performer created through a GAI system is used in a human role that would otherwise be performed by a human. For those reasons, the Producer agrees to give the Union notice and an opportunity to bargain in good faith over appropriate consideration, if any, if a Synthetic Performer is used in place of a performer who would have been engaged under this Agreement in a human role.

"The parties acknowledge that the Producers have customarily used digital technologies to generate non-human characters without the services of a performer covered under this Agreement, and that the foregoing does not apply to such uses.

"If a Producer intends to create, and does create, a Synthetic Performer with a principal facial feature (i.e., eyes, nose, mouth and/or ears) that is recognizable as that of a specific natural performer through the use of such identified natural performer's name and facial feature in the prompt to a GAI system, the Producer shall obtain such identified natural performer's consent and bargain with such natural performer for the use of the Synthetic Performer in connection with a motion picture and no additional discussion with the Union, consideration or remuneration, is required under this Section [XX.1]. For clarity, the foregoing provision shall apply to each such identified natural performer if more than one specific natural performer's recognizable principal facial feature is used in the described manner (e.g., Performer 1's eyes, Performer 2's mouth). No consent is required when the use is of the type protected by the First Amendment to the United States Constitution, including but not limited to instances when the First Amendment would protect a use for purposes of comment, criticism, scholarship, satire or parody, or would protect a use in a docudrama, or historical or biographical work. . . ."

c. Digital Replication and Alteration of Background Actors

"*Add a new Section to Schedule X-1 and Schedule X-11 of the SAG-AFTRA Codified Basic Agreement as follows:*

"**[__]. Digital Replication and Alteration**

"This Section [__] applies when a background actor is employed by the Producer under this Agreement . . . to appear in a motion picture and, in connection with the background actor's employment on the motion picture, the Producer (directly or through a third party):

"**(i)** requires the background actor to provide services for purposes of creating a Background Actor Digital Replica;

"**(ii)** uses a Background Actor Digital Replica as provided herein; or

"**(iii)** digitally alters the background actor's voice or likeness. . . .

"For purposes of this Section, a 'Background Actor Digital Replica' of a background actor is a replica of the voice or likeness of the background actor which is created using digital technology with the background actor's physical participation and is for the purpose of depicting the background actor in a scene in which the background actor did not actually appear. . . ."

B. WORKFORCE TRAINING

1. AI Upskilling and Workforce Training

The U.S. government has continued its efforts to build an "AI-ready" workforce that will be sufficiently equipped to meet the demands of the upcoming AI job market. As the following acts will show, one of the government's primary focuses is workforce development and AI upskilling to maximize the potential benefits and promise of an AI economy.

a. AI in Government Act of 2020

The *AI in Government Act of 2020* was enacted by Congress to modernize AI systems and procedures in the U.S. federal government. It created multiple programs and initiatives to enhance AI utilization, including the formation of the AI Center of Excellence within the General Services Administration, as well as the development of federal agency guidance for AI use and creation of positions that are related to AI, and capitalized on core AI skills and competencies.

AI in Government Act of 2020

P.L. 116-260, Division U—Homeland Security and Governmental Affairs Provisions Title I—AI in Government Act of 2020, Consolidated Appropriations Act, 2021

Sec. 105. Update of Occupational Series for Artificial Intelligence

(a) In General.—Not later than 18 months after the date of enactment of this Act, and in accordance with chapter 51 of title 5, United States Code, the Director of the Office of Personnel Management shall—

(1) identify key skills and competencies needed for positions related to artificial intelligence;

(2) establish an occupational series, or update and improve an existing occupational job series, to include positions the primary duties of which relate to artificial intelligence;

(3) to the extent appropriate, establish an estimate of the number of Federal employees in positions related to artificial intelligence, by each agency; and

(4) using the estimate established in paragraph (3), prepare a 2-year and 5-year forecast of the number of Federal employees in positions related to artificial intelligence that each agency will need to employ. . . .

b. AI Training Act

The *AI Training* Act was signed into law in 2022 to fund and develop AI training programs for AI workforce readiness. The federal law encourages public-private cooperation in the development of training programs that deepen research and knowledge of the technical aspects of AI systems. The overall aim is to further understanding of the risks and benefits of AI.

AI Training Act

P.L. 117-207, Sec. 1 ("This Act may be cited as the 'Artificial Intelligence Training for the Acquisition Workforce Act' or the 'AI Training Act'.")

An Act [t]o require the Director of the Office of Management and Budget to establish or otherwise provide an artificial intelligence training program for the acquisition workforce, and for other purposes. . . .

Sec. 1. Short Title

This Act may be cited as the "Artificial Intelligence Training for the Acquisition Workforce Act" or the "AI Training Act."

Sec. 2. Artificial Intelligence Training Programs

(b) Requirement.—

(1) In General.—Not later than 1 year after the date of enactment of this Act, and not less frequently than annually thereafter, the Director, in coordination with the Administrator of General Services and any other person determined relevant by the Director, shall develop and implement or otherwise provide an AI training program for the covered workforce.

(2) Purpose.—The purpose of the AI training program shall be to ensure that the covered workforce has knowledge of the capabilities and risks associated with AI.

(3) Topics.—The AI training program shall include information relating to—

(A) the science underlying AI, including how AI works;

(B) introductory concepts relating to the technological features of artificial intelligence systems;

(C) the ways in which AI can benefit the Federal Government;

(D) the risks posed by AI, including discrimination and risks to privacy;

(E) ways to mitigate the risks described in subparagraph (D), including efforts to create and identify AI that is reliable, safe, and trustworthy; and

(F) future trends in AI, including trends for homeland and national security and innovation.

(4) Updates.—Not less frequently than once every 2 years, the Director shall update the AI training program to—

(A) incorporate new information relating to AI; and

(B) ensure that the AI training program continues to satisfy the requirements under paragraph (3).

(5) Format.—The Director is encouraged to develop and implement or otherwise include under the AI training program interactive learning with—

(A) technologists;

(B) scholars; and

(C) other experts from the private, public, and nonprofit sectors.

(6) Metrics.—The Director shall ensure the existence of a means by which to—

(A) understand and measure the participation of the covered workforce; and

(B) receive and consider feedback from participants in the AI training program to improve the AI training program. . . .

C. EDUCATION AND RESEARCH

1. AI in Education and Research

a. National Artificial Intelligence Initiative Act of 2020

The *National Artificial Intelligence Initiative Act of 2020* focuses its national education efforts primarily on workforce development. This act also establishes the National Artificial Intelligence Research Institutes, which aims to support AI research through partnerships among public and private organizations.

National Artificial Intelligence Initiative Act of 2020

P.L. 116-283, Division E—National Artificial Intelligence Initiative Act of 2020, William M. (Mac) Thornberry National Defense Authorization Act for Fiscal Year 2021
Title LII—National Artificial Intelligence Research Institutes

Sec. 5201. National Artificial Intelligence Research Institutes

(a) In General.— . . . the Director of the National Science Foundation shall establish a program to award financial assistance for the planning, establishment, and support of Institutes (as described in subsection (b)(2)) in accordance with this section.

(b) Financial Assistance to Establish and Support National Artificial Intelligence Research Institutes.—

(1) In General.— . . . the Secretary of Energy, the Secretary of Commerce, the Director of the National Science Foundation, and every other agency head may award financial assistance to an eligible entity, or consortia thereof, as determined by an agency head, to establish and support an Institute.

(2) Artificial Intelligence Institutes.—An Institute described in this subsection is an artificial intelligence research institute that—

(A) is focused on—

(i) a particular economic or social sector, including health, education, manufacturing, agriculture, security, energy, and environment, and includes a component that addresses the ethical, societal, safety, and security implications relevant to the application of artificial intelligence in that sector; or

(ii) a cross-cutting challenge for artificial intelligence systems, including trustworthiness, or foundational science;

(B) requires partnership among public and private organizations, including, as appropriate, Federal agencies, institutions of higher education, including community colleges, nonprofit research organizations, Federal laboratories, State, local, and Tribal governments, industry, including startup companies, and civil society organizations, including civil rights and disability rights organizations (or consortia thereof);

(C) has the potential to create an innovation ecosystem, or enhance existing ecosystems, to translate Institute research into applications and products, as appropriate to the topic of each Institute;

(D) supports interdisciplinary research and development across multiple institutions of higher education and organizations;

(E) supports interdisciplinary education activities, including curriculum development, research experiences, and faculty professional development across undergraduate, graduate, and professional academic programs; and

(F) supports workforce development in artificial intelligence related disciplines in the United States, including increasing participation of historically underrepresented communities.

(3) Use of Funds.—Financial assistance awarded under paragraph (1) may be used by an Institute for—

(A) managing and making available to researchers accessible, curated, standardized, secure, and privacy protected data sets from the public and private sectors for the purposes of training and testing artificial intelligence systems and for research using artificial intelligence systems pursuant to subsections (c), (e), and (f) of section 22A the National Institute of Standards and Technology Act (as added by section 5301 of this division);

(B) developing and managing testbeds for artificial intelligence systems, including sector-specific test beds, designed to enable users to evaluate artificial intelligence systems prior to deployment;

(C) conducting research and education activities involving artificial intelligence systems to solve challenges with social, economic, health, scientific, and national security implications;

(D) providing or brokering access to computing resources, networking, and data facilities for artificial intelligence research and development relevant to the Institute's research goals;

(E) providing technical assistance to users, including software engineering support, for artificial intelligence research and development relevant to the Institute's research goals;

(F) engaging in outreach and engagement to broaden participation in artificial intelligence research and the artificial intelligence workforce; and

(G) such other activities that an agency head, whose agency's missions contribute to or are affected by artificial intelligence, considers consistent with the purposes described in section 5101(a).

(4) Duration.—

(A) Initial Periods.—An award of financial assistance under paragraph (1) shall be awarded for an initial period of 5 years.

(B) Extension.—An established Institute may apply for, and the agency head may grant, extended funding for periods of 5 years on a merit-reviewed basis using the merit review criteria of the sponsoring agency.

(5) Application for Financial Assistance.—

(A) A person seeking financial assistance under paragraph (1) shall submit to an agency head an application at such time, in such manner, and containing such information as the agency head may require.

(6) Competitive, Merit Review.—In awarding financial assistance under paragraph (1), the agency head shall—

(A) use a competitive, merit review process that includes peer review by a diverse group of individuals with relevant expertise from both the private and public sectors; and

(B) ensure the focus areas of the Institute do not substantially and unnecessarily duplicate the efforts of any other Institute.

(7) Collaboration.—

(A) In General.—In awarding financial assistance under paragraph (1), an agency head may collaborate with Federal departments and agencies whose missions contribute to or are affected by artificial intelligence systems.

(B) Coordinating Network.—The Director of the National Science Foundation shall establish a network of Institutes receiving financial assistance under this subsection, to be known as the "Artificial Intelligence Leadership Network," to coordinate cross-cutting research and other activities carried out by the Institutes.

(8) Limitation.—No funds authorized in this title shall be awarded to Institutes outside of the United States. All awardees and subawardees for such Institute shall be based in the United States, in addition to any other eligibility criteria as established by each agency head.

b. UNESCO Readiness Assessment Methodology

In 2021, the United Nations Educational, Scientific and Cultural Organization (UNESCO) published a *Recommendation on the Ethics of Artificial Intelligence*, adopted by almost 200 member states.[13] UNESCO's *Readiness Assessment Methodology*, published in 2023, proposed a methodology for the implementation of the 2021 UNESCO AI ethical framework.[14] The assessment questions posed in the *Readiness Assessment Methodology* included inquiries intended to help nations gauge AI research readiness. The research assessment particularly focused on quantitative measures to ensure ethical AI research.

The UNESCO *Readiness Assessment Methodology* includes several metrics, such as measuring the level of research and development related to AI within a member state. The assessment tool, in addition to research and development metrics, also proposes assessments of the nation's education infrastructure and the public's access to AI education. It further proposes other relevant assessments to the measurement of AI education and research.

Readiness Assessment Methodology: A Tool of the Recommendation on the Ethics of Artificial Intelligence

United Nations Educational, Scientific and Cultural Organization (UNESCO)
August 28, 2023

4. THE SCIENTIFIC/EDUCATIONAL DIMENSION

4.1 Background

This dimension aims to assess the level of research and development related to AI in a country, including the number of AI-related publications and patents, and the number of AI researchers and engineers involved in R&D. It will also look into AI ethics research, e.g., reflecting

13. *193 Countries Adopt First-Ever Global Agreement on the Ethics of Artificial Intelligence*, UN News (Nov. 25, 2021).

14. UNESCO, Readiness Assessment Methodology: A Tool of the Recommendation on the Ethics of Artificial Intelligence, 6-7, 10, 14, 19 (2023).

the number of publications focusing on the ethics of AI. The educational dimension could include the availability of education opportunities for students such as AI-related degree programmes, life-long education programmes for AI developers and education opportunities for the general public. This aspect will examine, for example, whether there are dedicated programmes that familiarize the general public and provide them with technology-related skills that could be useful for keeping up to date with new job requirements. Apart from the education opportunities the dimension will examine the numbers of students (graduates), professionals and the general public in AI- or ICT-related disciplines. It could also include the number of graduates in STEM, as an important precondition for AI development and deployment. Potentially, the dimension could address the level of AI and e-skills in the population. Finally, the dimension will include the availability of AI ethics education for students of both AI-related and non-AI-related degrees as well as AI ethics courses for professionals including managers, developers or product designers.

2. *AI and GDPR: Data Privacy in Research Rules*

a. GDPR, Articles 5(1)(b) and 21(6) [Research]

Although the EU's *GDPR* provides comprehensive privacy requirements for data processors, the regulation provides certain regulatory carve-outs if data collections are done in the "public interests," which, among other things, include academic research.

GDPR

Article 5(1)(b). Principles Relating to Processing of Personal Data

1. Personal data shall be

(b) collected for specified, explicit and legitimate purposes and not further processed in a manner that is incompatible with those purposes; further processing for archiving purposes in the public interest, scientific or historical research purposes or statistical purposes shall, in accordance with Article 89(1), not be considered to be incompatible with the initial purposes ('purpose limitation');

GDPR

Article 21(6). Right to Object

6. Where personal data are processed for scientific or historical research purposes or statistical purposes pursuant to Article 89(1), the data subject, on grounds relating to his or her particular situation, shall have the right to object to processing of personal data concerning him or her, unless the processing is necessary for the performance of a task carried out for reasons of public interest.

3. *Incentivizing AI Research*

Domestically and globally, governmental entities recognize the need to invest in AI research, often incentivizing collaboration between the public and private sectors. This is seen as critical to advance the aims of safe and trustworthy AI and to promulgate ethical AI research principles.

a. AI in Government Act of 2020

The following legislation established the AI Center of Excellence within the General Services Administration, which aims to ensure excellence in the research and deployment of AI throughout all federal agencies. To ensure that the Center effectively achieves its mission, the legislation specifically calls for the Center to collaborate with the Department of Defense, the Department of Commerce, the Department of Energy, the Department of Homeland Security, the Office of Management and Budget, the Office of the Director of National Intelligence, and the National Science Foundation to use multiagency expertise for developing effective operational strategies for the federal government.

AI in Government Act of 2020

P.L. 116-260, Division U—Homeland Security and Governmental Affairs Provisions Title I—AI in Government Act of 2020, Consolidated Appropriations Act, 2021

An Act to authorize an AI Center of Excellence within the General Services Administration, and for other purposes. . . .

Sec. 103. AI Center of Excellence

(a) In General.—There is created within the General Services Administration a program to be known as the "AI Center of Excellence", which shall—

(1) facilitate the adoption of artificial intelligence technologies in the Federal Government;

(2) improve cohesion and competency in the adoption and use of artificial intelligence within the Federal Government; and

(3) carry out paragraphs (1) and (2) for the purposes of benefitting the public and enhancing the productivity and efficiency of Federal Government operations.

(b) Duties.—The duties of the AI CoE shall include—

(1) regularly convening individuals from agencies, industry, Federal laboratories, nonprofit organizations, institutions of higher education, and other entities to discuss recent developments in artificial intelligence, including the dissemination of information regarding programs, pilots, and other initiatives at agencies, as well as recent trends and relevant information on the understanding, adoption, and use of artificial intelligence;

(2) collecting, aggregating, and publishing on a publicly available website information regarding programs, pilots, and other initiatives led by other agencies and any other information determined appropriate by the Administrator;

(3) advising the Administrator, the Director, and agencies on the acquisition and use of artificial intelligence through technical insight and expertise, as needed;

(4) assist agencies in applying Federal policies regarding the management and use of data in applications of artificial intelligence;

(5) consulting with agencies, including the Department of Defense, the Department of Commerce, the Department of Energy, the Department of Homeland Security, the Office of Management and Budget, the Office of the Director of National Intelligence, and the National Science Foundation, that operate programs, create standards and guidelines, or otherwise fund internal projects or coordinate between the public and private sectors relating to artificial intelligence;

(6) advising the Director on developing policy related to the use of artificial intelligence by agencies; and

(7) advising the Director of the Office of Science and Technology Policy on developing policy related to research and national investment in artificial intelligence. . . .

Sec. 104. Guidance for Agency Use of Artificial Intelligence

(a) Guidance.—Not later than 270 days after the date of enactment of this Act, the Director, in coordination with the Director of the Office of Science and Technology Policy in consultation with the Administrator and any other relevant agencies and key stakeholders as determined by the Director, shall issue a memorandum to the head of each agency that shall—

(1) inform the development of policies regarding Federal acquisition and use by agencies regarding technologies that are empowered or enabled by artificial intelligence, including an identification of the responsibilities of agency officials managing the use of such technology;

(2) recommend approaches to remove barriers for use by agencies of artificial intelligence technologies in order to promote the innovative application of those technologies while protecting civil liberties, civil rights, and economic and national security;

(3) identify best practices for identifying, assessing, and mitigating any discriminatory impact or bias on the basis of any classification protected under Federal nondiscrimination laws, or any unintended consequence of the use of artificial intelligence, including policies to identify data used to train artificial intelligence algorithms as well as the data analyzed by artificial intelligence used by the agencies; and

(4) provide a template of the required contents of the agency plans described in subsection (c). . . .

b. CHIPS and Science Act [CHIPS Act of 2022]

To ensure that the United States remains competitive in manufacturing, research, and development of new technology, the following legislation includes funding for a multitude of federal government research projects in technology and sciences, including AI.

CHIPS (Creating Helpful Incentives to Produce Semiconductors) Act of 2022 [CHIPS and Science Act]

P.L. 117-167, Division B—Research and Innovation
Title II—National Institute of Standards and Technology for the Future, Subtitle B—Measurement Research

Sec. 10232. Artificial Intelligence

(a) In General.—The Director shall continue to support the development of artificial intelligence and data science, and carry out the activities of the National Artificial Intelligence Initiative Act of 2020 authorized in division E of the National Defense Authorization Act for Fiscal Year 2021 (Public Law 116–283), including through—

(1) expanding the Institute's capabilities, including scientific staff and research infrastructure;

(2) supporting measurement research and development for advanced computer chips and hardware designed for artificial intelligence systems;

(3) supporting the development of technical standards and guidelines that promote safe and trustworthy artificial intelligence systems, such as enhancing the accuracy, explainability, privacy, reliability, robustness, safety, security, and mitigation of harmful bias in artificial intelligence systems;

(4) creating a framework for managing risks associated with artificial intelligence systems; and

(5) developing and publishing cybersecurity tools, encryption methods, and best practices for artificial intelligence and data science.

(b) AI Testbeds.—Section 22A of the National Institute of Standards and Technology Act (15 U.S.C. 278h–1) is amended—

(1) by redesignating subsection (g) as subsection (h); and

(2) by inserting after subsection (f) the following:

"(g) Testbeds.—In coordination with other Federal agencies as appropriate, the private sector, and institutions of higher education (as such term is defined in section 101 of the Higher Education Act of 1965 (20 U.S.C. 1001)), the Director may establish testbeds, including in virtual environments, to support the development of robust and trustworthy artificial intelligence and machine learning systems, including testbeds that examine the vulnerabilities and conditions that may lead to failure in, malfunction of, or attacks on such systems."

c. Identifying Outputs of Generative Adversarial Networks Act

The following legislation shows Congress's specific efforts to direct the National Institute of Standards and Technology and other federal entities to evaluate threats posed by generative AI (noted as generative adversarial networks, which are one of the major artificial neural networks capable of synthesizing data).

Identifying Outputs of Generative Adversarial Networks Act

P.L. 116-258

Sec. 2. Findings

Congress finds the following:

(1) Gaps currently exist on the underlying research needed to develop tools that detect videos, audio files, or photos that have manipulated or synthesized content, including those generated by generative adversarial networks. Research on digital forensics is also needed to identify, preserve, recover, and analyze the provenance of digital artifacts.

(2) The National Science Foundation's focus to support research in artificial intelligence through computer and information science and engineering, cognitive science and psychology, economics and game theory, control theory, linguistics, mathematics, and philosophy, is building a better understanding of how new technologies are shaping the society and economy of the United States.

(3) The National Science Foundation has identified the "10 Big Ideas for NSF Future Investment" including "Harnessing the Data Revolution" and the "Future of Work at the Human-Technology Frontier", with artificial intelligence is a critical component.

(4) The outputs generated by generative adversarial networks should be included under the umbrella of research described in paragraph (3) given the grave national security and societal impact potential of such networks.

(5) Generative adversarial networks are not likely to be utilized as the sole technique of artificial intelligence or machine learning capable of creating credible deepfakes. Other techniques may be developed in the future to produce similar outputs.

Sec. 3. NSF Support of Research on Manipulated or Synthesized Content and Information Security

The Director of the National Science Foundation, in consultation with other relevant Federal agencies, shall support merit-reviewed and competitively awarded research on manipulated or synthesized content and information authenticity, which may include—

(1) fundamental research on digital forensic tools or other technologies for verifying the authenticity of information and detection of manipulated or synthesized content, including content generated by generative adversarial networks;

(2) fundamental research on technical tools for identifying manipulated or synthesized content, such as watermarking systems for generated media;

(3) social and behavioral research related to manipulated or synthesized content, including human engagement with the content;

(4) research on public understanding and awareness of manipulated and synthesized content, including research on best practices for educating the public to discern authenticity of digital content; and

(5) research awards coordinated with other federal agencies and programs, including the Defense Advanced Research Projects Agency and the Intelligence Advanced Research Projects [Activity], with coordination enabled by the Networking and Information Technology Research and Development Program.

Sec. 4. NIST Support for Research and Standards on Generative Adversarial Networks

(a) In General.—

The Director of the National Institute of Standards and Technology shall support research for the development of measurements and standards necessary to accelerate the development of the technological tools to examine the function and outputs of generative adversarial networks or other technologies that synthesize or manipulate content.

(b) Outreach.—

The Director of the National Institute of Standards and Technology shall conduct outreach—

(1) to receive input from private, public, and academic stakeholders on fundamental measurements and standards research necessary to examine the function and outputs of generative adversarial networks; and

(2) to consider the feasibility of an ongoing public and private sector engagement to develop voluntary standards for the function and outputs of generative adversarial networks or other technologies that synthesize or manipulate content. . . .

Sec. 6. Generative Adversarial Network Defined

In this Act, the term "generative adversarial network" means, with respect to artificial intelligence, the machine learning process of attempting to cause a generator artificial neural network (referred to in this section as the "generator"[)] and a discriminator artificial neural network (referred to in this section as a "discriminator") to compete against each other to become more accurate in their function and outputs, through which the generator and discriminator create a feedback loop, causing the generator to produce increasingly higher-quality artificial outputs and the discriminator to increasingly improve in detecting such artificial outputs.

D. SUSTAINABILITY AND THE ENVIRONMENT

1. Sustainable Development Goals

a. Corporate Sustainability Reporting Directive of the EU (CSRD)

The EU's *Corporate Sustainability Reporting Directive* (*CSRD*) requires corporate reporting to facilitate transparency and accountability. The *CSRD* extends to non–EU companies that have been identified as maintaining significant economic activities in the EU market. Sustainability reports cover a wide range of disclosures, including environmental and social impact, and governance protocols. AI has and will continue to impact *CSRD* reporting and the future of environmental, social, and governance (ESG) frameworks, and vice versa. The excerpts below from the Recitals and Directive are not legally binding but serve as important interpretive tools.

Corporate Sustainability Reporting Directive

EU Directive 2022/2464
December 14, 2022

. . .

(2) In its Communication of 8 March 2018 entitled 'Action Plan: Financing Sustainable Growth' (the 'Action Plan on Financing Sustainable Growth'), the Commission set out measures to achieve the following objectives: reorient capital flows towards sustainable investment in order to achieve sustainable and inclusive growth, manage financial risks stemming from climate change, resource depletion, environmental degradation and social issues, and foster transparency and long-termism in financial and economic activity. The disclosure by certain categories of undertakings of relevant, comparable and reliable sustainability information is a prerequisite for meeting those objectives. The European Parliament and the Council have adopted a number of legislative acts as part of the implementation of the Action Plan on Financing Sustainable Growth. Regulation (EU) 2019/2088 of the European Parliament and of the Council[15] governs how financial market participants and financial advisers are to disclose sustainability information to end investors and asset owners.

Regulation (EU) 2020/852 of the European Parliament and of the Council[16] creates a classification system of environmentally sustainable economic activities with the aim of scaling up sustainable investments and combatting greenwashing of financial products that unduly claim to be sustainable. Regulation (EU) 2019/2089 of the European Parliament and of the Council,[17] complemented by Commission Delegated Regulations (EU) 2020/1816,[18] (EU) 2020/1817[19] and (EU) 2020/1818,[20] introduces environmental, social

---

15. [Fn. 5 in original] Regulation (EU) 2019/2088 of the European Parliament and of the Council of 27 November 2019 on sustainability-related disclosures in the financial services sector (OJ L 317, 9.12.2019, p. 1).

16. [Fn. 6 in original] Regulation (EU) 2020/852 of the European Parliament and of the Council of 18 June 2020 on the establishment of a framework to facilitate sustainable investment, and amending Regulation (EU) 2019/2088 (OJ L 198, 22.6.2020, p. 13).

17. [Fn. 7 in original] Regulation (EU) 2019/2089 of the European Parliament and of the Council of 27 November 2019 amending Regulation (EU) 2016/1011 as regards EU Climate Transition Benchmarks, EU Paris-aligned Benchmarks and sustainability-related disclosures for benchmarks (OJ L 317, 9.12.2019, p. 17).

18. [Fn. 8 in original] Commission Delegated Regulation (EU) 2020/1816 of 17 July 2020 supplementing Regulation (EU) 2016/1011 of the European Parliament and of the Council as regards the explanation in the benchmark statement of how environmental, social and governance factors are reflected in each benchmark provided and published (OJ L 406, 3.12.2020, p. 1).

19. [Fn. 9 in original] Commission Delegated Regulation (EU) 2020/1817 of 17 July 2020 supplementing Regulation (EU) 2016/1011 of the European Parliament and of the Council as regards the minimum content of the explanation on how environmental, social and governance factors are reflected in the benchmark methodology (OJ L 406, 3.12.2020, p. 12).

20. [Fn. 10 in original] Commission Delegated Regulation (EU) 2020/1818 of 17 July 2020 supplementing Regulation (EU) 2016/1011 of the European Parliament and of the Council as regards minimum standards for EU Climate Transition Benchmarks and EU Paris-aligned Benchmarks (OJ L 406, 3.12.2020, p. 17).

and governance ('ESG') disclosure requirements for benchmark administrators and minimum standards for the construction of EU Climate Transition Benchmarks and EU Paris-aligned Benchmarks.

Regulation (EU) No 575/2013 of the European Parliament and of the Council[21] requires large institutions which have issued securities that are admitted to trading on a regulated market to disclose information on ESG risks from 28 June 2022. The prudential framework for investment firms established by Regulation (EU) 2019/2033 of the European Parliament and of the Council[22] and Directive (EU) 2019/2034 of the European Parliament and of the Council[23] contains provisions concerning the introduction of an ESG risk dimension in the Supervisory Review and Evaluation Process ('SREP') by competent authorities, and contains ESG risk disclosure requirements for investment firms, applicable from 26 December 2022. On 6 July 2021, the Commission also adopted a proposal for a Regulation of the European Parliament and of the Council on European green bonds, following up on the Action Plan on Financing Sustainable Growth. . . .

(6) In its resolution of 25 September 2015 entitled 'Transforming our world: the 2030 Agenda for Sustainable Development' (the '2030 Agenda') the United Nations (UN) General Assembly adopted a new global sustainable development framework. The 2030 Agenda has at its core the UN Sustainable Development Goals ('SDGs') and covers the three dimensions of sustainability: economic, social and environmental. The Commission Communication of 22 November 2016 entitled 'Next steps for a sustainable European future: European action for sustainability' linked the SDGs to the Union policy framework to ensure that all Union actions and policy initiatives, both within and outside the Union, take those goals on board at the outset. In its conclusions of 20 June 2017 on 'A sustainable European future: The EU response to the 2030 Agenda for Sustainable Development', the Council confirmed the commitment of the Union and its Member States to the implementation of the 2030 Agenda in a full, coherent, comprehensive, integrated and effective manner, in close cooperation with partners and other stakeholders.

(7) Directive 2014/95/EU of the European Parliament and of the Council[24] amended Directive 2013/34/EU as regards disclosure of non-financial information by certain large undertakings and groups. Directive 2014/95/EU introduced a requirement on undertakings to report information on, as

---

21. [Fn. 11 in original] Regulation (EU) No 575/2013 of the European Parliament and of the Council of 26 June 2013 on prudential requirements for credit institutions and amending Regulation (EU) No 648/2012 (OJ L 176, 27.6.2013, p. 1).

22. [Fn. 12 in original] Regulation (EU) 2019/2033 of the European Parliament and of the Council of 27 November 2019 on the prudential requirements of investment firms and amending Regulations (EU) No 1093/2010, (EU) No 575/2013, (EU) No 600/2014 and (EU) No 806/2014 (OJ L 314, 5.12.2019, p. 1).

23. [Fn. 13 in original] Directive (EU) 2019/2034 of the European Parliament and of the Council of 27 November 2019 on the prudential supervision of investment firms and amending Directives 2002/87/EC, 2009/65/EC, 2011/61/EU, 2013/36/EU, 2014/59/EU and 2014/65/EU (OJ L 314, 5.12.2019, p. 64).

24. [Fn. 16 in original] Directive 2014/95/EU of the European Parliament and of the Council of 22 October 2014 amending Directive 2013/34/EU as regards disclosure of non-financial and diversity information by certain large undertakings and groups (OJ L 330, 15.11.2014, p. 1).

a minimum, environmental, social and employee matters, respect for human rights, anti-corruption and bribery matters. With regard to those topics, Directive 2014/95/EU required undertakings to disclose information under the following reporting areas: business model; policies, including due diligence processes; the outcome of those policies; risks and risk management; and key performance indicators relevant to the business. . . .

(9) If undertakings carried out better sustainability reporting, the ultimate beneficiaries would be individual citizens and savers, including trade unions and workers' representatives who would be adequately informed and therefore able to better engage in social dialogue. Savers who want to invest sustainably will have the opportunity to do so, while all citizens would benefit from a stable, sustainable and inclusive economic system. To realise such benefits, the sustainability information disclosed in the annual reports of undertakings first has to reach two primary groups of users. The first group of users consists of investors, including asset managers, who want to better understand the risks and opportunities that sustainability issues pose for their investments and the impacts of those investments on people and the environment. The second group of users consists of civil society actors, including non-governmental organisations and social partners, which wish to better hold undertakings to account for their impacts on people and the environment. Other stakeholders might also make use of sustainability information disclosed in annual reports, in particular to foster comparability across and within market sectors.

The business partners of undertakings, including customers, might rely on sustainability information to understand and, where necessary, report on their sustainability risks and impacts throughout their own value chains. Policy makers and environmental agencies can use such information, in particular on an aggregate basis, to monitor environmental and social trends, to contribute to environmental accounts, and to inform public policy. Few individual citizens and consumers directly consult undertakings' annual reports, but they might use sustainability information indirectly, for example, when considering the advice or opinions of financial advisers or non-governmental organisations. Many investors and asset managers purchase sustainability information from third-party data providers, who collect information from various sources, including public corporate reports.

(10) The market for sustainability information is rapidly growing, and the role of third-party data providers is gaining in importance given the new obligations that investors and asset managers need to fulfil. With the increased availability of disaggregated data, sustainability information should come at a more reasonable cost. The amendments to Directive 2013/34/EU provided for in this amending Directive are expected to increase the comparability of data and harmonise standards. It is expected that the practices of third-party data providers will improve and that expertise will grow in this area, with a potential for job creation.

(11) There has been a very significant increase in demand for corporate sustainability information in recent years, especially on the part of the investment community. That increase in demand is driven by the changing nature of risks to undertakings and growing investor awareness of the financial implications of those risks. That is especially the case for climate-related financial risks. There is also growing awareness of the risks and opportunities for undertakings and for investments resulting from other environmental issues, such as biodiversity loss, and from health and social issues, including child labour and forced labour. The increase in demand for sustainability information is also driven by the growth in investment products that explicitly seek to meet certain sustainability standards or achieve certain sustainability objectives and to ensure coherence with the ambition of the Paris Agreement under the United Nations Framework Convention on Climate Change adopted on 12 December 2015 (the 'Paris Agreement'), the UN Convention on Biological Diversity and Union policies. Part of that increase is the logical consequence of previously adopted Union legislation, notably Regulations (EU) 2019/2088 and (EU) 2020/852. Some of that increase would have happened in any case, due to fast-changing citizen awareness, consumer preferences and market practices. The COVID-19 pandemic has further accelerated the increase in users' information needs, in particular as it has exposed the vulnerabilities of workers and undertakings' value chains. Information on environmental impacts is also relevant in the context of mitigating future pandemics, with human disturbance of ecosystems being increasingly linked to the occurrence and spread of diseases.

(12) Undertakings themselves stand to benefit from carrying out high-quality reporting on sustainability matters. The growth in the number of investment products that aim to pursue sustainability objectives means that good sustainability reporting can enhance an undertaking's access to financial capital. Sustainability reporting can help undertakings to identify and manage their own risks and opportunities related to sustainability matters. It can provide a basis for better dialogue and communication between undertakings and their stakeholders, and can help undertakings to improve their reputation. Moreover, a consistent basis for sustainability reporting in the form of sustainability reporting standards would lead to relevant and sufficient information being provided and thus significantly decrease ad hoc requests for information. . . .

b. UN Resolution—Enhancing International Cooperation on Capacity-Building of Artificial Intelligence

The following UN General Assembly Resolution outlines recommendations for cooperation among member states to bridge technical divides between developed and developing nations through AI capacity-building efforts.

UN Resolution 78/311—Enhancing International Cooperation on Capacity-Building of Artificial Intelligence

UN General Assembly Resolution
July 2024

The General Assembly

. . . *Recognizing* that rapid technological change, including the rapid advancement of artificial intelligence has the potential to bring new opportunities for socioeconomic development and accelerate the progress and achievement of the Sustainable Development Goals and sustainable development in its three dimensions—economic, social and environmental—in a balanced and integrated manner, while recognizing also that the improper or malicious design, development, deployment and use of artificial intelligence systems, such as without adequate safeguards or in a manner inconsistent with international law, could pose potential risks and challenges,

Recognizing that eradicating poverty in all its forms and dimensions, including extreme poverty, is the greatest global challenge for sustainable development and an indispensable requirement for sustainable development,

Stressing that that artificial intelligence systems should be safe, secure and trustworthy—whose life cycle includes the stages: pre-design, design, development, evaluation, testing, deployment, use, sale, procurement, operation and decommissioning, are such that they are human-centric, reliable, explainable, ethical, inclusive, in full respect, promotion and protection of human rights and international law—in line with the principle of artificial intelligence for good for all, with the vision of a people-centred, inclusive and development-oriented information society, bearing in mind that this resolution focuses on international cooperation on artificial intelligence capacity-building in the non-military domain and does not touch the development or use of artificial intelligence for military purposes,

Emphasizing that Member States should enjoy equal opportunities in the design, development, deployment, decommissioning and use of artificial intelligence, while respecting intellectual property rights and promoting innovation,

Noting with concern that that artificial intelligence and other digital divides between and within countries continue to widen, and developing countries face unique challenges in keeping pace with the rapid acceleration of artificial intelligence development, in particular in terms of the design, development, deployment and use of artificial intelligence, thus stressing the need and urgency to narrow the disparities and assist developing countries in artificial intelligence capacity-building so that they will not be further left behind,

Noting also with concern that actions inconsistent with international law and the Charter of the United Nations could hinder the development and innovation of artificial intelligence and global cooperation,

Noting both the positive benefits of open-source software, open models and open data, among other methods and business models, in spreading the benefits of artificial intelligence, as well as the potential risks, and recognizing the importance of the participation of developing countries in relevant global cooperation,

Recognizing that the lack of digital infrastructure connectivity and skills, including education, expertise and human capacity, remains a fundamental challenge in many developing countries, in particular the least developed countries, which can contribute to artificial intelligence and other digital divides, including different levels of readiness to make use of and benefit from artificial intelligence,

Stressing the need and urgency to bridge artificial intelligence and other digital divides between and within countries, and emphasizing the quality of access to the benefits of artificial intelligence, therefore stressing the importance of providing adequate public and private financing, mobilizing action-oriented means of implementation, such as knowledge sharing activities and the transfer of technology on mutually agreed terms, and capacity-building assistance for developing countries in line with their national needs, policies and priorities,

Noting the important role that international, regional and subregional organizations and international financial institutions, the private sector, companies, civil society, the media, academia and research institutions and technical communities and individuals, and other relevant stakeholders could play in enhancing artificial intelligence capacity-building and promoting safe, secure and trustworthy artificial intelligence systems for sustainable development,

Stressing the importance of enhancing coordination and cooperation among and within countries and increasing investment in artificial intelligence capacity-building, with specific consideration of the needs, priorities and conditions of developing countries, and encouraging developed countries and developing countries in a position to do so, as well as international organizations and all relevant stakeholders, to take active measures,

Recognizing that the United Nations system has an important role to play in artificial intelligence capacity-building, and emphasizing that it is important to enhance international cooperation and multi-stakeholder collaboration on capacity-building and support developing countries' effective, equitable and meaningful participation and representation in international processes and forums on the governance of artificial intelligence systems,

1. *Resolves* to bridge the artificial intelligence and other digital divides between and within countries, and to enhance international cooperation on capacity-building in developing countries, including through North-South, South-South and triangular cooperation, with full consideration of the needs, policies and priorities of developing countries, with the aim of harnessing the benefits of artificial intelligence, minimizing its risks, and accelerating innovation and progress toward the achievement of all 17 Sustainable Development Goals;

2. *Encourages* Member States, where appropriate and in line with their national circumstances and priorities, to incorporate capacity-building and the design, development, deployment and use of artificial intelligence into their national development plans and strategies, in full respect, promotion and protection of human rights and international law, and make necessary investments in this regard, and also encourages the international community, as well as relevant stakeholders, to increase financing and technical assistance to developing countries in the field of capacity-building, including by drawing on voluntary cooperative initiatives;

3. *Calls upon* the international community to foster an enabling environment for international cooperation on artificial intelligence capacity-building, and emphasizes that international law, in particular the Charter of the United Nations, as well as human rights and fundamental freedoms, must be respected;

4. *Calls upon* Member States to strengthen cooperation and partnerships that bring benefits for all to address major structural impediments and lift obstacles, including through expansion of access to infrastructure, knowledge and skills, with a view to promoting universal and meaningful digital connectivity, which can help lay the foundation for digital transformation and equitable and inclusive access to the benefits of digital and artificial intelligence development and innovations;

5. *Encourages* Member States, in particular developed countries and those developing countries in a position to do so, to increase capacity-building cooperation, including policy exchanges, knowledge sharing activities and the transfer of technology on mutually agreed terms, technical assistance,

lifelong learning, personnel training, skilling of workforce, international research cooperation, voluntary joint international research laboratories and artificial intelligence capacity-building centres, with full consideration of developing countries' national needs, policies and priorities, and to hold training courses, seminars and workshops, among others for sharing experiences and best practices;

6. *Calls upon* the international community to provide and promote a fair, open, inclusive and non-discriminatory business environment across the life cycle of safe, secure and trustworthy artificial intelligence systems;

7. *Encourages* Member States to consider the benefits and risks when scaling up the responsible use of digital solutions, such as open-source artificial intelligence and digital public infrastructure, among other methods and business models; to promote, protect and preserve linguistic and cultural diversity, taking into account multilingualism in their training data, particularly for the large language models; to adopt proactive measures to counteract racism, discrimination and other forms of algorithmic bias; and to enable fair competition in the artificial intelligence market place, promote an innovation environment and the use of digital public goods to harness the potential of safe, secure and trustworthy artificial intelligence systems;

8. *Encourages* Governments, the private sector, international, regional and subregional organizations, civil society, the media, academia and research institutions and technical communities and individuals, to strengthen international cooperation on artificial intelligence capacity-building and take necessary and positive steps, as appropriate, to eliminate barriers faced by all people, women and girls, persons with disabilities, Indigenous Peoples, local communities, children and youth, those living in poverty and in rural and remote areas, and those in vulnerable situations, and to ensure the full enjoyment of artificial intelligence benefits for all, improve digital inclusion and realize gender equality and the empowerment of women and girls, through investment, education, training, technological innovation, use and application;

9. *Calls upon* specialized agencies, funds, programmes, other entities, bodies and offices, and related organizations of the United Nations system, within their respective mandates and resources, to leverage the opportunities and address the challenges in enhancing international cooperation on artificial intelligence capacity-building, including through using appropriate interagency mechanisms, conducting research, mapping and analysis, reporting on progress and challenges in this field, and leveraging their resources and expertise to provide tailored assistance;

10. *Calls upon* other international, regional and subregional organizations and international financial institutions and all relevant stakeholders, within their respective mandates and resources, to strengthen artificial intelligence capacity-building in developing countries, and to carry out relevant cooperation and coordination, fully utilizing the existing international and regional mechanisms and platforms;

11. *Encourages* Member States, in particular developing countries, to make use of capacity-building resources relating to artificial intelligence in the United Nations system and other international, regional and subregional organizations, to enhance capacity-building, including support for the preparation of national digital and artificial intelligence strategies in line with their national needs, policies and priorities, ensuring that those investments lead to long-term and sustainable results;

12. *Supports* the United Nations in playing a central and coordinating role in international development cooperation;

13. *Calls upon* the United Nations system to enhance action-oriented international cooperation on artificial intelligence capacity-building, including through voluntary and transparent cooperation frameworks or initiatives, which also promotes the meaningful participation of developing countries in artificial intelligence processes;

14. *Looks forward* to the final report of the High-level Advisory Body on Artificial Intelligence, and the discussions on capacity-building related to artificial intelligence in the context of the Global Digital Compact, the Pact for the Future, and relevant follow-up processes in the United Nations as appropriate;

15. *Requests* the Secretary-General to report to the General Assembly at its eightieth session, within existing resources, processes and documents, on unique challenges faced by developing countries in artificial intelligence capacity-building, with recommendations that address those challenges. . . .

2. *AI and the Environment*

The most powerful computing systems are often referred to as high-performance computing (HPC) systems or supercomputing. HPC systems often use several supercomputers for the real-time processing of enormous amounts of data and engage in multiple complex calculations and statistical processes. Advanced computing and AI, including generative AI, require enormous energy expenditure. The operation of AI systems, cloud computing and data centers, and other network systems consumes a significant amount of energy resources produced in the United States and globally. This issue is often discussed within broader conversations on sustainability policy.

a. EU AI Act, Article 40 [Harmonised Standards and Standardisation Deliverables]

A significant aspect of AI governance involves the creation and harmonization of technical standards and the development of AI standardization. The excerpt of the *EU AI Act* below includes the development of reporting requirements and standards that are aimed at reducing energy consumption and improving energy efficiency.

EU AI Act

Article 40. Harmonised Standards and Standardisation Deliverables

2. In accordance with Article 10 of Regulation (EU) (No) 1025/2012, the Commission shall issue, without undue delay, standardisation requests covering all requirements set out in Section 2 of this Chapter and, as applicable, standardisation requests covering obligations set out in Chapter V, Sections 2 and 3, of this

Regulation. The standardisation request shall also ask for deliverables on reporting and documentation processes to improve AI systems' resource performance, such as reducing the high-risk AI system's consumption of energy and of other resources during its lifecycle, and on the energy-efficient development of general-purpose AI models. When preparing a standardisation request, the Commission shall consult the Board and relevant stakeholders, including the advisory forum.

When issuing a standardisation request to European standardisation organisations, the Commission shall specify that standards have to be clear, consistent, including with the standards developed in the various sectors for products covered by the existing Union harmonisation legislation listed in Annex I, and aiming to ensure that high-risk AI systems or general-purpose AI models placed on the market or put into service in the Union meet the relevant requirements or obligations laid down in this Regulation.

The Commission shall request the European standardisation organisations to provide evidence of their best efforts to fulfil the objectives referred to in the first and the second subparagraph of this paragraph in accordance with Article 24 of Regulation (EU) No 1025/2012. . . .

b. White House Executive Order on the Safe, Secure, and Trustworthy Development and Use of Artificial Intelligence (Rescinded)

The 2023 White House *Executive Order on the Safe, Secure, and Trustworthy Development and Use of Artificial Intelligence* calls for the U.S. Department of Energy to lead an effort on investigating the uses of AI to mitigate the risks of climate change. Although the incoming White House rescinded[25] the 2023 executive order, the excerpt below is included for historical reference.

White House Executive Order 14110 (Rescinded): Safe, Secure, and Trustworthy Development and Use of Artificial Intelligence

October 30, 2023

5.2 Promoting Innovation

(g) Within 180 days of the date of this order, to support the goal of strengthening our Nation's resilience against climate change impacts and building an equitable clean energy economy for the future, the Secretary of Energy, in consultation with the Chair of the Federal Energy Regulatory Commission, the Director of OSTP, the Chair of the Council on Environmental Quality, the Assistant to the President and National Climate Advisor, and the heads of other relevant agencies as the Secretary of Energy may deem appropriate, shall:

(i) issue a public report describing the potential for AI to improve planning, permitting, investment, and operations for electric grid infrastructure and to enable the provision of clean, affordable, reliable, resilient, and secure electric power to all Americans;

---

25. Exec. Order No. 14148, 90 Fed. Reg. 8237, *Initial Rescissions of Harmful Executive Orders and Actions* (Jan. 20, 2025) (rescinding E.O. 14110).

(ii) develop tools that facilitate building foundation models useful for basic and applied science, including models that streamline permitting and environmental reviews while improving environmental and social outcomes;

(iii) collaborate, as appropriate, with private sector organizations and members of academia to support development of AI tools to mitigate climate change risks;

(iv) take steps to expand partnerships with industry, academia, other agencies, and international allies and partners to utilize the Department of Energy's computing capabilities and AI testbeds to build foundation models that support new applications in science and energy, and for national security, including partnerships that increase community preparedness for climate-related risks, enable clean-energy deployment (including addressing delays in permitting reviews), and enhance grid reliability and resilience; and

(v) establish an office to coordinate development of AI and other critical and emerging technologies across Department of Energy programs and the 17 National Laboratories.

(h) Within 180 days of the date of this order, to understand AI's implications for scientific research, the President's Council of Advisors on Science and Technology shall submit to the President and make publicly available a report on the potential role of AI, especially given recent developments in AI, in research aimed at tackling major societal and global challenges. The report shall include a discussion of issues that may hinder the effective use of AI in research and practices needed to ensure that AI is used responsibly for research. . . .

c. Artificial Intelligence Environmental Impacts Act (Proposed)

The following proposed Senate bill seeks to direct the U.S. Environmental Protection Agency to conduct a study on the environmental impact of AI and publish a publicly available report.

Artificial Intelligence Environmental Impacts Act of 2024 (Proposed)

S. 3732
118th Congress (2023-2024)
Introduced to the U.S. Senate February 1, 2024

A Bill [t]o require the Administrator of the Environmental Protection Agency to carry out a study on the environmental impacts of artificial intelligence, to require the Director of the National Institute of Standards and Technology to convene a consortium on such environmental impacts, and to require the Director to develop a voluntary reporting system for the reporting of the environmental impacts of artificial intelligence, and for other purposes. . . .

Sec. 2. Findings.

Congress finds the following:

(1) Multiple estimates indicate that the amount of computational power being used for artificial intelligence applications has increased rapidly over the last decade. A 2022 estimate suggested that the number of computational operations being used to create each of the largest artificial intelligence models is currently doubling every 10 months.

(2) Accelerating use of artificial intelligence has the potential to greatly increase energy consumption due to the power utilization of computer hardware required for training and operating artificial intelligence models, despite ongoing efficiency gains in both artificial intelligence models and hardware.

(3) Rapid growth in data center infrastructure, including cooling systems and backup power equipment, supporting artificial intelligence and other computing-intensive technologies contributes to pollution, water consumption, and land-use changes.

(4) Resource and energy-intensive manufacturing processes are required for the hardware that runs artificial intelligence and other computing-intensive technologies, leading to significant environmental impacts.

(5) Yearly increases in electronic waste (known as "e-waste") pose increasing environmental and health risks, and will likely be exacerbated by outdated and discarded hardware used for artificial intelligence and other computing-intensive technologies.

(6) Many applications of artificial intelligence can have direct and indirect positive environmental impacts. Positive environmental impacts may include optimizing systems for energy efficiency, developing renewable energy, advancing planetary systems research, enabling discovery of new materials, and automatically monitoring environmental changes. However, artificial intelligence applications may also have direct and indirect negative environmental impacts, including rebound effects, behavioral impacts, and accelerating high-pollution activities.

(7) Estimates of the current and future environmental impacts of artificial intelligence are currently uncertain.

(8) Negative environmental effects may have a disparate impact across different regions and communities.

(9) Various options exist to reduce the negative environmental impacts of artificial intelligence, including using more efficient models, hardware, and data centers, using renewable energy, and examining the impacts of artificial intelligence applications.

(10) Promoting transparency and environmental protection measures may help mitigate negative environmental impacts of the rapid growth in artificial intelligence use, while promoting artificial intelligence uses with net positive environmental impacts.

Sec. 3. Definitions.

In this Act:

(1) Artificial Intelligence.—The term "artificial intelligence" has the meaning given such term in section 5002 of the National Artificial Intelligence Initiative Act of 2020 (15 U.S.C. 9401).

(2) Artificial Intelligence Model.—The term "artificial intelligence model" means a component of an information system that implements artificial intelligence technology and uses computational, statistical, or machine-learning techniques to produce outputs from a given set of inputs.

(3) Artificial Intelligence System.—The term "artificial intelligence system" means any data system, software, hardware, application, tool, or utility that operates in whole or in part using artificial intelligence.

(4) Voluntary Reporting Entity.—The term "voluntary reporting entity" means any company, organization, or other entity that—

(A) develops or operates an artificial intelligence system; and

(B) chooses to participate in the reporting system developed under section 6.

Sec. 4. Study of Environmental Impacts of Artificial Intelligence.

(a) In General.—Not later than 2 years after the date of enactment of this Act, the Administrator of the Environmental Protection Agency, in collaboration with the Secretary of Energy, the Director of the National Institute of Standards and Technology, and the Director of the Office of Science and Technology Policy, shall carry out, and submit to Congress and make publicly available a report describing the results of, a comprehensive study on the environmental impacts of artificial intelligence.

(b) Requirements.—The study required under subsection (a) shall include an examination of—

(1) the energy consumption and pollution associated with the full lifecycle of artificial intelligence models, including the design, development, deployment, and use of those artificial intelligence models;

(2) the energy consumption and pollution associated with the full lifecycle of artificial intelligence hardware, including the extraction of raw materials, manufacturing, and electronic waste associated with that hardware;

(3) the energy and water consumption for the cooling of the data centers used in the design, development, deployment, and use of artificial intelligence models;

(4) how choices made during the design, development, deployment, and use of artificial intelligence models, including the efficiency of the artificial intelligence models used, the location, power source, and design of data centers used, and the type of hardware used, impact the resulting environmental impacts;

(5) potential environmental impacts that could be acute at local scales, which may include added power loads that create grid stress, water withdrawals that create water stress, or local noise impacts;

(6) the positive environmental impacts associated with applications of artificial intelligence, which may include optimizing systems for energy efficiency, developing renewable energy, advancing planetary systems research, enabling discovery of new materials, and automatically monitoring environmental changes;

(7) the negative environmental impacts associated with applications of artificial intelligence, which may include rebound effects, behavioral impacts, and accelerating high-pollution activities;

(8) disparate impacts in the negative environmental impacts of artificial intelligence;

(9) other environmental impacts, as determined by the Administrator of the Environmental Protection Agency; and

(10) the results of the updated data center study carried out under section 453(e)(2) of the Energy Independence and Security Act of 2007 (42 U.S.C. 17112(e)(2)).

(c) Public Comment Required.—In conducting the study required under subsection (a), the Administrator of the Environmental Protection Agency shall solicit and consider public comments.

Sec. 5. Artificial Intelligence Environmental Impacts Consortium.

(a) In General.—The Director of the National Institute of Standards and Technology shall, in consultation with the Administrator of the Environmental Protection Agency, the Secretary of Energy, and such others as the Director considers appropriate, convene a consortium of stakeholders, including members from academia, civil society, and industry, to identify the future measurements, methodologies, standards, and other appropriate needs, in order to measure and report the full range of environmental impacts of artificial intelligence.

(b) Location.—The Director may determine the location of the consortium within the National Institute of Standards and Technology.

(c) Goals.—The goals of the consortium shall include the following:

(1) Facilitating consistent, comparable reporting on the environmental impacts of the full lifecycle of artificial intelligence models, systems, and hardware.

(2) According to technical feasibility, the development or cataloging of open source software and hardware tools and other resources designed to facilitate the measurement of environmental impacts of artificial intelligence models, systems, and hardware.

(3) Providing recommendations on how to mitigate the negative, and promote the positive, environmental impacts of artificial intelligence.

Sec. 6. Reporting System for Voluntary Reporting of Environmental Impacts of Artificial Intelligence.

(a) Voluntary Reporting System.—The Director of the National Institute of Standards and Technology shall, in consultation with the Administrator of the Environmental Protection Agency, the Secretary of Energy, the consortium convened under section 5, and such others as the Director considers appropriate, develop a system for voluntary reporting by voluntary reporting entities of the full range of environmental impacts of artificial intelligence.

(b) Guidelines.—

(1) In General.—The Director shall develop guidelines for voluntary reporting entities on how to participate in the voluntary reporting system developed under subsection (a). Such guidelines may include guidelines on how to calculate and report energy consumption, water consumption, pollution, and electronic-waste associated with the full lifecycle of artificial intelligence models and hardware, as well as other positive and negative impacts of artificial intelligence use, as determined by the Director.

(2) Public Comments.—Before finalizing the guidelines under paragraph (1), the Director shall solicit comments from the public on a draft version of the guidelines.

(c) Availability.—The Director shall, to the maximum extent practicable and with consideration to privileged business information, make submissions to the voluntary reporting system under subsection (a) available on a public website.

Sec. 7. Report to Congress.

Not later than 4 years after the date of the enactment of this Act, the Administrator of the Environmental Protection Agency, the Secretary of Energy, and the Director of the National Institute of Standards and Technology shall jointly submit to Congress a report detailing the following:

(1) The main findings of the consortium convened under section 5.

(2) A description of the reporting system created under section 6.

(3) Recommendations for legislative or administrative action to mitigate the negative and promote the positive environmental impacts of artificial intelligence. . . .

The WGA and SAG-AFTRA strikes of 2023 and other recent labor strikes represent concerns that AI might not work as a tool to enhance the workforce, but, rather, will replace the existing workforce along with human creativity and knowledge production, in significant and profound ways. That concern is coupled with a concern that the displacement will occur at an unprecedented pace, threatening livelihoods and human enterprises when they are challenged and outperformed by a digital equivalent.

In the years preceding the strikes, executive and legislative actions recognize the need for the expansion of AI research, training, and education. The *National Artificial Intelligence Initiative Act of 2020*[26] codified within a federal statute multiple policy priorities that had been previously promulgated by the Trump administration's Executive Order 13859, *Maintaining American Leadership in Artificial Intelligence*.[27] The priorities included expanding research investment in AI and emerging technologies, such as an investment in federal government AI computing and data capacities, establishing technical standards for AI, facilitating AI workforce training, and developing international relations and collaboration on AI research and policy coordination. The *AI in Government Act of 2020* also emphasized the need to expand AI training, research, and educational development. The energy and environmental demands of AI development necessitate more research and debate on how sustainable AI growth will be. Other federal actions, coordinated with international bodies, further recognizes the need to elevate the issue of AI and environmental protection.

AI and automation efficiency promise a new iteration of the Industrial Revolution. As AI continues to grow in ubiquity and utility, the uses and development of AI will also grow. This chapter shows how governing bodies are calling for actions that can address humanity concerns and sustainability objectives on a long-term scale in light of the exponential growth in AI development and its far-reaching impacts. The demands of law and policy will necessitate adaptation and innovation as the demands and risks of AI and its users change and are more widely recognized.

---

26. National Artificial Intelligence Initiative Act of 2020, H.R. 6216, 116th Cong. (2020).

27. Exec. Order No. 13859, 84 Fed. Reg. 3967, *Maintaining American Leadership in Artificial Intelligence* (Feb. 11, 2019).

CONSTITUTION OF THE UNITED STATES

We the People of the United States, in Order to form a more perfect Union, establish Justice, insure domestic Tranquility, provide for the common defence, promote the general Welfare, and secure the Blessings of Liberty to ourselves and our Posterity, do ordain and establish this Constitution for the United States of America.

Article I

Section 1. All legislative Powers herein granted shall be vested in a Congress of the United States, which shall consist of a Senate and House of Representatives.

Section 2. The House of Representatives shall be composed of Members chosen every second Year by the People of the several States, and the Electors in each State shall have the Qualifications requisite for Electors of the most numerous Branch of the State Legislature. . . .

The House of Representatives shall chuse their Speaker and other Officers; and shall have the sole Power of Impeachment.

Section 3. The Senate of the United States shall be composed of two Senators from each State, [chosen by the Legislature thereof,][1] for six Years; and each Senator shall have one Vote. . . .

The Senate shall have the sole Power to try all Impeachments. When sitting for that Purpose, they shall be on Oath or Affirmation. When the President of the United States is tried, the Chief Justice shall preside: And no Person shall be convicted without the Concurrence of two thirds of the Members present.

Judgment in Cases of Impeachment shall not extend further than to removal from Office, and disqualification to hold and enjoy any Office of honor, Trust or Profit under the United States: but the Party convicted shall nevertheless be liable and subject to Indictment, Trial, Judgment and Punishment, according to Law.

1. Changed by the Seventeenth Amendment to read "elected by the people thereof."

Section 4. The Times, Places and Manner of holding Elections for Senators and Representatives, shall be prescribed in each State by the Legislature thereof; but the Congress may at any time by Law make or alter such Regulations, except as to the Places of chusing Senators.

The Congress shall assemble at least once in every Year, and such Meeting shall [be on the first Monday in December,][2] unless they shall by Law appoint a different Day.

Section 5. . . . Each House shall keep a Journal of its Proceedings, and from time to time publish the same, excepting such Parts as may in their Judgment require Secrecy; and the Yeas and Nays of the Members of either House on any question shall, at the Desire of one fifth of those Present, be entered on the Journal. . . .

Section 6. The Senators and Representatives shall receive a Compensation for their Services, to be ascertained by Law, and paid out of the Treasury of the United States. They shall in all Cases, except Treason, Felony and Breach of the Peace, be privileged from Arrest during their Attendance at the Session of their respective Houses, and in going to and returning from the same; and for any Speech or Debate in either House, they shall not be questioned in any other Place.

. . . [N]o Person holding any Office under the United States, shall be a Member of either House during his Continuance in Office.

Section 7. All Bills for raising Revenue shall originate in the House of Representatives; but the Senate may propose or concur with amendments as on other Bills.

Every Bill which shall have passed the House of Representatives and the Senate, shall, before it becomes a Law, be presented to the President of the United States; If he approve he shall sign it, but if not he shall return it, with his Objections to that House in which it shall have originated, who shall enter the Objections at large on their Journal, and proceed to reconsider it. If after such Reconsideration two thirds of that House shall agree to pass the Bill, it shall be sent, together with the Objections, to the other House, by which it shall likewise be reconsidered, and if approved by two thirds of that House, it shall become a Law. . . . If any Bill shall not be returned by the President within ten Days (Sundays excepted) after it shall have been presented to him, the Same shall be a Law, in like Manner as if he had signed it, unless the Congress by their Adjournment prevent its Return, in which Case it shall not be a Law.

Every Order, Resolution, or Vote to which the Concurrence of the Senate and House of Representatives may be necessary (except on a question of Adjournment) shall be presented to the President of the United States; and

2. Changed by section 2 of the Twentieth Amendment to read "begin at noon on the 3d day of January."

before the Same shall take Effect, shall be approved by him, or being disapproved by him, shall be repassed by two thirds of the Senate and House of Representatives, according to the Rules and Limitations prescribed in the Case of a Bill.

Section 8. [1] The Congress shall have Power To lay and collect Taxes, Duties, Imposts and Excises, to pay the Debts and provide for the common Defence and general Welfare of the United States; but all Duties, Imposts and Excises shall be uniform throughout the United States;

[2] To borrow Money on the credit of the United States;

[3] To regulate Commerce with foreign Nations, and among the several States, and with the Indian Tribes;

[4] To establish an uniform Rule of Naturalization . . . ;

[9] To constitute Tribunals inferior to the supreme Court;

[10] To define and punish Piracies and Felonies committed on the high Seas, and Offences against the Law of Nations;

[11] To declare War, grant Letters of Marque and Reprisal, and make Rules concerning Captures on Land and Water;

[12] To raise and support Armies, but no Appropriation of Money to that Use shall be for a longer Term than two Years;

[13] To provide and maintain a Navy;

[14] To make Rules for the Government and Regulation of the land and naval Forces;

[15] To provide for calling forth the Militia to execute the Laws of the Union, suppress Insurrections and repel Invasions;

[16] To provide for organizing, arming, and disciplining, the Militia, and for governing such Part of them as may be employed in the Service of the United States, reserving to the States respectively, the Appointment of the Officers, and the Authority of training the Militia according to the discipline prescribed by Congress; . . .

[18] To make all Laws which shall be necessary and proper for carrying into Execution the foregoing Powers, and all other Powers vested by this Constitution in the Government of the United States, or in any Department or Officer thereof.

Section 9. . . . [2] The Privilege of the Writ of Habeas Corpus shall not be suspended, unless when in Cases of Rebellion or Invasion the public Safety may require it. . . .

[3] No Bill of Attainder or ex post facto Law shall be passed. . . .

[7] No Money shall be drawn from the Treasury, but in Consequence of Appropriations made by Law; and a regular Statement and Account of the Receipts and Expenditures of all public Money shall be published from time to time.

[8] No Title of Nobility shall be granted by the United States: And no Person holding any Office of Profit or Trust under them, shall, without the

Consent of the Congress, accept of any present, Emolument, Office, or Title, of any kind whatever, from any King, Prince, or foreign State.

Section 10. [1] No State shall enter into any Treaty, Alliance, or Confederation; grant Letters of Marque and Reprisal; coin Money; emit Bills of Credit; make any Thing but gold and silver Coin a Tender in Payment of Debts; pass any Bill of Attainder, ex post facto Law, or Law impairing the Obligation of Contracts, or grant any Title of Nobility. . . .

[3] No State shall, without the Consent of Congress, lay any Duty of Tonnage, keep Troops, or Ships of War in time of Peace, enter into any Agreement or Compact with another State, or with a foreign Power, or engage in War, unless actually invaded, or in such imminent Danger as will not admit of delay.

Article II

Section 1. The executive Power shall be vested in a President of the United States of America. He shall hold his Office during the Term of four Years, and, together with the Vice President, chosen for the same Term, be elected, as follows . . .

Before he enter on the Execution of his Office, he shall take the following Oath or Affirmation:—"I do solemnly swear (or affirm) that I will faithfully execute the Office of President of the United States, and will to the best of my Ability, preserve, protect and defend the Constitution of the United States."

Section 2. The President shall be Commander in Chief of the Army and Navy of the United States, and of the Militia of the several States, when called into the actual Service of the United States; he may require the Opinion, in writing, of the principal Officer in each of the executive Departments, upon any Subject relating to the Duties of their respective Offices, and he shall have Power to grant Reprieves and Pardons for Offences against the United States, except in Cases of Impeachment.

He shall have Power, by and with the Advice and Consent of the Senate, to make Treaties, provided two thirds of the Senators present concur; and he shall nominate, and by and with the Advice and Consent of the Senate, shall appoint Ambassadors, other public Ministers and Consuls, Judges of the supreme Court, and all other Officers of the United States, whose Appointments are not herein otherwise provided for, and which shall be established by Law: but the Congress may by Law vest the Appointment of such inferior Officers, as they think proper, in the President alone, in the Courts of Law, or in the Heads of Departments. . . .

Section 3. He shall from time to time give to the Congress Information of the State of the Union, and recommend to their Consideration such Measures as he shall judge necessary and expedient; he may, on extraordinary

Occasions, convene both Houses, or either of them, and in Case of Disagreement between them, with Respect to the Time of Adjournment, he may adjourn them to such Time as he shall think proper; he shall receive Ambassadors and other public Ministers; he shall take Care that the Laws be faithfully executed, and shall Commission all the Officers of the United States.

Section 4. The President, Vice President and all civil Officers of the United States, shall be removed from Office on Impeachment for, and Conviction of, Treason, Bribery, or other high Crimes and Misdemeanors.

Article III

Section 1. The judicial Power of the United States, shall be vested in one supreme Court, and in such inferior Courts as the Congress may from time to time ordain and establish. The Judges, both of the supreme and inferior Courts, shall hold their Offices during good Behaviour, and shall, at stated Times, receive for their Services, a Compensation, which shall not be diminished during their Continuance in Office.

Section 2. The judicial Power shall extend to all Cases, in Law and Equity, arising under this Constitution, the Laws of the United States, and Treaties made, or which shall be made, under their Authority;—to all Cases affecting Ambassadors, other public Ministers and Consuls;—to all Cases of admiralty and maritime Jurisdiction;—to Controversies to which the United States shall be a Party;—to Controversies between two or more States;—[between a State and Citizens of another State;—] between Citizens of different States,—between Citizens of the same State claiming Lands under Grants of different States, [and between a State, or the Citizens thereof, and foreign States, Citizens or Subjects.][3]

In all Cases affecting Ambassadors, other public Ministers and Consuls, and those in which a State shall be Party, the supreme Court shall have original Jurisdiction. In all the other Cases before mentioned, the supreme Court shall have appellate Jurisdiction, both as to Law and Fact, with such Exceptions, and under such Regulations as the Congress shall make. . . .

Section 3. Treason against the United States, shall consist only in levying War against them, or in adhering to their Enemies, giving them Aid and Comfort. No Person shall be convicted of Treason unless on the Testimony of two Witnesses to the same overt Act, or on Confession in open Court.

The Congress shall have Power to declare the Punishment of Treason, but no Attainder of Treason shall work Corruption of Blood, or Forfeiture except during the Life of the Person attainted.

---

3. The bracketed material in this section is changed by the Eleventh Amendment.

Article IV . . .

Section 4. The United States shall guarantee to every State in this Union a Republican Form of Government, and shall protect each of them against Invasion; and on Application of the Legislature, or of the Executive (when the Legislature cannot be convened) against domestic Violence. . . .

Article VI

. . . This Constitution, and the Laws of the United States which shall be made in Pursuance thereof; and all Treaties made, or which shall be made, under the Authority of the United States, shall be the supreme Law of the Land; and the Judges in every State shall be bound thereby, any Thing in the Constitution or Laws of any State to the Contrary notwithstanding.

The Senators and Representatives before mentioned, and the Members of the several State Legislatures, and all executive and judicial Officers, both of the United States and of the several States, shall be bound by Oath or Affirmation, to support this Constitution; . . .

Amendments to the Constitution of the United States of America

Amendment I

Congress shall make no law respecting an establishment of religion, or prohibiting the free exercise thereof; or abridging the freedom of speech, or of the press, or the right of the people peaceably to assemble, and to petition the Government for a redress of grievances.

Amendment II

A well regulated Militia, being necessary to the security of a free State, the right of the people to keep and bear Arms, shall not be infringed.

Amendment III

No Soldier shall, in time of peace be quartered in any house, without the consent of the Owner, nor in time of war, but in a manner to be prescribed by law.

Amendment IV

The right of the people to be secure in their persons, houses, papers, and effects, against unreasonable searches and seizures, shall not be violated, and no Warrants shall issue, but upon probable cause, supported by Oath or affirmation, and particularly describing the place to be searched, and the persons or things to be seized.

Amendment V

No person shall be held to answer for a capital, or otherwise infamous crime, unless on a presentment or indictment of a Grand Jury, except in cases arising in the land or naval forces, or in the Militia, when in actual service in time of War or public danger; nor shall any person be subject for the same offence to be twice put in jeopardy of life or limb, nor shall be compelled in any criminal case to be a witness against himself, nor be deprived of life, liberty, or property, without due process of law; nor shall private property be taken for public use without just compensation.

Amendment VI

In all criminal prosecutions, the accused shall enjoy the right to a speedy and public trial, by an impartial jury of the State and district wherein the crime shall have been committed; which district shall have been previously ascertained by law, and to be informed of the nature and cause of the accusation; to be confronted with the witnesses against him; to have compulsory process for obtaining witnesses in his favor, and to have the assistance of counsel for his defence. . . .

Amendment VIII

Excessive bail shall not be required, nor excessive fines imposed, nor cruel and unusual punishments inflicted.

Amendment IX

The enumeration in the Constitution of certain rights shall not be construed to deny or disparage others retained by the people.

Amendment X

The powers not delegated to the United States by the Constitution, nor prohibited by it to the States, are reserved to the States respectively, or to the people. . . .

Amendment XIV

Section 1. All persons born or naturalized in the United States and subject to the jurisdiction thereof, are citizens of the United States and of the State wherein they reside. No State shall make or enforce any law which shall abridge the privileges or immunities of citizens of the United States; nor shall any State deprive any person of life, liberty, or property, without due process of law; nor deny to any person within its jurisdiction the equal protection of the laws. . . .

Section 3. No person shall be a Senator or Representative in Congress, or elector of President and Vice-President, or hold any office, civil or military, under the United States, or under any State, who, having previously taken an oath, as a member of Congress, or as an officer of the United States, or as a member of any State legislature, or as an executive or judicial officer of any State, to support the Constitution of the United States, shall have engaged in insurrection or rebellion against the same, or given aid or comfort to the enemies thereof. But Congress may by a vote of two-thirds of each House, remove such disability. . . .

Section 5. The Congress shall have power to enforce, by appropriate legislation, the provisions of this article. . . .

Table of Statutes and Regulations

State Statutes

Table of Cases

Principal cases are italicized.

Index